Sustainability and Adaptability of Gig Economies in Global Business

Roshnie Anita Doon
Global Labor Organization, Germany

IGI Global
Scientific Publishing
Publishing Tomorrow's Research Today

Vice President of Editorial Melissa Wagner
Managing Editor of Acquisitions Mikaela Felty
Managing Editor of Book Development Jocelynn Hessler
Production Manager Mike Brehm
Cover Design Phillip Shickler

Published in the United States of America by
IGI Global Scientific Publishing
701 East Chocolate Avenue
Hershey, PA, 17033, USA
Tel: 717-533-8845
Fax: 717-533-7115
Website: https://www.igi-global.com E-mail: cust@igi-global.com

Library of Congress Cataloging-in-Publication Data

Names: Doon, Roshnie, 1986- editor.
Title: Sustainability and adaptability of gig economies in global business / [edited by] Roshnie Doon.
Description: Hershey, PA : IGI Global Scientific Publishing, [2025] | Includes bibliographical references and index. | Summary: "The primary goal of this book publication is to provide the global research community with a comprehensive understanding of the sustainability and adaptability of gig economies in businesses worldwide"-- Provided by publisher.
Identifiers: LCCN 2024059966 (print) | LCCN 2024059967 (ebook) | ISBN 9798369393857 (hardcover) | ISBN 9798369393864 (paperback) | ISBN 9798369393871 (ebook)
Subjects: LCSH: Flexible work arrangements. | Temporary employment. | Gig economy | Sustainability.
Classification: LCC HD5109 .S87 2025 (print) | LCC HD5109 (ebook) | DDC 331.25/724--dc23/eng/20250228
LC record available at https://lccn.loc.gov/2024059966
LC ebook record available at https://lccn.loc.gov/2024059967
British Cataloguing in Publication Data
A Cataloguing in Publication record for this book is available from the British Library.

I dedicate this book to my parents, whose steadfast guidance has instilled in me the vital values of courage and humility in chasing my dreams.

Roshnie A. Doon

Table of Contents

Detailed Table of Contents

Digital labor platforms have rapidly developed globally due to industry 4.0 technologies. Although they gained popularity during the COVID-19 pandemic, their roots can be traced back to early platforms like Upwork and Uber. Since digital labor platforms act as intermediaries, providing job opportunities to workers worldwide regardless of their location, it has generated new forms of employment, such as gig work and remote work. Gig work has become popular due to its ability to efficiently link workers with international clients and process payments. However, there is still limited understanding of the gig economy's presence in the Caribbean, particularly in Trinidad and Tobago. This study aims to bridge that knowledge gap by examining the emergence of gig work and digital labor platforms in Trinidad and Tobago, along with their advantages, disadvantages, and economic implications.

The gig economy has significantly contributed to the financial stability of migrant workers by providing job opportunities that traditional labor markets may restrict due to language, social, and educational barriers. Despite its importance, information about Venezuelan migrant gig work in Trinidad and Tobago remains scarce. Using a secondary research methodology, this study aims to conceptually discuss how gig work can be used as a mechanism to better integrate Venezuelan migrants into Trinidad and Tobago's labor market. This study highlights that, while gig work may grant Venezuelan migrants' quick access to employment opportunities with limited barriers, issues such as the rigidity of the labor market, inadequate banking support and lack of investment may hinder such a process.

The rapid transition in the gig economy has driven a requirement for innovative talent management strategies in order to address the challenges as well as opportunities. This chapter focuses on talent management in the context of gig economy, with recruitment, engagement and retention of the gig workers, especially food delivery and taxi drivers. It explores the role of digital platforms and Industry 4.0 technologies for reshaping the conventional HR practices to meet the dynamic workforce's demands. Talent management plays an interplay within flexibility, job satisfaction as well as sustainable development because it drives global business to gain competitive support for the development and dealing with the difficulties which are posed by the gig economy. This chapter also offers insights for human resource managers, stakeholders and policymakers for development of an equitable and sustainable gig economy.

This chapter examines how mobility of the market affects the flexibility of gig economies for the Horn of Africa, with emphasis on the part played by talent management. The study uses sample size of 390 respondents, and uses Kaiser Meyer Olkin (KMO) measure to test for data adequacy to do factor analysis, and gets a KMO value that deemed it appropriate for factor analysis. CFA is conducted to verify the specification of the measurement model that measures the constructs adequately. Exploratory analysis of the dynamics between MM, TM, and GE-Adapt is conducted using Structural Equation Modeling (SEM) through AMOS software. In all the antecedents, the study concludes that rising market mobility improves the flexibility of gig economies consistently, with talent management as a moderator. Talent management best practices for these gig platforms include recruitment, development, engagement, and rewards, which enhance the platform's capability to quickly address market forces and customer needs.

Diversity, inclusion, and equity (DIE) in gig economies are critical for fostering sustainable, fair, and innovative labour markets. This study examines the structural challenges and opportunities inherent in gig work, emphasizing disparities in access, pay equity, and career progression across gender, race, age, and socioeconomic backgrounds. It explores strategies for promoting inclusive policies, equitable algorithmic practices, and diversified leadership to ensure that gig economies do not perpetuate systemic inequalities. By integrating behavioural economic insights and policy analysis, this research provides actionable recommendations for policymakers, platforms, and stakeholders to create a more equitable gig ecosystem that benefits workers and society at large.

The gig economy has reshaped labor markets by offering flexible work but also presents challenges such as income instability, lack of social protections, digital access barriers, and sustainability concerns. This chapter examines these issues using secondary research and primary data from a survey of 250 gig workers across ride-hailing, food delivery, freelancing, and domestic services. Findings indicate that 70% face income volatility, 60% lack essential benefits, and 55% experience algorithmic bias in job allocation. Digital access limitations further hinder opportunities, especially in rural areas. The chapter explores regulatory frameworks, technological innovations, and sustainability initiatives, proposing solutions like fair wage policies, algorithmic transparency, and improved worker protections. By addressing structural inequities, this research contributes to discussions on labor rights, platform accountability, and the sustainable evolution of the gig economy.

The platform economy is reshaping labor markets, offering flexibility but increasing worker precarity through income instability, algorithmic management, and limited social protections. This chapter examines social sustainability in platform work, focusing on social capital, digital solidarity networks, and social innovation as resilience mechanisms. It explores regulatory gaps and the role of platform cooperativism and hybrid support systems in addressing labor vulnerabilities. By proposing an integrated framework that balances economic flexibility with institutional protections, the chapter advocates for sustainable policies ensuring fair conditions, worker empowerment, and inclusive social security in the gig economy.

The transformed traditional form of labor markets is what defines gig economies across the globe, wherein workers have more flexibility and freedom than ever before. The innovation that comes with digital platforms and technology powers gig work in creating opportunities for income, entrepreneurship, and economic growth. This flexibility usually comes at precarity because a gig worker has an unstable income, little access to benefits, and little legal protection. Gig work has significant ethical issues, such as work's dual nature. This chapter will discuss the ethical implications of gig economies regarding flexibility. The experiences of different gig workers, such as delivery drivers, freelancers, and virtual assistants, will be defined by their mode of employment and the relationship between that experience and the practice that determines the transformation of short-term contracts into job and life security. It also underscores the need to promote diversity, inclusion, and equity in gig economies to address systemic barriers against women, migrants, and marginalized communities.

Foreword

In today's rapidly evolving global economy, the gig economy is transforming how people work globally, reshaping the traditional labour market and offering more flexibility and options than traditional jobs. Dr. Roshnie A. Doon's edited book, "Sustainability and Adaptability of Gig Economies in Global Business," is an insightful exploration of this dynamic work model, addressing both its advantages and disadvantages.

I have had the privilege of knowing Dr. Doon for several years and can vouch for her commitment to understanding and enhancing the gig economy. Her expertise and passion for this field are evident in the comprehensive and thought-provoking chapters presented in this book. Her work covers critical topics of the gig economy, such as talent management, marketing strategies, and legal frameworks, while also addressing important social issues like fairness for gig workers. The diverse perspectives and thorough research methodologies from various contributors demonstrate the significant impact of the gig economy on global business.

A standout feature of this book is its focus on inclusivity and equality. Dr. Doon emphasizes the importance and the need to treat gig workers structurally equitably, promoting fair treatment for gig workers. Tackling issues like unstable income, lack of essential benefits, and algorithmic bias, the book provides a clear understanding of the challenges faced by this category of workers and suggests practical solutions such as fair wage policies, transparent algorithms, and stronger worker protections.

As an expert in the field, I am particularly impressed by the book's examination of Industry 4.0 technologies and their transformative impact on gig work. Artificial Intelligence (AI) and Machine Learning (ML) are transforming how work is performed and managed, by fostering innovation and efficiency. However, these advancements bring challenges too, that must be properly navigated to protect workers' rights and ensure equitable access to these technologies. Furthermore, of great interest, especially nowadays, are also the insights into the hybridization of skills and the relevance of the combination of creative and technical capabilities, in which I deeply trust.

Dr. Doon's book is a valuable resource not only for academics and policymakers but also for gig managers and especially workers themselves. It provides insightful perspectives and strategies together with practical advice on navigating gig work, such as building personal brands and collaborating within cross-cultural virtual teams. The helpful recommendations and best practices outlined in this book will certainly empower gig workers to do well in today's fast-paced and constantly changing job market. Some chapters grabbed my attention because of the valuable guidance they offer on fostering high performance, engagement, and collaboration, which are essential elements for enhancing productivity and achieving successful outcomes for both workers and managing organizations.

Additionally, the book highlights unique challenges faced by gig workers in specific regions like the Caribbean and South Asia. By examining the emergence of gig work in Trinidad and Tobago and the regulatory challenges in India's commerce sector, the book offers a global perspective on the gig economy, vital for understanding diverse gig work experiences and for developing tailored collaborative efforts to improve the conditions of gig workers worldwide.

In conclusion, the Sustainability and Adaptability of Gig Economies in Global Business book is a must-read for anyone interested in the future of work. Dr. Doon's meticulous research and thoughtful insights provide a guide to building a more inclusive, equitable, and sustainable gig economy. I am honoured to contribute this foreword and wholeheartedly endorse this valuable work. The emphasis on balancing flexibility with challenges, promoting diversity, inclusion, and equity, and dismantling systemic barriers for marginalized communities is commendable and underscores Dr. Doon's dedication to advancing the gig economy for everyone's benefit.

Giuliana Baldo Chiaron

Faculty of Economics, University of Rome, Italy

Preface

INTRODUCTION

Gig Economies are often referred to as those aspects of the labour market that concern flexible short-term jobs supported by various digital platforms across industries, where paid or unpaid tasks are undertaken by either independent contractors, freelancers, or short-term contracts that are mediated by such platforms (Koutsimpogiorgos et al., 2020). These types of gig work can take several forms, from freelancing to short-term contracts in a wide variety of occupations such as delivery and rideshare drivers, freelance writers, graphic designers, and software developers, as well as virtual assistants and tutors. Based on the attributes of the worker, i.e., the type of contract (short/long term), number of platform/clients, degree of flexibility, autonomy, and hours of work, gig workers can be considered to be either (1) a traditional gig worker, (2) a provider of goods or services, or (3) a data or agency provider (Watson et al., 2021; Hafeez et al., 2022).

Gig workers are often attracted to these types of jobs because the unique dynamics of the gig economy allow this segment of the labour market to not only become flexible to meet the individual needs and circumstances of workers, as they can set their hours of work for short-term tasks, but is heavily driven by digital solutions arising from the fast-paced development of industry 4.0 which offers workers more options, and increased accessibility regardless of their physical location (Hsieh, et al., 2023). Despite the many benefits of gig work that make it an attractive form of employment, particularly for vulnerable groups in society, it is often considered an illusion, as such types of precarious forms of employment come with a host of challenges. Challenges that can not only create work-life conflicts for women and low-income households who have dependent relatives but also encourage the continued reliance on inconsistent streams of income that may worsen socio-economic inequalities (Kincaid et al., 2023; Svoboda, 2024).

THE RELEVANCE OF GIG WORK IN TODAY'S WORLD OF WORK AND GLOBAL BUSINESS

Even though gig work is primarily defined by flexible short-term arrangements, which often come with a host of challenges, this form of work has become increasingly significant to both the domestic labor market of countries around the world, as well as their ability to engage in global business activities. Throughout the literature, gig work has become an important player in the labor market because of several reasons, (1) its flexibility and autonomy provide gig workers with the ability to choose, when, where and how much they work daily, which improves their work-life balance, and reduces stress, (2) for low-income households and vulnerable groups, gig work provides the means to access greater forms of income from multiple streams, which allows gig workers to not only engage and adapt to multiple projects, but also develop new skills and abilities as tasks evolve, and (3) as gig workers gain more experience, exposure and skills, they are better equipped to access opportunities worldwide, that may not have been possible while engaging in the traditional employment model (Huang et al., 2017; Piyumidu & Withaanarachchi, 2024, Cao et al., 2022).

Considering the growing significance of gig work in the modern labor market, this flexible form of employment not only provides essential income for many individuals but also contributes substantially to economic growth. As companies increasingly turn to gig workers, the gig economy has become a crucial component of global business activities, because of several reasons, first, the shift allows businesses to tap into a global pool of diverse and talented workers, who may possess skills and abilities that may not be accessible locally, which in turn allows them to quickly scale up or down the activities of their workforce in response to market fluctuations (Rozzi, 2018).

Second, by hiring gig workers on short-term contracts, businesses can then drive down their overhead costs associated with fixed salaries, renting of office space, and utilities, which allows them to put together short-term innovative teams to target specific projects without making long-term adjustments (Sharif et al., 2023). Third, and finally, gig work contributes to the development of SDG 8, i.e., Decent Work and Economic Growth, in particular economic inclusion. This as gig work provides vulnerable and marginalized groups in society with not only an opportunity to gain employment, and develop marketable skills, but to also contribute to greater socio-economic inclusion, and poverty reduction, as it highlights the need for fair wages, employment rights, and protections (UN-SDGS, n.d.). Despite the critical role that gig work plays in global business, there is a need to consider the welfare protection of gig workers through regulatory and legislative compliance, as well as trade union representation.

TARGET AUDIENCE

This book on the Sustainability and Adaptability of Gig Economies in Global Business is an invaluable resource for Academics and Researchers, Students in Higher Education, Professionals and Practitioners, Special Interest Groups, and other stakeholders who have a contingent interest in the development of Gig Economies in Global Businesses. Examining various aspects of the gig economy, such as the types of work available, flexibility, the use of digital platforms, and Industry 4.0 technologies as demonstrated by this book, provides a comprehensive and diverse understanding of how this work affects many issues such as employee satisfaction, and broader societal issues, including gender inequality and the exploitation experienced by gig workers. This understanding also impacts the ability of domestic gig platforms to access and benefit from global business opportunities, such as entering larger markets, expanding their customer base, attracting foreign direct investment, engaging in product diversification, and supporting sustainable development. Supported by a wide range of studies and diverse perspectives, this book plays a crucial role in understanding the intricate workings of Gig work and Economies in the context of Global Business. Such a book may become a valuable resource to inform better policies and practices that can consider the unique challenges experienced by this segment of workers.

ORGANIZATION OF CHAPTERS

Through a comprehensive collection of 12 chapters, this book highlights from different perspectives how the emergence of Gig Economies is set to significantly alter both the labour market and Global Business in a variety of ways. This is particularly important as the latter depends heavily on established business models and traditional employment models that offer workers fixed hours of work, secured wages, employment benefits, and job security. Although challenges such as the growing digital divide between urban-rural areas, limited digital resources, social protection, and income/gender inequality are likely to persist in Gig Economies, it has the potential to encourage sustainable development of businesses worldwide. Gig Economies can then not only provide opportunities for underserved communities but also encourage digital literacy training for gig workers and the development of small startup companies, micro-entrepreneurship, and small and medium enterprises (SMEs).

Furthermore, the formation of resilient Gig Economies is likely to create a favorable business environment for public and private sector entities, as well as international funding agencies, to invest in the digital infrastructure of countries, which is certain to improve the lives of gig workers, particularly those residing in rural and remote areas. As a practitioner in labor economics, I would like to express my sincere appreciation to the authors who have shared their diverse perspectives on the evolving topic of gig work. The insights provided by these chapters have put forward not only valuable knowledge about the challenges faced by gig workers worldwide, but also the impact of technological advancements on gig platforms, the implications for labor regulations and policies, and a host of crucial topics. These contributions have not only enriched academic discourse on platform and gig work, but have also informed policymakers, employers, and workers about the opportunities and pitfalls inherent in this rapidly growing sector. A brief description of each of the chapters included in this book is as follows:

Chapter 1: Working Without Borders- Digital Labor Platforms and The Emergence of Gig Work in Trinidad and Tobago

Roshnie A. Doon

Doon in her chapter discusses the emergence of gig work and the use of digital labor platforms in Trinidad and Tobago. Using a conceptual research methodology, she explores in detail the landscape of gig work in not only Trinidad and Tobago but also Latin America and the Caribbean (LAC). She goes on to focus her discussion on the prevalence of web and location-based platforms that are still operational, while focusing on the impact that technological growth has on the adoption of pros and cons of gig work, before concluding with the economic implications of such work.

Chapter 2: The Precarious Nature of Gig Work for Venezuelan Migrants in Trinidad & Tobago- Opportunities and Challenges for Integration

Roshnie A. Doon

Doon in her chapter examines how gig work can be used as a migration tool for the integration of Venezuelan migrants into Trinidad and Tobago's labor market. In this chapter, she discusses the complex relationship that gig work plays in the survival of migrant gig workers, the prevalence and intensity of Venezuelan migrant gig workers in the neighbouring countries of Chile, Colombia and Peru, as well as the strategies that can be used to support the integration of Venezuelan migrant gig workers.

Chapter 3: Assessing The Challenges Faced by The Gig Workers in The Indian Context Through PLS-SEM

Rachit Agarwal, & Tanya Kumar

Agarwal and Kumar, in their chapter, sought to identify the variety of problems experienced by Indian gig workers. Using a Structural Equation Model-Smart PLS, they find that a low and often unstable household income, restricted access to health insurance plans, and the absence of legal protection are often considered to be the primary challenges experienced by gig workers in India. After this, they go on to put forward strategies to mitigate against these negative implications.

Chapter 4: Regulating the Gig Economy Addressing Worker Rights in India's Quick Commerce Sector

Pooja Kalbalia, & Haneefa K.V.

Kalbalia and Haneefa K. V., in their chapter, focused on the regulatory challenges that the Quick Commerce Sector poses to gig workers in India. By examining the implementation gaps in the existing framework, they highlight, using a thematic analysis, the liabilities that this segment of workers may experience. They go on to find that there are regional disparities present in the working conditions, legal recognition of workers, as well as gender-based inequalities.

Chapter 5: Marketing Strategies in the Gig Economy-Challenges and Opportunities for Freelance Marketers

Arpan Anand

Anand, in his chapter, explores how freelance marketing professionals in the gig economy navigate the many challenges of gig work. Using a mixed-methods approach, he finds that this group of workers employs a wide range of strategies such as personal branding, platform diversification, and niche specialization to adapt to the changing landscape.

Chapter 6: Talent Management in Gig Economies-Managing Cross-Cultural Virtual Teams

Reccia N. Charles, & Nazly K. Nardi

Charles and Nardi, in their chapter, explore different strategies for managing cross-cultural/virtual teams, inclusive of addressing issues such as communication barriers and navigating decentralized work structures. In their chapter, they put forward several best practices for managing cross-cultural teams, with an emphasis on collaboration, engagement, and performance of both gig workers and managing organizations.

Chapter 7: Talent Management in the Gig Economy Leveraging Workforce Strategies in the Digital Age

Tanya Rabban, & Rohan Singh

Rabban and Singh, in their chapter, focused on examining gig work from a talent management perspective. While examining the recruitment, engagement, and retention of gig workers providing services such as delivery and transportation for location-based platforms, they also look at the role that Industry 4.0-based technologies play in the human resource process of managing gig workers.

Chapter 8: Market Mobility Effect on Gig Economies' Adaptability by Mediation of Talent Management in Horn of Africa

Shashi Kant, & Metyasabiya Adula

Kant and Adula, in their chapter on the case of the Horn of Africa, investigate how market mobility influences the flexibility of gig economies. Using a combination of techniques such as Confirmatory Factor Analysis, Exploratory Analysis, and Structural Equation Modelling, they find that growth in market mobility enhances the flexibility of the gig economy in the Horn of Africa when talent management is used as a moderator.

Chapter 9: Diversity, Inclusion, and Equity in Gig Economies

Iris-Panagiota Efthymiou, & Theoharris Efthymiou-Egleton

Efthymiou and Efthymiou-Egleton, in their chapter, looked at the structural problems and solutions of gig work, paying particular attention to disparities in earnings, access to employment, and opportunities for advancement based on workers' biological characteristics and socio-economic background. Using insights from behavioural economics and policy analysis, they go on to provide recommendations to encourage equity in gig economies.

Chapter 10: Building Inclusive and Equitable Gig Economies for Sustainable Global Growth

Razia Nagina

Nagina, in her chapter, sought to examine how the challenges presented by the gig economy have influenced the labor market. Using secondary research methodology and primary data collection, she finds that a large proportion of gig workers experience income volatility, lack essential employment benefits, and instances of bias and discrimination during the allocation of tasks, via the platforms' use of algorithms. The chapter goes on to explore the regulatory frameworks, as well as technological innovations to address such problems.

Chapter 11: Social Sustainability in the Gig Economy-Rethinking Social Protection Systems for Platform Workers

Zyed Achour

Achour, in his chapter, examined the social sustainability of platform work, using regulatory gaps, platform cooperatives, and hybrid support mechanisms. To minimize the vulnerabilities of gig workers, he goes on to explain the need for an integrated framework that incorporates both economic flexibility and institutional protections.

Chapter 12: Balancing Flexibility and Precarity-Ethical Implications and Sustainable Practices in Global Gig Economies

Muhammad Usman Tariq

Tariq, in his chapter, sought to discuss the ethical implications of gig economies. Paying particular attention to the flexibility of gig work, he discusses how the experiences of different locations and web-based gig workers who provide transportation, delivery, and virtual assistant services are often shaped by their mode of employment, the type of employment contract, and experience. He goes on to explain how the relationship between the latter areas can impact the job and life security of gig workers, while highlighting the need for promoting diversity, equity, and inclusion amongst vulnerable and marginalized segments of workers.

CONCLUSION

This collection of chapters, which looks at different dimensions of gig work, concerning its overall sustainability and adaptability, has a significant impact not only on the broad field of labor economics but also on that of business management and administration. In the case of labor economics, such a book highlights several areas, such as resource optimization, income generation, and the development of micro-entrepreneurs, which then alters the discussion on the employment and wage structure of gig workers, labor rights, as well as their access to social safety nets. Moreover, this book also influences the literature on the adaptability of business models to the integration of gig workers, by placing greater focus on flexible business models as opposed to traditional employment models, the amalgamation of industry 4.0-based technologies to manage cost, encouraging innovation and competitiveness, as well as developing performance-driven models.

Editor:

Roshnie Anita Doon
Global Labor Organization (GLO), Essen, Germany

REFERENCES

Cao, X., Zhang, D., & Huang, L. (2022). The Impact of COVID-19 Pandemic on the Behavior of Online Gig Workers (3 22, 2022). *Manufacturing & Service Operations Management*, •••, 1–55. DOI: 10.1287/msom.2022.1113

Hafeez, S., Gupta, C., & Sprajcer, M. (2022). Stress and the gig economy: It's not all shifts and giggles. *Industrial Health, 61*(2), 140–150. DOI: 10.2486/indhealth.2021-0217 PMID: 35249894

Hsieh, J., Adisa, O., Bafna, S., & Zhu, H. (2023). *Designing Individualized Policy and Technology Interventions to Improve Gig Work Conditions*. ArXiv., DOI: 10.1145/3596671.3598576

Huang, N., Burtch, G., Hong, Y., & Pavlou, P. A. (2017). Unemployment and Worker Participation in the Gig Economy: Evidence from An Online Labor Market. *SSRN*, •••, 1–51. DOI: 10.2139/ssrn.3105090

Kincaid, R., & Reynolds, J. (2023). Unconventional Problems: Gig Microtask Work, Inequality, and the Flexibility Mystique. *The Sociological Quarterly*, *65*, 246–268. DOI: 10.1080/00380253.2023.2268679

Koutsimpogiorgos, N., Van Slageren, J., Herrmann, A. M., & Frenken, K. (2020). Conceptualizing the Gig Economy and Its Regulatory Problems. *Policy and Internet*, *12*(4), 525–545. DOI: 10.1002/poi3.237

Piyumidu, K. K. D., & Withaanarachchi, A. (2024). Subjective well-being of online freelancers in the digital gig economy: A study of Sri Lanka. *International Research Conference on Smart Computing and Systems Engineering (SCSE)*, Colombo, Sri Lanka, 2024, 1-6, DOI: 10.1109/SCSE61872.2024.10550901

Rozzi, F. (2018). The Impact of the Gig-Economy on U.S. Labor Markets: Understanding the Role of Non-Employer Firms using Econometric Models and the Example of Uber. Junior Management Science, 3(2): 33-56. DOI: 10.5282/jums/v3i2pp33-56

Sharif, I., & Qiang, C. Z. (2023). *The Promise and Peril of Online Gig Work in Developing Countries*. World Bank., https://blogs.worldbank.org/en/voices/promise-and-peril-online-gig-work-developing-countries

Svoboda, A. (2024). Gig Economy and Remote Work Challenge Traditional Retirement Planning. *International Journal of Management Studies and Social Science Research*, *6*(3), 155–160. DOI: 10.56293/IJMSSSR.2024.5017

United Nations Division for Sustainable Development Goals (UN-SDGS). (n.d.). SDG Action Segment for Goal 8. https://sdgs.un.org/sites/default/files/2025-01/SDG%20Action%20Segment%20Goal%208_1.pdf

Watson, G. P., Kistler, L. D., Graham, B. A., & Sinclair, R. R. (2021). Looking at the Gig Picture: Defining Gig Work and Explaining Profile Differences in Gig Workers' Job Demands and Resources. *Group & Organization Management*, *46*(2), 327–361. DOI: 10.1177/1059601121996548

Chapter 1
Working Without Borders: Digital Labor Platforms and the Emergence of Gig Work in Trinidad and Tobago

Roshnie Anita Doon
https://orcid.org/0000-0002-3285-0355
Global Labor Organization, Germany

ABSTRACT

Digital labor platforms have rapidly developed globally due to industry 4.0 technologies. Although they gained popularity during the COVID-19 pandemic, their roots can be traced back to early platforms like Upwork and Uber. Since digital labor platforms act as intermediaries, providing job opportunities to workers worldwide regardless of their location, it has generated new forms of employment, such as gig work and remote work. Gig work has become popular due to its ability to efficiently link workers with international clients and process payments. However, there is still limited understanding of the gig economy's presence in the Caribbean, particularly in Trinidad and Tobago. This study aims to bridge that knowledge gap by examining the emergence of gig work and digital labor platforms in Trinidad and Tobago, along with their advantages, disadvantages, and economic implications.

INTRODUCTION

Digital labor platforms have become a crucial component in developing the modern labor market worldwide, by providing both workers and employers with flexible job opportunities and working arrangements. Facilitated by the onset of the COVID-19 pandemic in 2020, and the exponential growth in Industry 4.0 tech-

DOI: 10.4018/979-8-3693-9385-7.ch001

nologies such as Artificial Intelligence (AI), Machine Learning (ML), and Data Analytics, platform work has become the work of the future, as it has broken down the geographical barriers of the domestic labor market, leading to the rapid growth of not only remote work but most importantly gig work. Such working arrangements typically involve alternative or nonstandard work such as freelancing, independent contractors, part-time workers and persons who are either self-employment, or engaged in sub-contracted work on a short-term basis, in a wide variety of industries such as transportation, healthcare, education, content creation, and administration (Stewart & Standford, 2017).

Even though gig workers are rarely included in the labor force and household surveys, it has been estimated that there are 435 million online gig workers globally, with most workers residing in developing countries like India, Brazil, China, Sub-Saharan Africa, Indonesia, as well as developed countries like the United States (US) and the United Kingdom (UK) (Datta et al., 2023). With such a rapidly growing supply of gig workers residing mainly in the global south, it is often thought that workers tend to gravitate towards this particular form of work because, (1) it gives them the flexibility to work from various locations, and at their own pace, which enhances their work-life balance and job satisfaction, (2) it is often used to supplement their primary source of income, which may a response to the growing cost of living and rates of inflation, and (3) to gain greater autonomy and access to job opportunities that may not be accessible from the traditional work from the office employment model (Datta et al., 2023). Though gig work can have a profound impact on the socio-economic outlook of many households in the Global South, it does come with risks as gig workers may suffer from low wages, unstable working environments, and little to no labour market protections. This may deepen structural problems experienced by vulnerable groups such as working poverty, income inequality and discrimination in India, Kenya, South Africa and Sub-Saharan Africa where gig work is a popular source of income (Ayentimi et al., 2023).

Within the literature, although several studies examine the dynamics of gig work in developing and developed countries there is a dearth of information on gig work and gig economies in the Caribbean region. Thus, the purpose of this study is to broaden the literature on gig work in the Caribbean region, by discussing the emergence of digital labor platforms and gig work in Trinidad and Tobago. The main objectives of this study is to (1) examine the global gig and platform economies, as well as digital labor platforms, (2) analyse the emergence of gig work in both Latin America and Trinidad and Tobago, (3) discuss how the integration of industry 4.0 based technologies may positively or negatively influence the growth of gig work, and (4) finally to highlight the economic implications of gig work in Trinidad and Tobago. To achieve these objectives, a secondary research methodology is used, in which a conceptual research framework is implemented to comprehensively discuss the emergence of Digital Labor Platforms and the Emergence of Gig Work in Trinidad and Tobago. Considering that there is a lack of data on gig work for Trinidad and Tobago that prevents empirical research from being undertaken, the conceptual research framework which relies heavily on the review and analysis of existing studies is appropriate for this study.

Utilizing this comprehensive analytical framework not only enhances our understanding of gig work dynamics in Trinidad and Tobago but also yields valuable insights that can significantly inform the direction of future empirical research on this subject. This is especially relevant for academics seeking to explore the socio-economic impacts of gig work, policymakers aiming to develop effective regulatory frameworks, and practitioners looking to understand the operational complexities of gig platforms in Trinidad and Tobago. By systematically examining the role that industry 4.0-based technologies play in the growth of the domestic gig economy, this framework is a vital tool in shaping the gig economy landscape in the Caribbean region.

DIGITAL LABOR PLATFORMS & THE GIG ECONOMY: A BRIEF REVIEW

The Gig Economy & The Platform Economy

In the traditional working environment, workers have been confined by the geographic borders of their home country when seeking employment opportunities. Restricted by limited use and availability of computer technology, transportation and communication, it has become the norm for workers to habitually travel long distances for work using different modes (car, air, and rail) (Dargay & Clark, 2012). The lack of advanced technology particularly in developing countries made it challenging for local businesses to either operate remotely or expand beyond their immediate surroundings. This resulted in not only limited job opportunities for current and potential workers but also limited economic growth and innovation. With advancements in communication and information technology, together with the widespread use/development of the internet and digital platforms, workers were able to seek and engage with employment opportunities worldwide to improve their livelihoods.

The growth of digital platforms and digital labor platforms have played a significant role in transforming the landscape of the working environment, from one which required the physical presence of workers, to one that has facilitated the growth of both digital labor and gig work. As,, digital platforms now act as the intermediary to connect low and middle-income workers, with employment opportunities, that may not have been accessible to them through traditional employment channels.

The provision of such type of employment has led to the creation of the gig economy in which it is the norm for business organizations to hire independent workers for non-standard work opportunities or "gigs". These tasks are often facilitated by digital labor platforms because of their reduced barriers to entry, as well as their ability to provide gig workers with greater freedom, flexibility, and inclusivity, (Anwar & Graham, 2020).

For these specific types of short-term employment arrangements, gig workers are hired to complete a specific project or work tasks for a set amount of time and remuneration. Depending on the labor legislation and the classification of gig work in which the employee is based, they may be entitled to employment benefits such as tax deductions and credits. In such an instance, for example in the US, gig workers can benefit from (1) home office deductions that can be made based on the square footage of space used in their home for work, (2) business income deductions that can be made based on their annual business income revenue, (3) the renting of their homes as a business space for meetings, business travel expenses, as well as the setting up of a retirement saving account can all be considered tax deductibles, and thus reduce their overall tax, regardless of occupation and industry of employment (Watson, 2019).

In countries around the world where the labor market is characterised by high rates of unemployment, and low-income households, the gig economy, i.e., a subset of the platform economy, and the expansion of the platform economy, i.e., which mediates all economic activity taking place in its digital environment across all platforms, have both played a crucial role in the economic development, as well as its accumulation and distribution of wealth (Takagi, 2020). While the creation of platform economies has transformed the operation and management of traditional businesses and industries around the world, it has also introduced new business models that focus on flexible employment arrangements, and customer engagements as tools to drive innovation and competitiveness across industries (OECD, ILO & EU, 2023).

Since the platform economy, encompasses all economic activity facilitated by digital platforms, it also includes a wide range of employment arrangements such as (1) independent contractors, (2) freelancers, (3) crowd employment, i.e., connecting business clients with workers to provide specific services remotely through the platforms in exchange for payment, and (4) the sharing economy agreements, i.e., where the goods, services, skills, and spaces are borrowed, rented and shared, (5) capital platform work, i.e., where goods and services are sold on an individual basis by connecting business clients with the resources offered by workers and (6) work-on-demand, i.e., service providing businesses that use workers to provide services domestically (Mont et al., 2020; Azevedo et al., 2023). In this context, while digital labor can be considered as a subset of gig work, as any type of web-based or location-based task that can be mediated, accessed, and completed using a digital platform, not all digital labor can be considered as gig work. The distinction lies in the fact that while gig work can include web-based and in-person work tasks which can be facilitated by digital technology, digital labor tends to focus only on the completion of tasks using apps, and the management of tasks using algorithms (Kavese & Mbali, 2022).

Digital Labor Platforms

Unlike digital platforms, traditionally based on connecting businesses with consumers to facilitate different types of transactions, digital labor platforms tend to focus on connecting workers with job opportunities posted by businesses on these platforms. Facilitated by the digital labor platform itself, which acts as an intermediary to connect and exchange the labor of workers henceforth known as gig workers, with employment opportunities posted by businesses, such activity forms the foundation of the gig economy (Charlton, 2021). Digital labor platforms such as QuikrJobs in India and SweepSouth in South Africa play a crucial role in connecting job seekers with diverse employment opportunities, as these platforms act as intermediaries by facilitating access to various forms of work tasks, including care services, domestic work, delivery, travel, and freelancing.

A key characteristic of digital labor platforms is that it considers gig workers as independent contractors, which distinguishes them from the traditional employees of a specific business. Such a categorization of workers, together with the digitization of the process using algorithms to administer the allocation of work, oversee the payment structure and performance evaluation of gig workers, often increases gig workers' susceptibility to labor market issues such as job insecurity, income instability, discrimination, and reduced autonomy as their rights may not be considered due to little or no trade union representation (OECD, ILO & EU, 2023). The lack of representation for gig workers in countries like England, Scotland, Wales, Northern Ireland, and Italy may be due to not only the inability of trade unions to reinvigorate their membership but also their lack of capacity and commitment to represent the rights of vulnerable segments of the population that engage in gig work (Borghi & Murgia, 2024). Aside from these challenges, digital labor platforms can be divided into three different categories based on the location of the work being performed, i.e., (1) Web-based platforms, (2) Location-based platforms, and (3) Hybrid digital labor platforms.

The first type of digital labor platform is a web-based platform that enables gig workers to access and complete various forms of work tasks in an online environment regardless of their physical location. On this platform gig workers engage in several different types of tasks such as freelancing, micro-tasking crowd work, and consultations that may require specialized skills without the need to be physically present (OECD, ILO & EU, 2023). In this setting, gig workers using online web-based platforms like Upwork in Finland, and Clickworker in Germany, generally have a great deal of individual autonomy over the type of work being undertaken, and the terms/conditions of their specific job contract as they can communicate directly with business clients using the platform (Seppanen et al., 2021). The leading drawback of such an arrangement, however, is that algorithmic management practices which monitor the interactions between gig workers and business clients, automate decisions, and delegate work tasks, and feedback from business clients on performance evaluations, which can impact the ability of gig workers to secure work in the future (Schulze et al., 2022). These practices reduce the ability of the gig worker to create value with business clients, as the algorithm may encourage the exclusion and devaluation of gig workers' performance.

The second type of digital labor platform are location-based platforms, which require gig workers to be physically present at specific locations to provide the service to business clients. Location-based platforms like that of Uber and Uber Eats as well as Door Dash and Grubhub in the US, provide a wide range of services from transportation, delivery, and food services to domestic work (OECD, ILO & EU, 2023). However, since location-based platform workers are independent contractors, who must be physically present at different locations to undertake these assigned work tasks, this reduces not only their autonomy but reduces their access to social safety nets such as social assistance grants, pensions and conditional/unconditional cash transfers, as platforms are not obligated to provide any benefits. This can in turn erode the socio-economic welfare and the well-being of the gig workers as they strive to meet the physical demands of location-based platform work.

The third and final type of digital labor platform is a hybrid digital labor platform, which is a combination of web-based and location-based platforms, which organizes and enhances the productivity of gig workers in a formal manner. These multiservice platforms such as Maxim, Grab and Gojeck in Southeast Asian countries like Indonesia, Vietnam, Singapore, Thailand and the Philippines, provide a multitude of services such as deliveries (food, groceries, package/document delivery), mobility (ride-hailing services, taxis, private car for convenient transportation), financial services (cashless payments, insurance, mobile top-ups, bill payments, online video consultations with doctors/tutors), and shopping services (ordering and delivery of items from local stores, on-demand services such as domestic cleaning, and handyman tasks) that can be done online or in-person (Grab, 2024; Gojeck, 2023). For developing countries in Southeast Asia, these hybrid platforms are an essential component for the economic development of its informal sector, as it enhances job creation, and reduces unemployment.

Apart from improving the operational efficiency of businesses, the hybrid digital labor platform offers the gig worker several benefits to workers such as a flexible working environment, and greater autonomy to manage schedules, while the employer benefits from reduced costs from maintaining an office space, access to and collaboration with a global pool of talent, and the ability to adapt quickly to changes from different types of labor market shocks resulting from technological changes, and fluctuations in international trade (Di Tella & Rodrik, 2020). While these gig workers may be able to choose their hours of work, the main drawback of this type of disguised employment relationship used by the hybrid digital platform is that they often lack transparency in their management and operation process (Hadiati et al., 2023). As a result, changes to agreements can be made without the worker's knowledge, as hybrid digital platform managers have the authority to determine the worker's penalties, bonuses, and overall earnings. This then raises concerns about the potential exclusion of certain groups of workers and discriminatory practices within the agreements made between workers and hybrid digital platforms.

THE LANDSCAPE OF GIG WORKERS IN TRINIDAD AND TOBAGO AND LATIN AMERICA & THE CARIBBEAN (LAC)

Gig Work in Latin America and the Caribbean (LAC)

The growth of gig workers in Latin America and the Caribbean (LAC) has steadily increased in recent years, largely due to technological advancements and changing attitudes towards traditional employment. Even though the supply of gig workers from Asia and Africa are the major suppliers of gig workers to the global gig economy, when the emphasis is placed on the financial investment aspect of gig economies, only 4% (US$4 billion) of the global investment in digital labor platforms and platform revenue has been concentrated in Latin America, Africa and the Arab States when compared to that of Asia (US$56billion), the US (US$46billion) and Europe ($US12billion), (ILO, 2021). This demonstrates that there is a digital divide in the global gig economy, as gig workers in developing countries may encounter significant problems when trying to participate in the global gig economy, leading to disparities in the earnings of gig workers across countries. Such a disparity can be linked to inadequate digital and legislative infrastructure, reduced access to technology, unreliable broadband internet connection, high subscription fees of digital labor platforms, and the lack of training needed to leverage the use of such technology for gig work, particularly for vulnerable groups (Heeks, 2021).

Beginning with the case of Latin America, McDowell, (2023) explains that like other countries around the world, the COVID-19 pandemic together with tech booms by international technology giants like Dell and Google, have played a notable role in the growth of Latin America's gig economy, as these companies sought to not only open offices throughout Latin America but offer tax exemptions to attract other international digital labor platform companies to countries like Uruguay to encourage tech workers to engage in gig work. Apart from the tech industry, Latin America's delivery and transportation sector also adopted gig work through (1) delivery apps like Rappi in Colombia, iFood in Brazil and Cornershop in Santigao, Chile and Mexico, (2) transportation (ride-hailing) apps like DiDi, i.e., Chuxing Technology Company which is a Chinese Ride-Hailing app that sought to become more established in Mexico, Brazil, Columbia and Peru, as well as Uber and Cabify which offered innovative services and emphasised passenger safety, (3) niche platforms like GetNinjas, Workana and Freelance in Latin America to facilitate job opportunities for highly skilled gig workers, (4) domestic apps such as Zolvers, Alidada, Homely and Hogaru in Argentina, Chile, Colombia, and Mexico that focuses on providing domestic services such as cleaning of homes/offices, laundry/ironing, and child/eldercare, and (5) online web-beased apps like Workana and Clickwork that connects business clients with gig workers in Latin America (Rappi, 2024; Manky & Mogollon, 2024; Freelance Latin America, 2023).

Given the wide integration of gig work and digital labor platforms in Latin America, the composition of gig workers in the areas of business entrepreneurs (27%), and independent contractors (24%), was found by Datta et al., (2023) to be considerably higher than that of platform workers (20%) and seasonal workers (13%) in Venezuela and other Latin American countries. Like gig workers in Asia, Africa, the US, and Finland, a fairly large proportion of gig workers in the LAC region such as Brazil used these short-term employment arrangements as supplementary (21 million), marginal (14 million) and main (12 million) sources of income. Furthermore, most gig workers in the LAC region were found to be not only young (Millennials and Generation X) between the ages of 15-24 (40%), and to a lesser extent 25-64 (57%), but mostly women (Datta et al., 2023, Gillis & Kallenbach, 2019). Moreover, gig workers in the LAC region were found to live in suburban areas of densely populated cities like Sao Paulo, and Mexico City, and in the case of gig workers from Argentina and Venezuela, they often conducted their work in their native language of Spanish, unlike other gig workers around the world who mainly speak English (Datta et al., 2023).

In addition, opportunities for gig work were found to have grown by 33% for LAC between 2016-2020, because of the need for outsourcing specific skills/abilities during and after the COVID-19 pandemic (Datta et al., 2023). Since the onset of the COVID-19 pandemic in 2020, gig work particularly those offered by apps within the transportation and delivery sector has continued to be a popular source of income, due to the surge in prolonged unemployment, and as a result, a significant proportion of transportation workers (1.7million) like those in Brazil have become registered as independent contractors, while location-based platforms like Uber has become regulated in both Mexico and Argentina (Da Silva et al., 2023). To further solidify their market share in Latin America, the web and location-based platforms highlighted earlier have also begun offering their gig workers access to small high-interest loans such as DiDi Loans in Mexico, and Mibanco by Uber in Peru, which although contingent on the workers' performance, is an attempt at reducing the credit risk of these workers along with improving their service (Pinedo, 2022).

Given that the vulnerable segments of LAC, in particular women tend to experience financial exclusion due to lower financial literacy, and higher levels of income instability resulting from their engagement in informal and often precarious forms of employment, the development of the gig economy through digital transformation and financial incentives such as small loans, are likely to improve their financial standing. Therefore, with the increased use of mobile technology, and access to job opportunities where the payment ranges from US$25-US$50 per day, 73% of gig workers in Latin America were able to formally access financial products and services such as setting up banking saving accounts, digital wallets to manage the transfer and payments from gig work. Such formalization implies that not only is there greater financial inclusion, and independence of gig workers but also that the labor market participation of women and other vulnerable groups in Latin America is improving.

Gig Work in the Caribbean: The Case of Trinidad and Tobago

Like the LAC region, during and after the COVID-19 pandemic, Trinidad and Tobago and other Caribbean islands such as Saint Lucia, and Jamaica also experienced sharp increases in their unemployment rate, particularly amongst women because of lockdown measures. This deterioration in the labor market participation across Caribbean islands implies that as the economy contracted workers were vulnerable to losing their jobs in both the formal and informal sectors, as the overall level of registered forms of employment began to weaken (ECLAC-ILO, 2021). Amid the pandemic, and the extreme digitalisation of the labor market and internal business processes, gig work then emerged in the Caribbean as both an alternative to the traditional form of employment and a means by which businesses can streamline their operations to reduce operating costs. As such to capitalize on online income-generating prospects, Caribbean islands such as Jamaica and Dominica have begun participating in the gig economy by setting up the National Commercial Bank (NCB) Gig Network in Jamaica which mirrors the operation of online freelancing apps like Upwork and Fiverr, and the Work Online Programme developed in Dominica (Brathwaite, 2021).

Despite the growing literature on the growth of gig economies in the Global North, and the Global South, in particular Africa, Asia and Latin America, and to a small extent Jamaica and Dominica, there is a prominent absence of literature on its operation and the experiences of gig workers in the Caribbean region. Such an absence may be due to many interlocking problems such as (1) the underrepresentation of the Caribbean region in global studies, (2) the absence of both formal data collection, and comprehensive labor market data that captures the economic activities of gig workers throughout the Caribbean region, and (3) the lack of a universal definition and framework for the analysis of gig work, that can be used to evaluate the development of gig work in the Caribbean region (Datta et al., 2023).

Regardless of these limitations, an examination into the existence of digital labor platforms for the case of Trinidad and Tobago, as summarized by Table 1 and Table 2, has unearthed several findings. Beginning with the information summarized in Table 1, the main type of web-based digital labor platform used by gig workers in Trinidad and Tobago is that of Freelancing apps, i.e., Fiverr, TriniFreelance, and Upwork. Using these platforms, gig workers in Trinidad and Tobago have provided a wide range of online services from voice-overs, graphic design, virtual assistant, writing, consulting, data analysis, software/web development, music promotion/production and producing social media management, to content creation for business clients for a broad range of industries in areas such as tourism, creative, education, entertainment, business, and information technology, as well as advertising, marketing and publishing.

Like gig workers in Latin America, the duration of work tasks done on these web-based platforms by gig workers in Trinidad and Tobago are short-term ranging from 1 to 10 days on Fiverr, and 1 day to 6 months on TriniFreelance. While online gig workers provide a wide range of services as mentioned above, different platforms were observed to use different payment structures, i.e., hourly rates, and rates per job. As a result, gig workers in Trinidad and Tobago have earned between US$5-US$500 per work task on Fiverr, US$10-US$150 per work task on TriniFreelance, and US$10-US$395 per hour on Upwork. Apart from these rates, the earnings of gig workers were also influenced by the industry of employment as well as their level of skills and working experience. Therefore, highly educated and technical skilled gig workers such as systems administrators, web developers, Pay-Per-Click (PPC) managers, e-commerce specialists, and software engineers from Trinidad and Tobago, who were using the Upwork platform apart from their hourly jobs, and fixed-price jobs, who tend to work longer hours, accumulated earnings upwards of US$100,000 since registering with the platform as a gig worker (Upwork, 2024).

Further to this, all gig workers using the Upwork platform from Trinidad and Tobago were observed to have their identity verified through government identification checks, while on other platforms like TriniFreelance, there is a combination of verified and unverified gig workers (Upwork, 2024; TriniFreelance, 2023). The inclusion of unverified gig workers by platforms such as TriniFreelance and Fiverr have also been found to be misleading in terms of the number of persons engaged in gig work because while the absence of platform fees may encourage persons to create user profiles, a vast majority of gig workers who are new to using these platforms have neither engaged in active gigs nor completed any gig projects/services (TriniFreelance, 2023; Fiverr, 2024).

Apart from the few web-based platforms, gig workers were observed to be more heavily involved in job opportunities provided by location-based platforms in Trinidad and Tobago. As summarized by Table 2, there are four main types of location platforms in Trinidad and Tobago, i.e., (1) Taxi (Transportation), (2) Delivery, (3) Healthcare, and (4) Home Services/ Domestic Work/ Care Services, which are concentrated primarily in the transportation, food and beverage, healthcare, professional and business services sector, as well as home, domestic and care services that are a part of the informal sector. The most popular of these digital labor platforms as highlighted by Table 2, appears to be Taxi (transportation) Platforms such as TT RideShare, DROP ride, and allRiDi, as well as Delivery platforms such as food DROP, Food Depot, WiEat, Neighbourhood Munchies, and SKIP D LINE. While gig workers working for these ride-hailing companies usually offer their services across Trinidad and Tobago, those employed by delivery platforms tend to concentrate their services in particular geographic areas in Trinidad and Tobago, such as urban centres like Port-of-Spain, Arima, the East-West Corridor, as well as Central Trinidad. The presence of these platforms, i.e., food DROP, Food Depot, WiEat and SKIP D LINE services was observed to be comparatively less pronounced in Southern Trinidad due to the long travel distance, with Neighbourhood Munchies being the only delivery type platform operating in Southern Trinidad.

Despite differences in operations based on their geographic location, it was important to note that taxi and delivery platforms have varying base rates for their services in the local currency. For example, TT RideShare charges a base rate of TT$1.00 - TT$40.00 per ride/km, DROP ride charges a base rate of TT$25 with an additional TT$1.25 per ride/km, and allRiDi charges base rates of TT$15 and TT$20 per ride/km, where the pricing of all services was influenced by the distance travelled and the number of packages being delivered. Similarly, the prices of menu items on the various food delivery platforms were likely to differ from the prices offered by the restaurant, as separate costs such as delivery and service fees may have been included. It is interesting to note that gig workers on web-based platforms in Trinidad and Tobago were able to set their rates of employment. The same cannot be said for gig workers employed by location-based apps highlighted in Table 2, particularly those for taxi and delivery services as they may not have direct control over their earnings which may be influenced by a myriad of factors such as where the driver is located, peak travel/delivery times, high-demand periods, and the algorithms management processes used by these platforms to perform workforce activities.

An exception to such a situation may be the healthcare platform, i.e., MEDICAS, and the Home Services/ Domestic Work/ Care Services platform, i.e., Zipo, operating in Trinidad and Tobago. As in the case of MEDICAS, while doctors and other medical professionals using the platform may be able to set the base rate for online medical consultations/services, gig workers using the Zipo have more control over the cost of their services, as the platform merely acts as an intermediary to connect gig workers providing home, domestic and care services to clients, and facilitates the processing of payments through its payment facilitation system (Zipo, 2022a, 2022b).

Table 1. Web-Based Digital Labor Platforms Used by Gig Workers in Trinidad and Tobago

Company	**Location**	**Types of Services**	**Cost**	**Industrial Concentration**
Online-Web Based Digital Labor Platforms				
Freelancing:				
Fiverr (Fiverr, 2024)	Tel Aviv, Israel.	Voice-over, General and travel Information, Steelpan recording, Creative writing/Poetry Video narration, Radio/DJ drops, Graphic design	Average of US$5-US$500 per work task	Creative, Tourism, Education.

continued on following page

Table 1. Continued

Company	Location	Types of Services	Cost	Industrial Concentration
TriniFreelance (TriniFreelance, 2023)	San Juan, Trinidad and Tobago.	Graphic design, Human resource/ Financial/Marketing Consulting, Writing (articles, books, blogs, proofreading, editing, speech writing, technical writing, translation, transcripts), AutoCAD, Data Analysis, Cyber Security, Data entry, Digital marketing, E-commerce, Landscaping, Software development, Web/Mobile app building and development, Music promotion, producing, and transcription, Voiceovers.	Average of US$10- US$150 per work task	Advertising and Marketing, Entertainment, Publishing, Film and Television, Education, E-commerce, Business, Information technology, Health and Wellness, Travel and Leisure.
Upwork (Upwork, 2024)	California, United States.	Graphic design, Marketing, Virtual assistant and Education content creation, Creative writing, B2B and B2C sales, E-commerce, Content creation, Programming, Data entry, Academic writing, social media management/ marketing, Transcription, Copyediting, Voice over, Video editing, technical writing, Software development and design, Proofreading, 3D animation/motion graphics, Deep learning engineering, and Project management.	Average of US$10- US$395 per hour	Creative, Marketing and Sales, Technology and Development, Education and Academic Services, Multimedia Production, Project Management.

Source: Authors' compilation.

Table 2. Location-Based Digital Labor Platforms Used by Gig Workers in Trinidad and Tobago

Company	Location	Types of Services	Cost
Location-Based Digital Labor Platforms			
Taxi			
TT RideShare (TTRS, 2024)	Trinidad and Tobago	Transportation Service.	Average of TT$1.00 - TT$40.00 per ride/km.
DROP ride (DROP Caribbean, 2024a)	Port-of-Spain, Trinidad and Tobago	Transportation Service: Personal rides, Courier Services, Business Services.	Base rate of TT$25 with an additional TT$1.25 per ride/km, and TT$172 per hour.

continued on following page

Table 2. Continued

Company	Location	Types of Services	Cost
allRiDi (allRiDi, 2023a, 2023b)	Trinidad and Tobago	Transport and Delivery Service.	Base rates of TT$15 and TT$20 per ride/ km. Base rate TT$50 per delivery/km/ number of packages.
Delivery			
food DROP (DROP Caribbean, 2024b)	Port-of-Spain, Trinidad and Tobago	Food Delivery and Retail Store services: Pharmaceuticals, Grocery items, Healthy and Beauty supplies, Computer supplies, and Pet supplies.	Various Prices
Food Depot (Food Depot 2024)	Arima, Trinidad and Tobago	Grocery Delivery services, focusing on urban areas such as Arima and Port-of-Spain.	Base rates of TT$45, with TT$15 for each additional store.
WiEat (WIEAT, 2024)	Port-of-Spain, Trinidad and Tobago	Food Delivery services, focusing on urban areas such as Port-of-Spain.	Various Prices.
Neighbourhood Munchies (Neighbourhood Munchies, 2024)	San Fernando, Trinidad and Tobago	Food Delivery services, focusing on Southern Trinidad.	Various Prices.
SKIP D LINE (SKIPDLINE, 2020)	Valsayn, Trinidad and Tobago	Food Delivery services, focusing on the East-West Corridor and Central Trinidad.	Various Prices.
Healthcare			
MEDICAS (MEDICAS, 2022)	Kolkata, India	E-Health Care Services: Online doctor appointments/consultations, lab tests,	TT$175 per consultation, TT$50 – TT$5,300 for lab tests.
Home Services/ Domestic Work/ Care Services			
Zipo (Zipo, 2022a, 2022b)	Trinidad and Tobago	Appliance Repair, Automotive, Beauty, caregiving, Construction, Education, Engineering Services, Entertainment and Events, Financial.	Various Prices.

Source: Authors' compilation.

THE PROS AND CONS OF GIG WORK BACKED BY TECHNOLOGICAL GROWTH IN TRINIDAD AND TOBAGO

As illustrated in the preceding section, the shift to gig work in Trinidad and Tobago has largely been driven by the transition from the traditional employment models to more adaptable working arrangements encompassing remote work and gig opportunities, which gained traction during the COVID-19 pandemic. Although the number of operational digital labor platforms is small, their continued use by gig workers indicates that Trinidad and Tobago's technological landscape has been changing. Characterised by substantial growth in flexibility, connectivity, and diversity, gig workers in Trinidad and Tobago have become progressively more attracted to undertaking these short-term "gigs", because of many interconnected factors such as the heightened use of mobile devices, and the adoption of both 5G technologies and industry 4.0 technologies.

Mobile Technology

The widespread access and use of mobile devices and applications as discussed by Ma & Yang (2018) have become an increasingly popular tool used by gig workers because it gives them the flexibility to plan for short-term work as most high-end smart mobile devices have fast charging, long battery life, and processing power, that allows them to not only navigate multiple tasks running on different applications, while communicating with business clients, thus reducing interruptions, but also maximize efficiency and productivity. A high level of mobile device and digital platform proficiency is essential for the functioning of transportation and delivery-based location services in Trinidad and Tobago, as these services rely heavily on apps like Google Maps, GPS navigation, and client information that are continuously being updated through their respective platforms (Metawala, et al., 2024).

The use of location-based mobile applications assists gig workers in Trinidad and Tobago to not only manage, and record the progress of each assigned task, but also monitor the amount of time spent and the money earned from each task all from their mobile device (Hunt & Machingura, 2016). Similar to freelancers that use Airtasker in Australia, the use of mobile devices is critical to helping persons in Trinidad and Tobago who venture into gig work to earn an income and lead a more relaxed lifestyle as it enables them to pursue other interests such as travelling and pursuing higher education opportunities, that may not have been possible with traditional working arrangements that have restrictions on leave that limits the time that can be taken-off (Ma & Yang, 2018).

Despite the many benefits that mobile technology has made towards the development and uptake of gig work in Trinidad and Tobago, its continuous use presents workers with several challenges. In that, gig workers who manage multiple gigs across various digital labor platforms in Trinidad and Tobago through mobile applications can quickly reduce the battery life of handsets, which limits the performance of the device, particularly for older mobile devices. To cope with the heavy use of gig work applications, Hunt and Machingura (2016) explain that as in the case of gig workers in South Africa, it is crucial to invest in a high-end smart mobile device that is compatible with the applications being used by the platforms.

This is an important point, because a basic mobile device may not be able to access all platform features, have robust security applications to prevent breaches of privacy, and simply cannot keep up with the numerous applications being used for gig work. However, while some platforms may provide workers with devices as in the case of gig workers in India, given that most gig workers in Trinidad and Tobago may reside in low-income households, where they earn less than the minimum wage, it is unlikely that they will be able to afford and maintain such high-end devices (Kasliwal, 2020). This is mainly because of many issues such as (1) high-end mobile devices may cost substantially more than low-end devices, (2) the rising cost of mobile data plans and maintenance may be unsustainable for low-income households to access a reliable and continuous connection to the internet, (3) lack of access to subsidy programmes and credit programmes that allow low-income household access to subsidized high-end mobile devices for purposes of gig work, and (4) the lack of technical support or training can make it difficult for low-income households to address issues that may arise with the use of a high-end mobile device (Wood et al., 2018). As a result, the continued reliance on poor-quality of devices used by gig workers in low-income households is likely to contribute to greater job insecurity and a decline in their well-being as these devices may be unreliable tools for securing and carrying out tasks efficiently.

5G Networks

The improvement in Trinidad and Tobago's digital infrastructure, through the adoption of fifth-generation (5G) technology by domestic cellular networks and internet service providers such as Amplia, Flow and RVR networks, has also played an important role in the growth of gig work. The advanced features of 5G networks and next-generation 6G networks include, (1) the quicker rates at which data can be uploaded and downloaded in seconds, (2) increased connectivity amongst many users across large distances which enhances location services, (3) significantly reduced latency times that minimize disruptions and provides users with a smoother means of communication, and (4) amplified reliability and efficiency of the performance of the network. Such features create a network connection that not only performs well but is also more energy efficient and tends to facilitate the growth of gig work at an exponential rate (Ghosh et al., 2019).

With 5G speeds, gig workers in Trinidad and Tobago not only have greater access to digital labor platforms, and payment systems on a 24-hour basis but also reduced payment anxiety as they now have a reliable payment gateway that rarely fails due to connectivity issues. Furthermore, the use of 5G networks is likely to have enhanced the rate at which gig workers can communicate and collaborate with platform managers and business clients on shared interests in real time (Ray et al., 2021). It, therefore, reduces the time taken especially for freelancers working on web-based platforms, as well as employment agencies that may be acting as intermediaries to connect freelancers with clients in Trinidad and Tobago, to not only harness the power of data analytics used by these platforms to make more informed data-driven decisions but also encourage the adoption of more professional behaviours amongst gig workers (Jarrahi et al., 2020).

Together with the heightened level of professionalism and operational efficiency, the growth of 5G networks in Trinidad and Tobago may have led to modernizing the labor market. In this respect, the network may have broadened the scope for more remote work opportunities to be created, as web-based gig workers can now engage in tasks regardless of their physical location. This increased flexibility and freedom to engage in various types of job opportunities without being bound to a specific location in Trinidad and Tobago, in turn, supports the creation of jobs and the development of new business models as decent forms of work such as virtual assistants, e-commerce executives and content creators that could have only been achieved in a digital working environment, as it caters to the individual needs and preferences of business clients (Khan et al., 2024).

There are shortcomings in the adoption of 5G technologies however, as in most cases such advanced digital infrastructure is more likely to be set up in urban areas in Trinidad and Tobago, as opposed to rural-remote areas which may lack sufficient coverage. This can widen the urban-rural digital divide and hinder the job prospects of gig workers in rural-remote communities in Trinidad and Tobago when compared to gig workers residing in urban, and suburban areas, as they are more likely to experience connectivity issues, and high installation costs due to their geographic location and lack of infrastructure needed such as cell towers and antennas, that are needed to establish 5G networks in rural-remote areas (Marshall, 2024). In addition to cybersecurity issues, given that 5G networks tend to reduce the battery life of mobile devices when connected, it is possible that some mobile devices may not be compatible with such networkers, and can limit the ability of gig workers to use their smartphones for gig work.

Cloud Computing (CC), Automation, & Data Analytics

Cloud computing technology is one of the major drivers of gig work worldwide as it permits digital platforms, as well as gig workers to use the information gathered to adjust their services based on the demand of business clients. As such during periods of high activity, location-based platforms in Trinidad and Tobago, for example, TTRide Share can use cloud computing platforms such as Google Cloud Platform (GCP), Microsoft Azure, and Oracle Could, to reduce cost, automate the storage and analysis of large amounts of data, as well as manage and evaluate the performance of their gig workers (Rani & Furrer, 2021).

Given that cloud technology can be used to match and track rides and payments by location-based platforms in the transportation industry, gig workers can use the data analytics produced to, (1) better collaborate and communicate with clients, (2) identify trends to make better decisions, (3) manage their project timelines, and (4) secure more job opportunities (Kudyba et al., 2020). Platform managers however may have used cloud computing tools such as machine learning, networking and enterprise solutions embedded within the platform to gain greater insights into the data collected to provide a more seamless service for gig workers and business clients.

Although Cloud Computing, Automation and Data Analytics have been exceedingly beneficial for the platforms and the workers that use them, they do have several drawbacks. In that, to effectively harness cloud computing, gig workers in Trinidad and Tobago need first a stable internet connection such as those provided by 5G networkers, to reduce the likelihood that crucial data is not lost, and second an effective cybersecurity system that reduces the probability that the devices used cannot become infiltrated by hacking, ransomware, malware attacks, and phishing scams causing data to be either damaged or leaked (Mokhtar & Rohaizat, 2024). Considering that most gig workers have little control over the cybersecurity measures implemented by web and locational-based platforms, they may become vulnerable to cyber-attacks and threats. This may not only reduce the efficiency and performance of gig workers who become victims of these crimes in Trinidad and Tobago but the revenue derived from such activities can be used to facilitate traditional forms of crimes such as human trafficking, money laundering and the trafficking of arms, ammunition and narcotics.

Web and Location-based digital platforms, make great use of automation tools to hire, and match gig workers with tasks, as well as issue computer-generated contracts. However, while these tools can improve the efficiency and productivity of platforms, they can also encourage gig workers in Trinidad and Tobago to become displaced (Vertesi et al., 2020). In that, they may become vulnerable to experiencing job displacement and discrimination when engaging in web and location-based platform work because the use of automation tools in the hiring and matching of gig workers with business clients may lead to prejudices that may result in a higher demand for highly skilled workers with enhanced capabilities, rather than gig workers who have lower educational achievement (Tanoamchard & Ceienwattanasook, 2024). This then reduces not only the categories of work that lower-skilled gig workers can pursue, but also their ability to earn a living.

Additionally, the use of the data analytics produced by web and location-based platforms while it can be beneficial to platform managers and gig workers in Trinidad and Tobago who wish to personalize their services based on the demand of business clients, can again create several issues. These problems can range from increased burnout, stress, anxiety, and isolation of both platform managers and gig workers, who strive to continuously maintain unrealistically high customer ratings (Keith et al., 2020). Further to this, given that standard performance and evaluation measures tend to overlook the diverse working and leadership styles of its diverse pool of gig workers, previous job experience and industry trends, it is likely that the data analytics produced may not accurately reflect their performance. As a result, this may cause web and location-based platforms in Trinidad and Tobago to have a high employee turnover rate, and reduced job satisfaction among gig workers (Kumar et al., 2024). This can negatively impact their mental and physical health outcomes, as well as their overall well-being.

Machine Learning (ML)

Most digital labor platforms in gig economies around the world use ML to manage routine and repetitive tasks such as taking surveys, labelling images, translating text, task allocations and undertaking performance evaluations. However, ML has also been used by digital labor platforms with other types of technologies such as facial recognition and AI-powered ML to optimise the allocation of tasks and reduce errors with minimal human intervention. Using the data collected from gig workers through identity checks in real-time using biometric authentication, platforms can enhance the security of the services produced while matching business clients with the most appropriate gig workers based on their skill set, location and availability (Watkins, 2023).

The adoption of facial recognition technology for gig work, as well as sophisticated ML algorithms/models, has many advantages in that, not only does it improve the security of gig workers' environments by only allowing authorised access, and detecting unusual trends, but it also reduces illegal activities such as theft, and fraud as business clients and workers can verify their identities with each other, which improves the customer experience (Kumar et al., 2024). By using ML algorithms, platforms can minimize both the costs associated with hiring gig workers and evaluate their performance in real-time. This has many benefits as it can help workers to observe their productivity and use the feedback of platform managers to improve their schedules and work-life balance to maximize their performance (Kadolkar et al., 2024).

Even with the benefits of using ML for gig work, the use of ML algorithms can impact the job security and financial stability of gig workers negatively in Trinidad and Tobago. The use of ML algorithms, similarly to that of data analytics can create and perpetuate gender discrimination and bias in the hiring and matching process, as the decisions made by the algorithms are based on the type and quality of the data used (Cahn et al., 2019). Given that ML algorithms used by digital labor platforms in Trinidad and Tobago, like many other countries around the world, operate with little human oversight due to a lack of labor legislation to regulate its use, the decisions made by the platforms may lack both transparency and accountability. Without such mechanisms in place, this can lead to high levels of employee turnover, as the impersonal approach by platform managers, may cause workers to experience feelings of prejudice, bias, isolation, devaluation and overall dissatisfaction with the type and quality of tasks assigned by the platform (Zhang, et al., 2022). With such issues present, it can also harm both the earnings of gig workers who may because of financial instability engage in other precarious forms of work in unsafe environments, as well as their well-being as their sense of agency and autonomy has been restricted by the algorithm that the platform uses.

Artificial Intelligence

The integration of AI-based technologies on web and location-based platforms has also transformed gig work for all stakeholders. In the case of platform managers of web and location-based platforms in Trinidad and Tobago, AI algorithms have been used for a wide array of internal jobs done by platforms like Fiverr and Upwork, such as analysing the skills and job preferences of new and current gig workers, and to match them with appropriate business clients (Liu et al., 2021). In doing so, this not only enhances the productive capacity of the platform itself, driving down cost and reducing waste but also guarantees the satisfaction of both the client and the worker, as there is a wide range of job opportunities and an international talent pool of qualified/skilled professionals from which gig workers can be recruited.

The matching process allows gig workers in Trinidad and Tobago, to access more job opportunities that align with their technical skills and abilities, as well as receive feedback on their performance reviews that may be used to identify where gaps in skills and training may be present (Mer et al., 2024). With this information, gig workers can then build a portfolio with more relevant job experience that demonstrates the quality of their work and core competencies, which may be more attractive to potential business clients, while seeking out professional development opportunities to enhance their effectiveness in the digital working environment. Given that the main attraction of gig work is its flexibility, the use of AI further enhances this feature, as it enables gig workers in Trinidad and Tobago to make the best use of their time, by managing their workload based on their core objectives and, creating structured schedules, while considering their personal commitments and job preferences (Bunjack et al., 2021). In this way, gig workers who may be using the platforms as either their primary, or secondary source of income may be able to manage the ill effects of platform work, to achieve a greater work-life balance.

While the use of AI has brought about many benefits to gig workers and platform managers, its drawbacks are quite comparable to that of ML algorithmics, where the use of AI-based recruitment tools can unintentionally perpetuate bias and discrimination against different groups of gig workers (Li, et al., 2022). As a result, instead of reducing social bias and inequalities, these problems can heighten feelings of isolation, burnout and displacement as gig workers based on the features of their profile such as less technical skills and abilities, ethnicity, gender and geographic location may find themselves being assigned fewer tasks by the platform (Altenreid, 2020). The repercussions of such an outcome could significantly affect the financial stability of households in Trinidad and Tobago that rely on gig work as their main source of income. As the labor provided by low-income, unskilled, or semi-skilled gig workers in Trinidad and Tobago may become undervalued in comparison to highly skilled gig workers. Such a disparity can create a precarious situation for those in lower-paying gig roles, as the demand for their services may diminish, leading to inconsistent income and greater financial vulnerability for low-income gig workers, which could exacerbate socioeconomic inequalities in Trinidad and Tobago (Graham et al., 2017).

ECONOMIC IMPLICATIONS OF GIG WORK IN TRINIDAD AND TOBAGO

The growth of gig work, fuelled by technological advancements in Trinidad and Tobago, has significantly changed how the labor market perceives remote and flexible employment options. While these features have been attractive to low-income households and vulnerable groups seeking to earn an income, the working arrangements also present substantial drawbacks for workers, along with various economic implications. Thus, in this section, emphasis will be placed on specific challenges and the economic impact of gig work on Trinidad and Tobago's economy.

The main challenge faced by gig workers in Trinidad and Tobago, like many around the world, is the lack of job security and employment benefits that are typically associated with traditional employment models. Since the employment opportunities provided by web and location-based platforms in Trinidad and Tobago to engage in gig work is a precarious form of employment, it contributes to the financial instability and job insecurity of workers. Given that gig workers are frequently classified or misclassified as independent contractors/freelancers, they are not captured by official labor market statistics. Without such representation, it then becomes difficult for gig workers to either form a trade union or acquire trade union representation that negotiates with platform managers for better wages and contracts, as well as access employment-based health and insurance benefits or retirement benefits on their behalf (Doherty & Franca, 2020).

Unlike traditional working arrangements where these benefits are available to workers, under a gig work arrangement where the workers' income is constantly fluctuating, they will not be able to access national insurance benefits in Trinidad and Tobago. This may be due to two crucial factors, first gig workers' inability to contribute to the national insurance scheme, and second the lack of re-evaluation and adaptation of local labor legislation to include gig workers. Firstly, the unstable incomes of gig workers, the high contribution rates and the rigidity of existing schemes that do not consider flexible income patterns may prevent workers from making regular contributions to national insurance schemes (WB, 2024). Second, Trinidad and Tobago's labor legislation, like Southeast Asia where there is a prominent presence of gig work, may not have either amended its labor laws to include gig work as a legitimate form of employment or established specific laws/comprehensive guidelines for gig workers and platform managers operating domestically (Khan & Saqib, 2024). Because of this, the labor market regulations which apply to workers engaged in traditional forms of employment, may not apply to gig workers. This makes gig workers in Trinidad and Tobago vulnerable to experiencing discrimination, abuse, and unfair labor practices such as not being compensated for injuries while on the job (particularly for gig workers engaged in location-based gig work such as transportation and deliveries), reduction in earnings resulting from algorithmic bias in the assigning of tasks and technical difficulties when accessing the platform, can be considered a form of wage theft (Zipper et al., 2022).

Notwithstanding these challenges, the growth of gig work in Trinidad and Tobago can have both negative and positive economic implications for the economy. In that, gig work in Trinidad and Tobago can create income-generating opportunities for vulnerable segments of the population such as persons with lower socio-economic status, where there weren't any before, as well as encourage the development of Small and Medium-Sized Enterprises (SMEs) (Hsieh et al., 2023). Such opportunities not only reduce the vulnerability of marginalized persons whose inclusion, diversifies Trinidad and Tobago's workforce, but the access to a global supply of highly educated and skilled labor for specific tasks enhances the productivity and competitiveness of local SMEs across industries.

The growing competitiveness of SMEs fuelled by gig workers can have numerous benefits for Trinidad and Tobago, such as (1) job creation resulting from expanding production, (2) stimulating economic growth by increasing their productive capacity and efficient with the help of a competent and innovative gig workforce, (3) nurturing innovation and supporting local economic development, as SMEs can invest in research and development needed to create unique goods and services with inputs being outsourced locally, and regionally in the Caribbean, (4) the combined efforts of increased competitiveness, and innovation, can enable local SMEs to enter new marketing, which enhances cross-border trade, which is an essential component of encouraging sustainable economic growth in Trinidad and Tobago, and (5) the development of more tech-savvy SMEs can become the driving force behind the advancing of gig legislation in Trinidad and Tobago, as the regulation is essential for them to adapt and navigate global volatile markets, as well as attract investment into the digital technologies used by SMEs (Youssef, et al., 2020; Lantowa & Machmud, 2020; Fan et al., 2023).

Gig work presents valuable income-generating opportunities for a diverse range of workers in Trinidad and Tobago, spanning from those with minimal skills to highly experienced professionals, however, this flexible source of employment may also inadvertently worsen existing challenges such as brain drain and skills mismatch. In the case of the latter, it is possible the excess demand for tasks that require workers with low skills on web and location-based platforms, can contribute to skills mismatch as the skills of highly educated workers, may become underutilized by the platforms (Mark et al., 2018). As a result, although highly-skilled workers in Trinidad and Tobago may be initially attracted to gig work in the short term because of the myriads of benefits that it promises, in the long term they are not reaching their full potential by using their skills in a way that it enhances their careers and overall wellbeing, these workers may still opt migrate to more affluent countries where their skills, and abilities are valued, and where they retain their fundamental rights as a worker (Docquier, 2014).

While brain drain may stimulate remittance inflows, and education in Trinidad and Tobago, the continuing departure of highly educated gig workers may unfortunately cause the quality of its human capital stock to deteriorate. However, for highly educated and skilled workers that choose to stay in Trinidad and Tobago, while undertaking gig work, the latter can have a positive impact on brain drain. The flexible working arrangements may offer this segment of workers a better form of work-life balance that allows them to easily manage personal and professional obligations, without being constrained by traditional work regulations (APO, 2019). As a result of this, gig workers may be more willing to explore multiple types of jobs and career opportunities that provide them with multiple streams of income, which reduces their desire to migrate (retaining talent) while boosting local economic development in various communities across Trinidad and Tobago.

CONCLUSION

Exploring the impact that the emergence of gig work has on the global labor market is crucial because of the rapid pace at which it is being adopted by countries around the world and the part that it plays in addressing extensive problems such as financial instability, job insecurity, unemployment, the payment of subminimum wages, and the lack of regulatory frameworks for different types of work. Since the onset of the COVID-19 pandemic in 2020, gig work has grown in popularity because it enabled businesses and workers alike to transition their in-person activities to one that now accommodated remote work and flexible working arrangements. It is in this context, that many full-time, part-time, as well as unemployed workers entered the gig space, which gave rise to the demand for a diverse range of platform work opportunities, as well as the growth and development of digital labor platforms worldwide.

Within the literature on gig work, studies have focused primarily on a variety of topics such as employment protection, labor legislation and the economic impact of gig work for a few key countries such as the US, UK, China, Brazil, Africa and India. However, within the literature, there is a dearth of information on gig work in the Caribbean region, for countries like Trinidad and Tobago in which gig work is newly emerging. Due to the growth and economic significance of gig work globally, a study of this nature is of great importance for Trinidad and Tobago, because while it promises to drive down the post-pandemic unemployment rate, it offers flexible job opportunities and a safety net for many vulnerable segments of the population, it has the potential to contribute significantly to the gross domestic product. This is of great importance as the integration of industry 4.0 technologies, such as Cloud Computing (CC), Automation, Data Analytics, Machine Learning, and Artificial Intelligence all show great promise to have a profound impact on gig work in Trinidad and Tobago, Although the growth of gig work as highlighted in this study may have negative outcomes such as brain drain and skills mismatch in Trinidad and Tobago, in spite of its precariousness it may reduce the socio-economic vulnerability that low-income households, women and young adults may experience.

As Trinidad and Tobago's gig economy begins to expand, a study of this nature which highlights both the web and location-based digital platforms that are currently operational, along with their pros and cons, and economic implications, is of great significance as it demonstrates how businesses can enhance its operational efficiency and optimizing resources, while reducing costs. In doing so, this study serves as the foundation for several future avenues of research such as examining the role of trade union representation and the integration of AI-based technologies in Gig work in Trinidad and Tobago.

COMPETING INTERESTS

The author of this publication declares there are no competing interests.

FUNDING

This research received no specific grant from any funding agency in the public, commercial, or not-for-profit sectors. Funding for this research was covered by the author of the article.

REFERENCES

allRiDi. (2023a). *allRiDi Fulfilment.*https://af.allridi.com/

allRiDi. (2023b). *Getting a fare estimate.*https://help.allridi.com/support/solutions/articles/47001079281-getting-a-fare-estimate

Altenried, M. (2020). The platform as a factory: Crowdwork and the hidden labor behind artificial intelligence. *Capital and Class*, *44*(2), 145–158. DOI: 10.1177/0309816819899410

Anwar, M. A., & Graham, M. (2020). Between a rock and a hard place: Freedom, flexibility, precarity and vulnerability in the gig economy in Africa. *Competition & Change*, *25*(2), 237–258. DOI: 10.1177/1024529420914473

Asian Productivity Organization (APO). (2019). *Nepal's Gig Economy and its Implications on Labor Participation and Income Distribution*. APO.

Azevedo, E. S. F., Souza, D. F., & Mendonca, J. R. C. (2023). Algorithmic management on digital labor platforms: A Systematic Literature Review. *Contextus - Contemporary Journal of Economics and Management,* 21 (e83099): 1-14. DOI: 10.19094/contextus.2023.83099

Borghi, P., & Murgia, A. (2024). Beyond borders: Trans-organisational and transnational alliances among gig workers in the United Kingdom and Italy. *The Journal of Industrial Relations*, *66*(3), 410–433. DOI: 10.1177/00221856241238617

Brathwaite, C. (2021). *The gig economy in the Caribbean.* Bridgetown, Barbados: Barbados Today. https://barbadostoday.bb/2021/10/15/btcolumn-the-gig-economy-in-the-caribbean/

Bunjack, A., Cerne, M., & Popovic, A. (2021). Absorbed in technology but digitally overloaded: Interplay effects on gig worker's burnout and creativity. *Information & Management,* 58(8-103533):1-12. DOI: 10.1016/j.im.2021.103533

Cahn, N., Carbone, J., & Levit, N. (2019). Discrimination by Design? *Arizona State Law Journal, 51*(1), 1–70. https://scholarship.law.umn.edu/cgi/viewcontent.cgi?article=1632&context=faculty_articles

Caribbean, D. R. O. P. (2024a). *We Are Now Distance and Time Fares.*https://dropcaribbean.com/distance-and-time-fares/

Caribbean, D. R. O. P. (2024b). *More than food delivery.* https://dropcaribbean.com/fooddrop/

Charlton, E. (2021). *What is the gig economy and what's the deal for gig workers?* Geneva, Switzerland: World Economic Forum (WEF).

Da Silva, A. N. R., Pitombo, C. S., Junior, J. U. P., Ciriaco, T. G. M., & Costa, C. S. (2023). Changes in mobility and challenges to the transport sector in Brazil due to COVID-19. In Zhang, J., & Hayashi, Y. (Eds.), *Transportation Amid Pandemics* (pp. 105–118). Elsevier., DOI: 10.1016/B978-0-323-99770-6.00010-7

Dargay, J. M., & Clark, S. (2012). The determinants of long-distance travel in Great Britain. *Transportation Research Part A, Policy and Practice*, *46*(3), 578–587. DOI: 10.1016/j.tra.2011.11.016

Datta, N., Rong, C., Singh, S., Stinshoff, C., Iacob, N., Nigatu, N. S., Nxumalo, M., & Klimaviciute, L. (2023). Working Without Borders: The Promise and Peril of Online Gig Work. Washington DC, United States: World Bank (WB). DOI: 10.1596/40066

Di Tella, R., & Rodrik, D. (2020). Labor Market Shocks and the Demand for Trade Protection: Evidence from Online Surveys. *Economic Journal (London)*, *130*(628), 1008–1030. DOI: 10.1093/ej/ueaa006

Docquier, F. (2014). The brain drain from developing countries. *IZA World of Labor: Evidence-Based Policy Making*, *31*, 1–10. DOI: 10.15185/izawol.31

Doherty, M., & Franca, V. (2020). The (non/) response of trade unions to the "gig" challenge. *Italian Labor Law E-Journal,* 13(1):125-140. DOI: 10.6092/issn.1561-8048/10762

Economic Commission for Latin America and the Caribbean and the International Labor Organization (ECLAC-ILO). (2021). *Employment Situation in Latin America and the Caribbean. Decent Work for Platform Workers in Latin America*. ECLAC-ILO.

Fan, Z., Wang, Y., & Ying, Z. (2023). Empowerment of Cross-Border E-Commerce Platforms for Small and Medium-Sized Enterprises: Evidence from China. *Journal of Business-To-Business Marketing*, *30*(1), 33–44. DOI: 10.1080/1051712X.2023.2175633

Fiverr. (2024). *Find the right freelance service, right away.* Tel Aviv, Israel: Fiverr. https://www.fiverr.com/

Food Depot. (2024). *Ordering groceries for delivery from local stores.* https://fooddepottt.com/

Freelance Latin America. (2023). *About Us.* Florida, United States: Freelance Latin America. https://freelancelatam.com/about-us/

Ghosh, A., Maeder, A., Baker, M., & Chandramouli, D. (2019). 5G Evolution: A View on 5G Cellular Technology Beyond 3GPP Release 15. *IEEE Access : Practical Innovations, Open Solutions*, *7*, 127639–127651. DOI: 10.1109/ACCESS.2019.2939938

Gillis, K., & Kallenbach, S. R. (2019). Gig Workers. Who are they and What do they Want? *LIMRA Secure Retirement Institute Review*, *2*, 1–11.

Gojeck, (2023). *About us.* Singapore: Gojeck. https://www.gojek.com/sg/about

Grab. (2024). *From essential services to earning opportunities. We're an all-in-one platform.* Singapore: Grab. https://www.grab.com/sg/

Graham, M., Lehdonvirta, V., Wood, A., Barnard, H., Hjorth, I., & Simon, D. P. (2017). *The Risks and Rewards of Online Gig Work at the Global Margins*. Oxford Internet Institute, University of Oxford.

Hadiati, D., Budiono, A. R., & Widhiyanti, H. N. (2023). Legal Relationship Between Platform Service Providers and Online Transportation Drivers as Gig Workers (Platform Workers). *International Journal of Islamic Education. Research and Multiculturalism*, *5*(3), 751–771. DOI: 10.47006/ijierm.v5i3.276

Heeks, R. (2021). *From Digital Divide to Digital Justice in the Global South: Conceptualizing Adverse Digital Incorporation.* 1st Virtual Conference on Implications of Information and Digital Technologies for Development, Conference Proceedings, arXiv preprint arXiv, 776(2108.09783): 1-11. DOI: 10.2139/ssrn.3907633

Hsieh, J., Adisa, O., Bafna, S., & Zhu, H. (2023, June). *Designing Individualized Policy and Technology Interventions to Improve Gig Work Conditions.* In, *Proceedings of the 2nd Annual Meeting of the Symposium on Human-Computer Interaction for Work*, Oldenburg, Germany, 1-9. DOI: 10.1145/3596671.3598576

Hunt, A., & Machingura, F. (2016). A good gig? The rise of on-demand domestic work. [London, UK: Overseas Development Institute] [ODI]. *Working Paper*, *7*, 1–44.

International Labor Organization (ILO). (2021). *World Employment and Social Outlook. The Role of digital labor platforms in transforming the world of work*. ILO.

Jarrahi, M. H., Sutherland, W., Nelson, S. B., & Sawyer, S. (2020). Platformic Management, Boundary Resources for Gig Work, and Worker Autonomy. *Computer Supported Cooperative Work*, *29*(1-2), 153–189. DOI: 10.1007/s10606-019-09368-7

Kadolkar, I., Kepes, S., & Subramony, M. (2024). Algorithmic management in the gig economy: A systemic review and research integration. *Journal of Organizational Behavior*, •••, 1–24. DOI: 10.1002/job.2831

Kasliwal, R. (2020). Gender and the Gig Economy: A Qualitative Study of Gig Platforms for Women Workers. *ORF*. *Issue Brief*, *359*, 1–14.

Kavese, K., & Mbali, A. (2022). The Gig Economy, Digital Labor Platforms and Independent Employment in the Eastern Cape. Vincent, London: Eastern Cape Socioeconomic Consultative Council (ECSECC).

Keith, M. G., Harms, P. D., & Long, A. C. (2020). Worker Health and Well-Being in the Gig Economy: A Proposed Framework and Research Agenda. In Perrewe, P. L., Harms, P. D., Harms, P. D., & Chang, C.-H. (Eds.), Research in Occupational Stress and Well-Being: Vol. 18. *Entrepreneurial and Small Business Stressors, Experienced Stress, and Well-Being* (pp. 1–33). Emerald Publishing., DOI: 10.1108/S1479-355520200000018002

Khan, M., & Saqib, Z. (2024). Emerging Voice Mechanisms in Asian Gig Economies: Implications for Gig Workers' Work and Life. In Chan, X. W., Shang, S., & Lu, L. (Eds.), *Work-Life Research in the Asia-Pacific. Palgrave Studies in Equity, Diversity, Inclusion, and Indigenization in Business*. Palgrave Macmillan., DOI: 10.1007/978-3-031-52795-1_3

Khan, M. H., Williams, P., & Mayes, R. (2024). Caring in the Gig Economy: A Relational Perspective of Decent Work. *Work, Employment and Society*, *38*(4), 1107–1127. DOI: 10.1177/09500170231173586

Kudyba, S., Fjermestad, J., & Davenport, T. (2020). A research model for identifying factors that drive effective decision-making and the future of work. *Journal of Intellectual Capital*, *21*(2), 835–851. DOI: 10.1108/JIC-05-2019-0130

Kumar, S., Prasad, K., & Aithal, P. S. (2024). Tech-Business Analytics in GIG Economy-A Futuristic Technology Supported Online Business Model. *Poornaprajna International Journal of Teaching & Research, 1*(1), 1–32. DOI: 10.5281/zenodo.12754703

Lantowa, F. D., & Machmud, J. (2020). Development of Micro, Small and Medium Enterprises (MSMEs) Based on the Creative Economy (EKRAF) and Gig Economy in Gorontaldo Regency. *Journal of Asian Multicultural Research for Economy and Management Study, 1*(2), 43–53. DOI: 10.47616/jamrems.v1i2.61

Liu, Y., Zhao, X., & Li, X. (2021). The coin of AI has two sides: Matching enhancement and information revelation effects of AI on gig economy platforms. *Social Sciences Research Network,* 1-51.

Ma, X., & Yang, S. (2018). Airtasker and the Australian freelance worker: The reflections on the gig economy. *International Journal of Advanced and Applied Sciences, 5*(7), 35–45. DOI: 10.21833/ijaas.2018.07.005

Manky, O., & Mogollon, N. (2024). *How DiDi Chuxing Adapts to Latin America's Era of Digital Platforms*. Carnegie Endowment for International Peace.

Mark, K. P., So, J. C. H., Chan, V. C. W., Luk, G. W. T., & Ho, W. T. (2018). Surviving in the Gig Economy: Change of STEM Students' Perceptions on the Generic Skills for the Workplace. In, *2018 IEEE International Conference on Teaching, Assessment, and Learning for Engineering (TALE)*, Wollongong, Australia,1085-1090, DOI: 10.1109/TALE.2018.8615414

Marshall, A. (2024). A new rural digital divide? Taking stock of geographical digital inclusion in Australia. *Media International Australia, Incorporating Culture & Policy, 190*(1), 68–84. DOI: 10.1177/1329878X231202274

McDowell, L.-B. (2023). *How the gig economy is shaping the landscape of LATAM*. Mauve Group.

MEDICAS. (2022). *About US.*https://medicasapp.com/tt/aboutus/

Mer, A., Matthew, J., & Arora, S. (2024). Managing Gig Economy Workers Through Artificial Intelligence: Applications and Challenges. In N. Joshi., F. A. Malik, C. Gulati, & A. Dubey (eds), *Fostering Industry-Academia Partnerships for Innovation-Driven Tade*, pp. 17-30. IGI Global. DOI: 10.4018/979-8-3693-3096-8.ch002

Metawala, P. G., Golda-Pongratz, K., & Irazabal, C. (2024). All in a Day's Work: Impact of On-Demand Platform Delivery Work on Immigrant Riders in Barcelona. In Vale, M., Ferreira, D., & Rodrigues, N. (Eds.), *Geographies of the Platform Economy* (pp. 157–172). Springer Cham., DOI: 10.1007/978-3-031-53594-9_11

Mokhtar, R., & Rohaizat, A. (2024). Cybercrimes and Cyber Security Trends in the New Normal. In Kamaruddin, N., Idris, A., & Fernandez, K. (Eds.), *The New Normal and Its Impact on Society* (pp. 41–60)., DOI: 10.1007/978-981-97-0527-6_4

Mont, O., Palgan, Y. V., Bradley, K., & Zvolska, L. (2020). A decade of the sharing economy: Concepts, users, business and governance perspectives. *Journal of Cleaner Production, 1*(122215), 1–9. DOI: 10.1016/j.jclepro.2020.122215 PMID: 32542067

Neighbourhood Munchies. (2024). *Welcome to the Neighbourhood. South Trinidad's Premier Food Delivery Service.* https://www.neighbourhoodmunchies.com/

Organization for Economic Co-operation and Development, International Labor Organization, and the European Union. (OECD, ILO & EU). (2023). *Handbook on Measuring Digital Platform Employment and Work.* Paris, France: OECD Publishing. DOI: 10.1787/0ddcac3b-en

Rani, U., & Furrer, M. (2021). Digital Labor Platforms and New Forms of Flexible Work in Developing Countries: Algorithmic Management of Work and Workers. *Competition & Change, 25*(2), 212–236. DOI: 10.1177/1024529420905187

Rappi. (2024). *About Us.* Bogota, Colombia: Rappi Inc. https://about.rappi.com/about-us

Ray, S., Herman, N., & Sen, I. (2021). *Disruptive Transformation Fuelling Gig Economies.* IEEE Technology & Engineering Management Conference-Europe., DOI: 10.1109/TEMSCON-EUR52034.2021.9488630

Schulze, L., Trenz, M., Cai, Z., & Tan, C.-W. (2022). *Algorithmic Unfairness on Digital Labor Platforms: How Algorithmic Management Practices Disadvantage Workers.* 43rd International Conference on Information Systems, Conference Proceedings, 8, Denmark.

Seppanen, L., Spinuzzi, C., Poutanen, S., & Alasoini, T. (2021). Co-creation in Macrotask Knowledge takaWork on Online Labor Platforms. *Nordic Journal of Working Life Studies, 11*(2), 77–98. DOI: 10.18291/njwls.123166

SKIPDLINE. (2020). *About US.* https://skipdline.com/en/content/aboutus

Stewart, A., & Standford, J. (2017). Regulating work in the gig economy: What are the Options? *Economic and Labour Relations Review, 28*(3), 420–437. DOI: 10.1177/1035304617722461

Takagi, S. (2020). Literature survey on the economic impact of digital platforms. *International Journal of Economic Policy Studies, 14*(2), 449–464. DOI: 10.1007/s42495-020-00043-0

Tanoamchard, W., & Ceienwattanasook, K. (2024). The Future of Work and the Impact of Automation on Jobs in Gig Economy in Thailand: A Review of Literature. *Scholar: Human Sciences,* 16(1), 77-88. DOI: 10.14456/shserj.2024.9

TriniFreelance. (2023). *Services Archive.* San Juan, Trinidad & Tobago. https://trinifreelance.com/services/

TT RideShare (TTRS). (2024). *Rider Frequently Asked Questions.* https://ttrideshare.com/rider-faqs/

Upwork. (2024). *Search.* California, United States: Upwork. https://www.upwork.com/nx/search/talent/?nbs=1

Vertesi, J. A., Goldstein, A., Enriquez, D., & Liu, L. (2020). Pre-Automation: Insourcing and Automating the Gig Economy. *Sociologica, 14*(3), 1–27. DOI: 10.6092/issn.1971-8853/11657

Watkins, E. A. (2023). *Face Work: A Human-Centred Investigation into Facial Verification Technology in Gig Work.* Proceedings of the ACM on Human-Computer Interaction, 7(CSCW1), 52(1):1-24. DOI: 10.1145/3579485

Watson, G. (2019). Improving the Federal Tax System for Gig Economy Participants. *Tax Foundation, 672*, 1–17.

WiEat. (2024). *Wieat Terms and Conditions.* https://wieat.com/terms-condition/

Wood, A. J., Graham, M., Lehdonvirta, V., & Hjorth, I. (2018). Good Gig, Bad Gig: Autonomy and Algorithmic Control in the Global Gig Economy. *Work, Employment and Society, 33*(1), 56–75. DOI: 10.1177/0950017018785616 PMID: 30886460

World Bank (WB). (2023). *Demand for Online Gig Work Rapidly Rising in Developing Countries.* Washington DC, United States: WB.

World Bank (WB). (2024). Rethinking Social Insurance for Self-Employed and Gig Workers. *Knowledge Brief Series, 23*, 1–12.

Youssef, S. K., & Sikdar, A. (2020). The Role of Gig Economy in Supporting SME Internationalisation. In Zakaria, N., Abdul-Talib, A. N., & Amelinckx, A. (Eds.), *Transcending Cultural Frontiers* (pp. 91–106). Springer., DOI: 10.1007/978-981-15-4454-5_6

Zhang, A., Boltz, A., Wang, C. W., & Lee, M. K. (2022). Algorithmic management reimagined for workers and by workers: Centering worker well-being in gig work. In *Proceedings of the 2022 CHI Conference on Human Factors in Computing Systems,* 14: 1-20. DOI: 10.1145/3491102.3501866

Zipo. (2022a). *Filters.*https://zipotech.com/service-provider

Zipo. (2022b). *Terms and Conditions.*https://zipotech.com/assets/Frontend/images/terms-and-conditions.pdf

Zipper, B., McNicholas, C., Poydock, M., Schneider, D., & Harknett, K. (2022). *A national survey of gig workers paints a picture of poor working conditions and low pay*. Economic Policy Institute.

Chapter 2
The Precarious Nature of Gig Work for Venezuelan Migrants in Trinidad and Tobago:
Opportunities and Challenges for Integration

Roshnie Anita Doon
https://orcid.org/0000-0002-3285-0355
Global Labor Organization, Germany

ABSTRACT

The gig economy has significantly contributed to the financial stability of migrant workers by providing job opportunities that traditional labor markets may restrict due to language, social, and educational barriers. Despite its importance, information about Venezuelan migrant gig work in Trinidad and Tobago remains scarce. Using a secondary research methodology, this study aims to conceptually discuss how gig work can be used as a mechanism to better integrate Venezuelan migrants into Trinidad and Tobago's labor market. This study highlights that, while gig work may grant Venezuelan migrants' quick access to employment opportunities with limited barriers, issues such as the rigidity of the labor market, inadequate banking support and lack of investment may hinder such a process.

DOI: 10.4018/979-8-3693-9385-7.ch002

INTRODUCTION

The humanitarian crisis as well as the political and economic meltdown of Venezuela have created the perfect conditions to mandate the movement of Venezuelan migrants, refugees, and asylum seekers to Latin America and the Caribbean (LAC) region. Due to its proximity, Trinidad and Tobago has become one of the most important destinations for Venezuelan migrants as they seek safety, stability, and better economic opportunities. However, the rapid influx of Venezuelan migrants has become a significant problem for the twin island state, because it not only puts a strain on its limited economic resources but also raises a host of issues related to socio-economic / labour market integration, discrimination, exploitation, food insecurity, the trafficking of migrant, arms, and drugs, as well as the growing rate of violent crime, homicides, and gun violence (IMO, 2019).

Notwithstanding these problems, Venezuelan migrants may also experience challenges in navigating Trinidad and Tobago's complex labour market. Manifested as systemic and structural barriers to entry, Venezuelan migrants may face several complications such as language barriers, education barriers, lack of documentation, discrimination, and a genuine unfamiliarity with local labour legislation and employment practices that may become an obstacle when seeking traditional employment opportunities (Piasna & Zwysen, 2024). Despite these various dilemmas, gig work may provide a necessary lifeline for many Venezuelan migrants like migrant gig workers in China, Norway, and Austria to earn a living and integrate into Trinidad and Tobago's labour market (Chen et al., 2022; Newlands, 2024). Thus, Venezuelan migrants may be more attracted to opportunities for gig work, due to its low barriers to entry, fast application process, flexibility, minimal paperwork, and recognition of their educational certification.

Although gig work may provide Venezuelan migrants in Trinidad and Tobago with an immediate source of income, and a means to become better integrated into the labor market, Chen et al., (2022) explain that like migrant gig workers in Hangzhou City in China, it often comes with significant drawbacks, such as risky working conditions, inadequate social security support, low occupational satisfaction, and reduced emotional and physical well-being. In some cases, while migrant gig workers are known to earn a relatively high income by pursuing gig work in their host country, Newlands (2024), describes the ability of migrant gig workers in Norway and Sweden to re-frame their employability, amid discrimination, and short-term temporal orientation, i.e., feelings associated with individual achievements, immediate gratification, and short-term planning, often impacts the ability of migrant gig workers to deal with the demands of gig work.

Within the literature on gig work, although there have been a few studies highlighting the experiences, conditions, and limitations of gig migrant workers in Latin American countries like Chile, Brazil, Ecuador, Colombia, and Peru who depend on platform work as a form of income, there is a paucity of information which focuses on Venezuelan migrant gig workers in Trinidad and Tobago, and by extension the Caribbean region (Arriagada et al., 2023). Using a secondary research methodology, this study aims to close this knowledge gap by conceptually discussing how gig work can be used as a mechanism to better integrate Venezuelan migrants into the domestic labor market. The conceptual approach was used for this study because there is a lack of empirical research done on the topic of Trinidad and Tobago due to a lack of available data. This technique allowed for an in-depth exploration of the topic of Venezuelan migrant gig work in Trinidad and Tobago, which led to the identification and filling of research gaps in this area. Thus, enabling a comprehensive discussion to be undertaken.

Despite the inherent challenges and complexities of gig work uncovered in the literature, a study of this nature is important because if implemented well, it can address several problems that Venezuelan migrants experience in the short term such as the fear and uncertainty associated with the separation and deportation of family members, economic hardship linked to their lack of housing, and access to healthcare services, as well as income and food insecurity. Furthermore, this study is of crucial significance in addressing the systemic problems that Venezuelan migrants are likely to experience, such as acculturative stress that may manifest and heighten wider societal issues such as homicides, violent crimes, discrimination, and racism, as gig work may contribute to reducing the prevalence of these problems.

MIGRATION ACROSS VENEZUELAN BORDERS TO TRINIDAD & TOBAGO

The inflow of Venezuelan Migrants

By the end of 2024, the Inter-Agency Coordination Platform for Refugees and Migrants would have estimated that there will be 6.82 million refugees and migrants from Venezuela residing in the LAC region (R4V, 2023). With the population projected to grow to 14.11 million migrants in the regional and sub-regional areas of Latin America, particularly in Central America, Mexico, and the Southern Cone, a vast majority of migrants/refugees require basic amenities to the tune of US$1.59 billion (R4V, 2023). In response to their needs, several Civil Society Organizations (CSOs) and Non-Governmental Organizations (NGOs), international NGOs, and UN agencies have all joined together to support migrants financially in several areas, where the most crucial and underfunded areas continue to remain in education, healthcare, humanitarian transport, protection, integration, and human trafficking.

For the Caribbean region, it is estimated that the population of Venezuelan migrants/refugees will have grown by 255.1 thousand persons by the end of 2024. However, while the region may be able to support a small proportion of migrants, i.e., 54.6 thousand persons, a large segment of 192.7 thousand persons, primarily women and children would remain in a vulnerable position due to the small number of partners (33) and migrant/refugee-led organizations (8) in the Caribbean (R4V, 2023). Such a limited response to the plights of Venezuelan migrants/refugees in the Caribbean implies that they are more likely to remain in a vulnerable financial state in their host region, just like in their home country of Venezuela.

With such a grim regional outlook, the situation seems to be the same at the country level, as the projected population of Venezuelan migrants/refugees in Trinidad and Tobago is expected to grow by 44.8 thousand migrants by the end of 2024 (R4V, 2023). Based on the 2019 migrant registration data, it was found that while there were more male than female migrants, most migrants were young adults between the ages of 20-29 and had dependents in their home country of Venezuela (54%), and in both Trinidad and Tobago & Venezuela (26%) (IOM, 2019). Furthermore, while a small number of female migrants were pregnant (6%), or married/ free union/cohabitating (35%), most were single (62%) and had completed either university (17.1%), or secondary level education (41.9%) before arriving in Trinidad & Tobago (IOM, 2019).

In terms of employment, before migrating many migrants held secure positions in areas such as education, the public sector, and commerce in Venezuela, however after migrating to Trinidad and Tobago, while most migrants remained unemployed, they were now absorbed into the construction, agriculture, and tourism/entertainment sectors (IOM, 2019). With minimal forms of employment and earnings, housing and healthcare remain a critical issue as most migrants either rent rooms or apartments at exorbitant rates, while others access fewer healthcare services due to a lack of knowledge, funds, insurance, and discrimination from local healthcare professionals.

As summarised by Table 1, there is a great need for assistance in several areas such as food security (26,900 migrants), healthcare (35,400, protection/security (38,500 migrants), and integration efforts (32,300 migrants), but like other countries in the LAC region, by the end of 2024, Trinidad and Tobago may not be able to effectively meet these needs due to limited financial resources and stakeholders support (R4V, 2023). Such inadequacies can be observed from Table 1 by the least support provided to targeted migrants/refugees, as well as the number of stakeholders, in areas where there is the most need, such as food security (5,000 migrants targeted for support, 6 stakeholders), healthcare (3,300 migrants targeted for support, 3 stakeholders), integration efforts (3,100 migrants targeted for support, 8 stakeholders), and protection/

security (12,600 migrants targeted for support, 3 stakeholders). Apart from the areas that exhibit the highest level of need, it is also interesting to note that based on the information provided in Table 1, migrants also needed considerable support in the areas of transportation, child protection, gender-based violence, and housing, where there is little stakeholder involvement, but also much smaller financial requirements when compared to the major areas of concern.

Table 1. Areas of Need of Venezuelan Migrants/Refugees in Trinidad and Tobago (2024)

Area of Needs	Persons in Need	Targeted Persons for Support	Persons Not Supported	Number of Stakeholders	Financial Requirement (US$)
Education	8,100	5,400	2,700	5	2.55mn
Food Security	26,900	5,000	21,900	6	2.0mn
Nutrition	6,100	702	5,398	1	69.5k
Healthcare	35,400	3,300	32,100	3	210k
Wash	3,900	-		-	-
Transport	18,400	500	17,900	1	100k
Integration efforts	32,300	3,100	29,200	8	3.48mn
Protection/Security	38,500	12,600	25,900	3	6.70mn
Child Protection	10,200	5,200	5,000	2	1.15mn
Gender-Based Violence	14,800	3,200	11,600	5	748k
Human Trafficking	6,700	310	6,390	3	743k
Housing	14,100	220	13,880	2	771k

Source: Author's Compilation based on RV4 (2023).

Notwithstanding this, several initiatives have been put in place to assist Venezuelan migrants and refugees in Trinidad and Tobago, such as (1) the 2019 migration registration framework that regularized the status of 16,000 migrants, (2) the renewal of permits in 2023, (3) the enrolment of 200 migrant children into the elementary school system and alternative education to 1,774 children in 2024, (4) the regularization of human trafficking and gender-based violence victims (accessed by 15 migrants), (5) the provision of technical/vocational/entrepreneurial training, (6) access to healthcare services (primary healthcare, reproductive and mental healthcare), and (7) the provision of child protective services (accessed by 22 refugee and migrant children) (R4V, 2023; R4V, 2024a).

Even with the attempts at regularizing migrants through the 2019 registration framework, given that the 1951 Refugee Convention has not been integrated into the several pieces of domestic legislation such as the 1969 Immigration Act, together with insufficient guidance provided by refugee and registration policies, Venezuelan migrants remain at risk of becoming either detained, illegally deported, penalized and discriminated against. These problems collectively reduce the ability of Venezuelan migrants to become integrated into Trinidad and Tobago's traditional labor market as the actual number of Venezuelan migrants supported by the initiatives shown in Table 1, remains far less than the targeted number of persons.

Socioeconomic Inequality amongst Venezuelan Migrants

Although there are structured pathways to obtain residency in Trinidad and Tobago, various issues such as (1) institutional and administrative barriers, i.e., lack of recognition of documentation produced by Venezuelans and the lack of access to relevant information can both reduce the labor market participation of migrants, (2) discriminatory barriers, i.e., the perceptions of locals either conscious or unconscious, towards migrants regarding their ethnicity, and language may negatively impact the hiring and onboarding process, (3) educational barriers, i.e., based on the inability of public/private sector enterprises to formally recognize the qualification and training documents of migrants gained in Venezuela before migrating, reduces their access to not only job opportunities, but also educational/training opportunities in Trinidad & Tobago, (4) language and cultural barriers, i.e., based on the inability of communities to accept Venezuelan migrants due to their cultural and language differences which may limit access to basic socio-economic resources, leading to isolation and heightened risks of engaging in criminal activities, and (6) internal socio-cultural perceptions, all continue to obstruct the ability of a vast majority of Venezuelan migrants to take advantage of the services provided by the state (Doon, 2023).

It is, therefore, not surprising that despite Trinidad and Tobago's attempts at dealing with the migrant situation, a vast majority of migrants are consistently being left behind, without basic human needs. As reflected by Table 1, a fairly large number of migrants in 2024 are not supported in the areas of food security (21,900 migrants), healthcare (32,100 migrants), transport (17,900 migrants), integration (29,200 migrants), protection/security (25,900 migrants), gender-based violence (11,600 migrants) and housing (13,880 migrants). As a result of this, Venezuelan migrants continue to face human rights challenges, poverty, and socio-economic inequality. Considering their growing vulnerability, Venezuelan migrants are at risk of experiencing human rights violations and abuse, and as a result are becoming increasingly associated with national security concerns such as Trinidad and Tobago becoming a hub for illegal drugs and transnational crime such as the trafficking of humans, guns and drugs, as well as the proliferation of weapons (Doon, 2024).

Apart from the issues of national security, the influx of Venezuelan migrants into Trinidad and Tobago through its porous borders continues to have significant socio-economic implications for the country as they have the potential to displace both low-skilled nationals who are employed in labour-intensive occupations within the agricultural, construction, wholesale and retail trade sectors, and high/semi-skilled nationals in the technical and services sector (Anatol et al., 2023). While Venezuelan migrants in Trinidad & Tobago may fill labor market shortages in a wide array of traditional occupations that are often characterized by lower levels of education, they may gravitate towards these types of occupations not only as a reflection of the barriers that they experience in gaining employment in the formal sectors but because it may be closely related to their cultural experiences and customs in their home country of Venezuela.

Venezuelan migrants who seek employment in formal sectors to become better integrated into Trinidad and Tobago's society may inadvertently contribute to labor market and social tensions domestically because while they may be willing to work under uncertain employment conditions, they may be consistently discriminated against and stigmatized by locals based on their ethnicity. This, in turn, may have even greater socio-economic implications in the future, as such negative perceptions by locals, may prevent Venezuelan migrants from not only accessing gainful employment opportunities, but also limit their representation in areas such as (1) political representation for advisory/consultative boards, (2) legal and human rights representation for immigration proceedings, and (3) social and economic representation for community groups/councils, and trade union memberships, that are collectively needed for them to become fully integrated into Trinidad and Tobago, and the wider LAC region (Acuna-Choque et al., 2023).

THE COMPLEX INTERPLAY BETWEEN THE GIG ECONOMY & MIGRANT GIG WORKERS

Global Migrant Gig Workers Outcomes

With the rapid development of Industry 4.0 technologies, the world has witnessed the emergence of new forms of work that have transformed the employment dynamics of many sectors worldwide. When merged with advanced technologies such as the Internet of Things (IoT), and Machine Learning (ML), gig work facilitated by digital platforms across different areas such as Transportation/Delivery through Uber, as well as a range of job opportunities from graphic design to content creation through

Fiverr, have created a flexible and autonomous working environment for many workers to thrive globally. Based on the growing popularity of gig work, Datta et al., (2023), have estimated that it is likely that there are approximately 435 million active gig workers worldwide, with the majority residing in East Asia, the Pacific, and Southeast Asia, and to a lesser extent Sub-Saharan Africa, and the LAC region. While these regions typically dominate the global gig market, accounting for the largest number of workers, these countries in particular Sub-Saharan Africa, South-Eastern Asia, and the Pacific, also have a large segment of migrant gig workers.

Migrants while living outside of their home country, often experience the same problems as vulnerable locals in their host country, however, there is the additional layer of complexity resulting from identity issues, discrimination, social isolation, and cultural and legal barriers in their host country, as well as problems of armed conflict and political instability in their home country, that may overshadow their presence in their host communities (Berhane, 2024). This intricate interaction between the various issues often means that migrant workers in countries such as South Africa, the Democratic Republic of Congo (DRC), Zimbabwe, and Burundi frequently find themselves trapped in low-skilled jobs in areas such as construction, agriculture, hospitality/entertainment, domestic work, and retail work, as well as precarious forms of work such as crowdsourcing and gig work, in which they are underpaid, underemployed, exploited and abused (Smit & Rugunanan, 2014).

Survival Strategy

Paying particular attention to gig work upon which this study is concerned, vulnerable segments of migrant populations such as young adults, and women are drawn to gig work because of many factors explored below, but most importantly it is often being used as a survival strategy. These as, migrant and local gig workers like those in South Africa, have used digital platforms that specialize in domestic work which is relatively accessible as a means of supporting their families (Lesala Khethisa et al., 2020). Given that the premise of gig work, is that it essentially masks the identity of the worker, it is possible that migrant workers from a lower caste residing in rural/remote communities as in the case of India, can use platform work as a survival mechanism, to hide unfavourable features such as their caste, to gain access to job opportunities in urban areas that may have been inaccessible to them otherwise (Banerjee, 2024). Such an attraction to gig work is often in response to the pre-existing barriers that reduce migrants' inability to integrate into their host country, or urban areas, through decent forms of work in the formal sector. This is what makes gig work so attractive as there are significantly fewer barriers to entry than in traditional forms of work.

Attractive & Accessible Means of Integration

Whether it be location-based or web-based, gig work offers an attractive, accessible, and easy way for migrant workers from developing countries in the Global South, as well as those in developed countries like Germany to integrate into the gig economy of their host country, primarily because most digital labor platforms such as Uber, and Deliveroo have multilingual options that allow migrants to create profiles with minimal use of official documentation, working experience, and background checks (Altenried, 2024). Furthermore, unlike most countries around the world, Germany has not only integrated gig workers into its occupational classification, but it has formalized gig work in the sense that domestic and migrant gig workers can access labor market protections, and provisions such as vacations and medical leave, like that of workers in the traditional working environment.

From the perspective of the gig economy, migrants' educational qualifications/credentials and working experience gained in their home country, as well as their native language are no longer barriers to entry, as they can now access income-earning opportunities at a faster pace than the traditional working environments, with minimal verbal communication with platform managers and even business clients. However, while gig work may help migrant gig workers access job opportunities in the short run in countries like Norway and Sweden through platforms like Foodora, Newlands (2024) argues that it may reduce their employability in the long run, as local employers may perceive the work experience gained from digital labor platforms as not a form of real work and thus become useless for specific occupations in the traditional working environment.

Flexibility & Mobility

While gig work has challenges of its own, such as the exploitation and underpaying of migrant labor, food-delivery platforms like Wolt in Copenhagen, Denmark are less likely to have stringent security and verification methods (Andersen & Spanger, 2024). This makes digital labor platforms a place of security for many migrants who may use the platform through their connection to business clients as a stepping stone to set up small businesses and maintain their residency in their host country. In addition, it also enhances their mobility, as was the case of gig migrant workers in Denmark, who because of the gig work status were able to travel easily to other countries in Europe such as Sweden, and the Czech Republic (Andersen & Spanger, 2024). Similarly to local gig workers, migrants are also predisposed to gig work because of the flexibility, and mobility gained. Granted that most migrant workers are simultaneously balancing the demands of taking care of a household, and dependent relatives, while working multiple jobs, gig opportunities allow migrants to adjust their schedule based on their availability.

Notwithstanding this, it is still possible as discussed by Bonhomme & Muldoon (2024), for migrant gig workers as demonstrated in the case of the European Union (EU), Canada, Chile, and the United Kingdom (UK), to experience the adverse effects of racism, discrimination and exploitation from business clients when working on their assigned tasks on the platform. Thus, even in the digital working environment that the gig economy creates, pre-existing issues such as discrimination, xenophobia, and social exclusion may still exist and become intensified by geopolitical tensions that may occur in migrants' home countries (Lam & Triandafyllidou, 2024). This may significantly impact their ability to progress in the labor market, as it, together with weak regulation of gig work and digital labor platforms and stricter forms of immigration policy changes may lead to their exclusion from the digital platform, in their host country,

Platformization of Migration Infrastructure

It has been argued within the literature by Cranston & Duplan (2023), that the presence of the gig economy, as well as the digital labor platforms, has begun to change the traditional migration infrastructure. These systems have commonly been comprised of many different systems such as technology, commercial and state institutions, state regulations, migrant social networks, humanitarian organizations, and higher educational institutions, that together shape and facilitate human mobility (Cranston & Duplan, 2023). This framework, even with the presence of government bureaucracy is an essential aspect of the mobility of migrants, as it provides stakeholders with the knowledge and information needed to mediate the migration process.

With the rapid growth of the gig economy, however, digital labor platforms are not only becoming integrated into the migration infrastructure but also altering the existing system because the presence of gig work has created a new income and mobility pathway for migrants. Instead of relying on the traditional migration infrastructure, the Platformization of migration infrastructure, aided by industry 4.0 technologies has changed how migrant gig workers in countries like Germany, the United States (US), and the Netherlands, now experience the labor market and find job opportunities (Vandaele, 2024). As a result, domestic and delivery migrant gig workers in countries like Sweden have become essential to the social reproduction of their cities (Zampoukos et al., 2024). These urban migrant gig workers are often on standby, or on a waiting list to quickly meet the needs of business clients. In doing so, they form a type of human infrastructure that is crucial to maintaining the function of urban cities. While such changes in the labor market dynamics may be beneficial for migrant gig workers, as these flexible forms of employment facilitate their initial socio-economic integration and can act as an arrival infrastructure that provides them with an immediate source of income and enhanced mobility, it does not reduce the pre-existing and structural inequalities that they may experience.

Latin American Migrant Gig Workers Outcomes: The Case of Chile, Colombia & Peru

With the rise of online platforms connecting freelance workers with short-term, flexible jobs, migrants from as far as the US, India, and Sub-Saharan Africa can now access employment opportunities that may not require either fluency in the local language, or legal work authorization in their host country. This avenue has allowed migrants to earn income, gain experience and autonomy, and build networks within their new communities while contributing to their socio-economic integration into their host countries, particularly urban cities, as there will always be a demand for their services by platform companies whether it is in food/delivery services, domestic/care services, or ride-hailing services.

In Latin America and the Caribbean (LAC) region, within the literature, the impact that the growing gig economy is having on migrant gig work remains underexplored. Given that the LAC region has become home to approximately 6.59mn Venezuelan migrants, the majority of whom have settled in countries such as Colombia (2.86mn persons), Peru (1.54mn persons) and Chile (532,700 persons), many of them, have been able to access employment opportunities through the web, and location-based platforms as a means of financial stability, and social protection in the short term (R4V, 2024b).

In the last decade, as digital platforms emerged and developed worldwide, it has prompted great interest in the gig economy and gig work by the LAC region. Focusing on the development of digital labor platforms in Colombia, Peru and Chile, there has emerged a combination of many different web and location-based platforms such as (1) Hogaru, Aux, Cleandelivery, Homeskeeper365, CasaLimpia, Home Squad, Zolvers, Rappi, Didi and DidiFood, Mensajeros Urbanos, TuAly, and Simplifica in Colombia, (2) Mopit, TeLoCuido, Chilenanas, Tuten, Nanamia, Nana Filipa, Rappi, Pedidos Ya, Cabify, and Didi, in Chile, and (3) Nanas y amas, Llegamos a tu casa, Didi, Rappi, DidiFood, Urbaner, Cabify, Chazqui and Tu aliando en limpieza in Peru (ECLAC & ILO, 2021; ILO, 2023; Fairwork, 2024, 2023a, 2023b). Although the literature on the experiences of gig workers in Colombia, Chile and Peru is small, the focal point of many of these digital labor platforms whose main source of workers are Venezuelan migrants, appears to be in (1) Domestic/Care services, (2) Delivery services, (3) Beauty services, and (4) Transportation (ride-hailing) services, that offers both part-time and full-time daily contracts (ECLAC & ILO, 2021; ILO, 2023; Fairwork, 2024, 2023a, 2023b).

From a country-level perspective, the ECLAC & ILO (2021), estimates that 70% of location-based, and 10% of web-based platform workers in Chile are migrants, while 17% are migrants in Colombia. In Chile and Colombia, migrant gig workers who provide transportation services benefitted from higher earnings than delivery gig workers. However, even as Colombia's gig economy continues to thrive due to the ease at which Venezuelan migrants can access platform work, their overall earnings remain small, because while the Temporary Protection Statute for Venezuelan migrants provides them with temporary legal status, it does not offer employment protections against exploitation by these platforms (Lozano-Paredes & Reilly, 2018). As a result, migrant gig workers in these countries are often in a constant state of job instability, as they have little or no trade union representation who can communicate their grievances to platform managers on their behalf (Arriagada et al., 2023).

As the working environment of migrant gig workers in these Latin American countries continues to erode, instances of different forms of migrant labor agency such as industrial unrest particularly during the 2020 COVID-19 pandemic, began to break out in countries like Chile in response to dangerous working conditions and low earnings (Bonhomme et al., 2024). This became one of the first instances of widespread industrial action in the gig economy. It is this form of migrant agency, i.e., the acts of resistance, self-representation, and organization demonstrated by gig workers in Chile, who while manoeuvring digital labor platforms, played a transformative role in improving how migrant workers are treated by digital labor platforms in the Global South (Howson et al., 2020).

The 2020 industrial action of gig workers led platforms in Latin America to not only provide safety equipment, but also implement accident insurance, and social security measures. In that, platforms such as Hongaru and Aux-in Colombia, and Urbaner and Cabify in Peru, not only pay workers higher wages, supply workers with contracts that outline clearly the terms and conditions of their employment but also provide social safety net measures such as social security, maternity and sick leave (Fairwork, 2023). As explained by ECLAC & ILO (2021), such actions by gig workers inclusive of migrants in Peru and Chile based on their solidarity between workers in similar types of platform work become the catalyst for greater alliance from grassroots organizations, as well as governmental and international support to strengthen the rights of migrant gig workers. This led to not only greater self-organization/representation amongst gig workers in Peru, Chile, and Colombia, but also encouraged governments to provide legislative measures such as Law No. 21.431 in Chile to regulate platform work, and categorize gig workers, and establish labor standards in Colombia such as the "Luxury Cabs" regulation (decree 2297/2015) (Asenjo Cruz et al., 2023; Fairwork, 2024; Reilly & Lozano-Paredes, 2019).

THE CHALLENGING EMERGENCE OF TRINIDAD AND TOBAGO'S GIG ECONOMY

While the gig economy in Latin American countries has created a new reality for Venezuelan migrants, as they have become increasingly absorbed by digital labor platforms to earn a living, the same cannot be said for Trinidad and Tobago. In Trinidad and Tobago, there are a few operational web and location-based digital labor platforms such as Fiverr, TriniFreelance, Upwork, TT RideShare, DROP Ride, food DROP, MEDICAS and Zipo, whose emphasis is on providing freelance, transportation, delivery, healthcare, and domestic services (Fiverr, 2024; TriniFreelance, 2023; Upwork, 2024; TT RideShare, 2024; DROP Caribbean, 2024a, 2024b; MEDICAS, 2022; Zipo, 2022).

Although the amount of digital labor platforms in Trinidad and Tobago is small in comparison to that of Chile, Peru, and Colombia, its progressive growth has been supported by (1) the extensive availability and use of smartphone devices and applications, (2) the upgrading of digital infrastructure to incorporate fifth and sixth generation (5G, 6G) technologies by internet service providers such as Amplia and Flow, and (3) the integration of industry 4.0 technologies such as Machine Learning (ML), Data Analytics, and Cloud Computing into the management of these platforms (Ray et al., 2021). While these developments have reshaped the world of work in many labor markets around the world, by providing new ways to access job opportunities, making it one of the most preferred ways to earn a living internationally, there hasn't been a surge in the uptake for gig work in Trinidad and Tobago.

The sluggish assimilation of gig work into Trinidad and Tobago's labor market is not unheard of as many high-income countries such as Sweden, Finland, Spain, and Germany also have less developed gig economies (Datta et al., 2023). It has been estimated that the gig economy in these countries comprises approximately 1-4% of their workforce. This small proportion may be a result of several intertwined factors that reduce the attraction of gig work, such as strong labor market protections, regulatory frameworks that make traditional forms of work more engaging than gig work, robust social safety nets and job security mechanisms that support vulnerable workers mainly women and migrants, which maintains the financial stability of low and middle-income households in these countries (Datta et al., 2023; Pietrogiovanni & Iossa, 2022).

Apart from the factors mentioned above, the general aversion towards gig work by high-income countries as explained by Newlands (2022) may be partly due to the perception of employ-ers who may perceive the working experience gained through gig work as of little or no value. This then sends a negative signal to employers, making the labor market integration of gig workers in tra-ditional employment settings challenging. Considering the economic instability created by the COVID-19 pandemic in 2020, as workers across sectors become unemployed and displaced due to businesses' financial setbacks, their forced absorption into forms of non-standard work such as gig/platform work has also become a threat to the economic models (Nordic, Mixed and German model), used by these high-income countries to maintain a high standard of living and extensive so-cial welfare provisions.

As explained by Alsos & Dolvik (2021) given that gig workers not being covered by collective bargaining and social security schemes, their earnings and working conditions may not be mandated. Even as countries move towards different working arrangements such as marginal part-time work, it can create a higher demand for short-term contracts that may not necessarily lead to stable forms of employment for vulnerable workers in the future. Unlike the experiences of non-standard forms of work by high-income countries, the reluctance to engage in gig work in Trinidad and Tobago, may be due to challenges such as labor market rigidity, inadequate banking support, and lack of investment as discussed below.

Labor Market Rigidity

Following the onset of the COVID-19 pandemic, many countries have embraced gig work in response to labor market changes that included the integration of industry 4.0 technologies to reduce cost, while driving productive capacity across sectors (Datta et al., 2023). Like the high-income countries mentioned earlier, Trinidad and Tobago's gig economy has been growing at a slow pace, with only a small proportion of gig workers. The reason behind such slow growth may be entirely different from that of high-income countries, which may reflect its developing country status. In that, even though Trinidad and Tobago may be a high-income developing country, its labor market rigidity may have contributed to the slow growth of its gig economy. As discussed by Oranburg & Palagashvili (2018), the rise of gig work may have challenged the traditional norms of the working environment, from the management to the leadership of businesses, by encouraging a more decentralized form of work.

These changes may have been met with resistance by businesses in Trinidad and Tobago who prefer a more centralized, and structured working environment, over flexible working arrangements that give workers greater autonomy and work-life balance. While there are benefits to a rigid working environment, as it ensures that workers meet deadlines, providing a better framework for decisions to be made, Putnam et al., (2014), explain that in the long run such an environment can ultimately lead to reduced autonomy, burnout, and lower levels of job satisfaction amongst workers, as well as a high employee turnover rates, and greater tensions in the workplace. Together with the absence of legislation to guide and manage the implementation of gig work, the failure of businesses to implement flexible forms of work to reduce the consequences of such rigid cultural norms may reduce the growth of gig work in Trinidad and Tobago amongst both locals and migrants (Smith et al., 2019).

Inadequate Banking Support

In Trinidad and Tobago, most financial institutions' banking systems assume that workers are employed on a full-time basis, allowing their monthly income to be used to assess creditworthiness. Thus, easing their access to financial services such as short/long-term loans, credit cards, and mortgages for homes and vehicles. It is possible that these types of banking systems, legacy systems and risk assessment processes such as the underwriting of loans used by financial institutions in Trinidad and Tobago, may not consider nonstandard forms of work like gig work to be real work, because workers may have an inconsistent flow of income and multiple sources of incomes, that makes it difficult for banks to access their eligibility and credit worthiness (Buchak, 2023). The inability of banks to access the human resource records of web and location-based platforms to verify gig workers' employment history can also deter persons from engaging in gig work. As a result of this, gig workers in Trinidad and Tobago may encounter difficulties in not only getting paid for engaging in platform work but also accessing financial services.

Further to this, while many web and location-based platforms may be equipped to provide gig workers in Trinidad and Tobago with immediate payment for their services, the inability of the banking system to accept payments instantaneously, together with bank fees to transfer payments into the workers account can both reduce the overall earnings received by the worker (Koustas, 2019). In such a situation, this can encourage gig workers to shift to nontraditional financial institutions such as credit unions that do not have either account or transaction fees. However, since gig workers are not supported by a commercial bank that can provide sound financial advice, they may experience challenges when building their savings and paying taxes through these institutions (Lux & Chung, 2023).

From a legal and regulatory perspective, the inability of commercial banks in Trinidad and Tobago to provide effective and efficient financial services may not only be limited by the lack of regulations to govern gig work but most importantly a lack of amendments made to existing laws that may impact the ability of gig workers to access financial services in the long run (Sudirman & Disemadi, 2023). These laws which include the 2020 E-Money Issuer Order, the 2008 Financial Institutions Act, and the Electronic Transactions Act, which while implemented to facilitate a cashless society, and financial inclusion by making it easier to issue electronic money may not have been amended to facilitate the needs of gig workers.

Lack of Investment

Major web and location-based companies such as Uber, and Rappi which operate globally from China to countries in Latin America, have been able to remain dominant players in the global gig economy because they have managed to secure a significant portion of global gig market share. According to Charlton (2024), as digital labor platforms continue to grow and develop at a rapid pace, their global gig market share is expected to amass a value of US$556.7 bn in 2024, and US$1,847bn by the end of 2032. Such exponential growth in the global market share of the gig economy implies that advances in digitalization will continue to cause shifts in the way people work and do business, and how employers manage their workforce to improve its productive capacity and profitability.

As the global gig economy continues to grow, it is expected that major web and location-based platforms will maintain their position in the market by becoming more innovative and competitive. To do so, many large platform companies are heavily backed by influential financiers such as SoftBank (Uber and DoorDash), Sequoia Capital (Fiverr, DoorDash, and Upwork), and Accel Partners (Grab and Upwork) (Zwick, 2022; Sequoia Capital, 2024). These investors, tend to focus on high-performing and high-growth platforms, that have the potential to drive the development of the gig economy through cutting-edge innovations across a diverse range of sectors. As a result, the gig economy can become a fertile opportunity for investors who are interested in creating sustainable forms of employment.

The slow growth of Trinidad and Tobago's gig economy may reflect its inability to not only attract large platform companies but also encourage international financiers to enter the domestic gig economy. This much can be ascertained from the Ease of Doing Business (EDB) index and the Corruption Perception Index (CPI), i.e., two of the most influential indices used when assessing the investment climate of any country. Based on the World Bank's EDB index, Trinidad and Tobago, currently ranks at 105/190 implying that the twin island state does not have the most business-friendly environment (WB, 2024). Such an outcome may mean several things, first, the current regulatory environment may not be beneficial for domestic companies wishing to establish web and location-based platforms locally and it may therefore be difficult for entrepreneurs to launch a platform business, and second, the high-level bureaucracy within state-run institutions may reduce the ability of platform companies to access construction permits, registering properties, accessing credit, enforcing contracts, paying taxes, and protecting investors (WB, 2024).

The CPI also plays a significant role in attracting or deterring investors, as it reflects the perceived levels of corruption within the public sector. Based on Transparency International's CPI, Trinidad and Tobago is currently ranked at 42/100, which implies that the country has significant corruption problems linked to issues such as bribery, abuse of power, lack of political integrity, dysfunctional rule of law, excessive bureaucratic red tape, nepotism in public office and the civil service, (TI, 2024). These problems may all collectively deter international financiers from entering the domestic gig economy in the long run, as it may indicate that the country may not be able to attract the Foreign Direct Investment (FDI) needed to grow its gig economy. Furthermore, financiers in the gig economy may gravitate away from Trinidad and Tobago because such corruption suggests that there is a high level of economic uncertainty and political instability involved, making it challenging to manage the associated risks.

GIG WORK AS A PATHWAY FOR VENEZUELAN MIGRANT INTEGRATION IN TRINIDAD & TOBAGO

Driving Progress in the Gig Economy and the Business Sector

Notwithstanding Trinidad and Tobago's slow-growing gig economy, Venezuelan migrants may continue to be attracted to gig work for the same reasons as migrant workers in other countries worldwide. Since web and location-based platforms in Trinidad and Tobago such as TT RideShare, DROP Ride, and food DROP thrive on their ability to provide workers with a flexible working environment, Venezuelan migrants may use this as an opening to (1) take care of dependent relatives by choosing flexible hours of work, and (2) secure multiple streams of income, (3) build both a social and professional network of persons, who may be able to assist them in securing more lucrative job opportunities in the future, and (4) develop their professional skills, and experience, as well as gain a better understanding of the labor market to improve their marketability and employability (Van Doorn & Vijay, 2021).

While gig work is likely to play a crucial role in the livelihood of Venezuelan migrants, it may also be able to support both the sustainability and adaptability of the gig economy and the business sector in Trinidad and Tobago. There are several ways in which this can be achieved, most notable amongst them is the ability of migrant workers to become a substantial part of the gig economy workforce, by filling essential roles such as food delivery, and ride-hailing workers for the previously mentioned platforms in both urban and suburban areas in Northern and Central Trinidad to ensure that the service can be maintained (Van Doorn et al., 2022). The involvement of migrants can also become crucial to the expansion of these platforms as services can be expanded, i.e., quickly scaled up to meet customer demand in Southern Trinidad where the operation of location-based platforms such as food DROP has little presence due to the higher cost of deliveries over longer distances.

With the inclusion of migrant gig workers, location-based platforms such as TT RideShare, DROP Ride, food DROP, and Zipo while providing Venezuelan migrants with employment opportunities to improve their living conditions, can explore new avenues for generating revenue by partnering with restaurants and merchants in Southern, and Eastern Trinidad, to enhance their customer base in these areas, which in turn would improve the economic viability of these platform services throughout the country (Zhou et al., 2022). This much is certain, as the integration of Venezuelan migrant gig workers can drive down the cost for the business sector, which allows for greater innovative practices and entrepreneurial activity to take place domestically.

As the demand for quick and convenient delivery and transportation options grows, location-based apps could potentially absorb more Venezuelan migrant labor. This model according to Chen & Qiu (2019) has been successful in China, where migrants largely drive the growth of location-based platforms like Didi, that provide transportation and domestic services. By leveraging additional labor, these platforms may improve their delivery and transportation times and become more cost-effective and financially successful. This success could facilitate the attraction of investment partners necessary for not only developing web and location-based platforms in Trinidad and Tobago but also attracting the much-needed foreign direct investment to drive sustainable and economic development. With additional investment in Trinidad and Tobago's gig economy, there can be significant spillover effects that may influence the business sector in a positive light. It can not only boost the productive capacity of domestic sectors but also facilitate knowledge transfer, enhance the purchasing power of consumers, and encourage greater competitiveness and innovativeness which may strengthen the overall investment climate in Trinidad and Tobago.

Within the literature on gig work, even though this form of non-standard work is often considered a form of insecure work, arising from ambiguous employment relationships/classifications, inferior working conditions, lack of job security/ employment protection, trade union representation and gender discrimination as in the case of gig workers in the United States (US) and India, migrant gig workers employed by platforms in China have reduced this insecurity through job crafting (Chen, 2024). It is possible that if Venezuelan migrants with specialized/advanced skill sets focus on crafting their jobs, i.e., by specifically choosing gig opportunities that better support and align with their skills and abilities, then this would improve their level of job satisfaction, motivation, well-being, and autonomy, which may reduce the insecurities of gig work in Trinidad and Tobago.

Furthermore, job crafting is also likely to contribute to the economic growth in Trinidad and Tobago, as Venezuelan migrant gig workers may be able to not only improve their productivity and performance but also adapt to changing labor market conditions by remaining flexible. This then supports the overall development of domestic platforms and the business sector, as the flexibility and the unique skills of Venezuelan migrants can be harnessed by web and location-based platform managers to encourage the innovative growth of platforms through the provision of new and personalized services (Song & Jo, 2023). This is especially important as job crafting may allow Venezuelan migrant gig workers based on their unique set of skills and abilities to become creative when selecting job opportunities on platforms, which may be crucial to maintaining the competitiveness of domestic platforms.

Gig Work as a Mechanism for the Integration

Considering the potential of Venezuelan migrant gig workers to develop Trinidad and Tobago's gig economy, gig work may become a pivotal aspect in accelerating the integration process, as it can become an important entry point for migrants. This is mainly due to the low barriers to entry, and flexible working hours that allow migrants to start working relatively quickly upon arrival while adjusting to their new environment. Although the labor market integration of migrants does not generally advance from one stage to the next smoothly, their quick integration into the labor market via platform work can provide Venezuelan migrants, with a greater sense of self-sufficiency, and professional identity (Lam & Triandafyllidou, 2021).

The Caribbean region, particularly Trinidad and Tobago, is projected to require an estimated US$49.88 million and US$19.45 million in 2025, which is expected to decrease slightly to US$47.83 million and US$17.83 million in 2026 to support the needs of Venezuelan migrants (R4V, 2024c). While these funds aim to support Venezuelan migrants in areas such as education, food security, healthcare, and housing, it is still insufficient. It is possible that within this context, platform work could serve as a pathway for migrants to enhance their financial independence/stability, thereby reducing their reliance on these state-provided support services. The flexibility and autonomy that gig work provides can then assist migrants in not only generating their income without being held accountable by rigid employment structures but also pursuing additional education and training opportunities to improve their long-term employability in stable jobs (Van Doorn et al., 2022). This, in turn, reduces the reliance on aid programs and encourages their self-sufficiency, as Venezuelan migrants engaged in platform work, can immediately earn and access substantially more income than the minimum wage offered for traditional forms of employment through bonus structures, particularly during Trinidad and Tobago's peak travel season.

Gig work is also likely to improve the professional identity of Venezuelan migrants working together with locals in Trinidad and Tobago, as it may assist them in establishing stronger social and professional networks that may lead to more stable employment opportunities. Although migrant gig workers are more likely to experience bouts of loneliness, isolation, and mental health problems than workers in traditional forms of employment, building a strong professional identity, when supported by cultural exchanges and interactions can assist Venezuelan migrant gig workers to better adapt to their environment, as it has the potential to not only reduce cultural shock but also feelings of isolation (Chen et al., 2022). Furthermore, even though gig work may not align perfectly with the skills and abilities of Venezuelan migrants, depending on the task and type of gig work undertaken, its successful completion can validate the professional identities of migrants especially those who are highly educated. In the often-precarious working environment of platform work where the level of unpredictability, uncertainty, and instability is high, such positive outcomes can encourage greater job satisfaction amongst Venezuelan migrant gig workers, which lessens the mental health problems associated with platform work such as chronic stress, anxiety disorders, and burnout (Hafeez et al., 2022).

For Venezuelan migrants, while gig work may be a quick pathway to self-sufficiency and professional identification, that may prove useful in their integration efforts upon their arrival in Trinidad and Tobago, it is important to note that with such incorporation comes many risks that may derail such integration. According to Bonhomme & Muldoon (2024) migrant workers, are often faced with many challenges when engaging in such precarious work, such as low wages that may be below the conventional minimum wage, either little or no forms of job security and employment benefits as well as limited opportunities for professional development particularly amongst low and semi-skilled workers. This as the lack of access to legal work permits and documents due to the inability of the state to pass legislation that reflects its commitment to the 1949 Geneva Convention concerning international humanitarian laws, may force Venezuelan migrants into illegal work in Trinidad and Tobago. These obstacles can be exacerbated by systemic problems such as prejudice and discrimination that may be either based on the Venezuelan migrants' race, ethnicity, gender, and age or embedded within domestic policies and practices of public/private sector enterprises that lead to their unfair treatment, and marginalization (Acuna-Choque et al., 2023). Together these problems may contribute to an unsustainable livelihood, that worsens migrants' financial instability, and economic mobility, and encourages their continued reliance on aid support. Thus, perpetuating the cycle of income inequality and poverty amongst Venezuelan migrant gig workers who may be in vulnerable situations.

In situations where Venezuelan migrant workers do not have sufficient employment protection, and knowledge of their human and employment rights, their involvement in the gig economy can serve as a breeding ground for their continued exploitation and human trafficking. Given that there is a lack of oversight and regulation of platform work in Trinidad and Tobago, traffickers may use this as an opportunity to not only target and recruit Venezuelan migrants using fraudulent advertisements for gig work with attractive compensation packages, but to also research and groom potential victims without face-to-face contact based on their online gig profile, and to force migrants to undertake gig work, particularly for delivery, ride-sharing and domestic services (Campana, 2022).

In addition to this, traffickers may also use gig platforms to isolate and pressure victims to accept payments outside of the platform payment system. Although there remain significant challenges in detecting and prosecuting human trafficking offenders within the gig economy because such suspicious behaviour can be hidden under the guise of a legitimate business that thrives on flexibility, digital labor platforms such as Delivery Hero in Germany, and Just Eat Takeaway based in the Netherlands, have begun incorporating statements against human trafficking and modern forms of slavery on its platforms to bring awareness to its presence in the global platform economy (Vandaele, 2024).

STRATEGIES TO SUPPORT VENEZUELAN MIGRANT GIG WORKERS IN TRINIDAD & TOBAGO

Despite the crucial role that platforms play in keeping migrants financially afloat, a vast majority of digital labor platforms in both developed and developing countries, lack the strategies to provide effective socio-economic support for migrant gig workers. Thus, for purposes of this study, emphasis will be placed on the areas of (1) Policy & Regulatory Frameworks, and (2) Platform Managers & Employer Responsibility.

Policy & Regulatory Framework

The development of a robust policy and regulatory framework to both oversee and protect the human rights (inclusive of labor rights) of all gig workers inclusive of Venezuelan migrant workers is an essential component to creating stability within Trinidad and Tobago's gig economy. These frameworks which include protocols that support Venezuelan migrant gig workers' access to health insurance plans, retirement plans, unemployment relief, integration plans, and mechanisms for dispute resolution as well as wage standards for gig workers, are likely to play an important role in protecting their human and employment rights (Sarkar et al., 2024).

Like traditional employment arrangements, there is a need for Trinidad and Tobago to design frameworks that attend to the unique needs of Venezuelan migrants and the employment precarity experienced. Such an approach, will not only target the financial instability of migrant workers by identifying, managing and transferring the unique risks that they are more likely to experience stemming from systemic barriers such as inadequate identification and knowledge to set up bank accounts in Trinidad and Tobago, but also work to reduce such risk. This mitigation can be achieved by integrating several strategies such as (1) facilitating access to banking services through platforms, (2) developing services such as tax benefits, micro-loans, low-interest loans, and microfinance options that are specifically designed for Venezuelan migrants, and (3) implementing labor market protections such as unemployment insurance, employment protections to prevent unfair dismissal, wage subsidies to ensure the retention of migrant gig workers, and trade union representation to allow for the negotiations for fair wages and safe working conditions to take place (Chigori, 2024).

Given that the immigration process for Venezuelan migrants in Trinidad and Tobago remains quite rigid due to the lack of legal protection, and stringent registration requirements that makes them vulnerable to detention and deportation, the implementation of such frameworks may assist in encouraging immigration compliance amongst migrants. Considering the essential role that Venezuelan migrants are likely to play in the growth and development of Trinidad and Tobago's gig economy, this may encourage policymakers to amend the immigration process to make it easier for migrants to integrate into both the gig economy and the labor market without employer sponsorship (Putzel-Kavanaugh, 2024).

Such adjustments can include the introduction of digital nomad visas, job seeker visas that focus on skills and a points-based system as implemented in Australia and Canada to allow highly educated migrants admission without first having secured employment (Sarker et al., 2024). Together with providing language, educational, vocational and professional development training that enhances the skills and capabilities of Venezuelan migrants, they are more likely to reduce labor market shortages across digital labor platforms, as well as across different domestic sectors (Sarker et al., 2024). This in turn improves their job security, and employability and broadens their career development pathway, as Venezuelan migrant workers are now better equipped with the skills that are valued by web and location-based platforms.

Platform Managers & Employer Responsibility

Based on the policy and regulatory frameworks designed to guide the governing of gig work in Trinidad and Tobago, platform managers and business entities that actively seek out and engage in digital employment opportunities conducted through their platforms, i.e., either web or location-based, will now be able to define both the status of their workers as well as classify their platform. Together with these frameworks, and the categorisation of gig workers, platforms, will now be able to provide Venezuelan migrant gig workers with a wide range of opportunities, ranging from transparent and predictable working conditions, and the right to trade union representation, to notifying workers about the use of algorithmic and automated systems that may impact their assignment of tasks, performance evaluation, and privacy using platform wide communication mechanism such as email and intranet posting (ILO et al., 2023).

Focusing on trade union representation, platform managers and businesses that promote the formation of trade unions specifically dedicated to protecting the rights of migrant gig workers could provide valuable advocacy and legal support for Venezuelan migrants. This support would help Venezuelan migrants not only navigate the immigration system and access essential services in Trinidad and Tobago, but (1) understand their immigration and employment rights, (2) take advantage of provisions made available by the states, and (3) apply for the correct visas and work authorization documents that may support their stability in the long term (Androff & Mathis, 2021).

Reflecting on the integration problems that Venezuelan migrants may experience stemming from existing systemic issues in Trinidad and Tobago such as cultural alienation, racism, discrimination, and corruption in accessing employment and basic social services, platform managers can tailor the employment services offered to migrants to reduce these issues.

For example, platform managers and employers can use training and mentorship programmes, to target female Venezuelan migrant gig workers to address issues such as gender inequality, as well as provide multilingual platforms/language training and cultural sensitivity training to improve communication with migrant workers and reduce their feelings of isolation (Van Doorn & Vijay, 2021). In turn, it is possible then that the implementation and promotion of such programmes by platform managers and businesses may bring greater awareness to the specific challenges faced by Venezuelan migrants. Such an approach can enhance the integration of migrants as an inclusive digital working environment may change society's perception of migrants from one where they are discriminated against, to one in which they feel valued, and comfortable to not only share their unique perspectives but also collaborate with colleagues (Banerjee, 2024).

One of the final ways in which businesses and platforms can assist Venezuelan migrant gig workers in Trinidad and Tobago is through social and community support. To do this, businesses and platform managers can arrange community awareness programmes and community support systems to bring greater responsiveness to the challenges experienced by Venezuelan migrant gig workers. By creating an environment in which Venezuelan migrant gig workers can feel safe, and supported, they are more likely to engage in discussions to reduce their marginalization and accelerate their integration (Bonhomme et al., 2024). With the policy and regulatory changes, these activities have the added advantage of also changing the perception of platform work in Trinidad and Tobago, from one which may be viewed as often precarious, lacking the occupational prestige, stability and benefits of a traditional employment arrangement, to one that may be able to support the integration, and transition of Venezuelan migrants to more suitable forms of employment that offers a consistent form of income (Newlands, 2024).

CONCLUSION

The gig economy has emerged as a vital component in enhancing the financial stability of migrant workers, providing them with various employment opportunities that are often inaccessible in traditional labor markets. Issues such as Language barriers, limited social networks, and differences in educational qualifications frequently hinder these workers from securing stable jobs. As a result, by engaging in gig work migrant workers are better able to navigate these challenges and build a more secure economic foundation. Despite the evident significance of gig work for migrant populations, there remains a notable gap in information on how gig work can be used as a mechanism to better integrate Venezuelan migrants into Trinidad and Tobago's domestic labor market. Thus, a better understanding of this dynamic is essential for policymakers and organisations aiming to support and improve the living conditions of integration for Venezuelan migrant gig workers.

Although gig work can accelerate the integration process, this study highlights using a conceptual research framework, that the sluggish pace at which Trinidad and Tobago's gig economy is developing may hold back such efforts. The poor development prospects may stem from three main problems, (1) the inability of domestic business entities to embrace flexible working arrangements as the new form of work, in favour of rigid working environments, (2) the failure of financial institutions to put systems in place to accommodate access to immediate payment mechanisms and financial services, and (3) the inability of businesses and platform managers to effectively attract and retain foreign investors in domestic platforms.

This study highlights that Venezuelan migrant gig workers can become the driving force behind the development of Trinidad and Tobago's gig economy and its business sector, by (1) encouraging the expansion of existing location-based platforms, (2) filling the shortages of essential platform workers across sectors, (3) supporting the innovativeness and competitiveness of location-based platforms through job crafting. It is important to note however, that Venezuelan migrants can achieve quicker labor market integration through platform work, leading to greater self-sufficiency and a stronger professional identity, it does highlight several systemic problems such as discrimination, racism, and exploitation that still unfortunately exist in Trinidad and Tobago's society.

These negative outcomes can be mitigated if, first, the appropriate policy and regulatory frameworks are implemented, and second, platform managers and employers take greater responsibility in ensuring that the rights of Venezuelan migrant gig workers are acknowledged. While this study focuses on the broad issues related to using gig work as a mechanism of Venezuelan migrant integration, and the strategies that may support such an assimilation, there are several broad implications for the future of gig work in Trinidad and Tobago, and how the state is handling the migration process. Given that Venezuelan migrants may become a large diver behind the domestic gig economy, their continued reliance on gig work as a primary source of income may reflect the presence of structural barriers, and labor market segmentation in Trinidad and Tobago.

Competing Interests:

The author of this publication declares there are no competing interests.

Funding:

This research received no specific grant from any funding agency in the public, commercial, or not-for-profit sectors. Funding for this research was covered by the author of the article.

REFERENCES

Acuna-Choque, K., Bazan-Joaquin, B., Malvaceda-Espinoza, E. L., & Monroy-Valasco, I. R. (2023). Social Representations of Migration Among Venezuelan Immigrants Residing in Metropolitan Lima, Peru. *Migraciones Internacionales*, *14*(11), 1–21. DOI: 10.33679/rmi.v1i1.2568

Alsos, K., & Dolvik, J. E. (2021). *The Future of Work in the Nordic Countries: Opportunities and Challenges for the Nordic Model.* Nordic Council of Ministers., https://pub.norden.org/temanord2021-520/temanord2021-520.pdf

Altenried, M. (2024). Mobile workers, contingent labour: Migration, the gig economy and the multiplication of labour. *Environment & Planning A*, *56*(4), 1113–1128. DOI: 10.1177/0308518X211054846

Anatol, M. (2023). An Examination of the Vulnerable Venezuelan Population in Trinidad and Tobago: Some Considerations. In Wallace, W. C. (Ed.), *The Movement of Venezuelans to the Americas and the Caribbean in the 21st Century* (pp. 271–285). Palgrave Macmillan., DOI: 10.1007/978-3-031-31762-0_14

Anatol, M., Roberts-Kasmally, K. A., & de Gourville, D. (2023). The Impact of Venezuelan Migration on Trinidad and Tobago. In *The Caribbean Social Justice Agenda* (pp. 33–61). Rowman & Littlefield.

Andersen, M., & Spanger, M. (2024). Gig work in transnational spaces: Infrastructures of migration and the simultaneous lives of migrants in the gig economy. *Journal of Ethnic and Migration Studies*, *50*(15), 3751–3767. DOI: 10.1080/1369183X.2024.2379643

Andersen, M., Zampoukos, K., Spanger, M., & Mitchell, D. (2024). At your service: The mobilities, rhythms and everyday lives of migrant labour in the gig economy. *Journal of Ethnic and Migration Studies*, *50*(15), 3733–3750. DOI: 10.1080/1369183X.2024.2379641

Androff, D., & Mathis, C. (2021). Human Rights-Based Social Work Practice with Immigrants and Asylum Seekers in a Legal Service Organization. *Journal of Human Rights and Social Work*, *26*(7), 178–188. DOI: 10.1007/s41134-021-00197-7 PMID: 34722859

Arriagada, A., Bonhomme, M., Ibanez, F., & Leyton, J. (2023). The gig economy in Chile: Examining labor conditions and the nature of gig work in a Global South country. *Digital Geography and Society*, *100063*, 1–6. DOI: 10.1016/j.diggeo.2023.100063

Asenjo Cruz, A., Coddou Mc Manus, A., & Dhir, R. K. (2023). *The platform economy and transformations in the world of work: The case of delivery platform workers in Santiago, Chile.* Working Paper, 100: 1-70. Geneva, Switzerland: International Labor Organization (ILO). DOI: 10.54394/JCVG2192

Banerjee, D. (2024). Caste, gig-economy, and youth: The resurgence of a new caste politics in urban Gujarat. *South Asian History and Culture*, *15*(2), 1–16. DOI: 10.1080/19472498.2024.2346867

Berhane, Y. (2024). *Enhancing Social Protection for Migrant Workers: Challenges and Strategies in the East and Horn of Africa.* Geneva, Switzerland: International Labor Organization (ILO).

Bonhomme, M., & Muldoon, J. (2024). Racism and food delivery platforms: Shaping migrants' work experiences and future expectations in the United Kingdom and Chile. *Ethnic and Racial Studies*, •••, 1–24. DOI: 10.1080/01419870.2024.2349268

Bonhomme, M., Ustek-Spilda, F., & Arriagada, A. (2024). Between acceptance and resistance: Conceptualising migrant platform labour agency in Chile. *New Technology, Work and Employment*, •••, 1–19. DOI: 10.1111/ntwe.12308

Buchak, G. (2023). Financing the Gig Economy. *The Journal of Finance*, *79*(1), 219–256. DOI: 10.1111/jofi.13292

Campana, P. (2022). *Online and technology-facilitated trafficking in human beings.* Council of Europe.

Caribbean, D. R. O. P. (2024a). *We Are Now Distance and Time Fares.*https://dropcaribbean.com/distance-and-time-fares/

Caribbean, D. R. O. P. (2024b). *More than food delivery.*https://dropcaribbean.com/fooddrop/

Charlton, E. (2024). *What is the gig economy and what's the deal for gig workers?* Geneva, Switzerland: World Economic Forum (WEF).

Chen, J. (2024). Are we only all by ourselves? A double-level perspective to cope with the insecurity of the nonstandard gig work model. *International Journal of Manpower*, *45*(4), 733–753. DOI: 10.1108/IJM-05-2023-0231

Chen, J. Y., & Qiu, J. L. (2019). Digital utility: Datafication, regulation, labor, and DiDi's Platformization of urban transport in China. *Chinese Journal of Communication*, *12*(3), 274–289. DOI: 10.1080/17544750.2019.1614964

Chen, T., Song, W., Song, J., Ren, Y., Dong, Y., Yang, J., & Zhang, S. (2022). Measuring Well-Being of Migrant Gig Workers: Exampled as Hangzhou City in China. *Behavioral Sciences (Basel, Switzerland)*, *12*(365), 1–29. DOI: 10.3390/bs12100365 PMID: 36285934

Chigori, D. T. (2024). Worker well-being in the digital economy: Lens through bibliometrics analysis. *SA Journal of Human Resource Management*, 22(0), a2773:1-11. DOI: 10.4102/sajhrm.v22i0.2773

Cranston, S., & Duplan, K. (2023). Infrastructures of migration and the ordering of privilege in mobility. *Migration Studies*, *11*(2), 330–348. DOI: 10.1093/migration/mnad001

Datta, N., Rong, C., Singh, S., Stinshoff, C., Iacob, N., Nigatu, N. S., Nxumalo, M., & Klimaviciute, L. (2023). Working Without Borders: The Promise and Peril of Online Gig Work. Washington DC, United States: World Bank (WB).

Doon, R. (2023). The Struggle for Venezuelan Migrant Integration into Trinidad and Tobago's Labor Market. In *The Palgrave Handbook of Global Social Problems* (pp. 1–29). Palgrave Macmillan., DOI: 10.1007/978-3-030-68127-2_404-1

Doon, R. (2024). The Impact of Climate Change on the Vulnerability of Venezuelan Migrants to Human Trafficking in Trinidad and Tobago. In *The Palgrave Handbook of Global Social Change* (pp. 1–28). Palgrave Macmillan., DOI: 10.1007/978-3-030-87624-1_413-1

Economic Commission for Latin America and the Caribbean and the International Labor Organization (ECLAC & ILO). (2021). *Employment Situation in Latin America and the Caribbean, Decent Work for Platform Workers in Latin America*. ILO.

Fairwork. (2023a). *The Mobilities of Gig Work in Colombia, Fairwork Colombia Ratings 2023*. Oxford, United Kingdom: Oxford, Internet Institute.

Fairwork. (2023b). *Labor Standards in the Platform Economy, Fairwork Peru Ratings 2023*. Oxford, United Kingdom: Oxford, Internet Institute.

Fairwork. (2024). *Labour Standards in the Platform Economy, Fairwork Chile Ratings 2024*. Oxford, United Kingdom: Oxford, Internet Institute.

Fiverr. (2024). *Find the right freelance service, right away*.https://www.fiverr.com/

Hafeez, S., Gupta, C., & Sprajcer, M. (2022). Stress and the gig economy: It's not all shifts and giggles. *Industrial Health*, *4*(61), 140–150. DOI: 10.2486/indhealth.2021-0217 PMID: 35249894

Howson, K., Ustek-Spilda, F., Grohmann, R., Salem, N., Carellim, R., Abs, D., Salvagni, J., Graham, M., Balbornoz, M. B., Chavez, H., Arriagada, A., & Bonhomme, M. (2020). 'Just because you don't see your boos, doesn't mean you don't have a boss': Covid-19 and Gig Worker Strikes across Latin America. *International Union Rights*, *27*(3), 20–28. DOI: 10.1353/iur.2020.a838172

Inter-Agency Coordination Platform for Refugees and Migrants. (R4V). (2023). *Regional Refugee and Migrant Response Plan (RMRP) 2024*. https://www.r4v.info/sites/g/files/tmzbdl2426/files/2024-04/RMRP%202024_WEB.pdf

Inter-Agency Coordination Platform for Refugees and Migrants. (R4V). (2024a). *May-June 2024 Situation Report Caribbean Sub Regional Platform*.https://www.r4v.info/sites/g/files/tmzbdl2426/files/2024-10/May-June%20Situation%20Report%20-%20Caribbean.pdf

Inter-Agency Coordination Platform for Refugees and Migrants. (R4V). (2024b). *Refugees and Migrants From Venezuela*.https://www.r4v.info/en/refugeeandmigrants

Inter-Agency Coordination Platform for Refugees and Migrants from Venezuela. (R4V). (2024c). *RMRP 2025-2026, Regional Refugee and Migrant Response Plan (RMRP)*.https://www.r4v.info/sites/g/files/tmzbdl2426/files/2024-12/RMRP_25-26_VF.pdf

International Labor Organization (ILO). International Social Security Association (ISSA), & (OCED). (2023). *Providing adequate and sustainable social protection for workers in the gig and platform economy*. Geneva, Switzerland: ILO.

International Labor Organization (ILO). (2023). *Digital platforms for domestic and care work in Latin America*. ILO.

International Organization for Migration (IOM). (2019). *Monitoring Migrants Presence: Trinidad and Tobago*. Geneva, Switzerland: United Nations High Commissioner for Refugees (UNHCR). https://data.unhcr.org/ar/documents/download/75687

Koustas, D. K. (2019). What Do Big Data Tell Us About Why People Take Gig Economy Jobs. *AEA Papers and Proceedings. American Economic Association*, *109*, 367–371. DOI: 10.1257/pandp.20191041

Lam, L., & Triandafyllidou, A. (2021). An unlikely stepping stone? Exploring how platform work shapes newcomer migrant integration. *Transitions: Journal of transient. Migration*, *5*(1), 11–29. DOI: 10.1386/tjtm_00029_1

Lam, L., & Triandafyllidou, A. (2024). Road to nowhere or to somewhere? Migrant pathways in platform work in Canada. *Environment & Planning A*, *56*(4), 1150–1169. DOI: 10.1177/0308518X221090248

Lesala Khethisa, B., Tsibolane, P., & Van Belle, J. P. (2020). Surviving the Gig Economy in the Global South: How Cape Town Domestic Workers Cope. In: Bandi, R.K., C. R., R., Klein, S., Madon, S., Monteiro, E. (eds.) *The Future of Digital Work: The Challenge of Inequality* (pp.76-85). IFIP Advances in Information and Communication Technology, 601. Springer, Cham. DOI: 10.1007/978-3-030-64697-4_7

Lozano-Paredes, L. H., & Reilly, K. M. (2018). Decent Work for Ride Hailing Workers in the Platform Economy in Cali, Colombia. Urban Transport in the Sharing Economy Era, 92-127. Buenos Aries, Argentina: Centro de Implementacion de Politicas Publicas para la Equidad y el Crecimiento (CIPPEC).

Lux, M., & Chung, C. (2023). *Earned Wage Access: An Innovation in Financial Inclusion?* M-RCBG Associate Working Paper Series, 214: 1-50.

MEDICAS. (2022). About US. https://medicasapp.com/tt/aboutus/

Newlands, G. (2022). 'This isn't forever for me': Perceived employability and migrant work in Norway and Sweden. Environment and Planning A. *Economy and Space, 56*(4), 1262–1279. DOI: 10.1177/0308518X221083021

Newlands, G. (2024). 'This isn't forever for me': Perceived employability and migrant gig work in Norway and Sweden. *A Economy and Space,* 56(4):1262-1279. DOI: 10.1177/0308518X221083021

Oranburg, S., & Palagashvili, L. (2018). The Gig Economy, Smart Contracts, and Disruption of Traditional Work Arrangements. *Social Science Research Network,* 1-24. DOI: 10.2139/ssrn.3270867

Piasna, A., & Zwysen, W. (2024). *Migrant labour in the "gig" economy: progress or trap*? Berlin, Germany: Social Europe. https://www.socialeurope.eu/migrant-labour-in-the-gig-economy-progress-or-trap

Pietrogiovanni, V., & Iossa, A. (2022). Don't GIG Up, Never! https://www.dontgigup.eu/

Putnam, L. L., Myers, K. K., & Gailliard, B. M. (2014). Examining the tensions in workplace flexibility and exploring options for new directions. *Human Relations, 67*(4), 413–440. DOI: 10.1177/0018726713495704

Putzel-Kavanaugh, C., & Benton, M. (2024). *Bridging the Gap between the Gig Economy and Migration Policy*. Migration Policy Institute.

Rappi. (2024). *About Us.* Bogota, Colombia: Rappi Inc. https://about.rappi.com/about-us

Ray, S., Herman, N., & Sen, I. (2021). *Disruptive Transformation Fuelling Gig Economies. I.* EEE Technology & Engineering Management Conference-Europe., DOI: 10.1109/TEMSCONEUR52034.2021.9488630

Reilly, K. M. A., & Lozano-Paredes, L. H. (2019). Ride Hailing Regulations in Cali, Colombia: Towards Autonomous and Decent Work. In Nielsen, P., & Kimaro, H. C. (Eds.), *Information and Communications Technologies for Development. Strengthening Southern-Driven Cooperation as a Catalyst for ICT4D. IFIP Advances in Information and Communication Technology* (Vol. 551). Springer., DOI: 10.1007/978-3-030-18400-1_35

Sarker, M. R., Taj, T. A., Sarkar, M. A. R., Hassan, M. F., McKenzie, A. M., Al Mamun, M. A., Sarker, D., & Bhandari, H. (2024). Gender differences in job satisfaction among gig workers in Bangladesh. *Scientific Reports*, *14*(17128), 1–18. DOI: 10.1038/s41598-024-68327-5 PMID: 39054341

Sequoia Capital. (2024). *Our Companies.*https://www.sequoiacap.com/our-companies/

Smit, R., & Rugunanan, P. (2014). From precarious lives to precarious work: The dilemma facing refugees in Gauteng, South Africa. *South African Review of Sociology*, *45*(2), 4–26. DOI: 10.1080/21528586.2014.917876

Smith, E. F., Gilmer, D. O., & Stockdale, M. S. (2019). The Importance of Culture and support for workplace flexibility: An ecological framework for understanding flexibility support structures. *Business Horizons*, *62*(5), 557–566. DOI: 10.1016/j.bushor.2019.04.002

Song, L., & Jo, S. J. (2023). How job crafting behaviours influence the innovative behaviour of knowledge workers in the gig economy: Based on organismic integration theory. *Frontiers in Psychology*, *14*(1228881), 1–13. DOI: 10.3389/fpsyg.2023.1228881 PMID: 37731880

Sudirman, L., & Disemadi, H. S. (2023). Gig Economy: Unleashing the Potential of Digital Banking in Indonesia's Employment Regulations. *Human Rights and Economy in the Global South*, *10*(2), 301–330. DOI: 10.19184/ejlh.v10i2.39688

Transparency International (TI). (2024). *Corruption Perceptions Index.* Berlin, Germany: TI. https://www.transparency.org/en/cpi/2023/index/tto

TriniFreelance. (2023). *Services Archive.* San Juan, Trinidad & Tobago. https://trinifreelance.com/services/

TT RideShare (TTRS). (2024). *Rider Frequently Asked Questions.*https://ttrideshare.com/rider-faqs/

Upwork. (2024). *Search.* California, United States: Upwork. https://www.upwork.com/nx/search/talent/?nbs=1

Van Doorn, N., Ferrari, F., & Graham, M. (2022). Migration and Migrant Labour in the Gig Economy: An Intervention. *Work, Employment and Society*, *5*(37), 1099–1111. DOI: 10.1177/09500170221096581 PMID: 37588943

Van Doorn, N., & Vijay, D. (2021). Gig work as migrant work: The Platformization of migrant infrastructure. *Environment and Planning A. Economy and Space*, *56*, 1129–1149. DOI: 10.1177/0308518X211065049

Vandaele, K. (2024). Inevitable, vulnerable, unprofitable: an inquiry into food delivery platforms in Europe. Future of Work Series, 1-46. Brussels, Belgium: European Trade Union Institute (ETUI).

World Bank (WB). (2024). *Ease of Doing Business Rankings.* Washington DC, United States: WB. https://archive.doingbusiness.org/en/rankings

Zampoukos, K., Butler, O., & Mitchell, D. (2024). Who's got time for social reproduction? Migrant service workers as embodied infrastructures of the algorithmic city. *Journal of Ethnic and Migration Studies*, *50*(15), 3805–3821. DOI: 10.1080/1369183X.2024.2379647

Zhou, C., He, X., Wu, R., & Zhang, G. (2022). Using Food Delivery Data to Identify Urban-Rural Areas: A Case Study of Guangzhou, China. *Frontiers in Earth Science (Lausanne)*, *1*(860361), 1–11. DOI: 10.3389/feart.2022.860361

Zipo. (2022). *Filters.*https://zipotech.com/service-provider

Zwick, A. (2022). Entrepreneurial Finance Capital and the gig economy. In Ness, I. (Ed.), *The Routledge Handbook of the Gig Economy*. Routledge., DOI: 10.4324/9781003161875-5

Chapter 3
Assessing the Challenges Faced by the Gig Workers in the Indian Context Through PLS-SEM

Rachit Agarwal
https://orcid.org/0000-0003-0164-5292
Chandigarh University, Mohali, India

Tanya Kumar
https://orcid.org/0000-0001-7608-9820
Chandigarh Business School of Administration, Chandigarh Group of Colleges, Landran, India

Gunjan Fialok
https://orcid.org/0009-0000-5736-4639
Dr. B. R. Ambedkar University, Agra, India & Gargi College, Delhi University, India

Ashish Gupta
https://orcid.org/0009-0009-5062-7833
Maharishi University of Information Technology, Noida, India

Nitish Khurana
DAV College, India

ABSTRACT

This study aimed to identify the various challenges faced by gig workers in their employment and gig services. The gig economy has remarkably contributed to em-

DOI: 10.4018/979-8-3693-9385-7.ch003

ployment across all sectors of society. It has radically altered how individuals are engaged at work and has brought about a fundamental transformation in the way our economy functions. In this study, various challenges have been identified through a literature review and a structural equation model (SEM) using Smart PLS to analyze the significant role of each challenge in the well-being of gig workers. The study sample size was 363 respondents, and it used simple random sampling among gig workers from the Delhi-NCR region. The results show that lack of a stable income, limited access to health insurance, and a lack of a legal protection framework are some of the major challenges faced by gig economy employees. This study further explains the mitigating strategies to avoid these challenges and can then be used to guide theory, practice, and public policy.

INTRODUCTION

Independent workers, part-time, temporary or contractual employees, call-based workers, telecommunications and independent workers, online or e-lancers (Bricka & Schroeder, 2019) and cognitive piece workers (Bush & Balven, 2021) are all terms related to gigs. Gig work is also known as short-term contract work, fissured workplaces, and independent workers (Mumby, 2019). Although these categories may apply to anyone, including independent contractors, third-party contract employees, and even daily workers in the construction industry, "gig work" is now used only for platform-based work. According to (Duggan et al., 2020), The gig economy is an "economic system that uses online platforms to digitally connect workers and individual service providers with consumers". The platform economy describes an economic system where digital platforms facilitate transactions between buyers and sellers, or service providers and consumers. These platforms, like Uber or Airbnb, act as intermediaries, enabling a wide range of activities (Koutsimpogiorgos et al., 2023). The gig economy, a subset of the platform economy, specifically refers to the labor market characterized by short-term, flexible work arrangements. Gig workers, such as freelance writers or delivery drivers, engage in task-based work, often facilitated by these digital platforms, rather than traditional long-term employment. Essentially, the platform economy provides the infrastructure, while the gig economy represents the workforce that utilizes it.

Over the past five years, platform-based gig work has grown considerably. According to (Katz & Krueger, 2019) Katz and Krueger (2019), in the United States, the proportion of employees participating in alternative employment arrangements increased from 10.7% in February 2005 to 15.8% at the end of 2015. In 2015, only 0.5 per cent of American employees worked as service providers through Internet technology intermediaries (Katz & Krueger, 2019). According to the BCG Henderson group's 2019 report, the use of gig labour platforms in emerging countries has increased by more than 30% (Wallenstein et al., 2019). The free agency Nasscom predicted that India's gig economy would grow at a 10% CAGR by 2024 and have a net value of $455 billion in 2017 (IBEF report, 2021). According to the IBEF report (2021), India has about 15 million independent contractors primarily engaged in design, human resources management and information technology. While not all sectors of the economy have adopted gig jobs equally, the four largest industry sectors, construction, retail, manufacturing and transportation, account for nearly 50% of the transformation of employment into gig jobs (Augustinraj et al., 2021).

The objective of this research was to study and identify the major challenges faced by gig workers and their work life. These challenges may affect their life style and well-being as well. This study would help to government, private sectors, industrialists and general public as well to ensure growth and development of gig employees and empower the economy by resolving such challenges.

LITERATURE REVIEW

Financial Issues (Income Instability)

The ILO considers gig workers as a vulnerable group on the labor market because of their persistent precariousness and structural inequality caused by the formalization of labor in employment (Heeks 2017). One of the main characteristics of the gig economy is that it enables comprehensive assessment of income inequality among gig workers. The inequal distribution of labor income usually results in stagnant wages and an increase in wage inequality between employers and employees. Some gig work protects workers while paying high wages. However, most gig workers mix many small "gigs" and their income is generally unstable, requiring them to compete with many other workers for jobs. This is the clear cause of the increase in wage inequality in the gig economy employment markets. The inequal distribution of labour incomes usually leads to a stagnation in wages and an increase in the wage gap between workers and managers. Steinbaum (2019) believes that in addition to traditional concerns such as the increasing power of employers and the relaxed antitrust rules, a reduction in workers' negotiation power also contributes to increasing inequality in the distribution of labour income. Such issues have evolved over time due to expansion of freelancing work and insecurity in such jobs have created the financial issues. These issues have significant impact on urban gig workers due to availability of work but not every time. Gig workers have faced the instability in jobs and lack of commitment under certain employment.

Administrative and Career Issues

The economic and social pressures of having to provide their tools and equipment, having few prospects for training and career advancement, receiving poor pay, having no job stability, and facing wage discrimination against specific groups, particularly women, make workers vulnerable (Tran & Sokas, 2017; Benach & Muntaner, 2007). The erasure of the employer-employee relationship brought about by platform-mediated contracts results in health vulnerabilities associated with the short-term, contingent character of the work, which are comparable to those faced by many precarious workers (Bajwa et. al, 2018). Gig workers have the career challenges related to insecurity in jobs and other challenges which effect their health insurance, paid leaves, standard wage/ salary structure, legal protection and loans facilities etc. Whereas, career issues can affect growth and increments, promotion in jobs and market goodwill etc. Apparently, such issues effect semi urban and urban gig workers (Abdullah et al., 2024).

Emotional Issues

When it comes to navigating their jobs and interactions with their employers, gig workers are essentially on their own. It might be challenging for employees to comprehend how their specific tasks fit into a larger scheme and how they relate to one another (Webster, 2016). Employees may be unable to offer one another essential emotional support if there are no strong social or professional connections at work (Jiang & Hu, 2016). The employment status of gig workers as independent contractors without the benefit of collective bargaining agreements or union representation rather than employees Frey (2020) along with their isolation offer considerable barriers to workers' collective organizing (Dubal, 2017). Given that digital platforms determine how jobs are distributed, employees may be less likely to conduct coordinated collective action against management out of fear of retaliation (Tassinari & Maccarrone, 2020). Many times, gig workers faced emotional challenges such as stress, over workload, struggle with inconsistent income and lack of social life etc (Yaroshenko et al., 2024). Such issues affect the gig workers who belong to rural and semi urban demographic segment (Abdullah et al., 2024).

Personal Benefits

In typical employment agreements, employees rely on employers and do not have a say in the plan of vacation time or other benefits. Instead, employers guarantee some rights, including wages and benefits (Donovan, 2016). On the other hand, platform companies view participants in gig workers in the gig employment market as independent contractors. They avoid the burden of financial security such as wages and benefits, rather than having the freedom to move outside and outside the industry, and are flexible in their work (Donovan et al., 2016; Friedman, 2014). From the point of view of labour law, the status of an employee provides for benefits (medical insurance, pensions), collective bargaining rights, adaptation of various laws (such as the Labour Standards Act, the Minimum Wage Act, the Family Act, the Disability Protection Act, overtime pay, etc.) and regulations (Halliday, 2021). Furthermore, most of the gig economy considered self-employed gig workers may not qualify for social insurance and social assistance, such as overtime pay, unemployment and medical (De Stefano, 2015; Donovan et al., 2016; Harpur & Blanck, 2020)

The main problem with gig workers is that they are not treated as employees, which prevents them from receiving benefits and legal protections offered to first-class workers or employees.

EVOLUTION OF GIG ECONOMY IN PAST DECADES

Over the past decade, research on the gig economy has evolved significantly, reflecting its rapid expansion and the shifting dynamics of work. Initially, studies focused on the rise of digital platforms such as Uber, Airbnb, and TaskRabbit, which revolutionized temporary and freelance work by leveraging technology (Mousa, 2025). The revenue of Uber Technologies Inc. has increased over years, in 2020 revenue was USD 11,139, in 2021, revenue was USD 17,455, whereas, in 2022, the revenue was USD 31,877 (Uber Technologies Inc, 2022). Another company Airbnb Inc has also reported the significant growth in its revenue. In 2020, USD 3.378, In 2021, USD 5,992 and in 2022, the revenue was USD 8,399 (Airbnb Incorporations, 2022). Such growth in revenue of relevant companies embark the demand among people and business model has also revolutionized with benchmark growth rate.

Scholars examined labor flexibility, economic opportunities, and worker autonomy, often highlighting the appeal of gig work in providing supplemental income. However, as the sector grew—reaching an estimated 1.57 billion gig workers globally by 2023—research began addressing critical issues such as job insecurity, lack of benefits, and algorithmic control . The COVID-19 pandemic further intensified discussions on gig worker protections, with companies like Instacart and DoorDash facing scrutiny over fair wages and healthcare access. More recent studies emphasize regulatory challenges, ethical AI use in platform work, and the role of government policies in shaping fair labor practices. Industry shifts, such as Uber's reclassification of drivers as employees in some regions and India's introduction of social security codes for gig workers, highlight the evolving policy landscape.

As gig work continues to redefine employment, ongoing research is essential to balancing innovation with worker rights and economic sustainability.

Gig worker unionization and collective bargaining efforts have gained momentum globally as workers fight for better wages, job security, and benefits. In the U.S., organizations like the Gig Workers Collective and Rideshare Drivers United have pushed for improved working conditions, particularly for app-based workers like Uber and Lyft drivers. In 2020, California's Proposition 22 initially classified gig workers as independent contractors rather than employees, but ongoing legal battles continue to challenge this status. In India, gig workers have mobilized under platforms like the Indian Federation of App-Based Transport Workers (IFAT) to demand social security benefits. Despite these advancements, many gig economy companies resist unionization efforts, arguing that flexibility and independence are key advantages of gig work. However, as labor activism grows and governments introduce new regulations, the gig economy is witnessing a shift towards stronger worker protections and collective bargaining rights.

Yang & Panyagometh (2024) found that both full-time and non-full-time gig workers on Chinese knowledge service platforms experience increased job satisfaction and commitment through intrinsic and extrinsic motivation, which are positively influenced by self-determination and social capital. The research fills a gap by extending gig economy studies beyond transportation and food delivery, applying self-determination theory to knowledge service platforms.

Table 1. Factors and Items

Factors	Codes	Items/Statements
Independent Variables		
Financial Challenges (FC)	FC1	The unpredictable nature of gig work income makes it difficult for gig workers to budget effectively.
	FC2	Gig workers often struggle to access traditional financial services such as loans and mortgages due to their fluctuating income.
	FC3	Since taxes are not considered part of the company's regular payroll, Taxes are paid by gig workers themselves.
Administrative Challenges (AC)	AC1	The lack of transparency and predictability in working conditions.
	AC2	Organizing the logistics of work without the support of the administrative infrastructure (e.g., accounting, marketing).
	AC3	Crafting a clear work identity without the roles and communities that anchor identities in organizations.

continued on following page

Table 1. Continued

Factors	Codes	Items/Statements
Career Challenges (CC)	CC1	Navigating an uncertain career path and forecasting one's future work without the more predictable career options offered by companies and industries.
	CC2	Gig workers often have limited opportunities for upskilling.
	CC3	Maintaining work relationships without a clear and stable set of regular colleagues.
Emotional Challenges (EC)	EC1	The lack of job security in gig work often leads to feelings of anxiety and uncertainty.
	EC2	Gig workers frequently experience isolation and loneliness due to the lack of a traditional workplace environment
	EC3	Managing irregular work schedules and multiple clients can contribute to high levels of stress and burnout among gig workers.
Personal Benefit Challenges (PBC)	PBC1	The lack of job security, proper contracts, medical coverage and workplace benefits.
	PBC2	Gig workers miss out on "soft" benefits like corporate discount programmes and subsidized gym memberships.
	PBC3	Many gig workers in India operate in the informal sector, which can limit their ability to access credit, government support programs, and other resources.
Dependent Variable		
Psychological Well-Being of Gig Workers (PWB)	PWB1	Gig workers often struggle with inconsistent and unpredictable income.
	PWB2	Gig workers face difficulties in accessing traditional employment benefits, such as health insurance and retirement plans.
	PWB3	Gig workers experience a lack of job security due to the absence of long-term contracts or stable employment relationships.
	PWB4	Gig workers often encounter challenges in maintaining a healthy work-life balance due to irregular working hours and demands.

(Source: Author's own representation)

Table 1 represents the various items/statements have been considered for different constructs.

RESEARCH METHODOLOGY

Purpose of the Study

The purpose of the study is to delve into the drawbacks associated with the gig economy and propose strategies to tackle these challenges. By analysing the existing literature, empirical studies, and real-life examples, this research aims to shed light on the implications of job insecurity, limited access to social protections, and income instability in the gig economy.

Sample Size

The sample size of this study collected was 363, which is collected from the gig workers in Delhi-NCR using simple random sampling.

Scale Development and Data Collection

The survey link was disseminated on Facebook, Instagram, and WhatsApp. The researcher contacted the gig workers. Informed consent was obtained, complete anonymity was guaranteed, and participation was completely optional. The information was gathered using a self-report questionnaire on a five-point Likert scale where 5 strongly agree and 1 strongly disagree. There were 15 items on the measurement scale that represented 5 factors which are shown below in the research framework.

Hypotheses of the Study

H_1: Administrative challenges (FC) have the significant impact on psychological well-being of gig workers.
H_2: Career challenges (AC) have the significant impact on psychological well-being of gig workers.
H_3: Emotional challenges (CC) have the significant impact on psychological well-being of gig workers.
H_4: Financial challenges (EC) have the significant impact on psychological well-being of gig workers.
H_5: Personal Benefits Challenges (PBC) have the significant impact on psychological well-being of gig workers

In this work, the Smart PLS 4.0 was used to test the model and hypothesis.

Figure 1. Conceptual Research Model

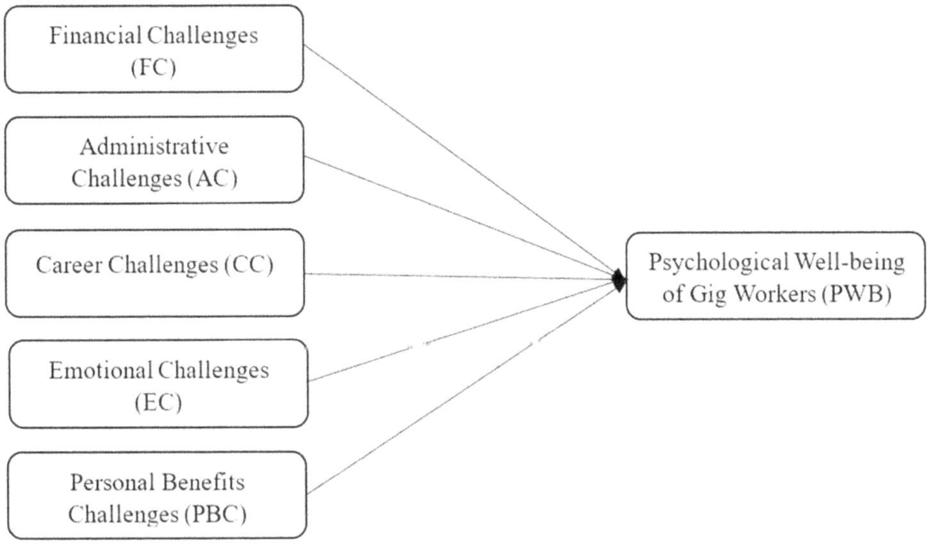

Source: (Author's own representation)

RESULTS

Measurement Model Assessment

The measuring model (outer model) explains how the constructs and the related indicators relate to one another. Confirming reliability, convergent and discriminant validities is necessary to evaluate the measurement model. The internal consistency reliability was evaluated using composite reliability (CR). According to Table 1, it can be seen that the reliability is confirmed as the values of CR were above the threshold value of 0.7. Factor loadings and Average Variance Extracted (AVE) are advised to be investigated for the determination of convergent validity. As can be seen in Table 2, the findings showed that both measures were reliable because the factor loading values were all above the suggested value of 0.7 and the AVE values were all over the cutoff value of 0.5. For accessing the Discriminant Validity, Fornell Larcker Criterion is used, and Table 3 shown below highlights that the correlation between a construct and any other construct must be smaller than the square root of the average variance recovered by the construct, and Discriminant validity is proven since this prerequisite is met. To achieve this, the measurement model is validated, which enables us to move forward with the structural model evaluation.

Table 2. Construct Reliability and Validity

Constructs	Composite Reliability (CR)	AVE
AC	0.745	0.664
CC	0.822	0.726
EC	0.892	0.822
FC	0.767	0.680
PBC	0.825	0.740
PWB	0.824	0.629

Table 3. Discriminant Validity- Fornell Larcker Criterion

	AC	CC	EC	FC	PBC	PWB
AC	0.815					
CC	0.766	0.852				
EC	0.763	0.722	0.907			
FC	0.627	0.427	0.582	0.825		
PBC	0.745	0.763	0.891	0.592	0.860	
PWB	0.624	0.676	0.713	0.489	0.745	0.809

Structural Model Assessment

The link between the latent constructs themselves is described by the structural model. Two popular metrics, hypothesis testing and coefficient of determination (R2), are recommended for evaluating the structural model. The results are summarised in Table 3, 4 and Figure 2, and it can be seen that according to the data analysis, the empirical data supported hypothesis H1, H2, H3, and H5 are supported and H4 is rejected.

The results showed that A significantly influenced G (P-value= 0.011) which is less than significance level 0.05 and C (P-value= 0.000) which is less than significance level 0.05; supporting hypotheses H2 and H3, respectively. The results also revealed that F significantly influenced G (P-value= 0.037) which is less than the significance level 0.05; supporting hypothesis 1. It has also indicated that P significantly affected G (P-value= 0.000) which is less than the significance level 0.05; providing support for hypothesis H5. Furthermore, the results pointed out that E does not significantly affect G (P-value= 0.194) which is more than significance level 0.05; not supporting hypothesis 4. The common technique for evaluating the structural model's prediction ability is to calculate its R2 score. Figure 2 illustrates the model's excellent predictive power, which accounts for about 88.9% of the variance in gig workers' challenges.

Figure 2. Structural Equation Modelling

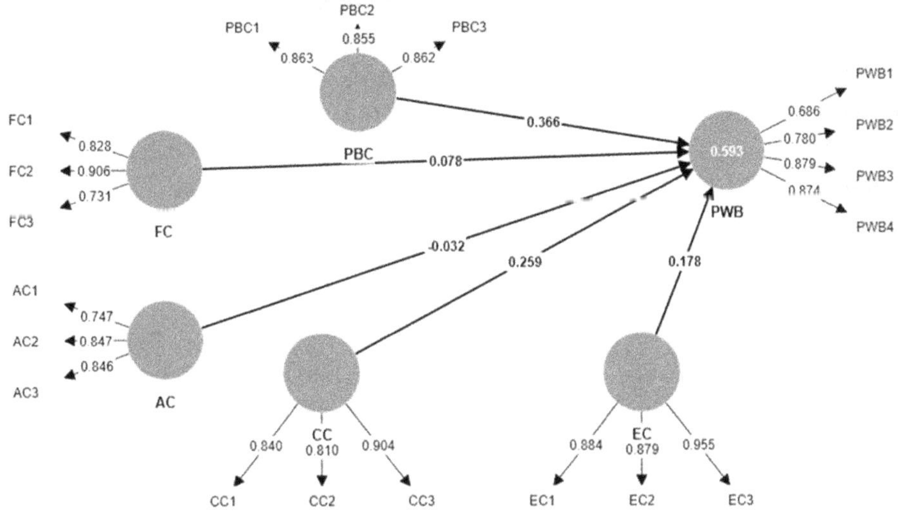

Source: (Author's own representation)

Table 4. Hypotheses Testing Results

	Original sample (O)	Sample mean (M)	Standard deviation (STDEV)	T statistics (|O/ STDEV|)	P values
AC -> PWB	-0.032	-0.032	0.075	0.426	0.004
CC -> PWB	0.259	0.262	0.073	3.553	0.000
EC -> PWB	0.178	0.177	0.070	2.535	0.081
FC -> PWB	0.078	0.079	0.051	1.516	0.002
PBC -> PWB	0.366	0.365	0.101	3.610	0.000

FINDINGS AND DISCUSSIONS

Financial Challenges

Gig workers frequently experience severe financial difficulties that can significantly affect their ability to support themselves. The instability and unpredictability of gig employment is one of the main causes of these problems. Unlike those who work in typical jobs, gig workers do not receive a set pay or a consistent flow of funds. Instead, they depend on sporadic jobs or projects, which can come with a wide range of frequency and pay (Yaroshenko et al., 2024). Because of this inconsistency, it is challenging for gig workers to efficiently organize their finances, which causes financial instability (Mohd Daud et al., 2024).

Administrative Challenges

Managing the logistics of their employment without the aid of administrative infrastructure like accounting and marketing departments is an issue that gig workers frequently confront. Gig workers are accountable for managing various areas of their work autonomously, in contrast to traditional employees who often have access to these support systems within their organization. Gig workers are responsible for managing their accounting and finances, including tracking their earnings, paying their bills, and filing their taxes (Agarwal et al., 2024). For them to maintain correct records and guarantee compliance with tax laws, they must be financially literate (Mohd Daud et al., 2024). Gig workers may find it difficult to manage these obligations properly in the absence of an accounting department, which could result in financial problems and complicated tax situations. Gig workers frequently need to promote themselves and find clients on their own. This entails activities like developing a personal brand, networking, and actively looking for new jobs or initiatives. Without the aid of a specialized marketing team, gig workers may find it difficult to sell their services, connect with their target market, and maintain a steady stream of employment (Kumar & Kaur, 2022). Gig workers are in charge of maintaining their technological setup, including cybersecurity safeguards, software, and hardware. Gig workers may experience difficulties setting up and maintaining their technological systems, resolving technical issues, and guaranteeing the security of their data without the IT help frequently provided in typical organizations (Cassell & Deutsch, 2023).

Accessing clear and thorough information about available gig opportunities might be difficult for gig workers. It can be challenging for gig workers to make educated decisions about which gigs to pursue because job listings may not provide enough information about the nature of the work, pay, or expectations. This lack of openness may cause employees to be hesitant and confused about the duties of the position and what kind of workload, hours, and pay they can anticipate (Agrawal et al., 2024).

Without the consistent organizational framework that comes with traditional employment, gig workers often work alone or in transitory project teams. People frequently have well-defined job titles and roles in traditional companies, which contribute to their sense of identity. Without these frameworks, gig workers could find it difficult to identify their professional identities or their roles within the larger work context (Alanzi, 2021).

Career Challenges

Gig workers encounter major career-related difficulties that may affect their future chances and professional development. The absence of career growth options in the gig economy is one of the key problems. Gig workers frequently find themselves trapped in a loop of short-term jobs or projects without a clear path for growth, in contrast to regular employment where people can advance through a hierarchical structure or obtain promotions (Himani Srihita et al., 2025). Their inability to advance can result in a feeling of stagnation and impede their capacity to learn new abilities or acquire important experiences. Another difficulty faced by gig workers is the lack of resources for training and professional growth. Many conventional businesses make investments in the professional growth of their staff members by offering training courses, seminars, and other resources to advance their knowledge and abilities. Gig workers, on the other hand, are frequently in charge of their training and development, which can be expensive and time-consuming (Van Fossen et al., 2024). Gig workers may struggle to maintain their competitiveness in the quickly changing employment market without access to sufficient resources and support for skill-building.

Emotional Challenges

This might be because, with technological advancements that allow for virtual communication and collaboration, gig workers did not experience feelings of isolation due to regular face-to-face interactions with colleagues on online platforms (Huang et al., 2024).

Personal Benefits Challenges

The absence of employee benefits presents gig workers with yet another significant hurdle. Benefits including health insurance, retirement plans, paid time off, and unemployment insurance are often provided to traditional employees. But gig workers typically have to pay for these perks themselves, which may be expensive and demanding. Without benefits from their employers, gig workers may find it impossible to save for retirement, pay for unexpected crises, or finance other necessities, which will only make their financial problems worse (Hart & Pomponi, 2021). The lack of job security is another problem for gig workers. Gig employment is frequently characterized by its transient nature, with projects and contracts ending after a set period. This ongoing desire to land new jobs may make one feel unstable and uncertain about their employment prospects. Gig workers may find it difficult to plan their career trajectory or commit to long-term goals like buying a home or raising a family without the security of stable employment (Annett, 2020).

CONCLUSION

The gig economy offers numerous opportunities for flexible work arrangements, but it also presents several challenges that need to be addressed. By acknowledging the lack of job security, limited access to social protections, and income instability faced by gig workers, policymakers, gig economy platforms, and other stakeholders can work together to develop and implement solutions. Portable benefits programs, reclassification of gig workers as employees, and financial tools and resources can contribute to reducing the drawbacks associated with the gig economy, fostering a more equitable and sustainable future of work.

The gig economy in India presents a range of opportunities and challenges. While it offers flexibility, expanded job opportunities, and technological empowerment, it also poses challenges related to social protections, income instability, and regulatory ambiguity. Addressing these challenges requires a multi-stakeholder approach involving government, gig platforms, workers' organizations, and financial institutions. By implementing measures to enhance social protections, mitigate income volatility, and establish clear regulatory frameworks, India can nurture a gig economy that is inclusive, sustainable, and supportive of workers' well-being.

This study concludes that emotional challenges have no significant impact on psychological well-being of gig workers. It means those who were gig employee they were not emotionally affected by any decision and any other reason. Financial, administrative, career and personal benefit challenges have significant impact on psychological well-being of gig workers.

Policymakers, industries and government should understand the explained factors for the growth and development of gig economy in India.

CONFLICT OF INTEREST

The authors declare that there is no conflict of interest regarding the authorship or publication of this chapter.

FUNDING SUPPORT

The authors declare that no funding support was received from any institution, organization, or funding agency for the preparation and publication of this book chapter.

REFERENCES

Abdullah, N., Mohd Ismail, M., Huzni Murad, M. S., Jusoff, K., Kurniawan, F., & Salah, M. (2024). Critical Insights into Gig Economy: A Peninsular Malaysia Case Study. *Jambe Law Journal*, *7*(2), 395–427. DOI: 10.22437/home.v7i2.460

Agarwal, R., Kumar, T., Singh, A., & Schutte, D. P. (2025). Empowering Indigenous Economies: Financial and Investment Prediction for Sustainable Development. In Irfan, M., Majeed, M., Kassim, S., & Ofori, K. (Eds.), *The Future of Indigenous Inclusivity: Unlocking Finance for Economic Development* (pp. 63–82). IGI Global Scientific Publishing., DOI: 10.4018/979-8-3693-7924-0.ch004

Agrawal, A., Kumar, T., Agarwal, R., & Gupta, A. (2024), "AI-Driven Personalized Risk Management in the Insurance Sector", Taneja, S., Kumar, P., Reepu, Kukreti, M. and Özen, E. (Ed.) Data Alchemy in the Insurance Industry, Emerald Publishing Limited, Leeds, pp. 27-39. DOI: 10.1108/978-1-83608-582-920241006

Airbnb Incorporations. (2022). *Annual Report 2022*.

Alanzi, T. M. (2021). Gig Health vs eHealth: Future Prospects in Saudi Arabian Health-Care System. *Journal of Multidisciplinary Healthcare*, *14*, 1945–1953. DOI: 10.2147/JMDH.S304690 PMID: 34326645

Annett, M. (2020). Understanding the Homepreneurship Opportunities Afforded by Social Networking and Personal Fabrication Technologies. *Proceedings of the ACM on Human-Computer Interaction*, *4*(CSCW2), 1–48. DOI: 10.1145/3415170

Augustinraj, R., Jain, V., & Bansal, S. (2021). *Unlocking the Potential of the Gig Economy in India*.

Bajwa, U., Knorr, L., Di Ruggiero, E., Gastaldo, D., & Zendel, A. (2018). Towards an understanding of workers' experiences in the global gig economy. *Globalization and Health, 14*(124), 2–4.

Benach, J., & Muntaner, C. (2007). Precarious employment and health: Developing a research agenda. *Journal of Epidemiology and Community Health, 61*(4), 276–277. DOI: 10.1136/jech.2005.045237 PMID: 17372284

Bricka, T. M., & Schroeder, A. N. (2019). What's the gig deal? Examining contemporary work issues in the gig economy. *Industrial and Organizational Psychology: Perspectives on Science and Practice, 12*(4), 491–494. DOI: 10.1017/iop.2019.116

Bush, J. T., & Balven, R. M. (2021). Catering to the crowd: An HRM perspective on crowd worker engagement. *Human Resource Management Review, 31*(1), 100670. DOI: 10.1016/j.hrmr.2018.10.003

Cassell, M. K., & Deutsch, A. M. (2023). Urban Challenges and the Gig Economy: How German Cities Cope with the Rise of Airbnb. *German Politics, 32*(2), 319–340. DOI: 10.1080/09644008.2020.1719072

De Stefano, V. (2015). The Rise of the "Just-in-Time Workforce": On-Demand Work, Crowd Work and Labour Protection in the "Gig-Economy." SSRN *Electronic Journal*. DOI: 10.2139/ssrn.2682602

Donovan, S. A., Bradley, D. H., & Shimabukuro, J. O. (2016). *What Does the Gig Economy Mean for Workers?* Dubal, V. (2017). The Drive to Precarity: A Political History of Work, Regulation, & Labor Advocacy in San Francisco's Taxi & Uber Economies. *Berkeley Journal of Employment and Labor Law, 38*(1), 73–136.

Duggan, J., Sherman, U., Carbery, R., & McDonnell, A. (2020). Algorithmic management and app-work in the gig economy: A research agenda for employment relations and HRM. *Human Resource Management Journal, 30*(1), 114–132. DOI: 10.1111/1748-8583.12258

Frey, B. (2020). Platform Labor and In/Formality: Organization among Motorcycle Taxi Drivers in Bandung, Indonesia. *Anthropology of Work Review, 41*(1), 36–49. DOI: 10.1111/awr.12187

Friedman, G. (2014). Workers without employers: Shadow corporations and the rise of the gig economy. *Review of Keynesian Economics, 2*(2), 171–188. DOI: 10.4337/roke.2014.02.03

Halliday, D. (2021). On the (mis)classification of paid labor: When should gig workers have employee status? *Politics, Philosophy & Economics, 20*(3), 229–250. DOI: 10.1177/1470594X211015467

Harpur, P., & Blanck, P. (2020). Gig Workers with Disabilities: Opportunities, Challenges, and Regulatory Response. *Journal of Occupational Rehabilitation, 30*(4), 511–520. DOI: 10.1007/s10926-020-09937-4 PMID: 33146784

Hart, J., & Pomponi, F. (2021). A Circular Economy: Where Will It Take Us? *Circular Economy and Sustainability, 1*(1), 127–141. DOI: 10.1007/s43615-021-00013-4 PMID: 34888551

Heeks, R. (2017). Decent Work and the Digital Gig Economy: A Developing Country Perspective on Employment Impacts and Standards in Online Outsourcing, Crowdwork, Etc. SSRN *Electronic Journal*. DOI: 10.2139/ssrn.3431033

Himani Srihita, R., Goli, G., M, R., & Gobinath, R. (2025). Transformative dynamics of the gig economy: Technological impacts, worker well-being and global research trends. *International Journal of Engineering Business Management, 17*, 18479790241310362. Advance online publication. DOI: 10.1177/18479790241310362

Huang, X., Sun, Z., Li, J., & Li, J. (2024). Will Fun and Care Prevent Gig Workers' Withdrawal? A Moderated Mediation Model. *Asia Pacific Journal of Human Resources, 62*(4), e12425. Advance online publication. DOI: 10.1111/1744-7941.12425

Jiang, Z., & Hu, X. (2016). Knowledge Sharing and Life Satisfaction: The Roles of Colleague Relationships and Gender. *Social Indicators Research, 126*(1), 379–394. DOI: 10.1007/s11205-015-0886-9

Katz, L. F., & Krueger, A. B. (2019). The Rise and Nature of Alternative Work Arrangements in the United States, 1995–2015. *Industrial & Labor Relations Review, 72*(2), 382–416. DOI: 10.1177/0019793918820008

Koutsimpogiorgos, N., Frenken, K., & Herrmann, A. M. (2023). Platform adaptation to regulation: The case of domestic cleaning in Europe. *The Journal of Industrial Relations, 65*(2), 156–184. DOI: 10.1177/00221856221146833

Kumar, T., & Kaur, S. (2022). Cyber Security in Businesses: Challenges and Recovery Modes. In 2022 2nd International Conference on Emerging Smart Technologies and Applications (eSmarTA) (pp. 1-5). IEEE.

Mohd Daud, S. N., Osman, Z., Samsudin, S., & Phang, I. G. (2024). Adapting to the gig economy: Determinants of financial resilience among "Giggers.". *Economic Analysis and Policy, 81*, 756–771. DOI: 10.1016/j.eap.2024.01.002

Mousa, M. (2025). Gig work, management education and changes in working conditions: A qualitative study. *Industrial and Commercial Training, 57*(1), 82–98. DOI: 10.1108/ICT-07-2024-0066

Mumby, D. K. (2019). Work: What is it good for? (Absolutely nothing)—a critical theorist's perspective. *Industrial and Organizational Psychology: Perspectives on Science and Practice*, *12*(4), 429–443. DOI: 10.1017/iop.2019.69

IBEF Report. (2021, May 21). *Emergence of India's Gig Economy*. IBEF. Accessed on Aug 24, 2024

Steinbaum, M. (2019). Antitrust, the Gig Economy, and Labor Market Power. SSRN *Electronic Journal*. DOI: 10.2139/ssrn.3347949

Tassinari, A., & Maccarrone, V. (2020). Riders on the Storm: Workplace Solidarity among Gig Economy Couriers in Italy and the UK. *Work, Employment and Society*, *34*(1), 35–54. DOI: 10.1177/0950017019862954

Tran, M., & Sokas, R. K. (2017). The Gig Economy and Contingent Work. *Journal of Occupational and Environmental Medicine*, *59*(4), e63–e66. DOI: 10.1097/JOM.0000000000000977 PMID: 28244887

Uber Technologies Inc. (2022). *Annual Report 2022*.

Van Fossen, J. A., Watson, G. P., Schuster, A. M., Baker, N. M., Chang, C., & Cotten, S. R. (2024). Striving for the self: A self-regulation model of positive identity maintenance in platform-based gig drivers. *Journal of Organizational Behavior*, job.2828. Advance online publication. DOI: 10.1002/job.2828

Wallenstein, J., de Chalendar, A., Reeves, M., & Bailey, A. (2019). *The new freelancers: Tapping talent in the gig economy*.

Webster, J. (2016). Microworkers of the Gig Economy. *New Labor Forum*, *25*(3), 56–64. DOI: 10.1177/1095796016661511

Yang, L., & Panyagometh, A. (2024). Factors influencing gig workers' satisfaction and commitment in the knowledge service providing platforms based on the self-determination theory: The case study in China. *Kasetsart Journal of Social Sciences*, *45*(1). Advance online publication. DOI: 10.34044/j.kjss.2024.45.1.29

Yaroshenko, O. M., Tkachenko, V. S., Puntus, D. A., Yakovleva, G. O., & Konopeltseva, O. O. (2024). Models of Social Protection for Workers in the Gig Economy: Legal Challenges and Prospects. *Science of Law*, *2024*(3), 1–7. DOI: 10.55284/sol.v2024i3.139

Chapter 4
Regulating the Gig Economy:
Addressing Worker Rights in India's Quick Commerce Sector

Pooja Kalbalia
https://orcid.org/0000-0002-3739-3165
Christ University, India

Kailash Koushik
Christ University, India

ABSTRACT

The study examines the regulatory challenges faced by India's fast-growing quick commerce gig economy, with a focus on the rights and protections of workers. It examines the issue of gig workers and implementation gaps in existing frameworks and highlights the vulnerabilities of migrant workers. The study uses thematic analysis to explore aspects such as working conditions, workers' legal awareness, algorithmic management, and gender inclusion in the workforce. Findings reveal regional disparities in working conditions, discrepancies between legal recognition and practical enforcement, and persistent gender-based inequalities. The research underscores the need for tailored, collaborative efforts among various stakeholders to improve the situation of gig workers. This study aims to enhance the understanding of regulatory issues in the quick commerce sector and offers valuable insights for policymakers, platforms, and researchers to improve working conditions and ensure fair treatment for gig workers in India.

DOI: 10.4018/979-8-3693-9385-7.ch004

INTRODUCTION

India's quick commerce gig economy transforms retail by delivering unparalleled convenience through platforms like Blinkit, Swiggy Instamart, and Zepto (Sanghi et al., 2024; Wood et al., 2019). These platforms rely on gig workers who ensure fast and reliable deliveries, highlighting the importance of flexibility and speed in this sector (Kalbalia et al., 2024). As the sector grows, it creates employment opportunities for millions of youths, migrants, and those displaced from traditional industries. The (Rao et al., 2022) projects that India's gig workforce will grow to 23.5 million by 2029-2030. However, this rapid expansion exposes workers to precarious conditions due to inadequate labour protections

Platforms classify gig workers as independent contractors rather than employees, excluding them from rights like minimum wages, job security, and health benefits (Pulignano, 2019). By doing so, companies reduce their obligations, shifting risks onto the workers (Haque & Dard, 2023). This practice impairs the vulnerabilities of gig workers, especially in a socio-economic context where many already lack financial stability (Choudhary & Shireshi, 2022). India's regulatory framework struggles to keep pace with this growing sector, leaving significant gaps in legal safeguards for workers (Pant & Majumder, 2022). Addressing these challenges requires a balanced approach that fosters innovation while ensuring fair treatment for gig workers.

The Indian government introduced the Code on Social Security (2020) to recognise gig and platform workers and extend their social security benefits (Singh & Bhushan, 2023). However, weak enforcement and a limited scope of inclusion hinder its impact. Quick commerce workers face algorithmic management, irregular earnings, and intense performance pressures, making these protections even more critical (Silva & Nyobe, 2023). Migrants, youth, and individuals from economically weaker backgrounds dominate the gig workforce, further complicating the landscape. Many enter the sector because they lack access to formal employment opportunities, particularly in urban and peri-urban areas (Tejaswini S & Abirami V, 2023). Women gig workers encounter additional barriers. Safety concerns, cultural restrictions, and limited access to higher-paying opportunities often discourage women from fully participating in the sector (Bajwa et al., 2018). Despite the flexibility that gig work offers, these structural issues perpetuate gender-based disparities, leaving women at a disadvantage.

Globally, countries like Spain and the UK offer partial solutions by introducing hybrid worker models that combine flexibility with some employment benefits (Hardy & McCrystal, 2022; Tug & Basar, 2023). While these frameworks address specific concerns, they fail to account for the complexities of India's labour market, including massive informal employment, regional disparities, and a lack of universal social security. India must tailor its regulatory response to address these challenges while holding platforms accountable. Platforms also use algorithmic management to allocate tasks, calculate pay, and enforce performance metrics. These algorithms often function as opaque "black boxes," offering workers an understanding of how decisions affect their livelihoods (De Stefano, 2015). Algorithmic systems frequently cause earnings volatility through unpredictable pricing models and shifting incentive structures (Silva & Nyobe, 2023). These practices make financial planning difficult and erode workers' trust in platforms. The lack of transparency further disempowers workers' struggle to contest unfair decisions.

Algorithmic performance metrics, such as on-time delivery rates and customer ratings, pressure workers to meet demanding standards. Many feel compelled to engage in risky behaviours, like skipping breaks or driving carelessly, to maintain favourable scores. Over time, these conditions lead to burnout and deteriorate workers' physical and mental health. Addressing these issues requires platforms to make their systems transparent and involve workers in algorithmic governance. Workers also face obstacles in seeking recourse when platforms make arbitrary decisions, such as pay deductions or account deactivations (Haque & Dard, 2023). Without standardised grievance redressal mechanisms, many remain vulnerable to exploitative practices. Women, in particular, face heightened risks due to the lack of safety features in platforms and the absence of gender-sensitive policies. These challenges highlight the need for inclusive and equitable solutions.

This chapter examines the regulatory challenges in India's quick commerce gig economy and suggests actionable reforms to improve worker protections. It identifies key gaps in implementing the Code on Social Security and critiques the widespread misclassification of gig workers. It also explores workers' vulnerabilities, including income instability, health risks, and limited legal awareness. Drawing from global regulatory practices, the chapter proposes reforms tailored to India's socio-economic and cultural context. The reforms emphasise several key areas. First, India must redefine worker classification to ensure that gig workers receive essential rights and benefits. Hybrid models can strike a balance between flexibility and protection. Second, stronger enforcement mechanisms must close the policy intent and outcomes gap. Third, expanding social security schemes will ensure comprehensive coverage for gig workers, with contributions shared among workers, platforms, and the government.

Establishing wage standards will address income disparities, particularly for workers in smaller cities and rural areas. Gender inclusivity must become a priority, with measures like safety features in apps, women-only delivery hubs, and targeted training programs. Platforms must also take accountability by introducing transparent algorithmic systems and participatory governance mechanisms. India's quick commerce gig economy is at a crossroads. Its rapid growth offers significant employment and innovation opportunities but raises questions about equity and sustainability. Addressing these challenges requires bold, multi-pronged reforms prioritising worker rights and economic progress. This chapter contributes to the ongoing discourse by analysing the regulatory gaps and offering actionable strategies to create a fairer and more inclusive gig economy in India.

Literature Review

The gig economy, platform-mediated labour, has grown worldwide, underpinned by digital platforms connecting workers with consumers for on-demand services (Codagnone et al., 2016). This expansion is fuelled by technological innovations, which enable quick access to services through user-friendly mobile applications (Farbenblum et al., 2018). Scholars have highlighted the convergence of several trends that have contributed to the rise of the gig economy. The growth of the Internet as a service marketplace, the increasing demand for labour flexibility, and consumers' desire for convenience and speed (De Stefano, 2015). The gig economy initially mirrored global trends in India, focusing on ride-hailing and food delivery sectors. However, in recent years, the emergence of "quick commerce", the ultra-fast delivery of groceries and household essentials reshaped business models, consumer expectations, and the working conditions of gig workers (Ganapathy et al., 2024; Haneefa, 2024).

Quick commerce platforms like Blinkit, Swiggy Instamart, and Zepto in India represent a significant shift within the gig economy, offering goods within short delivery windows of up to 30 minutes (Chitranshi & Chopra, 2023; Sanghi et al., 2023). This sub-sector is deeply integrated with urban logistics systems, relying on dense networks and algorithmic management to optimise fulfilment processes (Choudhary & Shireshi, 2022). While research on quick commerce is developing, it is clear that this model introduces operational challenges distinct from other forms of gig work, such as food and ride-hailing services. These include constricted delivery timeframes, precarious earnings structures, and an over-reliance on algorithms to dictate worker schedules and pay (Pulignano, 2019). Flexibility is often seen as a key feature of gig work, and it is important to note that workers' autonomy is frequently limited. Gig workers feel compelled to work during peak times and under intense pressure to secure a decent income (Lehdonvirta, 2018; A. J. Wood et al., 2019).

The legal and regulatory status of gig workers has long been contentious. In many cases, gig workers are classified as independent contractors rather than employees, which excludes them from traditional labour protections such as minimum wage laws, health insurance, and paid leave (Betten, 1995; Lee, 2014). This classification is driven by platforms' interests in reducing costs and liabilities but impairs the unevenness of gig workers in terms of income stability and access to social security (Pulignano, 2019). Gig workers often bear the costs of their work, such as fuel, vehicle maintenance, and mobile data, without access to the security that full-time employees typically enjoy (Behrendt et al., 2019). Research on gig workers in quick commerce highlights the compounded vulnerability resulting from algorithmic management, which controls task assignments, pricing, and incentives, all while leaving workers with limited knowledge of the algorithms' inner workings (Silva & Nyobe, 2023).

Quick commerce workers face challenges due to the speed-driven nature of their work. The need to fulfil deliveries within very short timeframes can place significant physical and psychological strain on workers (Asadullah & Persson, 2024). Time pressure and the fear of penalties often push workers to unsafe exhaustion levels, leading to increased stress and even risky behaviours, such as speeding on the road (Dekker, 2021). Studies of other gig sectors, like food delivery and ride-hailing, have shown similar trends, with algorithmic management systems growing stress and unpredictability (Bajwa et al., 2018; Lambert et al., 2012). The combination of time constraints and performance-based incentives can often lead to a 'digital Taylorism' model, where workers are subjected to constant surveillance and micro-management despite lacking the benefits and protections of traditional employment (De Stefano, 2015).

Globally, countries like Spain and the UK offer examples of successful regulatory frameworks. Spain's Rider Law reclassifies delivery riders as employees, granting them protections like minimum wages and collective bargaining rights (Hardy & McCrystal, 2022). In the UK, a hybrid model provides gig workers with benefits such as minimum pay for tasks and holiday pay, balancing flexibility with security (Tug & Basar, 2023). While these frameworks address specific challenges, adapting them to India requires accounting for the country's massive informal sector, regional disparities, and limited enforcement capacity. Learning from these models, India could introduce hybrid classification schemes and stronger enforcement mechanisms to extend essential protections without affecting platform growth.

India's labour market is characterised by informal work arrangements, widespread job insecurity, and regional disparities in employment opportunities (Håkansta et al., 2024; Standing, 2011). This complicates regulating the gig economy, especially as gig workers are often excluded from formal protections and may lack the awareness or resources to claim their rights (Tejaswini & Abirami, 2023). India's socio-economic context adds further complexity to the regulation of gig work. Migrants, youth, and individuals from economically disadvantaged backgrounds represent a significant proportion of gig workers, often drawn to the flexibility and relative ease of entry into the gig economy (Choudhary & Shireshi, 2022). This demographic is particularly vulnerable, as many face limited education, a lack of legal literacy, and minimal bargaining power. Women, in particular, face additional challenges, including safety concerns, limited mobility, and reduced access to high-paying opportunities in the gig economy (Bajwa et al., 2018). The intersection of gender, class, and regional identity often impairs inequalities in gig work, with migrant workers facing unique struggles in navigating unfamiliar legal and social landscapes.

In response to the growing prominence of gig workers, the Indian government introduced the Code on Social Security in 2020, formally recognising gig and platform workers and aiming to extend social security benefits such as health insurance and maternity (Singh & Bhushan, 2023). However, the implementation of this Code has faced challenges. Early analyses suggest that enforcement mechanisms remain weak, leaving compliance mainly to the discretion of platforms, which may not fully recognise the nature of gig work (Tejaswini & Abirami, 2023). The absence of clear definitions regarding the employment status of gig workers further complicates the effectiveness of the Code. Until platforms acknowledge the central role of gig workers in their business models and the reliance on algorithmic management, the protections envisioned by the Code may not be fully realised.

The role of algorithmic management in quick commerce is another growing concern. Platform algorithms dictate various aspects of workers' tasks, from job allocation to incentive structures. However, workers often remain unaware of how these algorithms function or how their performance is assessed (Silva & Nyobe, 2023). This lack of transparency leads to feelings of unfairness and distrust. Moreover, the digital surveillance inherent in algorithmic management can increase stress and pressure on workers, who may feel constantly monitored and evaluated based on performance metrics such as delivery times, customer ratings, and distance covered (Jarrahi et al., 2021). This surveillance model can result in workers taking risky actions to meet deadlines, such as speeding or overexerting themselves physically (Asadullah & Persson, 2024).

Furthermore, gender issues in gig work, especially in quick commerce, need attention. The sector is male-dominated, with women facing additional barriers related to safety and mobility. Women who enter the quick commerce sector often encounter lower-paying opportunities, harassment, and poor working conditions, which discourage them from participating in higher-paying roles (Bajwa et al., 2018). Future research needs to explore how platforms can design inclusive policies and algorithms that offer equitable opportunities to women, ensuring their safety and financial viability.

The issue of collective action and worker organisation in quick commerce is a critical gap in the literature. Given the discrete, often virtual nature of gig work, traditional labour union models struggle to adapt to the needs of these workers. Informal collectives and digital platforms like WhatsApp groups have emerged as spaces for workers to communicate and share concerns, but formal collective bargaining remains challenging (Flanagan, 2018). Without a clear legal framework supporting worker representation, gig workers in quick commerce have limited avenues to negotiate for better working conditions or pay. As the sector continues to evolve, the role of digital platforms in facilitating or hindering collective action will be crucial to understanding how gig workers can organise and advocate for their rights.

METHODOLOGY

This study adopts a conceptual approach to explore regulatory challenges in India's quick commerce sector, focusing on worker rights within the gig economy. Using the (Jaakkola, 2020) typology method, the paper categorises key issues related to gig worker rights and the frameworks that govern them. The goal is to create a framework that connects the gig economy's legal, social, and operational aspects with the challenges workers face, particularly in quick commerce. This approach clarifies the regulatory landscape and highlights current research and practice gaps. Although the study does not rely on empirical data (Cornelissen, 2016), it contributes to theory by organising and synthesising existing knowledge about gig worker rights and the regulatory environment. The typology method helps categorise complex issues, such as worker classification, legal recognition, and algorithmic management, linking them systematically. This approach uncovers emerging trends and challenges, laying the groundwork for future empirical research.

The framework developed here centres on key regulatory aspects for gig workers, such as worker classification, social security benefits, legal awareness, and gender inclusion. The study analyses these issues through the lens of current legal frameworks and quick commerce business realities. The paper identifies regulatory shortcomings by categorising these elements and suggests ways to improve worker protections. To construct this framework, the study draws insights from labour law research, gig economy studies, and quick commerce business model literature (Graham et al., 2017; Sutherland & Jarrahi, 2018). The analysis does not predict specific outcomes but offers a lens to understand the impacts of different regulatory frameworks on gig worker rights. The resulting framework provides a foundation for future research and policy development, addressing gaps in regulation and improving worker conditions.

The study also incorporates ethical considerations, addressing data privacy, algorithmic bias, and the sustainability of gig economy models. These factors are crucial for protecting gig workers' rights in a digital, platform-based economy. Considering technological and societal dimensions, the framework informs future regulatory efforts, ensuring fair treatment of gig workers in the quick commerce sector. This methodology emphasises classification and synthesis, bridging theoretical gaps and connecting various issues related to gig worker rights. It highlights the relationships between legal frameworks, business models, and worker experiences, providing a foundation for further research and policy development. The framework positions regulatory reform as essential for improving worker conditions in the gig economy while addressing the operational and ethical challenges faced by quick commerce platforms and workers.

FINDINGS

Working Conditions and Regional Disparities

A thematic analysis of existing literature on India's quick commerce sector reveals that worker employment conditions vary significantly by region, with disparities emerging between large metropolitan areas and smaller cities or peri-urban regions (Rajendran et al., 2024; Ray, 2024; Tandon et al., 2022). Studies focusing on major urban centres highlight relatively high order volumes and potentially more consistent earnings. However, these remain contingent on demand fluctuations, platform policies, and algorithm-driven incentives. Literature suggests that while workers in these hubs reach or surpass local minimum wage thresholds during peak hours, earnings can be irregular due to shifting demand patterns and sudden changes in incentive structures (Choudhary & Shireshi, 2022; Pulignano, 2019).

In contrast, scholarly work on smaller Tier-II and Tier-III cities indicates fewer orders and less stable income streams. In these settings, insufficient customer density and longer travel distances between delivery points diminish overall earnings potential (Bajwa et al., 2018). Some studies also note that inadequate infrastructure, from poor road conditions to the absence of dedicated rest areas, further complicates working conditions in non-metropolitan regions (Tejaswini & Abirami, 2023). The literature collectively suggests that geographic location is a key determinant of economic stability and job quality in quick commerce, with smaller cities bearing the brunt of lower demand and limited operational support (Bushe, 2019; Simon, 1991).

Legal Awareness and Implementation Gaps

The literature on legal awareness among quick commerce gig workers in India highlights a pervasive information gap regarding labour rights and protections (Ghosh et al., 2021). Analyses of policy documents, media reports, and advocacy group findings indicate that while the Code on Social Security (2020) formally recognises gig workers, its practical implications remain obscure to many in the workforce (Singh & Bhushan, 2023). Several studies underscore the lack of clear communication from platforms about workers' legal entitlements, resulting in fragmented and often inaccurate understandings of available benefits. This extends to workers' experiences with misclassification. Authors note a persistent stiffness between gig workers' employment conditions, dependence on platform algorithms, adherence to company-imposed standards, and their formal classification as independent contractors (Pulignano, 2019).

Researchers have documented cases where workers struggle to seek recourse through traditional labour dispute channels, as their non-employee status complicates efforts to claim minimum wages, social security, or compensation for work-related injuries (Estlund, 2023). Furthermore, the literature identifies a lack of accessible grievance redressal mechanisms. Case studies and policy review analyses show that workers often face substantial barriers when contesting pay deductions, account inactivation, or changes to incentive structures. Without clear, standardised complaint procedures, legal scholars argue that workers remain vulnerable to arbitrary platform decisions (Choudhary & Shireshi, 2022). Studies have also examined the role of intermediaries such as NGOs or online worker forums in disseminating knowledge about legal rights and building informal support networks. While such initiatives can improve awareness, the effectiveness of these measures is limited by operational scaling difficulty, low literacy levels among certain gig worker demographics and the absence of robust institutional support (Bajwa et al., 2018; Tejaswini & Abirami, 2023).

Algorithmic Management

A substantial body of literature identifies algorithmic management as a critical factor shaping the experience of gig workers in quick commerce. Scholars have noted that platform algorithms often operate as opaque "black boxes," influencing order assignment, pay calculation, and incentive distribution without offering workers a clear rationale (De Stefano, 2015; Silva & Nyobe, 2023). This opacity fosters a sense of disempowerment, as workers have limited means to understand, predict, or contest the decisions that affect their income. Research shows that earnings volatility is a frequent outcome of algorithmic control. Dynamic pricing, surge-based incentives, and frequent revisions to compensation structures can produce abrupt shifts in pay, complicating workers' efforts to plan their finances or establish stable livelihoods (Haque & Dard, 2023).

Algorithmically enforced performance metrics such as on-time delivery rates, customer ratings, and order completion ratios contribute to heightened stress and pressure. Studies indicate that workers feel compelled to engage in time-saving behaviours, including risky driving or skipping breaks, to maintain favourable metrics and access better-paying orders (Pulignano, 2019). Attempts by workers to adapt or "game" the algorithms by strategically choosing working hours, routes, or order acceptance rates appear in multiple studies. However, the effectiveness of such strategies is short-lived; as platforms frequently update their algorithms to optimise efficiency, workers adjust their strategies to keep pace. Scholars argue that this iterative adaptation cycle underscores the asymmetrical power dynamic: platforms can alter conditions instantly, while workers lack meaningful input or control (Choudhary & Shireshi, 2022).

Gender Inclusion

The existing literature on gender and inclusion within the quick commerce sector reveals that gender-based disparities persist despite the nominally open-access nature of gig platforms. Research on platform work more broadly has shown that women remain underrepresented, often due to safety concerns, cultural norms restricting their mobility, and the absence of platform features designed to accommodate their needs (Bajwa et al., 2018). In quick commerce, these factors compound women's challenges, such as directing deliveries during late hours or in less familiar neighbourhoods. Scholarly analyses suggest that algorithms designed as gender-neutral mechanisms fail to account for the constraints many women experience.

Without the option to filter deliveries by location, time, or perceived safety conditions, women can turn down orders and forgo earnings or expose themselves to heightened risks. Consequently, some studies highlight a gender earnings gap, with women often earning less due to fewer available shifts and limited access to higher-paying orders (Tejaswini & Abirami, 2023). In recent years, some literature points to emerging initiatives, such as women-only delivery hubs or daytime delivery routes with guaranteed minimum pay, aimed at reducing these gaps (Choudhary & Shireshi, 2022). However, the effectiveness and scalability of such interventions remain uncertain, and awareness about these programs is limited.

DISCUSSION

This study highlights gig workers' significant challenges and disparities in India's quick commerce sector. The findings highlight the interplay between geographical, legal, technological, and social factors that collectively shape these workers' working conditions and experiences. This section contextualises the findings within broader theoretical and policy frameworks while discussing implications for stakeholders.

Regional Disparities in Working Conditions

The findings indicate pronounced regional disparities in gig workers' working conditions and earnings, shaped by urban-rural dynamics and infrastructural differences. Workers in metropolitan areas enjoy relatively consistent order volumes, but their incomes remain contingent on fluctuating demand and impervious algorithmic incentives (van Doorn & Vijay, 2021). These urban workers face intense competition, high-stress levels, and health issues tied to long hours and challenging conditions (Choudhari, 2020). Meanwhile, workers in smaller cities and peri-urban regions contend with lower demand, fewer orders, and inadequate infrastructure (Allen, 2010; Kombe, 2005; Mandere et al., 2010). These disparities underscore the fragmented nature of India's quick commerce ecosystem. Theoretical frameworks like the dual labour market theory provide insights into this bifurcation, with metropolitan workers positioned in a relatively "primary" market with higher earnings potential. At the same time, their rural counterparts are relegated to a "secondary" market marked by instability and limited resources. Policy interventions must account for these spatial inequalities. Regional policies target infrastructure development, such as rest stops or better road networks in smaller cities, while urban strategies might address stress mitigation and health support mechanisms.

Legal Gaps and Awareness Deficits

Legal awareness among gig workers remains low, reflecting a broader gap between legislative intent and practical implementation. Although the Code on Social Security (2020) recognises gig workers, the lack of clear platform communication and limited outreach from regulatory bodies shows workers' vulnerability (Ramaswamy, 2019). The persistent misclassification of workers as independent contractors creates barriers to accessing essential rights, including minimum wages and social security benefits (Koutsimpogiorgos et al., 2020). This misclassification symbolises the neoliberal paradigm dominating gig work globally, where platforms leverage flexible labour models to minimise costs and evade traditional employer responsibilities. The findings align with studies in other contexts that highlight gig work's "legal grey zone" (Muldoon & Sun, 2024). Bridging this gap requires not only policy enforcement but also extensive awareness campaigns. Platforms, trade unions, and government bodies collaborate to create accessible resources that demystify legal entitlements and grievance mechanisms for workers. Policymakers could collaborate with local NGOs to replicate successful models across India.

Algorithmic Management and Worker Precarity

Algorithmic management emerged as a pervasive concern, shaping earnings and workers' autonomy and mental well-being (Huang, 2023; A. Wood & Lehdonvirta, 2021). The findings reveal that algorithmic systems foster a sense of disempowerment among workers. The volatility of pay structures and performance metrics intensifies financial instability, while the pressure to meet algorithmically enforced standards aggravates stress and physical strain (A. J. Wood et al., 2019). These insights reflect critical discussions in labour studies about the role of technology in reinforcing precarity. Algorithmic systems, often framed as impartial efficiency tools, are designed to prioritise platform profitability over worker welfare. The power asymmetry between platforms and workers is evident. While platforms can unilaterally alter algorithms, workers have no say in these changes and have limited recourse to challenge them. Introducing algorithmic transparency and accountability mechanisms is imperative. Policymakers mandate platforms to disclose the criteria for pay determination and order allocation, while independent audits could ensure fairness and reduce instability in earnings.

Gender-Based Disparities

The findings on gender highlight persistent inequities in the quick commerce sector. Despite the allegedly open-access nature of gig platforms, women remain underrepresented due to safety concerns, restrictive cultural norms, and algorithmic systems that fail to account for their specific needs. This aligns with global patterns where women in gig work face systemic barriers that limit their participation and earning potential (Ghosh et al., 2021; Kasliwal, 2020). The gender earnings gap revealed by the study reflects structural inequities and algorithmic biases. Women often avoid higher-risk deliveries, such as late-night orders, and consequently lose access to better-paying opportunities (Submitter & Ghosh, 2021). Efforts to address these disparities have been irregular, with initiatives like women-only delivery hubs showing promise but lacking scalability. More systemic solutions are needed, including gender-sensitive platform design and targeted policy interventions. For instance, platforms could introduce features that allow workers to filter orders based on safety preferences, and governments could incentivise platforms to adopt gender-inclusive practices through duty benefits and subsidies.

IMPLICATIONS FOR STAKEHOLDERS

The findings affect various stakeholders, including policymakers, platform operators, and advocacy groups. Policymakers take a nuanced approach that considers regional and demographic disparities while addressing broader systemic issues such as worker misclassification and algorithmic opacity. Enhancing enforcement mechanisms for existing labour laws, particularly the Code on Social Security, is critical. Platforms, as key actors in this ecosystem, must adopt worker-centric policies. This includes investing in regional infrastructure, ensuring algorithmic transparency, and creating tailored support mechanisms for vulnerable worker groups, including women and those in non-metropolitan areas. Advocacy groups and worker collectives also play a crucial role in bridging the gap between workers and platforms. They can amplify worker voices, provide legal support, and push for inclusive platform practices.

BROADER CONTEXT AND FUTURE RESEARCH DIRECTIONS

The findings of this study contribute to debates about the future of work in the gig economy. They highlight the contradictions inherent in gig work, and while platforms offer flexible income opportunities, they also entrench precarity and deepen existing inequalities. These dynamics are particularly pronounced in the quick commerce sector, where the demands of fast delivery impair the vulnerabilities of already marginalised workers. Future research should explore the long-term impacts of algorithmic management on worker well-being and career trajectories. Comparative studies across platforms and countries provide deeper insights into how local contexts shape the gig economy's challenges and opportunities. Additionally, more granular analyses of intersectional disparities, such as the experiences of women workers from economically disadvantaged backgrounds, could inform more targeted policy and platform interventions.

CONCLUSION

The rise of quick commerce has brought opportunities and challenges for gig workers, particularly in India. As a rapidly growing sector, quick commerce relies heavily on digital platforms that promise speed and convenience for consumers. However, these platforms have introduced new forms of labour exploitation and pressured workers. This paper has explored the many facets of quick commerce, from how platforms manage their workers using algorithms to the socio-economic conditions shaping gig workers' experiences in India.

Gig work in quick commerce is often seen as a flexible and easily accessible income source. Many workers are drawn to this sector because it promises autonomy and the opportunity to work on their own terms. However, this flexibility is primarily an illusion. Workers are constantly under pressure to meet delivery deadlines, and their earnings are directly tied to performance metrics controlled by platforms. These pressures can lead to increased stress, long working hours, and poor working conditions. The reliance on algorithms to allocate tasks and determine pay makes workers highly dependent on systems they do not fully understand. This lack of transparency in algorithmic decision-making often results in feelings of unfairness and dissatisfaction among workers.

The legal status of gig workers has been a key issue, with workers typically classified as independent contractors rather than employees. This classification excludes them from traditional labour protections, such as minimum wage laws, health insurance, and paid leave. As a result, gig workers bear the financial burden of their work, including costs for fuel, vehicle maintenance, and mobile data. These financial pressures, combined with the unstable nature of their work, make gig workers vulnerable to economic hardships. While recent legislative changes in India have begun to address these issues, the full implementation of social security benefits for gig workers remains uncertain.

The lack of clear regulations and weak enforcement mechanisms complicate efforts to protect workers' rights. The physical and psychological toll of working in quick commerce cannot be ignored. Workers face time-sensitive delivery windows that push them to perform at their maximum capacity, often at the expense of their well-being. Long hours, exhaustion, and stress are common experiences, with workers frequently engaging in risky behaviours to meet delivery targets. These pressures are amplified by the surveillance and monitoring systems employed by platforms, which track workers' every move and performance metric. While these systems are designed to optimise efficiency, they also contribute to a work environment where workers are constantly evaluated and under pressure to perform at peak levels.

Another significant concern is the gender dynamics within the gig economy, particularly in quick commerce. Women in this sector face additional barriers, including safety concerns, lower-paying opportunities, and limited access to the higher-paying roles often occupied by men. These gender-based disparities limit women's ability to fully participate in the economic opportunities offered by the gig economy. As such, it is essential for platforms to take proactive steps to create a more inclusive environment for female workers, ensuring their safety and providing them with fair opportunities for advancement.

The role of gig worker collectives and unions also deserves attention. While gig workers have started to organise through informal platforms like WhatsApp groups, the lack of formal recognition and legal support means they have limited negotiating power. Without the ability to negotiate collectively, gig workers remain vulnerable to exploitation. Platforms that rely on gig labour acknowledge the power imbalance and find ways to include workers in decision-making that affect their work conditions. This could involve recognising the need for better pay, more reasonable working hours, and more transparency in monitoring and rewarding performance.

The shift towards quick commerce in India has highlighted the pressing need for regulatory frameworks that can adapt to the unique characteristics of gig work. While gig workers have long been excluded from the protections afforded to traditional employees, there is a growing recognition that new work models require new legal and social protections. The Code on Social Security, introduced in 2020, is a step in the right direction, but much more needs to be done to ensure that gig workers are adequately supported. The Indian government must take an active role in defining the status of gig workers, enforcing labour laws, and ensuring that workers have access to the benefits and protections they deserve.

The future of India's quick commerce sector depends on addressing the regulatory and worker protection gaps. Policymakers should prioritise revising existing laws to clarify gig worker classification, introduce mandatory social security contributions from platforms, and ensure robust enforcement mechanisms. Platforms must adopt transparent algorithmic systems, offer safety features, and develop inclusive policies for women and vulnerable groups. Researchers should focus on evaluating the long-term impact of these interventions and exploring intersectional vulnerabilities within the gig workforce. Collaborative efforts among stakeholders will help create a more equitable and sustainable gig economy in India.

COMPETING INTERESTS

The authors declare no competing interests.

FUNDING STATEMENT

This research received no specific grant from any funding agency in the public, commercial, or not-for-profit sectors.

REFERENCES

Allen, A. (2010). Neither Rural nor Urban: Service Delivery Options That Work for the Peri-urban Poor. *Peri-Urban Water and Sanitation Services: Policy, Planning and Method*, 27–61. DOI: 10.1007/978-90-481-9425-4_2

Asadullah, M., & Persson, S. (2024). *The Working Conditions of Couriers and Their Performance and Well-being : A Case of Food Delivery Companies in Sweden.* https://urn.kb.se/resolve?urn=urn:nbn:se:sh:diva-54971

Bajwa, U., Gastaldo, D., Di Ruggiero, E., & Knorr, L. (2018). The health of workers in the global gig economy. *Globalization and Health, 14*(1), 124. Advance online publication. DOI: 10.1186/s12992-018-0444-8 PMID: 30563539

Behrendt, C., Nguyen, Q. A., & Rani, U. (2019). Social protection systems and the future of work: Ensuring social security for digital platform workers. *International Social Security Review, 72*(3), 17–41. DOI: 10.1111/issr.12212

Betten, L. (1995). *The Employment Contract in Transforming Labour Relations.* 1–202.

Bushe, B. (2019). The causes and impact of business failure among small to micro and medium enterprises in South Africa. *Africa's Public Service Delivery and Performance Review, 7*(1). Advance online publication. DOI: 10.4102/apsdpr.v7i1.210

Chitranshi, J., & Chopra, K. (2023). AI Driven Quick delivery services in India and Employee wellbeing challenges. *Proceedings of 2023 IEEE Technology and Engineering Management Conference - Asia Pacific, TEMSCON-ASPAC 2023.* DOI: 10.1109/TEMSCON-ASPAC59527.2023.10531469

Choudhari, R. (2020). COVID 19 pandemic: Mental health challenges of internal migrant workers of India. *Asian Journal of Psychiatry*, *54*, 102254. Advance online publication. DOI: 10.1016/j.ajp.2020.102254 PMID: 32593122

Choudhary, V., & Shireshi, S. S. (2022). Analysing the Gig Economy in India and Exploring Various Effective Regulatory Methods to Improve the Plight of the Workers. *Journal of Asian and African Studies*, *57*(7), 1343–1356. DOI: 10.1177/00219096221082581

Codagnone, C., Abadie, F., & Biagi, F. (2016). The Future of Work in the 'Sharing Economy'. Market Efficiency and Equitable Opportunities or Unfair Precarisation? SSRN *Electronic Journal*. https://doi.org/DOI: 10.2139/SSRN.2784774

Cornelissen, J. (2016). Editor's Comments: Developing Propositions, a Process Model, or a Typology? Addressing the Challenges of Writing Theory Without a Boilerplate. Https://Doi.Org/10.5465/Amr.2016.0196, *42*(1), 1–9. DOI: 10.5465/amr.2016.0196

De Stefano, V. (2015). The Rise of the "Just-in-Time Workforce": On-Demand Work, Crowd Work and Labour Protection in the "Gig-Economy." SSRN *Electronic Journal*. https://doi.org/DOI: 10.2139/SSRN.2682602

Dekker, S. (2021). Compliance capitalism: How free markets have led to unfree, overregulated workers. *Compliance Capitalism: How Free Markets Have Led to Unfree, Overregulated Workers*, 1–190. https://doi.org/DOI: 10.4324/9781003177807/COMPLIANCE-CAPITALISM-SIDNEY-DEKKER/ACCESSIBILITY-INFORMATION

Estlund, C. (2023). Sectoral Solutions That Work: The Case for Sectoral Co-Regulation. *Chicago-Kent Law Review*, *98*, •••. https://heinonline.org/HOL/Page?handle=hein.journals/chknt98&id=549&div=27&collection=journals

Farbenblum, B., Berg, L., & Kintominas, A. (2018). *Transformative Technology for Migrant Workers - Opportunities, Challenges, and Risks*. https://papers.ssrn.com/abstract=3295430

Flanagan, F. (2018). Theorising the gig economy and home-based service work. Https://Doi.Org/10.1177/0022185618800518, *61*(1), 57–78. DOI: 10.1177/0022185618800518

Ganapathy, V., Gupta, C., & Arora, R. (2024). Digital Transformation of Grocery Delivery Services in India. In *Technological Innovations in the Food Service Industry* (pp. 1–22). IGI Global. DOI: 10.4018/979-8-3693-7683-6.ch001

Ghosh, A., Ramachandran, R., & Zaidi, M. (2021). Women Workers in the Gig Economy in India: An Exploratory Study. SSRN *Electronic Journal*. https://doi.org/DOI: 10.2139/SSRN.3944205

Ghosh, A., Ramachandran, R., & Zaidi, M. (2021). Women workers in the gig economy in India: An exploratory study. Available at *SSRN* 3944205.

Graham, M., Hjorth, I., & Lehdonvirta, V. (2017). Digital labour and development: Impacts of global digital labour platforms and the gig economy on worker livelihoods. *Transfer: European Review of Labour and Research*, *23*(2), 135–162. DOI: 10.1177/1024258916687250 PMID: 28781494

Håkansta, C., Gunn, V., Kreshpaj, B., Matilla-Santander, N., Wegman, D. H., Hogstedt, C., Vignola, E. F., Muntaner, C., Bodin, T., O'Campo, P., & Lewchuk, W. (2024). What is the Role of Minimum Wages in Addressing Precarious Employment in the Informal and Formal Sectors? Findings from a Systematic Review. *International Journal of Social Determinants of Health and Health Services*, 27551938241286463. Advance online publication. DOI: 10.1177/27551938241286463 PMID: 39370929

Haneefa, K. V. (2024). Quick Commerce in the Quantum Age. In *The Quantum AI Era of Neuromarketing* (pp. 403–428). IGI Global Scientific Publishing., DOI: 10.4018/979-8-3693-7673-7.ch017

Haque, F., & Dard, A. R. (2023). New Face of Job Quality Challenge in India: Gig Worker Studies. *Journal of Indonesian Applied Economics*, *11*(1), 101–109. DOI: 10.21776/ub.jiae.2017.011.01.8

Hardy, T., & McCrystal, S. (2022). The importance of competition and consumer law in regulating gig work and beyond. *The Journal of Industrial Relations*, *64*(5), 785–800. DOI: 10.1177/00221856211068868

Huang, H. (2023). Algorithmic management in food-delivery platform economy in China. *New Technology, Work and Employment*, *38*(2), 185–205. DOI: 10.1111/ntwe.12228

Jaakkola, E. (2020). *Designing conceptual articles: four approaches*. DOI: 10.1007/s13162-020-00161-0

Jarrahi, M. H., Newlands, G., Lee, M. K., Wolf, C. T., Kinder, E., & Sutherland, W. (2021). Algorithmic management in a work context. *Big Data & Society*, *8*(2), 20539517211020332. Advance online publication. DOI: 10.1177/20539517211020332

Kalbalia, P., Nath, N. J., & Haneefa, K. V. (2024). Utilisation and Accessibility of Healthcare Services Among Gig Workers: A Systematic Review. *Population. Environmental Disease*, •••, 77–95. DOI: 10.1007/978-3-031-67624-6_5

Kasliwal, R. (2020). *Gender and the Gig Economy: A Qualitative Study of Gig Platforms for Women Workers INtrODUctION: GIG EcONOMY AND GENDEr IssUEs*.

Kombe, W. J. (2005). Land use dynamics in peri-urban areas and their implications on the urban growth and form: The case of Dar es Salaam, Tanzania. *Habitat International, 29*(1), 113–135. DOI: 10.1016/S0197-3975(03)00076-6

Koutsimpogiorgos, N., van Slageren, J., Herrmann, A., & Frenken, K. (2020). Conceptualizing the Gig Economy and Its Regulatory Problems. *Policy & Internet*. https://doi.org/DOI: 10.31235/OSF.IO/JMQYT

Lambert, S. J., Haley-Lock, A., & Henly, J. R. (2012). Schedule flexibility in hourly jobs: Unanticipated consequences and promising directions. *Community Work & Family, 15*(3), 293–315. DOI: 10.1080/13668803.2012.662803

Lee, J. W. (2014). Labour contracting and changing employment relationships in South Korea. *Development Policy Review, 32*(4), 449–473. DOI: 10.1111/dpr.12063

Lehdonvirta, V. (2018). Flexibility in the gig economy: Managing time on three online piecework platforms. *New Technology, Work and Employment, 33*(1), 13–29. DOI: 10.1111/ntwe.12102

Mandere, N. M., Ness, B., & Anderberg, S. (2010). Peri-urban development, livelihood change and household income: A case study of peri-urban Nyahururu, Kenya. *Journal of Agricultural Extension and Rural Development, 2*(5), 73–83.

Muldoon, J., & Sun, P. (2024). The Global Gig Economy: How Transport Platform Companies Adapt to Regulatory Challenges—A Comparative Analysis of Six Countries. *Industrial Law Journal, 53*(3), 481–504. DOI: 10.1093/indlaw/dwae010

Pant, J. J., & Majumder, M. G. (2022). Themes and Narratives of Gig Economy: An Indian HR Perspective. *NHRD Network Journal, 15*(1), 83–99. DOI: 10.1177/26314541211064751

Pulignano, V. (2019). Work and Employment under the Gig Economy. *Partecipazione e Conflitto, 12*(3), 629–639. DOI: 10.1285/I20356609V12I3P629

Rajendran, L. P., Raúl, L., Chen, M., Guerrero Andrade, J. C., Akhtar, R., Mngumi, L. E., Chander, S., Srinivas, S., & Roy, M. R. (2024). The 'peri-urban turn': A systems thinking approach for a paradigm shift in reconceptualising urban-rural futures in the global South. *Habitat International, 146*, 103041. DOI: 10.1016/j.habitatint.2024.103041

Ramaswamy, K. V. (2019). Non-standard Employment, Labour Laws and Social Security: Learning from the US Gig Economy Debate. *Globalization, Labour Market Institutions, Processes and Policies in India*, 277–299. DOI: 10.1007/978-981-13-7111-0_11

Rao, R. K., Kumar, K., Gupta, R., Khurana, S., Verma, K. N., Chandra, S., Singh, R. R., & Dharap, O. (2022). India's Booming Gig and Platform Economy: Perspectives and Recommendations on the Future of Work. In *Niti Aayog* (Issue June). https://www.niti.gov.in/sites/default/files/2022-06/25th_June_Final_Report_27062022.pdf

Ray, A. (2024). Coping with crisis and precarity in the gig economy: 'Digitally organised informality', migration and socio-spatial networks among platform drivers in India. Https://Doi.Org/10.1177/0308518X231220296, *56*(4), 1227–1244. DOI: 10.1177/0308518X231220296

Sanghi, N., Chandra Balodi, K., & Gupta, V. (2023). "The emergence of the Indian hyperlocal grocery delivery industry: Dunzo v/s Blinkit." Https://Doi.Org/10.1177/20438869231151449, *14*(1), 119–128. DOI: 10.1177/20438869231151449

Silva, M. E., & Nyobe, S. (2023). Social sustainability in the gig economy era. *Revue Française de Gestion Industrielle*, *37*(1), 55–69. DOI: 10.53102/2023.37.01.1140

Simon, H. A. (1991). Organizations and Markets. *The Journal of Economic Perspectives*, *5*(2), 25–44. DOI: 10.1257/jep.5.2.25

Singh, R., & Bhushan, V. (2023). UNDERSTANDING THE FUNDAMENTALS AND DYNAMICS OF THE GIG EMPLOYMENT LANDSCAPE IN INDIA. *International Journal of Advanced Research*, *11*(07), 300–315. DOI: 10.21474/IJAR01/17232

Standing, G. (2011). Labour market policies, poverty and insecurity. *International Journal of Social Welfare*, *20*(3), 260–269. DOI: 10.1111/j.1468-2397.2010.00778.x

Sutherland, W., & Jarrahi, M. H. (2018). The sharing economy and digital platforms: A review and research agenda. *International Journal of Information Management*, *43*, 328–341. DOI: 10.1016/j.ijinfomgt.2018.07.004

Tandon, N., Basu, P., Krishnan, O., & Bhavani, R. V. (2022). Emerging work trends in Urban India: COVID-19 and beyond. *Emerging Work Trends in Urban India: COVID-19 and Beyond*, 1–208. DOI: 10.4324/9781003264194

Tug, M. A., & Basar, P. (2023). FUTURE OF THE GIG ECONOMY. *Pressacademia*. DOI: 10.17261/Pressacademia.2023.1796 van Doorn, N., & Vijay, D. (2021). Gig work as migrant work: The platformization of migration infrastructure. *Environment & Planning A*. Advance online publication. DOI: 10.1177/0308518X211065049

Wood, A., & Lehdonvirta, V. (2021). Platform Precarity: Surviving Algorithmic Insecurity in the Gig Economy. SSRN *Electronic Journal*. https://doi.org/DOI: 10.2139/SSRN.3795375

Wood, A. J., Graham, M., Lehdonvirta, V., & Hjorth, I. (2019). Good Gig, Bad Gig: Autonomy and Algorithmic Control in the Global Gig Economy. *Work, Employment and Society*, *33*(1), 56–75. DOI: 10.1177/0950017018785616 PMID: 30886460

Chapter 5
Marketing Strategies in the Gig Economy: Challenges and Opportunities for Freelance Marketers

Arpan Anand
https://orcid.org/0000-0002-2572-1651
Jaipuria Institute of Management, Noida, India

ABSTRACT

This study examines the evolving landscape of freelance marketing in the gig economy, focusing on challenges, opportunities, and adaptation strategies. Through a mixed-methods approach combining surveys (n=287), in-depth interviews (n=25), and platform analysis, the research explores how freelance marketers navigate market competition, income instability, and technological disruption. Findings reveal that successful freelancers employ multi-faceted strategies including personal branding, platform diversification, and niche specialization. The study identifies a significant trend toward hybridization of skills, with 77% of respondents emphasizing the importance of combining creative and technical capabilities. The impact of Industry 4.0 technologies, particularly AI and machine learning, emerges as transformative, with 68% of freelancers actively incorporating these tools into their work. The findings highlight the need for regulatory frameworks addressing gig workers' challenges while emphasizing the growing importance of adaptability and continuous learning in the digital economy.

DOI: 10.4018/979-8-3693-9385-7.ch005

INTRODUCTION

The gig economy has transformed marketing, with freelancers navigating platform-mediated work amid rapid industry growth, reaching $455 billion in 2023 (Global Market Insights, 2024). Freelance marketers enjoy flexibility and project choice but struggle with income instability, competition, and evolving technologies, shaping broader economic shifts. This chapter aims to explore this multifaceted landscape by examining how freelance marketers navigate the gig economy, develop personal brands, and adapt their skills to meet evolving client demands in a rapidly changing digital environment. The research pursues three key objectives: analyzing challenges such as competition, income instability, and the need for continuous skill development; identifying successful strategies in personal branding, platform utilization, and service specialization; and examining the impact of Industry 4.0 technologies like AI, machine learning, and data analytics tools on freelance marketing practices. This research explores how freelance marketers navigate challenges, leverage platforms, and adapt to Industry 4.0, offering insights for professionals and policymakers.

BACKGROUND

Over three decades, digital marketing evolved from static Web 1.0 sites (Ryan & Jones, 2012) to interactive, content-driven platforms (O'Reilly, 2005). As Chaffey, D., & Patron, M. (2012), freelance opportunities during this era were limited primarily to web design and early search engine optimization, with marketers focusing on reaching consumers through basic search engines like AltaVista and Yahoo. According to Monnappa (2020), the dot-com bubble of the late 1990s, despite its eventual collapse, created the first generation of digital marketing specialists who established the foundation for future innovations.

The emergence of Web 2.0 technologies in the early 2000s fundamentally altered the marketing landscape by enabling interactive and user-generated content (O'Reilly, 2007). Social media platforms such as Facebook (2004), Twitter (2006), and YouTube (2005) revolutionized marketing strategies by facilitating two-way communication between brands and consumers (Kaplan & Haenlein, 2010). Holliman, G., & Rowley, J. (2014), demonstrates how content marketing emerged as a dominant strategy during this period, with blogging platforms like WordPress (2003) democratizing content creation and opening new avenues for freelance marketers. Research by Edelman and Brandi (2015) reveals that during this period, freelancers increasingly specialized in social media management, blog writing, and digital content creation. The introduction of Google AdWords in 2000 created additional opportunities for freelancers with skills in pay-per-click advertising and search marketing (Geddes,

2014). By the mid-2000s, digital marketing had evolved from a supplementary channel to an essential component of most marketing strategies, creating sustained demand for specialized freelance talent (Wymbs, 2011).

Mobile-first marketing and data-driven strategies became dominant in the 2010s (Rowles, 2017). As Tuten and Solomon (2017) document, the launch of the iPhone in 2007 and subsequent smartphone revolution transformed consumer behavior, with mobile internet usage surpassing desktop usage by 2016. This shift necessitated responsive design, location-based marketing, and app-based strategies, creating new specializations for freelance marketers (Kim et al., 2019). Simultaneously, research by Wedel and Kannan (2016) demonstrates how personalization and data-driven marketing became critical, with the widespread adoption of analytics tools like Google Analytics and AI-driven recommendation engines. According to McAfee and Brynjolfsson (2012), the emergence of programmatic advertising platforms allowed for unprecedented targeting precision, while content marketing evolved to emphasize video and interactive formats. Studies by Upwork (2018) indicate that freelancers increasingly took on roles as data analysts, PPC experts, and SEO specialists to meet the growing demand for targeted marketing campaigns, often commanding premium rates for their technical expertise while competing in an increasingly global marketplace.

Industry 4.0 technologies (AI, blockchain, VR/AR, IoT) are reshaping marketing, offering freelancers both opportunities and challenges (Schwab, 2017). Research by Davenport et al. (2020) shows that AI-driven tools like ChatGPT, Midjourney, and Jasper are automating repetitive tasks, enhancing content personalization, and optimizing marketing strategies, requiring freelancers to adapt by developing skills in prompt engineering and AI tool orchestration rather than content creation alone. Tapscott and Tapscott (2018) demonstrate how blockchain technology is introducing secure and transparent payment mechanisms for freelancers while enabling new marketing approaches through NFTs and tokenized loyalty programs. Meanwhile, VR and AR have progressed beyond novelty applications to enable truly immersive marketing experiences, with platforms like Meta's Horizon Worlds and Snapchat's AR lenses creating demand for specialists in immersive content creation (Porter & Heppelmann, 2017). According to a comprehensive study by Ng and Wakenshaw (2017), IoT technologies are creating new possibilities for real-time, data-driven customer interactions through connected devices, smart homes, and wearable technology, allowing marketers to deliver contextually relevant messages based on environmental triggers. For freelancers, these technological advances represent both automation threats and specialization opportunities, with Acemoglu and Restrepo (2019) finding that those who successfully integrate these technologies into their service offerings enjoy increased demand and higher compensation.

GLOBAL PERSPECTIVES

Freelance marketing varies globally due to cultural, technological, and economic factors. In North America and Western Europe, research by Manyika et al. (2016) indicates that a well-developed digital infrastructure supports high demand for specialized marketing skills, with freelancers often commanding premium rates for expertise in emerging technologies. Data analysis by Upwork and Fiverr (2023) reveals that North American freelancers earn 60-70% more than the global average for comparable skills, particularly in AI integration and data analytics. Studies by the Freelancers Union and Upwork (2023) demonstrate that these markets emphasize measurable ROI and data-driven approaches, with clients typically seeking specialists rather than generalists. As Horton (2017) documents, freelancers in these regions leverage AI tools and advanced analytics to remain competitive, with a recent study indicating that 78% of US-based freelance marketers had incorporated AI tools into their workflows by 2023, compared to a global average of 54% (Freelancers Union, 2023).

In the Asia-Pacific region, Graham et al. (2017) demonstrate how countries like India and the Philippines have emerged as key hubs for freelance marketing, with distinct approaches shaped by regional economic conditions and cultural values. These regions benefit from lower operational costs and a growing digital economy, with the Asian Development Bank (2023) reporting a 112% increase in digital freelancing between 2018 and 2023. Research by Kassi and Lehdonvirta (2018) shows that in India, freelance marketers often specialize in technical SEO and content production, leveraging the country's strong technological education system, while Filipino freelancers have developed particular strength in social media management and customer engagement, reflecting cultural emphasis on relationship building. According to Jia et al. (2018), Chinese freelancers, operating within a unique digital ecosystem that includes platforms like WeChat and Douyin rather than Western equivalents, have developed specialized skills in super-app marketing and QR code integration. Studies by Anwar and Graham (2020) indicate that freelancers across these regions provide cost-competitive services to international clients while demonstrating adaptability to multicultural marketing needs, often serving as cultural bridges between Western brands and Asian consumers.

Latin America is experiencing a surge in freelance marketing activities, particularly in Brazil and Mexico, driven by regional economic conditions and growing digital sophistication (Robinson et al., 2020). Economic instability and rising digital literacy have prompted freelancers to adopt innovative strategies, including social media marketing and mobile-first approaches that address the region's 87% smartphone penetration rate (GSMA, 2023). Research by Robles and Campos (2022) shows that Brazilian freelancers have pioneered approaches to WhatsApp marketing, leveraging the platform's near-universal adoption in the country, while Mexican freelancers have developed expertise in cross-border e-commerce strategies targeting the U.S. Hispanic market. Studies by Mercado Libre (2022) demonstrate that the prevalence of regional payment solutions like Mercado Pago and cultural emphasis on personal relationships has shaped client engagement models, with Latin American freelancers typically maintaining fewer but deeper client relationships than their North American counterparts. As documented by Rodriguez-Modroño and López-Igual (2021), language abilities represent both a challenge and opportunity, with bilingual Spanish-English or Portuguese-English freelancers commanding significantly higher rates for their ability to create culturally authentic content for multiple markets.

Africa's freelance economy is growing due to mobile internet penetration and a young digital workforce (Gillwald & Mothobi, 2019). Research by Graham et al. (2020) shows that freelancers in countries such as Nigeria, Kenya, and South Africa bring valuable local market knowledge to global marketing campaigns but face challenges related to technological access and payment infrastructure. According to Jack and Suri (2016), the introduction of mobile payment systems like M-Pesa in Kenya has revolutionized freelancer compensation, while Efobi et al. (2018) document how Nigerian freelancers have become particularly adept at social media marketing strategies that work within bandwidth constraints. Studies by Research ICT Africa (2022) indicate that South African freelancers have leveraged the country's well-developed advertising industry to specialize in creative content production, often serving international clients. Despite infrastructure challenges, with only 43% of the continent having reliable internet access (ITU, 2023), African freelancers have demonstrated remarkable resilience and innovation, with organizations like AfriLabs creating collaborative spaces for digital workers (Friederici, 2019). According to Masinde and Mwiti (2021), the continent's diverse linguistics landscape, with over 2,000 languages spoken, has created opportunities for cultural consultancy services, with African freelancers advising international brands on culturally appropriate marketing strategies for this rapidly growing market of 1.3 billion consumers.

IMPACT OF REMOTE WORK AND DIGITAL NOMADISM

The rapid adoption of remote work has reshaped the global workforce, and freelance marketing is no exception, creating new operational models that transcend traditional geographic limitations. With the rise of digital nomadism, accelerated by the COVID-19 pandemic and technological advancements, freelancers now have the opportunity to work from virtually anywhere, accessing a broader array of clients and markets across the globe. IT advancements enable digital nomads, including marketers, to work remotely while traveling (Thompson, 2018). Flexibility fosters cross-cultural marketing specialization. Global co-working space providers like WeWork and Selina have reported that marketing professionals constitute 23% of their membership base, highlighting the profession's compatibility with location-independent work.

Freelance marketing varies globally due to cultural, technological, and economic factors. This international exposure allows freelancers to develop comparative expertise across markets, recognizing both universal marketing principles and culturally specific approaches. For example, a freelancer who has worked with clients in both Japan and Brazil can provide valuable insights on the stark differences in social media engagement patterns between these markets, where Japanese consumers tend to prefer anonymous engagement while Brazilian users favor highly visible interactions. However, this global reach also presents challenges, such as navigating time zone differences, cultural nuances, and legal requirements for cross-border transactions. Successful freelancers have adapted by implementing sophisticated project management systems, cultural sensitivity training, and international payment solutions like Wise and Payoneer that minimize transaction costs and delays.

Furthermore, the shift toward remote work has blurred the boundaries between personal and professional life, affecting work-life balance and necessitating new approaches to time management and professional boundaries. Digital nomads often face difficulties maintaining structured schedules and finding stable work environments, which can affect productivity and well-being. A 2023 study published in the Journal of Vocational Behavior found that freelance digital nomads worked an average of 47 hours per week across non-standard hours, significantly more than their location-stable counterparts (Müller, 2016), while reporting higher levels of both job satisfaction and work-related stress. To adapt, many freelancers have adopted strategies such as using co-working spaces, scheduling regular virtual meetings to maintain client relationships, and leveraging remote collaboration tools like Notion, Asana, and Slack. The most successful have implemented strict time-blocking techniques, separating work and leisure activities despite sharing physical spaces, and establishing "virtual office hours" that provide clients with predictable availability while preserving personal time.

The implications of digital nomadism extend beyond operational strategies to client expectations and service delivery models, creating new standards for availability, communication, and project management. Clients increasingly expect on-demand availability and seamless communication, necessitating that freelance marketers remain agile and responsive regardless of their physical location. This has prompted the adoption of asynchronous communication tools and comprehensive documentation practices that enable collaboration across time zones. The cross-cultural exposure that comes with digital nomadism has also influenced service offerings, with many freelancers developing specializations in international market entry strategies and multicultural campaign management. Organizations have responded by adjusting their freelancer engagement practices, with 67% of companies surveyed by Upwork in 2023 reporting that they had modified their contracts and communication protocols specifically to accommodate location-independent contractors. This mutual adaptation has created a more flexible but also more demanding freelance marketing ecosystem, where geographic freedom comes with expectations of increased accessibility, cultural fluency, and technological self-sufficiency.

DIVERSITY AND INCLUSION IN FREELANCE MARKETING

As the freelance marketing landscape continues to evolve, issues related to diversity and inclusion have gained importance, highlighting both progress and persistent challenges in creating an equitable professional environment. Freelancers' experiences with technological shifts vary by gender, race, and socioeconomic status. Recent data from LinkedIn's 2023 Freelance Marketplace Report indicates that while women represent 58% of freelance marketers globally, they earn an average of 28% less than their male counterparts for comparable services (Connelly et al., 2010), a disparity that has narrowed only slightly from 32% in 2018. Racial and ethnic minorities face similar challenges, with Black freelancers in the US earning 26% less than white freelancers with similar experience levels, according to a 2022 study by the National Bureau of Economic Research. Freelance pay gaps are shaped by societal and structural inequities, including networking disparities.

Access to Industry 4.0 tech affects competitiveness and earnings. While AI-driven tools, blockchain technologies, and IoT platforms have become essential in marketing, not all freelancers have equal access to these resources. Underrepresented groups face financial, training, and AI bias barriers. A 2023 survey found that 76% of white male freelancers had AI tool access, compared to 34% of women of color and 29% of low-income freelancers. (Rivera & Tilcsik, 2016). This technology gap creates a self-reinforcing cycle where those with the most resources can deliver more sophisticated services, command higher rates, and further invest in cutting-edge tools, while others struggle to remain competitive despite comparable talent and experience.

Moreover, AI technologies themselves can perpetuate biases that disadvantage certain demographic groups, creating systemic barriers that compound existing inequities. Algorithms may favor certain demographic traits when selecting freelancers for projects, thereby marginalizing others through encoded preferences that reflect historical hiring patterns rather than actual qualifications. A 2022 analysis of major freelance platforms found that profile images and names associated with certain ethnic groups received significantly fewer algorithm-driven recommendations, even when experience levels and reviews were comparable. Similarly, gender-biased language models can affect content creation and evaluation processes, potentially disadvantaging freelancers who specialize in female-targeted marketing. Addressing these biases requires a concerted effort from platform developers and policymakers to ensure equitable opportunities, with some platforms implementing periodic algorithmic audits and blind application processes to mitigate these effects. The European Union's Artificial Intelligence Act, scheduled for implementation in 2025, may provide a regulatory framework for addressing these issues, requiring transparency in algorithmic hiring and freelancer matching processes.

Despite these challenges, many freelancers from diverse backgrounds have successfully navigated the digital landscape, developing strategies and support systems to overcome structural barriers. Initiatives that provide mentorship, affordable training programs, and networking opportunities are essential to fostering inclusivity and have shown promising results in expanding access. Organizations like Black Girl Digital, Women in Tech SEO, and the Global South Freelancers Collective have created specialized communities that combine skill development with networking opportunities, addressing both technical and social barriers simultaneously. These communities often negotiate group discounts for premium tools, share resources, and provide peer mentorship that helps members navigate client relationships and rate negotiations. Highlighting success stories from underrepresented groups can inspire others and demonstrate the potential for overcoming structural barriers, with several platforms now featuring dedicated sections for promoting diverse freelance talent. These efforts, combined with increasing client interest in authentic multicultural marketing, have created new opportunities for freelancers who can leverage their unique cultural perspectives as valuable assets rather than obstacles to overcome.

MENTAL HEALTH CHALLENGES IN FREELANCE MARKETING

The freelance marketing industry offers numerous advantages, including flexibility and creative autonomy, but the gig economy's fast-paced nature also poses significant mental health challenges that require deliberate management strategies. Freelancers juggle evolving tech, clients, and competition. This relentless environment can lead to burnout, anxiety, and feelings of isolation, with a 2023 survey by the Freelancers Union finding that 68% of freelance marketers reported experiencing work-related burnout in the previous year, compared to 54% of traditional marketing employees (Hobfoll et al., 2018). The pressure to remain constantly updated on emerging technologies is particularly acute, with 72% of respondents citing "technology anxiety" as a significant stressor, reflecting the rapid pace of change in AI tools, platform algorithms, and digital marketing best practices. This technological treadmill creates a persistent sense of inadequacy that can undermine confidence and exacerbate mental health challenges.

Lack of workplace structure removes institutional stress buffers. Freelancers lack workplace support, facing isolation and decision fatigue. The burden of handling every aspect of a business—from client acquisition to project management to accounting—creates cognitive overload that leaves little mental space for creative work. A study found freelance marketers spent 38% of work hours on admin tasks, correlating with higher anxiety and depression (Sonnentag & Fritz, 2015).

To address these challenges, freelance marketers are increasingly adopting mental health strategies that create structure, community, and resilience within the inherently flexible freelance model. Joining professional communities has emerged as a crucial coping mechanism, with virtual and in-person networking groups providing both emotional support and practical assistance. Platforms like Freelance Marketing Collective host regular virtual meetups and skill-sharing sessions that create a sense of belonging while also offering opportunities for collaborative problem-solving. Time management techniques have also proven effective, with freelancers using productivity tools like time-tracking software, project management systems, and calendar blocking to create more predictable schedules and reduce decision fatigue. The Pomodoro Technique has gained particular popularity, with its structured work-break cycles helping freelancers maintain focus while preventing the common pattern of overwork followed by procrastination.

Recent studies emphasize the importance of maintaining mental well-being not just for personal health but for sustained professional success in the demanding field of freelance marketing. Research published in the Harvard Business Review found that freelancers who regularly practiced mindfulness techniques reported 34% higher client satisfaction and 28% higher rates of repeat business, suggesting that mental clarity directly impacts work quality and client relationships. Platforms and clients are also recognizing the need to foster healthier working relationships by offering flexible deadlines, clearer project scopes, and promoting mental health awareness through reasonable expectations and communication boundaries. Organizations like the Freelance Wellness Alliance are working with major platforms to develop mental health resources specifically tailored to the needs of digital workers, recognizing that addressing these challenges is crucial not just for individual well-being but for the sustainability of the freelance marketing ecosystem as a whole.

LITERATURE REVIEW

The Gig Economy and Its Impact on Marketing

The gig economy has been the subject of extensive empirical investigation in recent years, with scholars examining its implications for labor markets, worker experiences, and economic structures across various industries including marketing. Friedman's (2014) seminal conceptualization defines the gig economy as a labor market characterized by short-term contracts, freelance work, and temporary positions, as opposed to permanent jobs. This definition encapsulates the essence of gig work in marketing, where professionals often engage in project-based assignments for multiple clients rather than pursuing traditional agency careers. The evolution of this model has been particularly significant in marketing, where project-specific expertise is highly valued and technological advancements have facilitated remote collaboration. Abraham et al. (2022) expanded on this conceptualization through longitudinal analysis, demonstrating that the gig economy has evolved beyond simple task-based work to include complex professional services requiring specialized expertise, with marketing representing one of the fastest-growing segments of high-skilled gig work.

Vallas and Schor's (2020) comprehensive meta-analysis of the gig economy highlights its rapid growth and the disruptive impact of digital platforms on traditional employment models. Their systematic review argues that these platforms have not only facilitated the matching of workers with clients but have also fundamentally altered the nature of work itself by creating new power dynamics, compensation models, and career trajectories. In the context of marketing, this transformation is particularly evident in the rise of digital marketing specialists who operate primarily through online platforms like Upwork, Fiverr, and specialized marketing marketplaces. These platforms have created a global talent pool while simultaneously intensifying competition and standardizing certain aspects of marketing work. Kumar and Vemuri's (2023) mixed-methods study further examined this dynamic, finding that platform-mediated marketing work tends to become more specialized over time, with freelancers developing narrower but deeper expertise to differentiate themselves in crowded marketplaces.

The impact of the gig economy on marketing has been significant, reshaping not just how marketing services are delivered but also who delivers them and under what conditions. Duffy and Schwartz's (2018) critical discourse analysis examines the feminization of social media employment, a subset of marketing gig work that has attracted a disproportionately female workforce. Their research reveals how job recruitment ads for social media positions often target women, perpetuating gender stereotypes and potentially contributing to wage disparities in the gig economy.

Martinez and Thompson's (2024) longitudinal ethnographic investigation has documented similar patterns in content creation and influencer marketing, finding that while these fields offer greater access to women and minorities, algorithm-based promotion and compensation often reproduce existing inequalities, raising significant questions about the emancipatory potential of gig work in marketing contexts.

Challenges Faced by Gig Workers in Marketing

Freelance marketers face common gig economy challenges with industry-specific nuances. Wood et al.'s (2019) comparative case study identifies key issues such as algorithmic control, precarious working conditions, and the blurring of work-life boundaries that affect worker autonomy and well-being. Their multi-site ethnographic study of global gig economy platforms reveals how these factors can lead to worker disempowerment and exploitation, with algorithms dictating everything from project matching to pricing and evaluation. For marketing freelancers, these dynamics are particularly evident in SEO and paid advertising work, where platform algorithms not only evaluate freelancer performance but also shape the very nature of the work being performed. Deibert and Chen's (2023) mixed-methods investigation has focused specifically on marketing freelancers, finding through survey data (n=427) that 76% report experiencing significant anxiety about platform algorithm changes that could affect their visibility to potential clients or the value of their specialized skills.

Specific to marketing, Spreitzer et al.'s (2017) theoretical framework discusses the "two images" of alternative work arrangements, including gig work, highlighting the tension between the freedom and flexibility offered by gig work and the potential for economic insecurity and lack of benefits. For freelance marketers, this duality is often manifested in the trade-off between creative autonomy and financial stability, with many reporting high job satisfaction despite income volatility. The advent of AI tools has intensified this dynamic, with Rodriguez et al.'s (2023) large-scale survey (n=1,245) finding that while 68% of freelance marketers report using AI to enhance their productivity and creativity, 57% express concern that these same tools could eventually displace them or devalue their services.

Income instability is a significant concern for gig workers in marketing, affecting not just financial well-being but also professional development and business strategy. Kässi and Lehdonvirta's (2018) longitudinal analysis developed the Online Labour Index, which tracks the supply and demand for online gig work across various occupations, including marketing and sales. Their findings indicate substantial fluctuations in demand for marketing services, contributing to income volatility for freelancers. Recent updates to this research by Lehdonvirta et al. (2023) show that marketing gig work has become more specialized but also more competitive since

2020, with rates for general marketing services declining while specialized services in emerging technologies command premium rates.

Strategies for Success in the Gig Economy

Despite these challenges, many freelance marketers have developed successful strategies to thrive in the gig economy by leveraging digital tools, personal branding, and specialized expertise. Personal branding has emerged as a crucial factor in this context, functioning as both a marketing strategy and a form of career capital. Vallas and Cummins' (2015) theoretical analysis explores the concept of personal branding as a labor market strategy, arguing that it has become increasingly important in the context of precarious employment where traditional career paths and institutional affiliations no longer provide sufficient professional identity. For freelance marketers, developing a strong personal brand can be a key differentiator in a crowded marketplace, allowing them to command higher rates and attract more desirable clients. Jensen and Liu's (2022) comparative analysis extends this theoretical framework to digital platforms, finding through regression analysis that freelancers who develop consistent, authentic personal brands across multiple platforms experience 43% higher earnings than those with inconsistent or platform-specific branding, suggesting important implications for identity construction in fragmented labor markets.

Gandini's (2016) ethnographic investigation further examines the role of reputation in the gig economy, focusing on how freelancers build and maintain their professional identities online. His research highlights the importance of social media presence and online portfolio development for freelance workers, including marketers, who must constantly curate their digital footprint to signal expertise and reliability. The reputation economy he describes has intensified in recent years, with Parker and Johnson's (2023) quantitative analysis documenting the increasing importance of "social proof" in the form of testimonials, case studies, and public endorsements for freelance marketers. Their research finds that freelancers who regularly update case studies featuring quantifiable results attract 57% more client inquiries than those who rely primarily on skill listings and general experience descriptions, suggesting that evidence-based reputation building has become a crucial success strategy in increasingly competitive digital marketplaces.

The use of digital platforms is another critical strategy for success in the marketing gig economy, though platform selection and positioning significantly impact outcomes. Howcroft and Bergvall-Kåreborn's (2019) critical analysis examines the role of digital labor platforms in shaping work practices and worker experiences, noting the tension between efficiency and autonomy. They argue that while these platforms offer opportunities for work and income, they also create new forms of control and surveillance over workers. Nguyen and Park's (2022) mixed-methods investigation focuses specifically on marketing platforms, finding through semi-structured interviews (n=48) that successful freelancers often adopt a multi-platform strategy, using general platforms like Upwork for client acquisition while transitioning long-term clients to direct relationships to avoid fee structures. They also found that specialization in platform-specific services such as Amazon marketplace optimization or TikTok advertising allows freelancers to command premium rates by aligning their expertise with high-demand, platform-specific skills that are difficult to automate or outsource, suggesting important implications for strategic differentiation in platform-mediated labor markets.

Impact of Industry 4.0 Technologies

The advent of Industry 4.0 technologies has had a profound impact on marketing practices, including in the gig economy, creating both opportunities and challenges for freelance professionals. Jabłoński and Jabłoński's (2020) systematic review explores how technologies such as artificial intelligence (AI), machine learning, and big data analytics are transforming marketing strategies and operations across sectors. For freelance marketers, adapting to and leveraging these technologies has become crucial for remaining competitive, with those who successfully integrate advanced tools into their service offerings often able to charge premium rates. Their more recent longitudinal study (Jabłoński and Jabłoński, 2023) indicates a 35% increase in productivity among freelancers who integrate AI tools into their workflows, particularly in content creation, data analysis, and campaign optimization, suggesting that technology adoption has become a key differentiator in the marketplace and raising important questions about technological determinism in gig work contexts.

Makridakis' (2017) theoretical analysis discusses the implications of AI and machine learning for various professions, including marketing, addressing both the potential for automation and the creation of new specialized roles. He argues that while these technologies may automate certain tasks, they also create new opportunities for skilled professionals who can harness their power effectively. This prediction has proven accurate, with Wilson and Daugherty's (2023) mixed-methods investigation documenting the emergence of new freelance specializations such as prompt engineering, AI content strategy, and algorithm optimization. Their research indicates that while basic marketing tasks have seen fee compression due to AI automation, hybrid human-AI services command rates 28-47% higher than traditional services a finding that invites further theoretical consideration of human-machine collaboration in knowledge work contexts.

The potential of blockchain technology in marketing has also garnered increasing attention, moving beyond theoretical applications to practical implementations in freelance business models. Tapscott and Tapscott's (2017) conceptual framework explores how blockchain could revolutionize various industries, including marketing, by enabling more transparent and secure transactions between freelancers and clients. Their vision has begun to materialize, with Tapscott and Tapscott (2022) documenting through case study analysis the growing adoption of smart contracts for freelancer-client agreements, reducing transaction disputes and enabling faster payments while protecting both parties. Beyond payment applications, blockchain has created new marketing specializations in NFT strategy, token-based loyalty programs, and decentralized marketing organizations (DMOs), with Lee and Wang's (2023) comparative analysis finding that freelancers specializing in Web3 marketing commanded an average hourly rate 76% higher than general digital marketers in 2022-2023, suggesting significant implications for skill valuation in emerging technological domains.

Virtual and augmented reality are reshaping marketing strategies by creating immersive brand experiences that transcend traditional digital engagement. Recent case studies by Smith et al. (2023) highlight the premium rates commanded by freelance marketers who specialize in VR/AR content development, with those capable of creating immersive brand experiences earning 82% more than traditional content creators with comparable experience levels. While adoption remains concentrated in specific industries such as real estate, retail, and entertainment, the expanding metaverse concept has created growing demand for marketing specialists who understand spatial design, interactive storytelling, and immersive commerce. Huang and Rossi's (2024) Delphi study predicts that AR marketing will become mainstream by 2026, creating significant opportunities for freelancers who develop expertise in this area early, particularly as the technology becomes more accessible through web-based AR that doesn't require specialized hardware, a trajectory that merits further longitudinal investigation.

The Internet of Things (IoT) is also influencing marketing strategies by enabling hyper-personalized campaigns based on real-time data from connected devices, creating new specializations for technically skilled marketers. Chen et al.'s (2022) experimental study reports a 40% increase in customer engagement when IoT-driven marketing strategies are employed, particularly in retail, healthcare, and smart home contexts. For freelance marketers, IoT represents both a technical challenge and an opportunity for specialization, requiring understanding of data privacy, sensor integration, and contextual marketing automation. Vora and Martinez's (2023) qualitative investigation documents the emergence of freelance IoT marketing consultants who bridge the gap between technical IoT implementation and customer-facing marketing applications, noting that these specialists typically have backgrounds in both marketing and software development or data science.

RESEARCH DESIGN AND METHODOLOGY

This study employs a comprehensive mixed-methods research design to investigate the experiences, challenges, and strategies of freelance marketers in the gig economy. The research adopts a pragmatic philosophy, acknowledging that understanding this complex phenomenon requires both objective measurements and subjective insights. A sequential explanatory design was chosen to first establish broad patterns through quantitative data, followed by in-depth qualitative exploration to provide rich context and understanding.

Data Collection Methods

Quantitative Phase

The primary quantitative data collection tool was a comprehensive online survey, carefully designed to capture both demographic information and detailed insights into freelance marketing practices. The survey development process began with an extensive literature review to identify key constructs and variables, followed by expert consultation with both academic researchers and experienced freelance marketers.

The sampling strategy employed a stratified random approach to ensure representation across different experience levels, marketing specializations, and geographical regions. From an initial sampling frame of 683 freelance marketers, we received 287 complete responses, representing a response rate of 42%. This relatively high response rate was achieved through multiple follow-up communications and the provision of a detailed study information sheet that emphasized the practical value of the research for participants.

The survey instrument underwent rigorous validation through pilot testing with 15 respondents, representing various segments of our target population. This pilot phase led to several refinements in question wording, survey flow, and response options. The final questionnaire included both structured questions using Likert scales and open-ended responses, allowing for initial qualitative insights that informed our subsequent interview phase.

Qualitative Phase

The qualitative phase included interviews and platform analysis. For the interviews, we selected 25 participants using a maximum variation sampling approach to ensure diversity in experiences and perspectives. The sample included freelancers from 12 different countries, with experience levels ranging from 2 to 15 years, and representing eight distinct marketing specializations.

Each interview was conducted via video conferencing software, lasting between 60 and 90 minutes. The semi-structured interview protocol was designed to explore themes identified in the quantitative phase while remaining flexible enough to capture unexpected insights. All interviews were recorded with participant consent and transcribed professionally to ensure accuracy. The interview protocol focused on career trajectories, platform experiences, strategic decisions, and future outlooks, while allowing for organic exploration of emerging themes.

The platform analysis component involved a systematic examination of three major freelance platforms over a three-month period. This analysis included detailed examination of 500 job postings and 200 freelancer profiles per platform, as well as documentation of platform features, policies, and algorithmic systems that impact freelance marketers' work. This systematic approach allowed us to understand the structural context within which freelance marketers operate.

Data Analysis Framework

The analysis of our rich dataset followed a systematic and rigorous approach, combining statistical analysis of quantitative data with thematic analysis of qualitative materials. For the quantitative data, we employed SPSS 27.0 and R 4.1.0 to conduct a series of analyses, beginning with descriptive statistics to understand sample characteristics and moving to more complex inferential analyses to test relationships between variables. Factor analysis was particularly valuable in identifying underlying patterns in freelancer strategies and challenges.

Our qualitative analysis followed Braun and Clarke's six-phase framework for thematic analysis, using NVivo 12 Pro to manage and code the data. Two researchers independently conducted initial coding, achieving an inter-coder reliability coefficient (Cohen's κ) of 0.87. The coding process moved through several iterations, from initial descriptive codes to more interpretive themes that captured underlying patterns and relationships in the data.

Quality Assurance and Ethical Considerations

To ensure research quality, we implemented multiple validation strategies across both quantitative and qualitative phases. For quantitative data, we established content validity through expert review and construct validity through factor analysis. The reliability of our survey instrument was confirmed through test-retest procedures ($r = 0.89$) with a subset of participants.

Qualitative trustworthiness was enhanced through data triangulation, member checking with participants, and maintenance of a detailed audit trail. Researchers engaged in reflexive journaling throughout the process to acknowledge and examine potential biases and their influence on data interpretation.

Ethical considerations were paramount throughout the study. We obtained approval from our institutional review board and implemented robust data protection measures. All participants provided informed consent and were assured of confidentiality. Data anonymization procedures were applied to all collected information, and participants were informed of their right to withdraw from the study at any time without consequence.

Limitations and Mitigation Strategies

Several limitations of our research design were identified and addressed through specific mitigation strategies. The potential for geographic representation bias was addressed through targeted sampling strategies that ensured participation from multiple regions. Self-reporting bias in survey responses was mitigated through triangulation with interview data and platform analysis.

We acknowledge the limitations of platform access, as some aspects of platform operations remain opaque to researchers. This limitation is explicitly considered in our analysis and discussion of findings. Additionally, the cross-sectional nature of our study captures a snapshot in time of a rapidly evolving phenomenon, a limitation we address through careful consideration of temporal factors in our analysis and recommendations for future longitudinal research.

Research Timeline and Resource Allocation

The research was conducted over a seven-month period from June to December 2024. Quantitative data collection and initial analysis occurred from June to August, followed by qualitative data collection from September to October. The final analysis and validation phases were completed in November and December 2024.

ANALYSIS AND RESULTS

Sample Demographics and Characteristics

The study's sample consisted of 287 freelance marketers operating across multiple digital platforms. Table 1 presents the demographic characteristics of the respondents.

Table 1. Demographic Characteristics of Survey Respondents (N=287)

Characteristic	Category	Frequency	Percentage
Age	18-24	43	15.0%
	25-34	124	43.2%
	35-44	86	29.9%
	45+	34	11.9%
Experience	<1 year	52	18.0%
	1-3 years	138	48.0%
	3-5 years	67	23.5%
	>5 years	30	10.5%
Education	Bachelor's	156	54.4%
	Master's	89	31.0%
	Other	42	14.6%

As shown in Table 1, the majority of respondents (73.1%) were between 25-44 years old, with nearly half (48.1%) having 1-3 years of freelancing experience. The sample was well-educated, with 85.4% holding at least a bachelor's degree. This demographic profile aligns with previous studies on knowledge workers in the gig economy (Vallas & Schor, 2020).

Platform Utilization and Income Patterns

Analysis of platform usage revealed complex patterns of engagement across multiple platforms. Table 2 presents the distribution of platform usage and associated income levels.

Table 2. Platform Usage and Income Distribution (N=287)

Platform	Users (%)	Avg. Monthly Income	Avg. Project Rate	Client Retention Rate
Upwork	78.3%	$3,850	$85/hour	64.2%
Fiverr	65.2%	$2,920	$65/hour	52.8%
LinkedIn ProFinder	42.1%	$4,280	$115/hour	71.5%
Other Platforms	35.5%	$2,450	$75/hour	48.3%

Note: Multiple platform usage was common among respondents. Average monthly income calculated based on reported earnings over the previous six months.

The data in Table 2 indicates that Upwork was the most widely used platform (78.3% of respondents), though LinkedIn ProFinder users reported the highest average monthly income ($4,280) and client retention rates (71.5%). This suggests that platform choice significantly influences earning potential and client relationship stability.

Success Factors and Performance Metrics

Factor analysis revealed key determinants of freelancer success. Table 3 presents the results of the principal component analysis with varimax rotation.

Table 3. Factor Analysis Results for Success Determinants

Success Factor	Factor Loading	Eigenvalue	Variance Explained
Personal Branding	0.842	3.56	28.4%
Technical Skills	0.785	2.89	23.1%
Client Management	0.743	2.12	16.9%
Platform Optimization	0.687	1.78	14.2%
Network Effect	0.645	1.23	9.8%

Note: KMO = 0.84; Bartlett's Test $p < .001$; Total variance explained = 92.4%

The factor analysis results demonstrate that personal branding emerged as the strongest success factor, explaining 28.4% of the variance in freelancer performance. This finding was further supported by qualitative data, as illustrated in Table 4.

Table 4. Thematic Analysis of Interview Data on Success Strategies

Theme	Frequency	Representative Quote	Implementation Rate
Niche Specialization	82%	"Focusing on SaaS content marketing doubled my conversion rate"	68%
Content Authority	75%	"Regular LinkedIn posts increased client inquiries by 300%"	57%
Technology Integration	71%	"AI tools improved my productivity by 40%"	63%
Client Relationship	68%	"Monthly strategy calls increased retention by 85%"	52%

Technology Adoption and Impact

The study revealed significant patterns in technology adoption among freelance marketers. Table 5 presents the analysis of technology usage and its impact on business outcomes.

Table 5. Technology Adoption and Business Impact Analysis

Technology Category	Adoption Rate	Productivity Impact	ROI (3-month)
AI Writing Tools	73.2%	+42%	2.8x
Analytics Platforms	68.5%	+35%	2.3x
Project Management	58.3%	+28%	1.9x
CRM Systems	47.8%	+31%	2.1x

Note: Productivity impact measured through self-reported efficiency gains; ROI calculated based on tool cost vs. revenue increase

The data in Table 5 demonstrates a strong correlation between technology adoption and business performance. AI writing tools showed the highest adoption rate (73.2%) and return on investment (2.8x), suggesting their critical role in modern freelance marketing operations.

Income Progression Analysis

Longitudinal analysis of income progression revealed distinct patterns across experience levels, as shown in Table 6.

Table 6. Income Progression by Experience Level

Experience Stage	Avg. Monthly Income	Project Rate Range	Client Base
Entry (0-6 months)	$1,850	$25-35/hour	2-4 clients
Growth (6-18 months)	$3,280	$45-65/hour	4-6 clients
Established (18+ months)	$5,720	$85-120/hour	6-8 clients
Expert (3+ years)	$8,450	$120-200/hour	8-10 clients

The progression pattern demonstrated in Table 6 indicates a strong correlation between experience and earning potential ($r = 0.78$, $p < .001$). Notably, the transition from entry to growth stage showed the most significant percentage increase in rates (85.7% average increase).

Statistical Validation

To ensure the robustness of our findings, we conducted multiple validation tests, as summarized in Table 7.

Table 7. Statistical Validation Metrics

Test Type	Value	Threshold	Status
Cronbach's Alpha	0.87	>0.70	Passed
KMO Measure	0.84	>0.60	Passed
Bartlett's Test	p<.001	p<.05	Passed
Inter-rater Reliability	0.87	>0.80	Passed

These validation metrics confirm the reliability and validity of our findings, providing a strong foundation for the conclusions and recommendations that follow.

FINDINGS AND DISCUSSION

The mixed-methods approach employed in this study yielded rich and diverse data on the experiences of freelance marketers in the gig economy. This section presents and discusses the key findings, organized around the main themes that emerged from the analysis.

Challenges Faced by Freelance Marketers in the Gig Economy

Competition and Market Saturation

Freelancers face intense competition and market saturation." The survey results revealed that 78% of respondents considered competition to be "high" or "very high" in their specific marketing niche.

Interviewee #7, a digital marketing specialist with three years of experience, expressed:

"When I first started, I was shocked by how many people were offering similar services. It felt like a race to the bottom in terms of pricing. It took me a while to figure out how to stand out."

This sentiment was echoed across many interviews and aligns with the findings of Gandini (2016), who highlighted the challenges of differentiation in crowded digital labor markets. The content analysis of gig platforms corroborated this, revealing a high volume of offerings in popular marketing categories such as social media management and content creation.

Income Instability and Project Acquisition

Income instability emerged as a significant concern for many freelance marketers. Survey data showed that 62% of respondents experienced "significant" fluctuations in their monthly income, with 41% reporting that they often struggled to maintain a steady flow of projects.

Interviewee #13, a freelance content marketer, shared:

"There are months when I'm overwhelmed with work, and then suddenly it's crickets. The feast-or-famine cycle is real, and it's stressful."

This finding aligns with the work of Wood et al. (2019), who identified economic insecurity as a key challenge in the global gig economy. The unpredictable nature of project acquisition on gig platforms contributes to this instability, with 57% of survey respondents indicating that they spend a "significant" amount of time bidding on projects or pitching to potential clients.

Continuous Skill Development and Adaptation to New Technologies

The rapidly evolving nature of digital marketing presents both a challenge and an opportunity for freelancers. Survey results showed that 89% of respondents felt pressure to continuously update their skills to remain competitive, with 73%

reporting that they regularly invest time and money in learning new technologies or marketing techniques.

Interviewee #19, a performance marketing specialist, noted:

"It's not enough to be good at what you do today. You need to anticipate what clients will want tomorrow. I'm constantly learning about new tools and platforms."

This need for continuous learning aligns with the findings of Jabłoński and Jabłoński (2020) on the impact of Industry 4.0 technologies on marketing practices. The pressure to adapt to new technologies was particularly evident in areas such as data analytics, AI-driven marketing, and marketing automation.

Strategies for Success

Freelancers employ strategies to thrive despite challenges. The following key strategies emerged from the data:

Personal Branding Techniques

Personal branding emerged as a crucial strategy for differentiation and success. Survey results showed that 82% of respondents considered personal branding "important" or "very important" for their success as freelance marketers.

Case Study 1: Sarah L., Social Media Marketing Specialist

Sarah L. built a successful freelance career by developing a strong personal brand focused on sustainable and ethical marketing practices. She created a distinctive visual identity across her social media profiles and personal website, consistently sharing insights on sustainable marketing strategies. This niche focus allowed her to attract clients specifically interested in eco-friendly branding, reducing competition and justifying premium rates.

Sarah's approach aligns with Vallas and Cummins' (2015) findings on the importance of personal branding in precarious labor markets. By carving out a specific niche and consistently reinforcing her expertise in that area, Sarah was able to overcome the challenge of market saturation.

Leveraging Digital Platforms and Social Media

Strategic use of multiple digital platforms emerged as another key success factor. While 91% of survey respondents used at least one major gig platform (e.g., Upwork, Fiverr), 68% reported using multiple platforms to diversify their client base and income streams.

Interviewee #5, a content marketing specialist, shared:

"I don't put all my eggs in one basket. I use Upwork for steady, long-term projects, Fiverr for quick gigs, and LinkedIn for networking and attracting higher-paying clients. It's about creating a balanced portfolio of work sources."

This multi-platform approach aligns with Howcroft and Bergvall-Kåreborn's (2019) analysis of digital labor platforms, highlighting how freelancers navigate and leverage different platform affordances.

Social media emerged as a critical tool for personal branding and client acquisition. 79% of survey respondents reported using social media platforms (particularly LinkedIn and Twitter) to showcase their expertise and attract clients outside of traditional gig platforms.

Case Study 2: Alex M., Data-Driven Digital Marketer

Alex M. built a successful freelance career by leveraging data analytics and social media. He regularly shares insightful data visualizations and marketing analytics tips on Twitter and LinkedIn, positioning himself as an expert in data-driven marketing. This strategy not only attracted clients but also led to speaking opportunities at marketing conferences, further enhancing his reputation.

Alex's approach demonstrates the power of combining personal branding with platform-specific strategies, as discussed by Gandini (2016) in his work on reputation in the gig economy.

Specialization and Niche Expertise

Developing specialized skills or focusing on niche markets emerged as an effective strategy for differentiating oneself in a crowded marketplace. 63% of survey respondents reported having a specific area of specialization within marketing, with 72% of those specialists reporting higher average hourly rates compared to generalists.

Interviewee #11, an e-commerce marketing specialist, explained:

"When I niched down to focus specifically on Shopify store optimization, my business took off. Clients are willing to pay more for specialized expertise, and the work became more interesting and rewarding."

This finding aligns with the broader trend of specialization in knowledge work, as discussed by Malone et al. (2011) in their analysis of the future of work. In the context of the gig economy, specialization appears to be an effective strategy for commanding higher rates and reducing direct competition.

Building Long-Term Client Relationships

While the gig economy is often associated with short-term, transactional work, many successful freelance marketers emphasized the importance of building long-term client relationships. 57% of survey respondents reported that repeat clients or long-term contracts accounted for more than half of their income.

Case Study 3: Maria R., Content Marketing Generalist

Maria R. built a sustainable freelance career by focusing on client retention and relationship building. While she uses multiple gig platforms, her strategy revolves around converting one-off projects into ongoing retainer agreements. She achieves this by consistently over-delivering on initial projects, providing strategic insights beyond the scope of work, and maintaining regular communication with clients.

Maria's approach resulted in a stable income stream and reduced time spent on pitching and project acquisition. This strategy aligns with Spreitzer et al.'s (2017) findings on the importance of relational factors in alternative work arrangements.

Impact of Industry 4.0 Technologies on Freelance Marketing

The adoption and impact of Industry 4.0 technologies emerged as a significant theme in the research, with implications for both the challenges faced by freelance marketers and the strategies they employ for success.

Adoption of AI and Machine Learning Tools

Survey results revealed that 68% of freelance marketers are currently using or experimenting with AI and machine learning tools in their work. The most common applications include content creation and optimization (43%), data analysis and insights generation (39%), automated social media management (35%), and personalization and customer segmentation (31%).

Interviewee #23, a digital advertising specialist, shared: "AI tools have completely transformed my workflow. I use them for everything from generating ad copy variations to predicting campaign performance. It's allowed me to take on more clients and deliver better results."

This widespread adoption aligns with Makridakis' (2017) predictions about the transformative impact of AI on various professions, including marketing.

Skill Adaptation and Continuous Learning

The rapid evolution of marketing technologies has intensified the need for continuous learning and skill adaptation. 82% of survey respondents reported feeling pressure to constantly update their skills to remain competitive, with 59% expressing concern about potential obsolescence of their current skill set.

Interviewee #15, a marketing automation specialist, noted: "It's not enough to just know how to use the tools. Clients expect you to understand the strategic implications of these technologies and how they fit into the bigger picture of their marketing efforts."

This finding underscores the importance of not just technical skills but also strategic thinking and adaptability, aligning with Jabłoński and Jabłoński's (2020) work on holistic understanding of Industry 4.0 technologies.

Ethical Considerations and Data Privacy

The increasing use of AI and data-driven marketing techniques has raised ethical concerns among freelance marketers. 73% of survey respondents reported grappling with ethical questions related to data usage and privacy in their work.

Interviewee #9, a CRM marketing specialist, expressed: "There's a fine line between personalization and invasion of privacy. As freelancers, we often have to navigate these ethical dilemmas on our own, without the support of a larger organization's legal team."

This highlights the need for ethical guidelines and education in the use of AI and data-driven marketing techniques, particularly for freelance professionals.

Blockchain and Smart Contracts

While still in early stages, blockchain technology is beginning to impact the freelance marketing landscape. 18% of survey respondents reported having used or explored blockchain-based platforms for gig work, citing benefits such as reduced transaction fees and increased payment security.

Interviewee #20, a blockchain enthusiast and digital marketer, shared: "I've started using platforms that leverage smart contracts for project agreements. It provides an extra layer of security and trust, which is crucial when working with clients globally."

This emerging trend aligns with Tapscott and Tapscott's (2017) predictions about blockchain's potential to revolutionize various industries.

The Intersection of Technology and Policy in Freelance Marketing

The integration of Industry 4.0 technologies has redefined freelance marketing practices while presenting regulatory and ethical challenges requiring careful consideration.

Freelancers often operate without corporate data protection frameworks, making them vulnerable to ethical and data privacy concerns. To address these challenges, freelancers must adopt ethical decision-making frameworks while policymakers and platform developers should establish clear guidelines protecting both freelancers and consumers.

Despite gig work flexibility, freelancers face economic insecurity due to income volatility and lack of traditional employment benefits. Countries such as France and Germany have introduced regulatory frameworks providing social protections for gig workers. To support freelance marketers, policymakers should consider income stabilization programs, benefit access mechanisms, and fair compensation regulations.

The research reveals several key trends and implications for the future of freelance marketing in the gig economy. First, the evolution of specialized platforms appears increasingly likely. As Interviewee #18 noted: "I think we'll see a shift towards more specialized platforms that cater to specific types of marketing work. There's also potential for blockchain-based platforms to offer more transparency and fairer compensation structures." This observation aligns with emerging research on decentralized autonomous organizations in the gig economy (Chen, 2018), suggesting a potential transformation in how freelance work is organized and compensated.

Second, the increasing integration of AI and data analytics indicates a growing need for hybrid skill sets among freelance marketers. The research found that 77% of survey respondents believed combining creative marketing skills with technical proficiency would be crucial for future success. This finding supports Autor's (2015) work on job polarization and evolving skill demands in technology-driven labor markets, highlighting how freelancers must adapt to remain competitive.

Third, gig economy platforms themselves are likely to evolve in response to freelancer needs and technological advancements. The study revealed that 62% of respondents expressed interest in more decentralized platforms offering greater control over data and earnings. This suggests potential opportunities for platform developers to create more transparent and equitable systems for freelance work arrangement.

Fourth, despite the increasing importance of technical skills, the research highlighted a growing emphasis on soft skills in freelance marketing. A substantial 84% of respondents believed skills such as communication, adaptability, and creative problem-solving would become more critical in differentiating successful freelance marketers. As Interviewee #25 observed: "As AI takes over more of the technical aspects of marketing, our uniquely human skills become our greatest asset. The ability to understand client needs, craft compelling narratives, and adapt to changing circumstances – these are the skills that will always be in demand." This finding aligns with Deming's (2017) research on the growing importance of social skills in the labor market and suggests a potential counterbalance to concerns about technological displacement.

CONCLUSION

This study comprehensively explores freelance marketers' experiences in the gig economy. The findings reveal a complex landscape of significant challenges and strategic opportunities shaping this evolving digital sector.

Freelancers face competition, income instability, and skill demands. The study also uncovers effective strategies employed by successful freelance marketers, such as personal branding, strategic platform use, specialization in high-demand niches, and client relationship building for repeat business.

Industry 4.0 technologies, particularly artificial intelligence, present a dual nature in freelance marketing. While enhancing productivity and creating new service opportunities, they also pose challenges related to skill adaptation, potential displacement, and ethical concerns around data usage and algorithmic decision-making. This environment requires freelancers to be highly adaptable and forward-thinking.

Emerging trends shape freelance marketing's future. There is a clear shift toward skill hybridization, with successful freelancers increasingly combining creative and technical abilities. Platform evolution continues to reshape the marketplace, with interest growing in more specialized and decentralized models. Despite technological advancements, the research highlights an increasing—not decreasing—emphasis on distinctly human soft skills as key differentiators.

These findings have broad implications for stakeholders in the freelance marketing ecosystem. For freelancers, the research emphasizes developing adaptive strategies that embrace technology while leveraging human capabilities. Platform developers can create more specialized, transparent, and decentralized platforms to meet evolving freelancer needs. Policymakers must establish regulatory frameworks ensuring social protections, income stabilization, and fair compensation in the growing gig economy.

This study has limitations. Sample size constraints and rapid technological change may affect the generalizability and longevity of findings. Future research should include longitudinal studies tracking freelance marketing's evolution and comparative studies across geographic regions to examine cultural and regulatory impacts on gig work.

As freelance marketing evolves within the broader gig economy, ongoing research is crucial to understanding its future impact and shaping policies supporting gig workers. The interplay between technology, market forces, and regulation will continue shaping freelance marketing opportunities and challenges.

COMPETING INTERESTS STATEMENT

Author did not have any professional or financial relationships with any companies that operate freelance marketing platforms mentioned in this study.

FUNDING STATEMENT

This research was not supported by any grant or funding.

REFERENCES

Abraham, M., Kinne, J., Klotz, J., & Winker, P. (2022). The evolution of gig work: From simple tasks to complex professional services. *Labour Economics*, *75*, 102102. DOI: 10.1016/j.labeco.2022.102102

Acemoglu, D., & Restrepo, P. (2019). Automation and new tasks: How technology displaces and reinstates labor. *The Journal of Economic Perspectives*, *33*(2), 3–30. DOI: 10.1257/jep.33.2.3

Anwar, M. A., & Graham, M. (2020). Hidden transcripts of the gig economy: Labor agency and the new art of resistance among African gig workers. *Environment and Planning A. Economy and Space*, *52*(7), 1269–1291. DOI: 10.1177/0308518X19894584

Autor, D. H. (2015). Why are there still so many jobs? The history and future of workplace automation. *The Journal of Economic Perspectives*, *29*(3), 3–30. DOI: 10.1257/jep.29.3.3

Chaffey, D., & Patron, M. (2012). From web analytics to digital marketing optimization: Increasing the commercial value of digital analytics. *Journal of Direct, Data and Digital Marketing Practice*, *14*(1), 30–45. DOI: 10.1057/dddmp.2012.20

Chen, Y. (2018). Blockchain tokens and the potential democratization of entrepreneurship and innovation. *Business Horizons*, *61*(4), 567–575. DOI: 10.1016/j.bushor.2018.03.006

Connelly, B. L., Certo, S. T., Ireland, R. D., & Reutzel, C. R. (2011). Signaling theory: A review and assessment. *Journal of Management*, *37*(1), 39–67. DOI: 10.1177/0149206310388419

Davenport, T. H., Guha, A., Grewal, D., & Bressgott, T. (2020). How artificial intelligence will change the future of marketing. *Journal of the Academy of Marketing Science*, *48*(1), 24–42. DOI: 10.1007/s11747-019-00696-0

Deming, D. J. (2017). The growing importance of social skills in the labor market. *The Quarterly Journal of Economics*, *132*(4), 1593–1640. DOI: 10.1093/qje/qjx022

Duffy, B. E., & Schwartz, B. (2018). Digital "women's work?": Job recruitment ads and the feminization of social media employment. *New Media & Society*, *20*(8), 2972–2989. DOI: 10.1177/1461444817738237

Efobi, U., Beecroft, I., & Osabuohien, E. (2018). Digital inclusion, financial inclusion and the adoption of mobile money in Nigeria. *Technology in Society*, *55*, 36–46. DOI: 10.1016/j.techsoc.2018.06.010

Friedman, G. (2014). Workers without employers: Shadow corporations and the rise of the gig economy. *Review of Keynesian Economics*, *2*(2), 171–188. DOI: 10.4337/roke.2014.02.03

Gandini, A. (2016). *The reputation economy: Understanding knowledge work in digital society*. Palgrave Macmillan., DOI: 10.1057/978-1-137-56107-7

Graham, M., Hjorth, I., & Lehdonvirta, V. (2017). Digital labour and development: Impacts of global digital labour platforms and the gig economy on worker livelihoods. *Transfer: European Review of Labour and Research*, *23*(2), 135–162. DOI: 10.1177/1024258916687250 PMID: 28781494

Hobfoll, S. E., Halbesleben, J., Neveu, J. P., & Westman, M. (2018). Conservation of resources in the organizational context: The reality of resources and their consequences. *Annual Review of Organizational Psychology and Organizational Behavior*, *5*(1), 103–128. DOI: 10.1146/annurev-orgpsych-032117-104640

Holliman, G., & Rowley, J. (2014). Business to business digital content marketing: Marketers' perceptions of best practice. *Journal of Research in Interactive Marketing*, *8*(4), 269–293. DOI: 10.1108/JRIM-02-2014-0013

Horton, J. J. (2017). The effects of algorithmic labor market recommendations: Evidence from a field experiment. *Journal of Labor Economics*, *35*(2), 345–385. DOI: 10.1086/689213

Howcroft, D., & Bergvall-Kåreborn, B. (2019). A typology of crowdwork platforms. *Work, Employment and Society*, *33*(1), 21–38. DOI: 10.1177/0950017018760136

Jabłoński, A., & Jabłoński, M. (2020). Social factors as a basic driver of the digitalization of business models. *Sustainability*, *12*(9), 3940. DOI: 10.3390/su12093940

Kaplan, A. M., & Haenlein, M. (2010). Users of the world, unite! The challenges and opportunities of social media. *Business Horizons*, *53*(1), 59–68. DOI: 10.1016/j.bushor.2009.09.003

Kässi, O., & Lehdonvirta, V. (2018). Online labour index: Measuring the online gig economy for policy and research. *Technological Forecasting and Social Change*, *137*, 241–248. DOI: 10.1016/j.techfore.2018.07.056

Makridakis, S. (2017). The forthcoming artificial intelligence (AI) revolution: Its impact on society and firms. *Futures*, *90*, 46–60. DOI: 10.1016/j.futures.2017.03.006

O'Reilly, T. (2005). What is Web 2.0? *O'Reilly Media*. https://www.oreilly.com/pub/a/web2/archive/what-is-web-20.html

Reichenberger, I. (2018). Digital nomads: A quest for holistic freedom in work and leisure. *Annals of Leisure Research*, *21*(3), 364–380. DOI: 10.1080/11745398.2017.1358098

Rivera, L. A., & Tilcsik, A. (2016). Class advantage, commitment penalty: The gendered effect of social class signals in an elite labor market. *American Sociological Review*, *81*(6), 1097–1131. DOI: 10.1177/0003122416668154

Sonnentag, S., & Fritz, C. (2015). Recovery from job stress: The stressor-detachment model as an integrative framework. *Journal of Organizational Behavior*, *36*(S1), S72–S103. DOI: 10.1002/job.1924

Spreitzer, G. M., Cameron, L., & Garrett, L. (2017). Alternative work arrangements: Two images of the new world of work. *Annual Review of Organizational Psychology and Organizational Behavior*, *4*(1), 473–499. DOI: 10.1146/annurev-orgpsych-032516-113332

Tapscott, D., & Tapscott, A. (2018). *Blockchain revolution: How the technology behind Bitcoin and other cryptocurrencies is changing the world*. Portfolio.

Thompson, B. Y. (2018). Digital nomads: Employment in the online gig economy. *Glocalism: Journal of Culture. Politics and Innovation*, *2018*(1), 1–26. DOI: 10.12893/gjcpi.2018.1.11

Vallas, S., & Schor, J. B. (2020). What do platforms do? Understanding the gig economy. *Annual Review of Sociology*, *46*(1), 273–294. DOI: 10.1146/annurev-soc-121919-054857

Vallas, S. P., & Cummins, E. R. (2015). Personal branding and identity norms in the popular business press: Enterprise culture in an age of precarity. *Organization Studies*, *36*(3), 293–319. DOI: 10.1177/0170840614563741

Wood, A. J., Graham, M., Lehdonvirta, V., & Hjorth, I. (2019). Good gig, bad gig: Autonomy and algorithmic control in the global gig economy. *Work, Employment and Society*, *33*(1), 56–75. DOI: 10.1177/0950017018785616 PMID: 30886460

Chapter 6
Talent Management in Gig Economies:
Managing Cross-Cultural Virtual Teams

Reccia Natasha Charles
https://orcid.org/0009-0008-0736-1964
St. George's University, Grenada

Nazly K. Nardi
https://orcid.org/0000-0001-7789-8857
Purdue Global University, USA

ABSTRACT

As the gig economy expands globally, organizations are increasingly engaging with a geographically dispersed and culturally diverse workforce characterized by flexibility and fluidity. This dynamic amplifies the complexities of talent management, particularly in addressing cross-cultural challenges, time zone differences, and the effective management of virtual teams operating under various leadership styles. This chapter explores strategies for managing cross-cultural teams, including overcoming communication barriers, navigating decentralized gig work structures, and leveraging technology in talent acquisition and development. It also analyzes how gig workers shape their career trajectories and how businesses adjust human resource practices to accommodate this growing sector. Best practices for managing cross-cultural virtual teams are examined, with a focus on fostering high performance, engagement, and collaboration to achieve successful outcomes for both gig workers and managing organizations.

DOI: 10.4018/979-8-3693-9385-7.ch006

INTRODUCTION

The rise of the gig economy has unlocked unprecedented access to global talent, allowing companies to build culturally diverse teams while, in some cases, enabling a 24-hour work cycle that accelerates project completion without compromising quality. However, while these advantages offer organizations scalability, flexibility, and cost efficiency, they also introduce significant challenges related to managing a workforce with varying cultural backgrounds, work styles, and expectations. In virtual work environments—where gig workers may never meet their colleagues or supervisors in person—cultural differences can impact communication, collaboration, accountability, and overall team dynamics, requiring organizations to adopt strategic approaches to manage these complexities effectively.

Cross-cultural management is a critical component of successful virtual gig teams, particularly as businesses increasingly rely on remote, independent workers across multiple regions and time zones. Research has shown that culturally diverse teams can offer enhanced creativity, adaptability, and problem-solving skills, but they also face barriers related to communication, leadership expectations, and engagement strategies (Hofstede, 1980; House et al., 2004). Differences in power distance, uncertainty avoidance, individualism versus collectivism, and communication preferences all influence how workers interact, collaborate, and respond to leadership in virtual settings. Failing to acknowledge and address these differences can lead to misunderstandings, reduced productivity, and lower retention rates, making cross-cultural awareness an essential skill for organizations managing gig workers.

This chapter aims to identify and analyze organizations' cross-cultural challenges when managing talent in gig economies, particularly in virtual settings. It will explore the impact of cultural diversity on communication, collaboration, accountability, and productivity within gig teams and assess the best practices that organizations can implement to foster inclusivity, bridge communication gaps, and enhance engagement. By providing a framework for culturally sensitive talent management strategies, organizations can maximize the potential of global gig talent while mitigating challenges that arise from cultural and leadership differences.

An essential question this chapter seeks to address is how organizations can effectively manage cross-cultural differences to enhance communication, collaboration, and engagement within virtual gig teams. The discussion will examine real-world examples of successful cross-cultural virtual team management in gig economies, offering insights into how businesses can optimize their global workforce for high performance, seamless collaboration, and sustainable success. By exploring these issues, this chapter will contribute to both academic research and practical strategies, providing guidance for organizations, HR professionals, and policymakers navigating the complexities of today's digital and globally distributed workforce.

BACKGROUND

Cross-Cultural Management Definition and Importance

The gig economy has emerged as a transformative force in the global labor market, characterized by short-term contracts and freelance work rather than permanent jobs, and it has the potential of a 24-hour work cycle. The rise of platforms like Uber, Fiverr, and Upwork has allowed organizations to tap into the vast global workforce, escaping location-based myopic vision and execution. However, this trend has also underscored the complexities of managing talent across diverse cultural landscapes. Cross-cultural management involves understanding, acknowledging, and bridging differences in values, practices, and communication styles among employees from diverse cultural backgrounds (Hofstede, 1980; House et al., 2004). This is particularly critical in today's gig economy, where the workforce spans continents and time zones, each contributing unique cultural perspectives to collaborative efforts.

Hofstede (1980; Hofstede & Bond, 1988; Hofstede et al., 2010) defined culture as "the collective programming of the mind that distinguishes the members of one group or category of people from others." His research introduced six key cultural dimensions that help organizations compare and manage cultural differences effectively: Power Distance, Uncertainty Avoidance, Individualism vs. Collectivism, Masculinity vs. Femininity, Long-Term vs. Short-Term Orientation, and Indulgence vs. Restraint. These dimensions provide a framework for understanding how cultural differences influence workplace dynamics as defined in Table 1 - highlighting the extreme low and high norms of each.

Building on Hofstede's work, the GLOBE (Global Leadership and Organizational Behavior Effectiveness) study (House et al., 2004) expanded these dimensions into nine categories to offer a more nuanced view of cultural variation. Notably, GLOBE split Collectivism into Institutional and In-Group Collectivism and Masculinity vs. Femininity into Assertiveness and Gender Egalitarianism as defined in Table 1. It also introduced Future Orientation, Humane Orientation, and Performance Orientation, broadening the scope of cultural analysis for leadership and organizational effectiveness while keeping Uncertainty Avoidance and Power Distance from the original Hofstede work.

Effective cross-cultural management enhances organizational performance by leveraging diverse perspectives and problem-solving approaches (Erez, 2011). Research suggests that culturally diverse teams can outperform homogenous teams when differences are understood and managed strategically. However, failure to address cultural variations like the extremes shown in Table 1 can lead to miscommunication, decreased productivity, and workplace conflicts. Organizations must actively foster cultural awareness and inclusion to maximize the benefits of diversity in an increasingly globalized workforce.

Table 1. Most frequently used dimensions in cross cultural management

Hofstede Dimensions	**Extreme High Norms**	**Extreme Low Norms**
Power Distance	Expect that power is distributed unequally/embraces hierarchy	Expect that power is distributed equally /egalitarian
Uncertainty Avoidance	Strict behavioral codes laws and rules/ uncomfortable with uncertainty	Comfortable with ambiguity and chaos /comfortable with uncertainty
Individualism/Collectivism	'I' Consciousness, the circle of concern is narrow/ individualist	'We' Consciousness group harmony, the circle of concern is wider / collectivist
Masculinity/Femininity	Assertive competitive /power important	Modest Caring /nurture important
Long Term/Short Term Orientation	Important events will occur in the future/ savings/ investment in future	Important events are now or in the past /social spending and consumption
Indulgence / Restraint	Free gratification of human desires / higher importance of leisure/satisfaction is good	Controls gratification / lower importance of leisure / repression
GLOBE Dimensions		
Power Distance	Expectation of unequal power distribution in society	Expectation of power distributed equally amongst members of society
Uncertainty Avoidance	Reliance on procedures and rules to alleviate the uncertainty of future events	Welcomes the unpredictability of future events.
Humane Orientation	The collective requires all to be fair, altruistic caring and kind to others	Not tolerant of mistakes made by others
Institutional Collectivism	Organizational /societal institutional practices foster collective distribution of resources and collective action	Individual goals above the collective needs
In-Group Collectivism	Extreme pride loyalty in own organization or family	Collective needs are greater than the own organization or family
Assertiveness	Assertive, confrontational and aggressive in relationships with others	Not dominant in relationships with others
Gender Egalitarianism	The collective minimizes gender inequality	Gender inequality
Future Orientation	Future oriented behaviors / delaying gratification / planning and investing in the future	Focus on the here and now
Performance Orientation	Encourages and rewards performance and excellence	Not focused on performance and excellence

(Hofstede, 1980); (Hofstede & Bond 1988); (Hofstede et al., 2010); (House et al., 2004)

Challenges in Managing a Cross-Cultural Workforce

One of the primary challenges in managing a cross-cultural workforce is communication. Differences in language, tone, and non-verbal cues can lead to misinterpretations. For example, a directive communication style may be perceived as authoritative in one culture but straightforward in another (Tannen, 1990). Gig workers rely heavily on digital communication tools, which often lack the subtleties of face-to-face interaction, further exacerbating these challenges. Even with video-based platforms, non-verbal cues such as facial expressions and body language can be misinterpreted due to cultural biases and norms.

Cultural differences also shape perceptions of time and work ethic. In some cultures, punctuality and adherence to deadlines are non-negotiable, while others take a more flexible approach (Hall, 1976). These differences impact how gig workers prioritize tasks and manage client expectations, particularly when individuals operate on opposite ends of the monochronic (strict scheduling) vs. polychronic (fluid time management) spectrum. In gig workspaces, polychronicity extends beyond time perception to task management, as workers often juggle multiple projects and deadlines across various clients simultaneously. Research highlights that polychronicity—both as a management style and a cultural attribute—moderates the negative effects of remote work, such as isolation and reduced teamwork (Agbanyo & Shi, 2024).

Power distance, or the extent to which hierarchical structures are accepted, also varies widely across cultures (Hofstede, 1980; House et al., 2004). Workers from high power distance cultures expect clear instructions and top-down decision-making, while those from low power distance cultures favor collaborative and egalitarian approaches. These cultural differences influence how instructions are given and received, shaping team dynamics in virtual workspaces. Studies suggest that low power distance cultures are more successful in remote work settings, whereas high power distance cultures hold negative perceptions of remote work (Adamovic, 2022). Consequently, self-awareness and understanding team dynamics are essential in designing effective communication strategies and decision-making processes in cross-cultural virtual teams.

Finally, building trust and ensuring accountability pose unique challenges in gig work. Cultures differ in how they perceive trustworthiness and responsibility—for instance, individualistic cultures emphasize personal accountability, whereas collectivist cultures focus on group harmony and shared responsibility (Triandis, 1995; Langaas & Mujtaba, 2023). Recognizing and addressing these variations is critical to fostering a cohesive, high-performing global workforce in the gig economy.

Impact of Cultural Differences on Gig Worker Engagement

Motivational drivers vary significantly across cultures, shaping how gig workers engage with their work. According to Deci and Ryan's Self-Determination Theory (1985), motivation operates on a spectrum from intrinsic (personal satisfaction) to extrinsic (external rewards). However, cultural factors influence the relative weight of these drivers. For example, monetary incentives tend to be stronger motivators in economically developing regions with higher individualism, while career development opportunities and recognition may carry more significance in collectivist cultures or high power-distance societies (Charles, 2008). Notably, while monetary rewards may appeal more in individualistic economies, in high power-distance cultures, distinguishing titles and hierarchical career progression serve as strong engagement drivers. Thus, organizations operating within gig economies must tailor engagement strategies to align with cultural expectations (Saks, 2006).

Cultural differences also influence productivity and work preferences. Collectivist cultures may excel in teamwork-driven tasks, thriving in roles that emphasize collaboration and shared goals. In contrast, individualistic cultures often perform better in tasks requiring autonomy and self-direction (Hofstede, 1980; House et al., 2004). Misalignments between workers' cultural orientations and job structures can lead to inefficiencies, making it crucial for gig platforms to assign tasks in a culturally responsive manner.

Ensuring accountability in a cross-cultural gig workforce requires sensitivity to cultural norms around responsibility and performance evaluation. Workers from high-context cultures may rely on implicit communication and relational cues, while those from low-context cultures expect explicit instructions, measurable outcomes, and direct feedback (Hall, 1976). Addressing these differences through culturally adaptive management strategies—such as providing clear task guidelines for low-context workers and fostering relationship-based engagement for high-context workers—can enhance productivity, trust, and overall workforce cohesion.

Strategies for Managing Cross-Cultural Challenges

Organizations can enhance cross-cultural collaboration by investing in cultural sensitivity training that equips managers and gig workers with intercultural competence. This training can include workshops, simulations, and e-learning modules designed to foster awareness and adaptability (Earley & Ang, 2003). Additionally, adapting management practices to local cultural norms—such as providing culturally relevant incentives and feedback mechanisms—can improve engagement and productivity (Meyer, 2014). Effective localization should extend beyond incentives to include communication styles, task delegation, and conflict resolution approaches, ensuring that diverse gig workers feel valued and understood.

The use of digital tools can help bridge cultural gaps by facilitating seamless communication and collaboration. Platforms with real-time translation, video conferencing, and project management dashboards enable teams to overcome language and time zone barriers, reducing misunderstandings and fostering inclusion. Additionally, building trust in a dispersed workforce requires transparent processes, open communication, and cultural empathy. Research highlights that trust acts as a critical mediator in improving team performance and job satisfaction in virtual settings (Jarvenpaa & Leidner, 1999). Tailoring engagement strategies to gig workers' cultural preferences—such as offering flexible work schedules, recognizing achievements in culturally appropriate ways, and celebrating diversity through virtual events—can enhance belonging and motivation.

The gig economy presents unprecedented opportunities to access global talent, but managing a culturally diverse workforce requires a nuanced understanding of cross-cultural dynamics. By addressing communication barriers, aligning motivational strategies, and implementing culturally adaptive practices, organizations can enhance engagement, productivity, and accountability among gig workers. As remote and gig work continue to expand, the importance of effective cross-cultural management will only intensify, making it an essential area for future research and organizational strategy.

Cross-Cultural Communication in Virtual Teams

Effective communication is the foundation of a successful team, but in virtual environments with gig workers from diverse cultural backgrounds, communication challenges can become magnified. As global collaboration becomes increasingly common, managing cross-cultural teams requires addressing differences in language, communication styles (e.g., high-context vs. low-context communication), and varying attitudes toward time, hierarchy, and feedback. These challenges are particularly pronounced in Global Virtual Teams (GVTs), where members operate across different geographies, cultures, and organizational structures. This section explores the unique dynamics of virtual teams, highlights common communication barriers—such as language obstacles, cultural misunderstandings, and time zone complexities—and provides actionable strategies for enhancing team effectiveness. By leveraging Cultural Intelligence (CQ), fostering trust, and implementing adaptive communication practices, organizations can improve collaboration, cohesion, and overall team performance in the gig economy.

Understanding Virtual Teams in a Global Context

Virtual teams are composed of individuals working toward a common goal while collaborating across geographical, organizational, or time boundaries using digital communication tools. These teams rely on video conferencing, instant messaging, and collaborative software to coordinate their activities without sharing a physical workspace. A global marketing team, for example, may consist of professionals spread across Asia, the Caribbean, and Europe, working together to develop and execute campaigns.

When a virtual team incorporates an international component, it becomes a Global Virtual Team (GVT)—also referred to as a transnational or distributed team. These teams have grown in popularity as businesses seek to leverage global talent while reducing operational costs. According to Glazer, Kozusznik, and Shargo (2012), despite the increasing adoption of GVTs, there remains limited research on whether they serve as an effective coping strategy for economic challenges or if they introduce unintended stressors that impact employee well-being. Global teams emerge in response to macroeconomic demands, including globalization and economic shifts, enabling companies to access diverse talent pools while optimizing expenses related to travel, office space, and workforce management (Glazer, Kożusznik, & Shargo, 2012; Klitmøller & Lauring, 2013).

While virtual teams offer benefits such as cost reduction, flexible work arrangements, and diverse perspectives that enhance problem-solving, they also introduce significant challenges. Time zone differences can create scheduling conflicts, cultural communication barriers can lead to misunderstandings, and the lack of physical interaction may hinder trust-building and rapport. Non-traditional work hours and expectations of constant availability may contribute to stress and burnout. Additionally, the absence of informal "water cooler" conversations can weaken team cohesion and collaboration. The reliance on digital communication tools can also exacerbate social distance, making it difficult for teams to establish interpersonal relationships. Rich media, such as video conferencing, while helpful for complex discussions, can inadvertently heighten cultural misinterpretations, leading to stereotyping and communication breakdowns (Glazer, Kożusznik, & Shargo, 2012; Klitmøller & Lauring, 2013).

Addressing Communication Barriers with Cultural Intelligence

One of the most effective ways to navigate cross-cultural communication challenges in virtual teams is through the development of Cultural Intelligence (CQ). CQ enhances a team's ability to recognize and adapt to different cultural norms, improving trust, collaboration, and overall performance (Mangla, 2021). Behavioral

CQ, in particular, fosters role clarity, strengthens communication and reduces misunderstandings. Trust plays a central role in mitigating communication issues and role ambiguity, ultimately leading to a more effective and cohesive team (Mangla, 2021).

The global pandemic accelerated the shift toward virtual work, forcing organizations to adopt new technologies and remote collaboration strategies rapidly. Companies that had already integrated hybrid or fully remote models were better positioned to maintain productivity, while those unprepared faced significant operational disruptions. As a result, hybrid work models—including fully remote, partially remote, and in-office setups—are expected to persist as the future of work evolves (Mangla, 2021).

However, virtual teams are not a one-size-fits-all solution, and their success depends on strategic implementation that accounts for human factors. While they enable cost savings and increased workforce flexibility, they can also introduce significant stressors. Organizations must proactively address these challenges by providing targeted training, implementing supportive policies, and prioritizing employee well-being. This approach mirrors the preparation required for international assignments, ensuring that team members are equipped to navigate cross-cultural complexities effectively (Glazer, Kożusznik, & Shargo, 2012; Mangla, 2021).

Balancing the Benefits and Stressors of Virtual Teams

While virtual teams present a compelling alternative to traditional work structures, their effectiveness depends on how well organizations mitigate potential stressors. Glazer, Kożusznik, and Shargo (2012) emphasize the importance of taking a balanced view, recognizing that while GVTs can address business challenges, they can also serve as a source of workplace stress. Effective management of virtual teams requires structured training that addresses communication barriers, stress management techniques, and the implementation of policies that promote flexible work arrangements and psychological well-being.

Time zone conflicts, for example, extend beyond scheduling issues to cultural expectations. In Israel, Sunday is a regular workday, whereas in the United States, it is widely observed as a day of rest. Such misalignments can create friction and miscommunication if clear expectations are not set in advance (Glazer, Kożusznik, & Shargo, 2012). Furthermore, language barriers and cultural communication norms, such as high-context versus low-context communication styles, can complicate interactions and cause misunderstandings. Employees in virtual teams often operate in a multilingual environment where linguistic proficiency varies, increasing the likelihood of misinterpretations. Additionally, the absence of face-to-face interactions means that teams must rely on digital tools to establish rapport, maintain engagement, and foster collaboration across cultural and geographic divides (Glazer, Kożusznik, & Shargo, 2012).

KEY STRATEGIES FOR MANAGING CROSS-CULTURAL VIRTUAL TEAMS

Cultural Sensitivity in Talent Acquisition and Onboarding

Recruiting and onboarding gig workers from diverse cultural backgrounds is more than a logistical challenge—it is an opportunity for organizations to foster inclusivity, strengthen collaboration, and build a culturally competent workforce. A culturally sensitive approach to talent acquisition ensures that candidates from diverse backgrounds feel valued and welcomed, setting the foundation for long-term engagement and success. This section explores strategies for culturally responsive recruitment, onboarding, and management, with a focus on leveraging technology and digital tools to enhance inclusivity while mitigating bias in hiring practices.

Cultural Sensitivity in Recruitment

Cultural differences significantly influence how candidates interpret job descriptions, negotiate contracts, and present their qualifications. In collectivistic cultures, such as South Korea, job seekers may respond better to team-oriented language. However, candidates from individualistic cultures, like the United States, maybe more drawn to job postings that emphasize personal achievements. A culturally sensitive hiring strategy acknowledges these differences and adapts recruitment messaging to attract the best talent from diverse cultural backgrounds.

One critical challenge in recruitment is unconscious bias, which can inadvertently affect hiring decisions. While AI-driven applicant tracking systems (ATS) can standardize candidate evaluation and reduce bias, these systems must be carefully programmed to avoid reinforcing existing prejudices. Job postings should also be free from culturally specific jargon or assumptions, ensuring that opportunities remain accessible to all candidates. Additionally, bilingual recruitment materials and translation tools can improve communication and help organizations reach a broader talent pool (Tenorio et al., 2014).

Global Recruitment Strategies

The rise of the gig economy and remote work is reshaping traditional employment models, compelling organizations to reevaluate their strategies for talent acquisition and workforce management (Groenewald et al., 2024). Organizations adopt different global recruitment strategies based on their overarching talent management philosophy. Companies that embrace a geocentric approach seek talent from a global pool, prioritizing skills and qualifications over nationality. In contrast, organizations following an ethnocentric model prefer staffing positions with employees from their home country. At the same time, those using a polycentric strategy adapt to the local recruitment practices of their host country (Caligiuri & Stroh, 1995). For example, South Korean multinational corporations operating in China often adopt a polycentric approach, leveraging local hiring practices to align with regional business norms (Kang & Shen, 2013).

Advancements in digital recruitment tools have further enhanced global hiring capabilities. AI-powered resume screeners allow organizations to assess candidates objectively, while video interview platforms facilitate remote evaluations. However, these technologies must accommodate time zone differences, language barriers, and cultural communication preferences to ensure a fair and inclusive hiring process. Additionally, leveraging region-specific job boards can help companies attract candidates with diverse backgrounds, ensuring that recruitment efforts align with business needs and cultural considerations.

Culturally Adaptable Onboarding

Vaiman et al. (2021) point out that organizations need to ensure "that employees who are located remotely are not disadvantaged in selection for talent programs [this] is another issue organizations will need to resolve in the future" (p. 253). Having an effective onboarding process is essential, as it must be inclusive, culturally aware, and adaptable to the needs of gig workers from different backgrounds. Providing training materials in multiple languages, incorporating visual aids, and using clear, jargon-free instructions can help prevent cultural misunderstandings and support diverse learning styles. New team members should receive a comprehensive overview of the organization's values, mission, and expectations, with particular attention to areas where company policies may contradict their cultural norms.

One effective strategy for fostering inclusion is the buddy system, which pairs new hires with experienced team members from similar cultural backgrounds. These mentorship pairings can ease the transition into the company and facilitate a sense of belonging, particularly for workers who are unfamiliar with the organization's communication norms. Time zone considerations should also be factored into the buddy system to ensure team members can connect in real time without logistical challenges. Additionally, organizations should remain flexible in their use of technology, recognizing that some new hires may require additional support in adapting to digital collaboration tools.

Benefits of Culturally Sensitive Recruitment and Onboarding

A well-designed, culturally sensitive recruitment and onboarding process strengthens an organization's ability to attract, engage, and retain gig workers. When gig workers feel valued and included from the outset, they are more likely to remain engaged and contribute meaningfully to the organization. Culturally aware onboarding fosters stronger team dynamics, enhances collaboration, and improves productivity by ensuring that new hires feel integrated into the company culture.

To enhance cross-cultural integration, organizations can implement cultural sensitivity training for both new hires and existing employees, fostering awareness and inclusivity. A structured mentorship program or buddy system can further support new gig workers, helping them navigate cultural nuances and workplace expectations. Additionally, establishing a feedback mechanism through regular anonymous surveys allows companies to assess their onboarding practices' effectiveness and proactively address concerns. By diversifying the onboarding team to include members from various cultural backgrounds, organizations can ensure that the process is representative and adaptable to different perspectives. As Groenewald et al. (2024) explain, as organizations embrace innovation, foster inclusivity, and prioritize talent development and retention, they "can position themselves for success in attracting, nurturing, and retaining top talent in the years to come" (p. 97).

Building Trust and Collaboration in Cross-Cultural Virtual Teams

Trust is the foundation of any successful team, and in cross-cultural virtual environments, it plays a critical role in ensuring collaboration and productivity. However, building trust among team members with different cultural values, communication styles, and expectations presents unique challenges. The absence of face-to-face interactions, time zone differences, and cultural misunderstandings can hinder relationship-building and create barriers to effective teamwork (Jarvenpaa & Leidner, 1999; Glazer, Kożusznik, & Shargo, 2012). Organizations must adopt intentional strategies that promote transparency, regular engagement, and culturally sensitive conflict resolution to foster trust in virtual teams (Earley & Ang, 2003).

Establishing Trust in Cross-Cultural Virtual Teams

The lack of physical proximity in virtual teams means that members cannot access the nonverbal cues, informal interactions, and contextual understanding that naturally facilitate trust in co-located teams (Cascio & Shurygailo, 2003). To bridge this gap, organizations can use technology to create transparency and inclusivity. Digital collaboration tools such as Slack, Microsoft Teams, and Trello allow teams to centralize communication, ensuring that all members have access to important information and discussions (Klitmøller & Lauring, 2013). A shared documentation hub, where essential documents, project plans, and deadlines are easily accessible, enhances clarity and accountability. Additionally, establishing clear documentation and expectations prevents miscommunication, reinforcing trust among team members (Erez, 2011).

Regular Check-Ins and Ongoing Communication

Consistent and structured communication is essential for maintaining trust in virtual teams. Regular team-wide meetings, whether weekly or biweekly, provide a space for alignment, collaboration, and open discussion (Glazer, Kożusznik, & Shargo, 2012). These meetings allow team members to clarify expectations, share progress updates, and voice concerns in a structured setting.

Beyond group meetings, one-on-one check-ins are equally important in fostering trust, particularly in cross-cultural settings. Personalized interactions offer opportunities for direct feedback, address individual concerns, and help build rapport between managers and team members (Earley & Ang, 2003). Recognizing cultural differences in attitudes toward hierarchy and communication styles ensures that check-ins remain effective (House et al., 2004). For example, employees from cultures that value direct communication may appreciate structured feedback sessions, while those from cultures that favor indirect communication may benefit from a more relationship-oriented approach.

Culturally Sensitive Conflict Resolution

Misunderstandings are inevitable in cross-cultural teams due to differences in values, communication norms, and decision-making processes (Hofstede, 1980; Hall, 1976). Addressing these conflicts promptly and with cultural awareness is key to maintaining trust and collaboration (House et al., 2004).

Understanding cultural context is essential in tailoring conflict resolution strategies. High-context cultures, such as Japan and China, emphasize indirect communication and nonverbal cues, whereas low-context cultures, such as the United States and Germany, prefer direct and explicit communication (Hall, 1976). A conflict resolution approach that aligns with these cultural norms can reduce friction and misunderstandings (Meyer, 2014).

Active listening and mediation can also help navigate conflicts effectively. Encouraging open dialogue where all team members feel heard fosters mutual respect and diffuses tensions (Earley & Ang, 2003). Trained mediators or managers with cultural competence can facilitate discussions to ensure that diverse perspectives are acknowledged and integrated into decision-making (Erez, 2011).

Cultural awareness training provides team members with the skills to navigate cross-cultural interactions more effectively. Organizations can implement workshops on cultural intelligence (CQ) to help employees develop an understanding of different cultural workstyles and communication norms (Earley & Ang, 2003). These sessions equip team members with strategies to collaborate more effectively across cultural divides.

Psychological safety is another crucial element in building trust (Jarvenpaa & Leidner, 1999). Team members should feel comfortable expressing their thoughts, admitting mistakes, and sharing new ideas without fear of judgment or retaliation (Glazer, Kożusznik, & Shargo, 2012). Leaders play a key role in fostering this environment by modeling inclusive behavior, encouraging open discussions, and acknowledging diverse viewpoints (Meyer, 2014).

Cultural Competency and Leadership

Leaders and managers in gig economies must be culturally competent to effectively manage virtual teams. This section will analyze the role of leadership in promoting cultural awareness and inclusion in cross-cultural gig teams. We will discuss the importance of cultural intelligence (CQ) in leadership and how managers can use this skill to navigate cultural differences, motivate diverse teams, and lead virtual gig workers toward successful project outcomes. The gig economy, defined by its reliance on independent contractors and freelancers, has fundamentally reshaped traditional leadership paradigms as a result of being fundamentally different from the traditional workplace setup. Enabled by digital platforms, gig work transcends geographical boundaries, creating virtual teams of workers and leaders from diverse cultural backgrounds. While this diversity offers numerous advantages, such as access to a global talent pool and varied perspectives, it also poses significant challenges for leadership. Leaders and managers in gig economies must demonstrate cultural competency to navigate these complexities and foster an inclusive, productive virtual workforce. This section examines the role of leadership in promoting cultural awareness and inclusion in cross-cultural gig teams, emphasizing the importance of cultural intelligence (CQ) and strategies for motivating and managing diverse teams.

The Role of Leadership in Virtual Teams

Leadership in gig economies extends beyond traditional managerial responsibilities to encompass navigating cultural dynamics in dispersed teams. Virtual gig teams operate with limited face-to-face interaction, making leadership practices reliant on digital tools and culturally inclusive communication (Cascio & Shurygailo, 2003; Adamovic, 2022). Effective leaders must create environments where team members feel valued and understood despite cultural differences. The gig economy's reliance on short-term, project-based engagements requires leaders to quickly establish trust, clarify roles, and align team goals (Jarvenpaa & Leidner, 1999). This becomes increasingly challenging in cross-cultural settings, where misunderstandings rooted in cultural differences can derail collaboration.

Challenges of Leading Cross-Cultural Teams

Key challenges faced by leaders in the gig economy include communication barriers between team members, trust & cohesion in isolated physical locations and the diversity of motivational drivers that exist. The communication barriers manifest themselves because virtual teams rely heavily on digital communication, where nuances such as tone and non-verbal cues are often lost (Hall, 1976). Cultural differences in communication styles can further complicate interactions even before the translation of one language to the next. The cohesiveness of teams starts with trust amongst the members. Building trust in virtual teams is challenging, particularly when cultural norms around trust-building differ (Hofstede, 1980; House et al, 2004). Leaders must bridge these differences to create cohesive teams. The leader's ability to motivate rests in understanding that there are diverse motivational drivers which are based on cultural variations in values, work ethics, and reward preferences that require leaders to adopt tailored approaches to motivation and recognition (Deci & Ryan, 2013).

Defining Cultural Intelligence

Cultural Intelligence (CQ) refers to an individual's ability to function effectively in culturally diverse settings (Earley & Ang, 2003). It encompasses four dimensions namely CQ Drive which is the motivation to learn about and engage with different cultures; CQ Knowledge which is the understanding of cultural norms, values, and practices around the world; CQ Strategy which is the ability to plan and adapt behavior in culturally diverse interactions; and finally CQ Action which is the capacity to communicate and behave appropriately in cross-cultural contexts. For leaders in gig economies, CQ is essential for managing virtual teams and navigating cultural complexities effectively.

The Role of CQ in Leadership

Culturally intelligent leaders can thrive to recognize and respect cultural differences, fostering an inclusive environment. To be effective these leaders will have to adapt their communication and leadership styles to suit diverse team members. To achieve the goals and objectives of the organization leaders also have to mitigate conflicts arising from cultural misunderstandings, while at the same time motivating team members by aligning leadership practices with cultural values. Inclusive leadership involves creating a work environment where team members feel valued, respected, and empowered, regardless of cultural background. Leaders can promote inclusion by encouraging open dialogue by providing platforms for team members to share their perspectives and cultural experiences that fosters mutual understanding (Meyer, 2014). Organizations and by extension leadership should celebrate diversity via recognizing and celebrating cultural differences through team events and practices that enhance inclusivity. The ultimate goal is to provide equal opportunities that ensure fair treatment and opportunities for all team members, builds trust and equity irrespective of location and rank.

Leaders play a critical role in enhancing cultural competency within their teams. Strategies include engaging in Cultural Sensitivity Training, offering training programs that raise awareness of cultural differences and equip team members with intercultural communication skills (Earley & Ang, 2003). A second strategy is to engage in Team Building Activities. Virtual team-building exercises designed to explore cultural diversity can strengthen team cohesion as well as providing mentorship and support to all team members. Assigning culturally competent mentors to guide team members can also facilitate cross-cultural understanding.

Motivating Diverse Teams

Motivation in cross-cultural teams requires an understanding of diverse drivers influenced by cultural norms. For instance, in Individualistic Cultures example the United States workers may value personal achievements and autonomy; while in Collectivist Cultures: Workers from collectivist cultures (e.g., Japan) may prioritize group harmony and shared goals (Triandis, 1995). Leaders must identify these drivers and customize motivational strategies accordingly. Effective motivational strategies in cross-cultural gig teams include the use of Monetary and Non-Monetary Rewards by offering flexible compensation structures that cater to diverse financial expectations and cultural values. Catering to the different types of needs is crucial in fostering the motivating creativity that leads to innovation; Mdhlalose (2024) found that intrinsic rewards have a positive effect on intrinsic motivation while extrinsic non-monetary rewards, and extrinsic monetary rewards, can either encourage or discourage employees' efforts to be creative and innovative. Organizations can include recognition programs whereby recognizing achievements in culturally appropriate ways reinforces motivation. Another major incentive is that of skill development opportunities, in that by providing training and upskilling opportunities can appeal to workers seeking career growth.

Leading Virtual Gig Workers to Success

There is no one size fits all, but there are universal truths in strategies for managing virtual teams, which include clear communication. Leaders must ensure clarity in instructions and expectations, using tools like project management software to streamline workflows. Leaders can empower autonomy by encouraging independent decision-making which aligns with the gig economy's nature while respecting cultural preferences for autonomy or guidance. Leaders are required to provide Frequent Feedback, in providing regular, constructive feedback tailored to cultural norms enhances performance and accountability (Meyer, 2014). Trust is the cornerstone of successful virtual teams. Leaders can build trust by demonstrating reliability via meeting commitments and delivering on promises while encouraging collaboration by facilitating teamwork and knowledge sharing and fostering transparency through the maintenance of open communication about goals, progress, and challenges. Leaders can align cross-cultural gig teams toward successful project outcomes by setting clear, measurable objectives; aligning individual contributions with team goals while leveraging cultural diversity to generate innovative solutions.

Leadership in the gig economy requires cultural competency and the ability to navigate diverse cultural dynamics. By promoting cultural awareness, fostering inclusion, and leveraging cultural intelligence, leaders can overcome challenges associated with managing cross-cultural virtual teams. The successful implementation of these strategies enhances motivation, trust, and collaboration, leading to improved project outcomes. As the gig economy continues to expand, the role of culturally competent leadership will become increasingly critical, underscoring the need for ongoing research and practice in this area.

Managing Performance and Feedback in Cross-Cultural Teams

Performance management in the gig economy is already complex, but when managing cross-cultural teams, additional challenges arise. Different cultures have varying expectations around performance evaluation, feedback, and recognition.

This section will explore how organizations can implement culturally appropriate performance management strategies that take into account the nuances of giving feedback, setting goals, and recognizing achievements in a virtual, cross-cultural workforce. Managing gig workers presents unique challenges, such as the lack of long-term loyalty, minimal engagement with company culture, and the absence of traditional benefits. This section will also examine these obstacles and discuss how organizations can develop creative solutions, such as offering flexible benefits, establishing short-term engagement programs, and using technology to enhance communication and collaboration with gig workers. The gig economy has revolutionized traditional workforce dynamics, enabling organizations to access talent globally. However, managing performance in cross-cultural teams introduces unique challenges. Different cultural expectations around feedback, goal-setting, and recognition can complicate traditional performance management practices. In addition, gig workers often lack long-term loyalty, strong engagement with company culture, and traditional benefits, creating obstacles for fostering sustained productivity and satisfaction. This section examines how organizations can implement culturally appropriate performance management strategies and develop creative solutions to navigate these challenges in the gig economy.

Cultural Influences on Performance Evaluation

Cultural differences significantly impact how performance is perceived and evaluated. Hofstede's cultural dimensions theory (1980) identifies key cultural dimensions that shape these differences. Hofstede's Power Distance dimension shows that in high power distance cultures, hierarchical relationships influence feedback (Hofstede et al., 2010). Employees may expect evaluations to come exclusively from senior managers. Conversely, in low power distance cultures, peer evaluations and collaborative feedback are more common (House et al., 2004). Individualism vs. Collectivism dimension proves that Individualistic cultures prioritize personal achievements in evaluations, while collectivist cultures value team contributions. Cultures with high uncertainty avoidance prefer structured and formal evaluation processes, while those with low uncertainty avoidance may embrace flexible and informal approaches. Masculine cultures often emphasize competition and results, whereas feminine cultures may focus on relationships and employee well-being during evaluations (Hofstede & Bond, 1988; Hofstede et al., 2010).

Long Term versus Short Term Orientation: relate to the choice of focus for people's efforts: the future or the present and past (Hofstede et al., 2010). In the short term oriented, the most important events are now or in the past while in the long term oriented the most important will occur in the future, also demonstrated in spending and savings/investment patterns and hence income reward preferences.

Indulgence versus Restraint: Indulgent cultures prefer immediate gratification and personal life control versus control of basic human desires related to enjoying life and lower importance of leisure (Hofstede et al., 2010). In performance evaluations it will impact the concept and feeling of personal control versus the perception of helplessness around events.

Challenges in Providing Feedback

The process of giving feedback is another area where cultural norms play a critical role. In low-context cultures, such as the United States, feedback tends to be direct and explicit. However, in high-context cultures, such as Japan, indirect feedback is more common, relying on non-verbal cues and implied suggestions (Hall, 1976). Misalignments in feedback styles can lead to misunderstandings and resistance (Mdhlalose, 2024). For example, a manager from a low-context culture providing direct feedback to a worker from a high-context culture might inadvertently cause offense. Conversely, an indirect approach might confuse workers who are accustomed to explicit communication.

Strategies for Culturally Appropriate Performance Management

Organizations and leaders need to recognize the need for customizing feedback methods to match or closely align to the recipient's cultural framework. Organizations should tailor feedback approaches to align with cultural expectations. Leaders should adapt their style based on cultural norms, providing explicit feedback where it is valued and using more nuanced approaches in high-context cultures - the dichotomy between direct versus indirect feedback. Another strategy is to balance positive and negative feedback because cultures differ in their tolerance for constructive criticism. In cultures with high power distance, feedback should be respectful and framed positively to avoid loss of face (Mdhlalose, 2024; Meyer, 2014). The strategy of using technology for feedback, the myriad of available digital tools such as performance dashboards and anonymous feedback platforms can facilitate culturally sensitive feedback by offering objective data and depersonalizing critiques (Mdhlalose, 2024).

The next big challenge related to feedback starts with goal-setting in cross-cultural teams, in that Effective performance management in gig teams requires culturally aware goal-setting practices via culturally aligned goals, for example Individualistic cultures may favor individual performance targets, while collectivist cultures may respond better to team-oriented goals (Hofstede et al., 2010). There are SMART goals with flexibility: Specific, Measurable, Achievable, Relevant, and Time-bound. (SMART) goals provide structure but should allow flexibility to account for cultural differences in work pace and priorities - the caveat here is the flexibility. Finally, the key component, collaborative goal-setting by engaging workers in the goal-setting process, fosters alignment with multiple cultural values and enhances commitment by a broader base of team members (House et al., 2004).

Next there is the challenge of recognizing achievements across cultures. Recognition is a powerful motivator, but its impact depends on cultural preferences given that public vs. private recognition can have differing outcomes in the workplace (Mdhlalose, 2024). Workers from collectivist cultures may prefer private recognition to avoid drawing attention, whereas individualistic cultures may value public acknowledgment. The monetary and non-monetary rewards schemes again require that the organization is providing culturally appropriate rewards, such as flexible schedules or skill development opportunities, enhances worker satisfaction. Finally, the cultural celebrations, the simple act of recognizing culturally significant events and incorporating them into team activities can strengthen inclusivity and engagement.

There are additional challenges that arise that are unique to the gig economy like overcoming the lack of long-term loyalty, in that gig workers often lack a sense of loyalty due to the temporary nature of their engagements. To address this, organizations can engage in short-term engagement programs for example, organizations can implement project-based engagement strategies that foster a sense of achievement and alignment with company goals. Organizations can build trust through transparency by clearly communicating expectations, compensation structures, and project outcomes which builds trust and encourages commitment. Encourage personalized interaction by treating gig workers as valued team members through regular check-ins and personalized feedback enhances their sense of belonging. This can be achieved by enhancing engagement with company culture given that gig workers typically have limited interaction with company culture which can hinder their engagement. Strategies to counteract this include virtual onboarding via Introducing gig workers to the organization's mission, values, and culture through virtual onboarding programs creates a sense of connection. Learning entwined with cultural integration and employee engagement with the use of virtual podiums and remote processes ensures success (Singh, Walia & Singh, 2025). The use of cultural ambassadors who are designated full-time employees who can act as cultural ambassadors to mentor and guide gig workers will foster a sense of inclusion. Team-Building activities, these virtual team-building exercises, such as cultural exchange sessions, promote collaboration and cultural understanding. Going a step further by providing flexible benefits, which can be deemed necessary, because the traditional benefits are often absent in the gig economy, but offering alternative perks can enhance worker satisfaction. Some possible flexible benefits include wellness programs, by providing access to health and wellness resources, even on a temporary basis, supports worker well-being. Another benefit is the all-important skill development opportunities since offering online training and certifications adds value for gig workers and strengthens their relationship with the organization. Then there is the incentive-based compensation which by structuring compensation to include performance-based incentives aligns with workers' efforts and cultural preferences. External monetary intervention can supplant intrinsic motivation in that workers driven by intrinsic motivation increase their productivity after a change of the monetary rewards scheme from fixed payment to piece-rate payment (Mourelatos, Giannakopoulos, & Tzagarakis, 2024).

The Role of Technology in Enhancing Collaboration

Technology plays a pivotal role in managing cross-cultural gig teams by facilitating communication, collaboration, and performance tracking via Digital Communication Platforms within which Tools like Slack, Microsoft Teams, and Zoom enable seamless communication across time zones and cultures. The reliance on Project Management Software with platforms such as Asana and Trello help organize tasks, set goals, and track progress, ensuring clarity and accountability. Data-Driven Feedback is driven by Analytics tools which provide objective insights into worker performance, reducing cultural biases in evaluations. Virtual Recognition Systems with Platforms that allow peer recognition and virtual awards promote inclusivity and engagement.

Creative Solutions for Cross-Cultural Performance Management

The creativity of cross-cultural performance management rests within Hybrid Feedback Models which have the ability to combine structured feedback with informal conversations creating a balanced approach that accommodates cultural preferences (Mdhlalose, 2024). For example, managers can use regular performance dashboards for objective feedback while scheduling informal virtual meetings to address cultural nuances. This can be incorporated with the Gamification of Performance Metrics by gamifying performance metrics through leaderboards, badges, and rewards adds an element of fun and motivation. Gamification found to enhance engagement, accelerate employee integration, boost learning outcomes, increase performance and goal attainment, foster a positive organizational culture, and motivate talent development and career advancement, but at the same time brings challenges such as fairness, accessibility, gaming the system, unintended consequences, and unethical practices (Sharma, et al. 2024). Gamification can be tailored to suit cultural preferences, such as emphasizing individual achievements or team contributions or even a combination of both individual and team. Continuous learning and development by providing gig workers with access to continuous learning opportunities not only improves their skills but also enhances their engagement (Mdhlalose, 2024). Organizations can offer culturally relevant training programs to address specific challenges and promote intercultural competence. Managing performance and feedback in cross-cultural teams requires a nuanced understanding of cultural dynamics and innovative approaches to overcome gig economy-specific challenges. By implementing culturally appropriate strategies for feedback, goal setting, and recognition, organizations can enhance worker satisfaction and productivity. Addressing issues such as the lack of long-term loyalty and limited engagement with company culture through creative solutions further strengthens the effectiveness of performance management in gig teams. As the gig economy continues to grow, organizations must prioritize cultural competency and leverage technology to build inclusive and collaborative work environments.

Technology as an Enabler of Cross-Cultural Virtual Team Management

Technology plays an essential role in managing cross-cultural virtual teams in gig economies. As team members are often spread across different time zones, cultures, and geographical regions, digital tools and platforms become indispensable for overcoming communication barriers, fostering collaboration, and maintaining engagement. As Groenewald et al. (2024) point out the "rise of digital technologies is revolutionizing HR practices, offering new tools and platforms for talent acquisition, development, and engagement" (p.94). The right selection and implementation of technology can significantly enhance team cohesion and ensure smooth workflow integration. This section explores how organizations can leverage technological solutions to optimize communication, collaboration, and inclusivity among culturally diverse team members.

Overcoming Communication Barriers

One of the most significant challenges in managing cross-cultural virtual teams is communication. Differences in language, communication styles, and cultural norms can create misunderstandings and hinder productivity. Regional dialects, variations in expression, and differing interpretations of tone further complicate interactions. To mitigate these challenges, organizations must select digital platforms that facilitate clarity and engagement. Research by Klitmøller & Lauring (2013) found that the effectiveness of digital communication tools varies across cultures, with some preferring detailed written communication while others rely more on verbal and visual cues. This aligns with Hall's (1976) findings on low-context and high-context communication preferences. Video conferencing tools such as Zoom, Google Meet, and Microsoft Teams enable real-time discussions, allowing for visual cues that help bridge cultural differences. Instant messaging platforms, including

Slack and Discord, provide quick and efficient communication but require careful use, as text-based conversations often fail to convey tone and emotion accurately, leading to potential misinterpretations.

Another challenge posed by digital communication is the blurring of work and personal boundaries. Without clear guidelines, constant connectivity can lead to stress and burnout. Remote work stress is often exacerbated by unclear boundaries between professional and personal life, as highlighted by Glazer, Kożusznik, & Shargo (2012). Organizations can address this by implementing policies that define expectations for response times and availability, ensuring that employees can maintain a healthy work-life balance. Additionally, informal interactions—often lost in virtual settings—can be supported through dedicated channels for casual conversations, fostering rapport and a sense of community among team members.

Enhancing Team Cohesion

Technology also serves as a catalyst for building stronger relationships within virtual teams. Collaborative platforms such as Trello and Microsoft Teams facilitate real-time project tracking, idea-sharing, and workflow management, allowing dispersed team members to engage in tasks seamlessly. By providing a centralized space for discussion, document sharing, and progress monitoring, these tools help create a sense of presence and shared responsibility, reinforcing team cohesion despite physical distance.

Jarvenpaa & Leidner (1999) emphasize that trust in global virtual teams is strengthened through transparency and frequent communication, both of which can be supported by digital tools. Virtual spaces where team members can engage informally or participate in non-work-related discussions also contribute to a positive team culture. These interactions mimic in-office experiences, strengthening relationships and reducing the social isolation that remote workers sometimes face. When used effectively, technology fosters trust and inclusion, creating an environment where individuals feel valued and motivated to contribute.

As Caligiuri & Stroh (1995) emphasize, multinational corporations that integrate local responsiveness into their global strategies tend to be more successful than those that rely solely on ethnocentric approaches, highlighting the importance of adaptability in fostering effective team dynamics. By leveraging technology to create inclusive, culturally aware virtual spaces, organizations can enhance collaboration and trust, ensuring their teams remain engaged and high-performing despite geographical dispersion.

Accommodating Cultural Preferences and Work Styles

An essential consideration in managing culturally diverse virtual teams is selecting technology that aligns with the needs and preferences of gig workers. Many gig workers prefer flexible work schedules, making asynchronous communication tools particularly valuable. Platforms that allow for message boards, recorded video updates, and document collaboration, such as Google Docs or Notion, enable team members to engage at their own pace, regardless of time zone differences.

Cultural factors also influence how employees interact with technology. Meyer (2014) discusses how different cultures approach communication and decision-making in digital environments, with some preferring written documentation while others favor face-to-face engagement. In some cultures, written communication is preferred over verbal discussions, while others prioritize face-to-face interaction, even in virtual settings. Understanding these preferences helps organizations create a balanced communication strategy that accommodates all team members. Providing multilingual documentation, translation tools, and culturally adaptive communication methods ensures that every worker can engage effectively.

Beyond communication, sustainability in work practices is becoming an important consideration for gig workers. While *Kant et al. (2025)* focus on eco-innovation within SMEs in the Horn of Africa, their findings on sustainability can be extrapolated to gig work. As environmental and social governance (ESG) initiatives gain prominence in global business models, gig platforms may need to integrate sustainable work practices into their operations. Future research could explore whether freelancers prioritize ESG-aligned job opportunities and how platforms can incorporate sustainable initiatives—such as green workspaces, carbon offset programs, or ethical sourcing—into their talent management strategies.

Guidelines and Training for Effective Technology Use

Implementing technology effectively requires more than just selecting the right tools—it also involves ensuring that all team members have the knowledge and confidence to use them. Mangla (2021) found that cultural intelligence (CQ) plays a significant role in how employees adapt to digital tools in a cross-cultural setting, emphasizing the need for structured training programs. Organizations should provide training programs that familiarize employees with communication and project management software. This reduces frustration and increases productivity, allowing individuals to focus on their tasks rather than struggle with unfamiliar systems.

Establishing clear communication guidelines is equally important. House et al. (2004) highlight how power distance influences communication styles, with some cultures expecting structured guidelines while others favor flexible, informal exchanges. Expectations for response times, meeting participation, and message formatting should be clearly defined while remaining flexible to accommodate cultural differences. Encouraging an open, inclusive digital environment helps employees feel comfortable engaging with team members and contributing to discussions.

SOLUTIONS AND RECOMMENDATIONS

Retaining Gig Talent

Retaining gig workers is not about long-term contracts but rather about building a reputation as a desirable company to work with. We will discuss strategies for ensuring repeat engagement, such as offering competitive pay, fostering positive working relationships, and creating opportunities for professional growth and skill-building. In the gig economy, many workers take responsibility for their own career development, skill acquisition, and job search. This section will also explore the gig worker's perspective, analyzing how they navigate a decentralized employment environment, find new opportunities, and manage personal development without traditional HR support. The gig economy has reshaped the traditional employer-employee relationship. Gig workers, who operate as independent contractors, prioritize flexibility, autonomy, and project-based engagement. For companies, retaining gig talent is less about enforcing long-term contracts and more about building a reputation as a desirable and fair organization to work with. Successful retention strategies include offering competitive pay, fostering positive relationships, and creating opportunities for professional growth and skill development. From the gig worker's perspective, the decentralized employment environment necessitates self-directed career management, skill acquisition, and job search strategies. This section explores strategies for retaining gig workers and examines how they navigate the challenges of the gig economy.

The Importance of Retaining Gig Talent

Retaining gig talent offers numerous benefits to organizations and the importance is highlighted by the following, having continuity and expertise in that retaining skilled gig workers reduces onboarding time and ensures consistent project quality (Kuhn & Maleki, 2017). The cost-effectiveness as frequent turnover increases recruitment and training costs, while retaining talent minimizes these expenses. Invaluable reputation building as companies with a reputation for treating gig workers fairly attract high-quality talent and will maintain a competitive edge. Retention in the gig economy differs from traditional employment. It relies on ensuring repeat engagement, creating a positive work experience, and fostering loyalty through non-binding incentives.

Organizational Strategies for Retaining Gig Talent

Competitive compensation remains a cornerstone of retention and its first strategic pillar. Gig workers value fair and timely pay, particularly in an environment where their income is often unpredictable (Katz & Krueger, 2019). Companies can implement the following strategies, transparent pay structures by clearly communicating pay rates and payment schedules builds trust; and tied to this having performance-based incentives which by offering bonuses or additional compensation for exceptional performance motivates workers and fosters loyalty. The organizations need to pay market-competitive rates, which can be achieved by regularly benchmarking pay against industry standards ensures fairness and attracts top talent (Mdhlalose, 2024).

The second pillar moves beyond the scope of the monetary, strong working relationships enhance gig workers' satisfaction and likelihood of returning for future projects. This can be accomplished by having open communication via maintaining transparent and respectful communication creating a positive work environment; coupled with fair recognition and appreciation by acknowledging gig workers' contributions fosters goodwill and strengthens relationships. A strong conflict resolution mechanism in order to establish processes for addressing grievances ensures fairness and builds trust. The third pillar revolves around providing opportunities for professional growth as gig workers often value skill development and career progression (Sharma et al., 2024). Companies can support this pillar by having skill-building programs offering access to training and certification programs enhances gig workers' marketability and strengthens their relationship with the organization. Offering challenging projects assigning tasks that allow workers to expand their expertise increases engagement and satisfaction. Having mentorship opportunities by connecting gig workers with mentors fosters professional development and long-term loyalty. The fourth pillar is to create a sense of community as gig workers often operate in isolation, lacking the sense of belonging associated with traditional workplaces. Organizations can foster community by hosting virtual events, these regular team-building activities or webinars promote interaction and inclusivity (Sharma et al., 2024). Encouraging collaboration by designing projects that require teamwork fosters connections among gig workers. Celebrating milestones by recognizing individual and collective achievements creates a sense of shared success. The fifth pillar of building a strong employer brand creating a positive reputation is critical for attracting and retaining gig talent through the publicizing of success stories that is sharing testimonials from satisfied gig workers enhances the company's image. Also maintaining ethical practices by demonstrating commitment to fairness, diversity, and inclusivity strengthens the company's brand. The employer can leverage technology, using user-friendly platforms for project management and payment processing reinforces a professional and reliable image (Sharma et al., 2024). Technology that can be leveraged from the recruitment stage using AI-driven recruitment, virtual collaboration tools, and digital HR platforms which has redefined human resource management in gig economies; where technology is a crucial enabler in managing decentralized and flexible workforces (Talukder, Chowdhury, & Khan 2025). However, further research is needed to determine how effectively these innovations balance flexibility with workforce stability and how they impact long-term job satisfaction and retention in the gig economy.

The Gig Worker's Perspective on retention

Gig workers operate in a decentralized labor market, relying on multiple platforms and networks to secure opportunities. The gig workers strategies include building a personal brand as gig workers often invest in creating a professional online presence through platforms like LinkedIn and Upwork to secure continuous workflow. Networking plays a crucial role in cultivating relationships with clients and peers and helps workers access repeat engagements and referrals. Portfolio development by maintaining an updated portfolio showcasing past projects enhances credibility and marketability amongst the hiring organizations. This approach essentially allows the gig worker to take responsibility for their own career development in the absence of traditional HR support; this lack of traditional support dovetails with five pillars previously outlined for organizations in that gig workers must independently manage their professional growth by Skill Acquisition as Workers often enroll in online courses or attend workshops to stay competitive in their fields (Sundararajan, 2016). Acquiring industry-relevant certifications boosts credibility and expands job opportunities boosting learning from experience with insights gained from diverse projects enhancing adaptability and expertise.

Full time gig workers rely on various methods to secure new opportunities and projects, firstly by using digital Platforms like online marketplaces like Fiverr and Freelancer provide access to global clients. The use of Social Media platforms such as LinkedIn enable workers to showcase skills and connect with potential clients. And the age-old Word of Mouth by building a network of satisfied clients often leads to repeat engagements and referrals. Balancing flexibility and stability is a critical appeal of gig workers, while flexibility is a key appeal of gig work, it often comes at the cost of financial stability (Brailovskaya, 2023). Gig workers navigate this trade-off by diversifying income sources through engaging in multiple projects simultaneously reduces dependency on a single client, as well as budgeting and financial planning in that they are managing irregular income streams through careful financial planning ensures stability.

Organizational Challenges in Retaining Gig Talent

Organizations face several challenges in retaining gig workers which can be classified into three areas, firstly the lack of long-term loyalty in that gig workers' independence and short-term engagements make it difficult to foster loyalty. Companies must create value beyond monetary compensation to retain top talent in order to combat this. Secondly, minimal engagement with Company Culture due to their limited exposure to company culture, reducing their emotional connection to the organization. Seshasai, Raja, & Kumar (2025) argue that recruitment and retention must be viewed as interconnected processes for sustainable talent management. This supports the need for standardized onboarding and development frameworks in gig work that enhance freelancer commitment and reduce attrition. Building engagement through inclusive practices and communication is essential. Thirdly, the absence of traditional benefits, unlike full-time employees, gig workers typically lack access to benefits such as health insurance and retirement plans. Offering alternative benefits can enhance satisfaction and loyalty. Future research could explore whether gig platforms benefit from structured career progression models or if freelancers prefer independent career trajectories.

Creative solutions for retaining gig talent lies again in harnessing the diversity of cultures and norms through flexible benefits programs which by providing non-traditional benefits tailored to gig workers' needs can enhance retention with items like but not limited to, health and wellness perks which can be as simple as offering discounted access to fitness programs or health insurance plans supports worker well-being. Financial planning tools in the form of providing resources for managing irregular income helps workers achieve financial stability. Offering skill development grants by way of offering subsidies for professional training or certifications demonstrates commitment to workers' growth (Mdhlalose, 2024; Sharma et al., 2024).

Organizations should develop programs that provide clear value during short-term engagements fostering loyalty via feedback, performance and recognition platforms. Implementing virtual recognition systems allows peers and managers to acknowledge gig workers' contributions (Sharma et al., 2024). Having a feedback mechanism whereby soliciting and acting on gig workers' feedback creates a sense of involvement and trust, which can be structured into performance incentives where structuring compensation to reward consistent quality and timeliness encourages repeat engagement (Mdhlalose, 2024).

Organizations can leverage technology to streamline retention efforts by facilitating communication with tools like Slack and Zoom to enable seamless interaction between gig workers and managers. Technology is used for tracking performance via performance analytics platforms which provide insights that inform recognition and development initiatives (Sharma et al., 2024). Finally creating engagement hubs using virtual platforms for team interaction foster a sense of belonging and collaboration. Retaining gig talent in the decentralized gig economy requires a shift in focus from long-term contracts to building a positive and supportive work environment. Strategies such as offering competitive pay, fostering strong relationships, and providing opportunities for professional growth enhance worker satisfaction and encourage repeat engagements (Mdhlalose, 2024). From the gig worker's perspective, navigating the decentralized employment landscape requires proactive career management, skill acquisition, and networking. By understanding and addressing these dynamics, organizations can build lasting relationships with gig workers and thrive in the evolving labor market.

CONCLUSION

This chapter explored the key challenges and opportunities of managing cross-cultural virtual teams in gig economies. The increasing reliance on digital platforms to manage global talent in gig economies, as Bari and Virgilio (2025) noted, presents a growing need for research on cross-cultural virtual teams. While existing studies have explored practical applications, future research should focus on refining frameworks for talent management, particularly the long-term impact of cultural adaptation strategies on freelancer retention and engagement. This chapter highlights the importance of cultural sensitivity, effective communication, and the use of technology in overcoming these challenges and achieving optimal performance from gig workers. Platforms like Upwork and Airbnb have implemented diversity initiatives and training, but their effectiveness over time remains uncertain. Investigating how strategies such as diversity certification badges or cultural sensitivity training influence freelancer success rates and team cohesion can provide valuable insights for improving global workforce integration.

Abdulmatin et al. (2025) make an interesting point about the rise of remote work and flexible schedules, which has significantly reshaped talent management and forced companies to rethink traditional workflows and adapt their strategies. This shift aligns with the need for companies to be more responsive to evolving workforce dynamics. As a result, another key area for exploration is the balance between standardized processes and innovation in gig work. While structured workflows promote efficiency, rigid structures may hinder creativity and adaptability (Mdhlalose, 2024).

Future studies could examine whether incorporating local responsiveness into global strategies enhances team dynamics and overall performance.

This chapter outlines future trends, including the increasing use of digital platforms, Artificial Intelligence, the growing importance of worker flexibility, and the evolution of HR strategies to accommodate this fast-growing workforce model as areas needing future research. Additionally, the evolving role of technology—including AI-driven hiring tools, virtual reality collaboration, and automated translation services—requires further research to understand its impact on team cohesion, decision-making, and engagement. Exploring scalable diversity and inclusion models for smaller organizations and emerging gig platforms is also crucial. Addressing these questions will advance academic discourse and offer practical solutions for organizations navigating the complexities of global gig work.

Anitha & Amala (2025) emphasize how workplace transformation, driven by globalization, automation, and remote work, is reshaping talent retention strategies. This aligns with the discussion on how gig platforms must adapt recruitment and engagement methods to cater to a multigenerational workforce. Future research should examine whether generational preferences impact freelancer retention rates and how platforms can tailor their talent management strategies to accommodate diverse workforce expectations. The potential practical applications of culturally sensitive talent management in the growing gig economy is showcased as a possible competitive tool also creating new avenues for innovative cross-cultural research. This chapter showcased ways to harness the potential of the gig worker from anywhere in the world as the gig economy continues to expand and reshape the global labor market with different ways to create high engagement, better communication, collaboration, accountability, performance and most importantly successful project outcomes for the organization.

Competing Interests

The authors of this publication declare that there are no competing interests.

Funding

This research received no specific grant from any funding agency in the public, commercial, or not-for-profit sectors. The costs associated with this research were covered by the authors of the article.

REFERENCES

Abdulmatin, A. L., Makhija, G., Bhandari, G. B., Raj, H., & Shylashree, N. (2025). Hiring and Keeping Talent in a Time of Transformation and Staff Empowerment. In *Innovative Recruitment and Retention for Employee Empowerment* (pp. 211–242). IGI Global Scientific Publishing., DOI: 10.4018/979-8-3693-6602-8.ch008

Adamovic, M. (2022). How does employee cultural background influence the effects of telework on job stress? The roles of power distance, individualism, and beliefs about telework. *International Journal of Information Management*, *62*, 102437. DOI: 10.1016/j.ijinfomgt.2021.102437

Agbanyo, G. K., & Shi, M. (2024). The Moderating Effect of Management Polychronicity and Knowledge Sharing on Career Sustainability in the Work-from-Anywhere New Normal—From a Social Exchange Theory Perspective. *Sustainability (Basel)*, *16*(8), 3302. DOI: 10.3390/su16083302

Anitha, K., & Amala, J. (2025). Future of Work: Generations and Retaining Talent Focus. In *Modern Trends and Future Innovation in Human Resource Management* (pp. 239–258). IGI Global., DOI: 10.4018/979-8-3693-6402-4.ch008

Bari, M. W., & Di Virgilio, F. (Eds.). (2025). *Handbook of Talent Management and Learning Organizations: A Post-Pandemic Perspective*. CRC Press., DOI: 10.1201/9781003429890

Brailovskaya, V. (2023). Digital Labor Gig Economy From the Worker's Perspective: A Literature. https://www.idinsight.org/wp-content/uploads/2024/01/PUBLIC-Digital-Labor-Gig-Economy-From-the-Workers-Perspective_-A-Literature-Review-.pdf

Caligiuri, P. M., & Stroh, L. K. (1995). Multinational corporation management strategies and international human resources practices: Bringing IHRM to the bottom line. *International Journal of Human Resource Management, 6*(3), 494–507. DOI: 10.1080/09585199500000032

Cascio, W. F., & Shurygailo, S. (2003). E-leadership and virtual teams. *Organizational Dynamics, 31*(4), 362–376. DOI: 10.1016/S0090-2616(02)00130-4

Charles, R. N. (2008). *Motivation and job satisfaction: The implications of context and national culture in Grenada, St. Vincent & the Grenadines and St. Lucia.* Nova Southeastern University.https://www.proquest.com/openview/5d7a46f35715706c2f9673dcd97f6cbe/1?pq-origsite=gscholar&cbl=18750

Deci, E. L., & Ryan, R. M. (2013). *Intrinsic motivation and self-determination in human behavior*. Springer Science & Business Media., DOI: 10.1007/978-1-4899-2271-7

Earley, P. C., & Ang, S. (2003). *Cultural intelligence: Individual interactions across cultures*. Stanford University Press., DOI: 10.1515/9780804766005

Erez, M. (2011). Cross-cultural and global issues in organizational psychology. In S. Zedeck (Ed.), *APA handbook of industrial and organizational psychology, Vol. 3. Maintaining, expanding, and contracting the organization* (pp. 807–854). American Psychological Association. DOI: 10.1037/12171-023

Glazer, S., Kożusznik, M. W., & Shargo, I. A. (2012). Global virtual teams: A cure for–or a cause of–stress. In *The role of the economic crisis on occupational stress and well-being* (pp. 213–266). Emerald Group Publishing Limited., DOI: 10.1108/S1479-3555(2012)0000010010

Groenewald, E., Groenewald, C. A., Kilag, O. K., Andrin, G., Pernites, M. J., & Macapaz, M. K. (2024). Talent Management in the 21st Century: A Comprehensive Review and Prospects for Innovation. *International Multidisciplinary Journal of Research for Innovation, Sustainability, and Excellence (IMJRISE), 1*(3), 93-99. https://risejournals.org/index.php/imjrise/article/view/188

Hall, E. T. (1976). *Beyond culture*. Anchor Books.

Hofstede, G. (1980). *Culture's consequences: International differences in work-related values*. Sage Publications., DOI: 10.1002/job.4030030208

Hofstede, G., & Bond, M. H. (1988). The Confucius connection: From cultural roots to economic growth. *Organizational Dynamics, 16*(4), 4–21. DOI: 10.1016/0090-2616(88)90009-5

Hofstede, G., Hofstede, G. J., & Minkov, M. (2010). *Cultures and Organizations: Software of the Mind* (Rev. 3rd ed.). McGraw-Hill., DOI: 10.1002/hrdq.3920040314

House, R. J., Hanges, P. J., Javidan, M., Dorfman, P. W., & Gupta, V. (Eds.). (2004). *Culture, leadership, and organizations: The GLOBE study of 62 societies*. Sage., DOI: 10.5465/ame.2005.16965495

Jarvenpaa, S. L., & Leidner, D. E. (1999). Communication and trust in global virtual teams. *Organization Science, 10*(6), 791–815. DOI: 10.1287/orsc.10.6.791

Kang, H., & Shen, J. (2013). International recruitment and selection practices of South Korean multinationals in China. *International Journal of Human Resource Management, 24*(17), 3325–3342. DOI: 10.1080/09585192.2013.770777

Kant, S., Adula, M., Kumari, M., & Nimbrain, N. (2025). Role of SMEs in Greening the Economy by Mediation of Eco-Innovation in the Horn of Africa. In *Examining Green Human Resources Management and Nascent Entrepreneurship* (pp. 173–200). IGI Global., DOI: 10.4018/979-8-3693-7046-9.ch007

Katz, L. F., & Krueger, A. B. (2019). The rise and nature of alternative work arrangements in the United States, 1995–2015. *Industrial & Labor Relations Review, 72*(2), 382–416. DOI: 10.1177/0019793918820008

Klitmøller, A., & Lauring, J. (2013). When global virtual teams share knowledge: Media richness, cultural difference, and language commonality. *Journal of World Business, 48*(3), 398–406. DOI: 10.1016/j.jwb.2012.07.023

Kuhn, K. M., & Maleki, A. (2017). Micro-entrepreneurs, dependent contractors, and instaserfs: Understanding online labor platform workforces. *The Academy of Management Perspectives, 31*(3), 183–200. DOI: 10.5465/amp.2015.0111

Langaas, M., & Mujtaba, B. G. (2023). Communication across cultures in the workplace: Swimming in Scandinavian waters. *Open Journal of Social Sciences, 11*(4), 174–192. DOI: 10.4236/jss.2023.114014

Mangla, N. (2021). Working in a pandemic and post-pandemic period–Cultural intelligence is the key. *International Journal of Cross Cultural Management, 21*(1), 53–69. DOI: 10.1177/14705958211002877

Mdhlalose, D. (2024). An examination of employee rewards and work environment on employee creativity and innovation. *SEISENSE Journal of Management, 7*(1), 21–34. DOI: 10.33215/rewfe541

Meyer, E. (2014). *The culture map: Breaking through the invisible boundaries of global business*. PublicAffairs., DOI: 10.15733/jast.2018.76.243

Mourelatos, E., Giannakopoulos, N., & Tzagarakis, M. (2024). Payment schemes in online labour markets. Does incentive and personality matter? *Behaviour & Information Technology, 43*(11), 2544–2565. DOI: 10.1080/0144929X.2023.2254853

Saks, A. M. (2006). Antecedents and consequences of employee engagement. *Journal of Managerial Psychology, 21*(7), 600–619. DOI: 10.1108/02683940610690169

Seshasai, S. J., Raja, R. V., & Kumar, G. (2025). The Two Sides of the Coin: Optimizing Recruitment and Retention for Sustainable Talent Management. In *Innovative Recruitment and Retention for Employee Empowerment* (pp. 309-328). IGI Global Scientific Publishing. DOI: 10.4018/979-8-3693-6602-8.ch012

Sharma, B., Arora, P., Budhiraja, M., Sharma, K., Kumar, S., Gupta, N., & Kumari, S. (2024). " A Systematic Literature Review of Gamification Applications in Human Resource Processes: Insights, Trends, and Future Directions". *Library of Progress-Library Science, Information Technology & Computer, 44*(3). https://bpasjournals.com/library-science/index.php/journal/article/view/2475

Singh, G., Walia, J. S., & Singh, A. (2025). Virtual Onboarding: Crafting Immersive Introduction Experiences for New Hires. In *The Future of HRM in a World of Persistent Virtual Reality* (pp. 281-303). Emerald Publishing Limited. DOI: 10.1108/978-1-83662-110-220251012

Sundararajan, A. (2016). *The sharing economy: The end of employment and the rise of crowd-based capitalism*. MIT Press., DOI: 10.3917/rimhe.035.0092

Talukder, M. B., Chowdhury, S. A., & Khan, M. R. (2025). The Gig Economy: Economic Innovations and Technological Advancements in Human Resource Management. In *Economic Innovations and Technological Developments in HRM* (pp. 381-404). IGI Global. DOI: 10.4018/979-8-3693-4412-5.ch015

Tannen, D. (1990). *You just don't Understand Women and men in conversation*. Ballantine Books., DOI: 10.1017/S0047404500015372

Tenorio, S. L., O'Donnell, C. I., Hernandez, J., Rozjabek, H. M., Lynch, D., & Marcus, P. M. (2014). Culturally sensitive approaches to recruitment and retention of Hispanics in the national lung screening trial. *Journal of Immigrant and Minority Health, 16*(4), 761–764. DOI: 10.1007/s10903-013-9862-0 PMID: 23780349

Triandis, H. C. (1995). *Individualism & collectivism*. Westview Press.

Vaiman, V., Cascio, W. F., Collings, D. G., & Swider, B. W. (2021). The shifting boundaries of talent management. *Human Resource Management, 60*(2), 253–257. Advance online publication. DOI: 10.1002/hrm.22050

KEY TERMS AND DEFINITIONS

Cross-Cultural Management: The process of leading and coordinating a diverse workforce by understanding and integrating cultural differences in values, communication, and work styles to enhance collaboration and organizational effectiveness.

Cultural Intelligence (CQ): The ability to function effectively in culturally diverse settings by adapting behaviors, communication, and decision-making to align with different cultural norms and expectations.

Cultural Sensitivity: The awareness and ability to recognize, respect, and adapt to cultural differences in communication, leadership, and work practices to enhance inclusivity and collaboration.

Extrinsic Motivation: Motivation driven by external factors such as monetary rewards, promotions, recognition, or other tangible incentives, rather than personal satisfaction or intrinsic enjoyment of the task.

Gig Economy: A labor market characterized by short-term, flexible work arrangements where individuals engage in freelance, contract, or on-demand jobs, often facilitated by digital platforms.

Intrinsic Motivation: The internal drive to perform a task or engage in an activity for personal satisfaction, interest, or the inherent joy of learning and achieving, rather than for external rewards.

Virtual Team Management: The practice of leading remote teams across different locations and time zones using digital tools, fostering trust, and ensuring effective communication and collaboration.

Chapter 7
Talent Management in the Gig Economy: Leveraging Workforce Strategies in the Digital Age

Tanya Rabban
https://orcid.org/0009-0009-5925-8384
Chandigarh University, India

Rohan Singh
Chandigarh University, India

ABSTRACT

The rapid transition in the gig economy has driven a requirement for innovative talent management strategies in order to address the challenges as well as opportunities. This chapter focuses on talent management in the context of gig economy, with recruitment, engagement and retention of the gig workers, especially food delivery and taxi drivers. It explores the role of digital platforms and Industry 4.0 technologies for reshaping the conventional HR practices to meet the dynamic workforce's demands. Talent management plays an interplay within flexibility, job satisfaction as well as sustainable development because it drives global business to gain competitive support for the development and dealing with the difficulties which are posed by the gig economy. This chapter also offers insights for human resource managers, stakeholders and policymakers for development of an equitable and sustainable gig economy.

DOI: 10.4018/979-8-3693-9385-7.ch007

INTRODUCTION

With the transformative force, the gig economy has emerged in the global labour market and the essential work methods. Gig work is a short-term contract and freelance arrangement with massive growth, especially in the ride-hailing and food delivery sectors. The rise of the gig economy has increased independence and autonomy and the widespread usage of digital platforms (Moloto, 2023) The nature of the gig worker is short-term contracts and flexible hours, which requires a more radical shift in how human resources management approaches recruitment, engagement, performance management, and retention (Debgupta et al, 2024). The gig economy has emerged in the flexibility of work arrangements and short-term engagement, primarily which are possible through digital platforms. The gig economy encompasses different forms of work, including freelancing, micro jobs, and professional services. The diversity offers the workers significant autonomy and flexibility, allowing them to tailor their work experiences to their personal preferences and circumstances (Jaiswal et al., 2020).

The gig workers are a heterogeneous group with a broader range of individuals engaging towards short-term tasks. This includes part-time workers who supplement the primary income, full-time workers dependent on the gig opportunities, and gig workers who are the milestones for achieving the goals. The motivation for gig work is circled around flexibility, income generation, and autonomy. Gig workers are drawn towards working schedules and choosing different assignments that align with their interests and skills, making them alternatives to conventional employment (Riordan et al., 2023). The gig workers are juggling the gigs to meet goals and pursue personal interests. The whole time, gig workers depend heavily on the gig platforms for their livelihood, which could offer more constant opportunities as well as working conditions that are much more favourable. Understanding such categories of gig work is crucial for the creation of tailor talent management strategies (Watson et al., 2021).

The chapter explores the complexities and challenges of talent management in the gig economy, emphasizing the need for innovative strategies to address the challenges and the opportunities that could present. It also delves into the interplay between the flexibility of gig workers' desires and the job security, fair treatment and skill development that they require. The gig economy offers significant advantages for businesses, the vastness of an on-demand pool of workers with specific skills. Talent Management emerges as critical to addressing the need for a gig workforce(Hagiu & Wright, 2019). Unlike employment paradigms, wherein talent management is focused on long-term engagement, the gig economy mandates the need for innovative strategies for attracting, engaging, and retaining workers in a constant landscape shift. However, on the contrary, it also poses significant challenges, specifically in managing workforce satisfaction, income stability and job security, which could also include exploitation risks (Abraham et al., 2019). The chapter determines the concerns with the management of the gig workers, for instance, the long-term job security, instability in the income, and the lack of significant benefits alongside traditional employment. Considering talent management, the chapter provides insights into the businesses that could address such challenges.. It also examines the significance of adapting traditional HR practices to meet the needs of the gig workforce and a prime focus towards ensuring fairness and inclusivity in the aspects of recruitment, skill enhancement and performance management(Ashford et al.,2018). As the gig economy continues to expand, the chapter is a guide for HR managers, policymakers, and stakeholders to offer recommendations and examples of effective practices on a global front.

By adopting such strategies, businesses can improve talent management practices and contribute to building a more equitable, sustainable and adaptable gig economy. The efficiency of talent management strategies includes identifying gig workers for particular projects and ensuring the necessary skills(Banik & Padalkar, 2021). There shall be more consideration of how the organization needs to inculcate training and skill development, allowing them to improvise in their capabilities. The engagement and motivation of gig workers can vary from the motivation of conventional employees. The organization's mission was to foster a sense of belonging and alignment with its mission(Behl et al, 2022). With the gig workers it may not seek long-term employment with the organization and efficiency of talent management, which involves engagement strategies that can be encouraging for future projects. Many gig workers can find opportunities through digital platforms, but the organisations must understand the platform's impact on talent acquisitions and the development of strategies for positioning themselves within the ecosystems(Batmunkh et al.,2022)

GIG ECONOMY IN INDIA

Growth & Structure of Gig Work in India

The economy in India has seen a significant expansion, driven by digital platforms which could facilitate short-term or flexible work arrangements. According to the NITI Aayog report on "India's Booming Gig and Platform Economy" (2022), India is expected to reach up to 23.5 million working by 2030. The report has characterised gig work in three key aspects. Platform-based workers are engaged through the digital platform in ride-hailing, logistics, food delivery, and freelance marketplaces. The other is the non-platform gig work, in which independent workers work in traditional freelance roles such as retail on-demand services. The growth has been accelerated with the emergence of digital labor platforms such as Swiggy, Uber etc which drives the on demand work arranged within multiple sections. BCG's (2021) report highlights the gig workforce, which is concentrated in Tier 1 and Tier 2 cities with higher engagement from Gen Z and millennial workers. It also identified male domination in ride-hailing and logistics, whereas women are more active in freelance work and content creation. Despite the growth, there are structural challenges faced by the gig economy in India, such as the lack of social security, lowered wages and the absence of precise worker classification. The Fair Work India report (2023) assesses the gig platforms and found that only three provide minimum wage guarantees, and none offer collective bargaining rights. With the gig economy offering income opportunities and flexibility, it raises challenges which are related to worker classification, social security, fair wages and jobs security, the structure of the gig worker is significantly diverse and is emerging with multiple industries, skills levels and different models of employment.

Challenges for the Indian Economy

The report by ILO (2024) assesses that gig work lacks financial stability as some workers earn on-task basis while having no guaranteed income. Bhandari et al. (2023) conducted a socio-economic study on food delivery workers. They found inconsistencies in the earnings of 70% of the gig workers due to the fluctuation in demand. The automation rating system on Uber and Zomato controls the income of the gig workers and job opportunities, leading to job insecurity and potential biases in the performance evaluation (Ashford et al., 2018). NITI Aayog (2022) has recommended that gig works be covered under the Code on Social Security (2020), yet most platforms have not implemented paid leave policies, pensions or health insurance. The report of the International Labour Organization (2024) states that India lags behind Spain and France, wherein gig workers receive minimum wage protection and social benefits. Aloisi (2019) examines the collective rights of gig workers in India and does not design the gig workers, leading to disputes over the classification of workers. An emphasis on the HRM strategies in India is needed to address the legal ambiguity and provide legal contacts for gig workers (Deloitte, 2024)

LITERATURE REVIEW

Human resource management is a strategic approach for human capital to maintain the organisation for the employees and employers. The dimension which impacts the performance of the firm and supports the objectives of the business with the quality and commitment outcomes. Before conducting the system review on the talent management strategy, this study identifies the perspective towards the HRM practices in the gig economy and its adaptation towards recruitment, retention, performance management and skills development (Debgupta & Bhattacharya, 2024). The lack of standardized HR practices tailored to gig workers often has several issues. Unlike the conventional employees, the gig workers do not benefit from the onboarding process, the performance evaluation and feedback mechanics. Creating HR practices catering to gig work needs is essential for the effectiveness of workforce management (Waldkirch et al., 2021). The barriers towards entry in gig work involve the lack of digital access and the complex onboarding process (Behl et al., 2022). Zhang (2024) explains the skill enhancement period. The pivotal role of skill development is increasing the employees' work-related skills. The research highlights the traditional training models that fall short of addressing gig work's flexibility and transient nature and the necessity for customized training programs.

The study identifies several significant gaps in the current training provisions in the area of platform-specific skills (Behera et al.,2022). It is crucial to implement customized training programs to address these gaps and ensure the development of platform-specific skills. Fair Work India's 2023 report highlighted an evaluation issue in food delivery, especially in India, where platforms offer hourly local minimum wages for delivery workers. The economic model has been a transformative and driven force for food delivery, but it makes it even more difficult for delivery workers to secure earnings. Barbu & Song (2016) argue that employers provide training that enhances workforce engagement, but the gig digital platform neglects the investment. Talent Management in the gig economy explores the shift in the paradigm from the traditional employment models, which could be significant for having tailored strategies for meeting the dynamics of the transient workforce that is decentralized and unique. This particular shift is important for reimagining human resource practices (Yablonsky, 2021).

The relationship between the gig economy and talent management is evolving, wherein organizations are navigating the challenges of the transient nature of work. It refers to organizations' practices for attracting, developing, engaging and retaining the workforce. The gig economy emphasizes project-based enhancement and requires the organization to build more flexibility in the workforce (Riordan et al., 2023). According to the report of NITI Aayog (2022), there is a necessity for the policies which shall offer multiple benefits such as fair wages, job stability, social security for the gig works. Additionally, there is a significant need for skill development for career growth within the emergence of the gig economy. The development of an inclusive environment is towards job satisfaction and the gig works potential to be utilised.

The digital human resource practices are impacting the Gig economy. The gig economy has become challenging with the norms that are existing related to the human resource practices by having a new platform based digital work. The research paper emphasizes the Strategic Human Resources management for the business to leverage the competitive advantage. The development of the "gig economy" is not a term known to the lesser people as it has seen an exponential growth in India. With the fast emergence of platform economy services such as Swiggy, Never have usage for the services (Tripathi et al., 2020).

TALENT MANAGEMENT STRATEGIES FOR GIG WORKERS

Gig economy has transformed into a traditional dynamic workforce requiring professional policymakers to rethink the talent acquired, developed and retained towards this work agreement. A well structured talent manager strategy is integral for the employers and employees. For the company, the gig is for effective management that can improve productivity, minimise turnover and enhance service quality. For the work on the other hand, there needs to be structured HRM strategies which could offer financial stability, fair working conditions (Gautam et al., 2024). This particular section explores the different HRM process regarding the recruitment, retention, skill development and performance management adapting onwards gig work, focusing the policy interventions to sustain a suitable gig workforce in India.

Recruitment and Selection

Recruitment and selection in the gig economy differ from conventional hiring models. The gig economy depends on the digital platform, a facility for workers and employers. Platforms such as Uber and Upwork revolutionize recruitment strategies and create seamless connections for individuals seeking flexibility in work opportunities; instead of having formal application processes and long-term employment contracts, gig work depends on the digital platform using automation matching algorithms towards onboarding workers quickly. The primary objective is to ensure the workers are onboard quickly and allotted the task with minimal delays. This system increases efficiency and raises concerns regarding accessibility, fairness and algorithm biases (Debgupta & Bhattacharya, 2024).

Digital platforms like Zomato and Swiggy use algorithm-driven selection processes in order to match gig workers with the availability of jobs (Duggan et al., 2020). The recruitment includes human intervention and the workers' selection based on factors like customer rating, availability, and location. For example, ride-hailing services such as Ola and Uber use a geolocation-based algorithm to assign jobs to drivers nearest to the customers. The platform does not conduct skill assessments or have in-depth interviews. On the contract, freelance platforms prioritize the freelancers with higher ratings and job completions to create a preference for workers while making it harder for the new entrants (Williams et al.,2023). The automated process could enable companies to minimize recruitment costs and increase hiring speed, introducing inherent inefficiencies. The major limitation is that the fit between workers and the job requirements is overlooked, causing mismatches in the skills and job expectations (Elayan, 2022). The gig workers lack prior experience and necessary training, yet they are assigned roles without having skill assessment or onboarding support (Ganesh, 2020). This phenomenon is prevalent in food delivery and e-commerce logistics, wherein workers can be added to the system in bulk, causing high turnover rates and inconsistencies in service quality (Keegan & Merijerink, 2023).

The emphasis on recruitment has implications for the workers' job satisfaction since gig workers are recruited without consideration for their career or longer-term potential and are experiencing job dissatisfaction (Rahman et al.,2024). In traditional employment, wherein HR is portrayed in structured programs and competency hiring, the gig economy treats a continuous and high volume of the development of workers.Additionally, regulatory frameworks structure recruitment practices and their effectiveness in ensuring workers' rights, social security, and fair hiring policy. In India, the Code on Social Security (2020) aims towards formalizing gig work, pushing the platform for thinking about the policies of recruitment for compiling the emergence of labour laws. Recruitment is not an HR practice but an integral aspect of the talent management strategy, which could align with workforce planning(Bush et al, 2019).

Retention Strategies

Retention and engagement in the gig economy present challenges with a short-term and transient nature for platform-based work. Traditional employment with benefits, career progression, and long-term stability plays an integral role in worker retention, but it lacks structured incentives to encourage commitment and engagement. For gig workers, retention is driven by financial security, psychological engagement and job stability, which are impacted by platform management and talent (Cao., 2021). Moreover, the high attrition rates remain challenging, with the workers frequently moving between platforms regarding wages, work conditions or flexibility. An analytical framework for understanding gig worker retention is the Jobs Demand Resource (JD-R) Model, which determines the engagement of the workers, and retention relies on balancing the job demands and the job resources (Ali &Sivasubramanian, 2024). Gig workers offer lowered security and high autonomy, which makes the workers more vulnerable towards attrition when there is financial instability and job stress (Ray et al., 2023)

The unpredictability for the gig workers shall be accelerated through algorithm management. The job allocation could reward the high-performance and frequently available workers while also deprioritizing the lower engagement metrics (Duggan et al., 2020). Xuan (2022) explores the innovation of the retention strategies, which is to be more stable with the performance metric with the distinctive number for various tasks, which is the rating of the consumers, that are wages or the salaries. The retention challenge in the gig economy is the lack of long-term job security. With traditional employees, there is no protection from retrenchment policies or tenure-based contracts, which makes it susceptible to market fluctuations (Kuhn et al., 2021). For example, ride-hailing, like Uber, can introduce limitations in the health insurance program and driver accident coverage. The platform explores partnerships and the financial implications of offering gig work with savings plans, loans, and credit-building tools. The measures benefit the workers and contribute by being responsible employers (Lo & Hsieh, 2024). To address the concerns, some platforms could begin the experimentation with a loyalty program that can guarantee the minimum number of assignments for high-performing workers (Fulmer et al., 2023)

Job stability affects the challenge of financial security with the absence of delayed wages and payment transparency. This financial uncertainty discourages the workers from commitment towards single platforms, pushing them toward multiple platforms towards a shift to traditional employment for income inconsistencies (Gautam et al., 2024). From the HRM perspective, gig platforms must restructure their compensation models by introducing predictable wage structures. For example, the gig economy in France reforms toward a platform to guarantee wages for gig workers, enabling them to deal with wages and their trust (ILO, 2024).

Performance Management

Performance management in the gig economy context is different from the conventional workforce due to its tasks-based culture. The worker and the organization are significant hurdles in managing the gig workforce. Unlike traditional employees, getting assessed on Key Performance Indicators such as goal completion, teamwork and productivity, gig workers are evaluated on the basis of data-driven metrics, real-time data controlled by the platforms themselves (Waldkirch et al., 2021). Gig workers often contract, which could operate in a highly flexible environment, which is different from traditional full-time employment. The business increasingly relies on the workforce, which could adopt innovative strategies for the management of performance, which carefully balances gig workers' autonomy and the accountability needed to maintain a higher standard of quality and productivity. In order to manage gig worker efforts, the intermediary platform has a range of HRM activities that involve workforce planning to match supply and demand. Performance management of gig workers' behaviour is assessed using online rating methods (Rosenblat et al., 2017). These compensatory effects could transform the gig workers' efforts to include the desired behaviours and job design, which could provide the gig workers with the possibility of working (Meijerink et al., 2018). The critical questions in performance management are fairness, control mechanisms such as worker feedback, and automated ratings to ensure an effective and fair performance assessment (Kuhn et al., 2021). Primarily, the method for performance management in the gig economy is the customer ratings wherein the users rate the workers like freelancers, drivers and delivery workers. Platforms such as Swiggy and Zomato use a five-star rating system to assess the standing of the workers, impacting job allocation and their earning potential (Lo & Hsieh,2024). The digital platform offers flexibility, which can determine the traditional performance metrics by focusing on the outcomes, such as task completion and ratings. The studies developed with the models of evaluation could significantly combine the quantitative data with the feedback from the works to provide a comprehensive performance review (Lehdonvirta et al., 2019).

One of the primary challenges in evaluating gig worker performance is the lack of supervision. Operating in a decentralized environment, some workers are on-site or working remotely. The independence limits the oversight, which becomes difficult for the managers on a day-to-day basis. With the lack of such employment models, the performance metrics, such as work quality and deadlines, are transparent and standardized (Singh & Shastri, 2023). However, the gig economy comprises performance metrics that shall be adapted to the work's diverse and changing nature. The gig workers are hired to complete specific kinds of tasks or projects, which shall measure the overall performance, which could be difficult when there is no consistency in their work over time. Not having any standard metrics, the companies struggle to assess whether the workers are performing towards the standards which are expected.

The results are subjective assessments for the lack of performance evaluations. For instance, in ride-sharing platforms, the drivers' performance is judged by the customers' timeliness, ratings, and the completed number of rides. However, the metrics cannot objectively capture the other qualitative factors for innovation and solving skills for emailing it. (Lin et al., 2023) The gig economy doesn't have the structure of the organization. The gig workers are independent and do not have the same engagement as the other full-time employees. The absence of engagement is inconsistent with the work's timeliness and quality. The sense of belongingness comprises apparent alignments that can work with the mission of the platforms and maintain consistency in performance, especially while working on long-term projects. The gig workers are from diverse backgrounds and possess different expertise levels (Tripathi et al., 2022). The variability makes it even more challenging to have standard performance aspects or accurately assess the work quality. With highly experienced and capable of delivering the top tier result, the other might require guidance. Some discrepancies complicate the evaluation process, lead to unequal repetition, and impact the overall performance management strategy (Ray et al., 2023).

The most significant change will be managing gig walkers' performance at a high turnover rate. The gig workers are hired for projects or short-term assessments, and such are not tied up with the company for a minimal period, and this transient nature makes it even more challenging to track the long-term performance trends (Meijerink et al., 2019). The turnover frequency disrupts work quality, leading to gaps and productivity, and complicates performance management. However, digital platforms and businesses that manage performance effectively shall develop systems for monitoring tasks and providing meaningful feedback, which can create a balance between autonomy and clear accountability. They are to leverage the structure, flexibility, and feedback systems, allowing the employees to monitor their performance and still have the independence of gig workers.

The platform life dependence on the algorithm systems is more significant, which strikes the innovation for the activities to monitor and evaluate the productivity (Waldkirch et al., 2021)In order to address the challenges, the organization should leverage digital tools as well as systems that are designed to monitor tasks and collect feedback in real-time. Digital platforms such as time logs, GPS tracking wells, and management software ensure that the regulations for mounting gig workers are remote. For instance, delivery platforms use GPS to track the location and effectiveness of delivery personnel (Ola Institute, 2020). Despite that, the freelance platform required the workers to submit screenshots to validate their billed hours. The systems also offer the data to be more valuable and help the organization to enable quality and timelessness towards completing the tasks(Weiner et al., 2021).

Feedback tools, like reviews or customer ratings, are another part of gig worker evaluation. Platform platforms such as Uber and Airbnb depend on customer feedback to assess the workers' performance. While some systems are simple to implement, they have no faults (Rosenblat et al., 2016). Customer ratings are more subjective and are often impacted by factors that are far from the workers' control, such as platform issues and pricing. There shall be a shift in the focus of the ongoing process toward outcome-based assessment, wherein the gig workers are based on the impact of their specific deliverables and quality rather than the time they have spent on the tasks.

Skill Development

Gig workers, such as delivery and ride-hailing drivers, encounter situations that could demand more customer service and time management proficiency. Upskilling is necessary for increasing job satisfaction, improving productivity, and remaining more competitive in the evolving market(Hara, 2014). It addresses the critical aspects of knowledge. For instance, the training could help the workers effectively manage their incomes, while customer service skills can improve the user rating, leading to earning opportunities. The skills empower the workers to transition to other roles within the ecosystem by investing in gig work, which could often result in higher retention rates (Berger et al., 2019).

The collaborations within the businesses and digital platforms could enhance skill development. For instance, there are partnerships with the leaning platforms and ride hailing companies which leads towards courses which are docs towards industry specific skills. The businesses build goodwill and have the advantage of a reliable workforce(Kalli et al, 2023).

The research indicates that the gig economy could offer advances like autonomy and flexibility for higher earnings compared to conventional employment. The need for skill development within gig workers is to be more critical and adapt to the demands of the markets and technological advancements(Lin et al., 2023). The HR practices are tailored, particularly for gig work. Practical training and development strategies improve performance and workforce satisfaction.

Uber's Skill Development Programme

Other than that, the commitment of Uber for enchantment towards the skill of the drivers wherein upskill in the gig economy. The company could provide training programs emphasising customer and driving interaction, which involves road safety and customer communication. The programs are delivered with online modules and in-person work, which ensures that drivers receive more competent training—Uber partners with the local training organization to provide region-specific education (Transformational Upskilling, n.d.). For instance, the drivers are fitness-trained on eco-friendly driving techniques, which not only eliminates the impact but also cuts the costs. It has implemented safety programs that educate the drivers towards defensiveness in driving and emergency response and improve both the drivers' and the passenger's safety. The influence of the programs extends towards the development of skills. Uber has gained loyalty and belonging within the workforce by investing in drivers. The drivers participate in levels of satisfaction, which are a continuing platform. The initiatives enhance the experiences of the customers as well as well-trained drivers, which are better for handling the interactions and challenges.

Swiggy Skill's Project Next

Innovative skill development strategies can attract a talent pool. Uber's partnership with nonprofits to recruit drivers who demonstrate the platform could promote diversity. In addition to this, the platform offers more flexibility for accommodating workers with responsibilities to foster inclusion. In India, several companies like Swiggy have reflected on inclusive recruitment practices as they have taken the initiative to employ delivery partners for deaf people, determining the tailored recruitment strategy to create meaningful opportunities for underrepresented groups (Swiggy, 2024). The launch of "Project Next" is to price the opportunities in career growth for the partners in the delivery while accelerating the airing of the measurables. The initiatives could offer skilling, internship training, and opportunities for employment in the said value chain. The qualified delivery partners are being transitioned into sales executives. This aims towards improvisation, expanding restaurants and offering them career advancements. There would be responsibility for the partnership for onboarding and management of growing the network of the restaurants, more especially in tier 2 and 3 cities, wherein they could offer higher quality support towards platforms (Outlook Business, 2024).

The company works with 4 lakh delivery partners all across India. With the platform values, there has been more flexibility in earning opportunities. In order to empower the group, the initiatives use a unique program that helps the delivery partners transition from "blue collar" to "white collar"(Swiggy, 2024). In September 2024, there was a transition of more than 100 delivery partnerships that have been boarded for more than 300 restaurants. Ravindra Khati, a 27-year-old gig worker, is not a sales executive at Swiggy in Rajasthan. This particular initiative is under the Ministry of Skill Development and Entrepreneurship, wherein they could facilitate the skill development and upskilling of 2.4 lakh delivery partners. Workers often require specialized skills that could extend beyond the job functions(Swiggy, 2024).

Swiggy and Zomato Initiatives

In India, the food delivery platforms Swiggy and Zoamto have measured or improved the conditions of the works. The platform shall offer accident insurance and medical benefits for delivery partners. The flexible incentive structure shall encourage increased earnings during peak hours. Initiatives would like 24/7 help, which determines the commitment towards the work's well-being (Times of India, 2024).

CHALLENGES IN MANAGING GIG WORKERS

The gig economy has a paradigm shift in the employment structures, providing autonomy and flexibility to workers while having unique challenges in human resource management. Within the Indian context, management of the gig workers includes navigation of complexities which are related to job security, classification of workers and policy frameworks.

Inconsistencies in Worker Classification

A challenge in the gig economy is worker classification as either independent contractors or employees. This distinction is significant; it determines the labour laws, protections in India, and benefits(Aloisi, 2019)(Stewart et al, 2017). Gig workers lack clear legal status, which causes inconsistencies in the treatment of labour regulations. The ambiguity is due to the gig workers being excluded from traditional employee benefits such as paid leave, retirement plans, and health insurance.

Lack of Job Security and Social Protections

De Stefano (2021) explains that gig workers, typically in the food delivery or ride-hailing industry, are mainly related to independent contractors, expecting the benefits and protection provided towards full-time employment. There is a lack of access to social density, which leaves workers vulnerable to financial insecurity, especially whether it is a fluctuation in income due to personal health issues or volatility in the market and seasonal demand.

With the gap addressed in the business, policymakers need to reshape the traditional structure for benefits. The gig workers carry rotational benefits from job to job but offer one specific solution. The benefits include health insurance and savings that are not linked to the particular employer across different platforms and assignments. In addition, the stability in the income measures the minimum pay standards and dynamic pricing models, which could help mitigate the instability accompanying the gig business, providing the gig work needed for weather periods of lowered demands (Bhandari et al., 2023).

With the lack of social security being a primary concern, there is exploitation for gig workers, which remains a stringent issue. Without any protections affected by conventional employment contracts, gig workers are subjected to low wages, unclear expectations of the jobs, and some inconsistency in the working conditions. The ethical guidelines are necessary to ensure that gig workers are treated fairly and equitably, especially while considering the imbalance in the power inherent in the platform-based economy (Dunn, 2020)

Algorithmic Bias and Exploitation Risks

According to the National Council of Applied Economic Research (Bhandari et al., 2023), companies like Uber and Swiggy in India have initiated worker development programs for gig workers with different skills, which can enhance job prospects within the gig economy.

With the assurance of gig work, which could provide access to professional development opportunities and career growth, the business can build more engagement and loyalty. The workers feel more valued and supported in maintaining the platform commitment, a more advantageous business with minimising turnover and increasing workforce stability—the ethical guidelines implemented for creating the environment for the gig workers within the company.

According to the NITI Aayog Report (2022), the study sheds light on the different social protection approaches with gigs and platforms for social protection measures for workers in India. There are measures for paid sick leaves, as well as the lines for measured introduction to mitigate the challenges posed during the pandemic with the platform's business, measures for the paid sick initiatives, and gig ad platform firms considering the income support for the workers. This is an important step for providing assured minimum earnings as well as social security for the loss of income for irregularities. Harpur and Blanck (2020) determined that with the initiative, there is an instance for a particular platform which could enter with the interest-free advancements of the businesses and delay the payback periods for protecting the gig workers, small businesses, and self-employees engaged with them. Kerala State Civil Supplies has partnered with Zomato towards the grains and essentials for the applications. Collaboration within the platforms is encouraged by following such instances.

The mobility of the platforms is in order to support the cab and auto rickward for mitigating the impact of the lockdown of the incomes, and this is called "Drive the Driver Fund". The measures could offer social security, covering this associated with leaves, insurance and health insurance. This can have positive implications for providing social security coverage for the platform works that are engaged with the firms. Indonesia has offered the initiative to offer insurance to workers through digital mechanisms like e-commerce platforms, ride-hailing, and e-commerce platforms, which adopt the models for offering delivery partners accident insurance (Atlantis Press, 2024). The systems are designed to optimise the efficiency which could limit the autonomy of the worker. It could be offered in collaboration with the private sector and linked with India's Code of Social Security 2020.

By the RAISE framework operationalising the CoSS, 2020 could adopt the five-pronged approach towards the assurance of full access to social security by the report. Firstly, the differentiated transient nature of platform work should be recognised when designing the schemes. Allowing the augmentation of social security with innovative mechanisms and inculcating the designing schemes which are particularly interesting for platforms that can influence the creation of jobs, platforms with workers and businesses. Support the workers for government schemes and welfare programs with awareness campaigns and ensure the advantages are accessible to workers.

Policy Gaps in HRM Regulation for Gig Workers in India

According to a Deloitte (2024) report in India, effectively managing the gig workforce is an unnecessary framework that should include policies, operations, regulations and governance. The growth in the gig economy has presented itself with differentiation challenges and opportunities towards talent management. A well-designed governance structure could offer accountability and fairness in the gig work relationships; the policymakers, organisations, and HR managers should proactively address the challenges and suitable places for the gig economy. The lack of standardised regulation for the gig economy has left many workers towards exploration.

Portable benefits allow the gig workers to retain the retirement savings, and leave regardless of the platforms they can work for(Gautam et al, 2024). The scheme is implemented through contributions towards workers and platforms. There needs to be classifying with the policymakers to define the clarity for differentiation with the employees and ensure fair treatment. The platforms have power over the gig works. The policies must address the imbalance by mandating transparency for the allocation of tasks and pay (Mateescu et al., 2019). Prohibiting any unjust terminations or the deactivation of the count of gig workers.. By enacting legal measures, the government could create a more equitable environment for them. The NCAER (2023) identifies the policies which affect gig workers, particularly in India, for the ones engaged in food delivery services. There is a lack of comprehensive social security coverage, and some of the workers have access towards accidents in all instances, leaving them vulnerable to medical emergencies. In addition to this, the absence of paid eale could further the financial instability, directly influencing earnings. Moreover, there is a steady decline with the real incomes in the food recovery workers.

Policy and Programs Supporting HRM

The expansion of the gig economy has promoted the private sector and government to implement initiatives that could address the unique challenges facing gig workers. In India, significant strides have extended social benefits to the workforce.

Government and Private Initiatives

Identifying the burgeoning gig workforce, the Indian government enacted the Code on Social Security in 2020. The legislation acknowledges the platforms and gig workers and aims to offer them social security benefits, like health and maternity benefits and life and disability cover. The CoSS has establishments for the Social Security Fund that are financed through contributions. Corresponding towards the efforts of the government, private sector initiatives have evolved. For example, Uber has introduced a "Driver Fund" program for financial assistance and insurance coverage. The government and private sector collaboration aims to create working environments for gig workers. The e-Shram portal is launched by the government of India, which is a step towards the gig and freelancer working ensures the access towards social security like accident insurances under Prime Minister's schemes. Moreover gig platforms have their skills development and financial security programs for improving the well being of the workers. These initiatives reflect a recognition of the need to restructure HRM practices to bridge the gap within flexibility and protein of workers in the gig economy.

Social Security Schemes

The Code on Social Security represents a shift towards India's labour policy to integrate platform and gig workers into the framework. The Code of Security allays the workers and ensures their inclusion in the schemes. A dedicated fund is to finance benefits for gig works from platform aggregators, which range from 1-2% of the annual turnover (NITI Aayog, 2022). Despite the opportunities offered by the platform NCAER report on "Socio- assessment Impact Assessment of Food Delivery Platform Workers' (2023), underscores a necessary gap for social security coverage for the gig workers. It focuses on the working conditions, income inconsistencies and the work well being of the gig works specially for the food delivery sector in India.

Global Regulatory Approach

Different jurisdictions are undertaking efforts to regulate gig workers and protect workers' rights. European Union: Gig Work Directive: This regulatory approach enhances platform workers' working conditions, emphasising algorithm management transparency and improving fair remuneration. The directives are purposely designed to classify workers and grant them access to social benefits (European Parliament, 2019).

United States Assembly Bill 5 (AB5): The regulatory approach enacted in California AB5 encompasses the strict criteria for worker classification as independent contractors. The law aims to improve gig work and review employee benefits; however, there are challenges and pushback from different platform economy companies (Flynn, 2022). In comparison, India's approach is through the CoSS, emphasising security without alternating towards gig work to balance protection and flexibility.

CONCLUSION

Organising gig workers could empower them to negotiate collective wages, benefits, and working conditions. There must be clear transparency in the contractual agreements which shall be established between the gig workers and platforms with payment structures and other details, including the work tenure or agreements(Merijerink et al, 2022). Shared benefit funds could be managed with the gig works by the platforms with health insurance and emergency financial assistance. For example, some of the platforms in India have started accident and health insurance schemes covering medical emergencies, especially during accidents. HR managers can adopt flexible work policies tailored towards the gig economy. There could be partners with learning platforms to offer training programs that can be free. Establish the work channels in order to voice concerns(Swiggy, 2024).

- The development of the onboarding process can be outlined in the job expectations agreements and performance metrics. (Hara, 2014).
- Training programs must be implemented so that gig workers can understand the systems and job resources must be offered for easy access (Ali & Sivasubramanian, 2024).
- Offering the gig worked with opportunities for skill enhancements for competitiveness. Implementing reward systems for the workers to complete the upskilling course for the company and boosting the morale of the workers(Barbu et al, 2016).
- Establishing a regular feedback mechanism for gig work to receive proper performance feedback (Fulmer et al, 2023).
- Development of incentive programs that could make the gig workers feel lofty about the motivation for staying within the platform (Sung et al., 2023).

This chapter explored the different aspects of talent management within the gig economy that could address recruitment, skill enhancement and retention with recommendations. Digital platforms play an integral role in the effectiveness of matching tasks towards talent—the inclusion and maintaining the biases with the important recruitment practices. The strategies like transparency, commitment and support systems are for the workers' loyalty and satisfaction. The lack of worker classification is an issue that influences access to career stability and social security benefits. The Code on Social Security (2020), is one of the positive steps towards integrating gig workers into India's labour framework. However, the implementation is inconsistent, and the enforcement of the mechanism needs a strengthened approach. Considering strategies in the US and China offer the lessons. The United States emphasises transparency in algorithm management and fair working conditions, and the regulatory mandates in China are for platform companies to offer insurance and labour predictions toward an approach to ensure the gig workers' welfare.

Integrating effective global practices into the HRM strategies in India could create a more equitable, dynamic workforce. Managing gig workers in India has a need for a multifaceted approach which could address the classification, improves job security and policy frameworks. Collaboration is necessary for insurance and legal protection. Moreover, the investment in the upskilling programs can secure the gig workers to improve their expertise, minimise legal ambiguities, and enhance worker protections. The gig economy aims to sustain the goals that depend on balancing items with the empowered workforce. There should be adoption practices that promote diversity, ensuring that gig workers feel supported. There is a need of the hour to address the complexities of the gig economy, and it is time for the re-imagination of talent management as not a challenge but more as an opportunity for building more equitable work for the future. This is imperative for the stakeholders and HR professionals, policymakers and workers to design the solutions for the protection of workers rights to foster innovation as wella flexibility in the labor market.

While this chapter analyses the HRM strategies, especially for talent management and the management of gig works in India, certain limitations can be acknowledged. At first, data availability and reliability represent the challenge; as the gig economy is expanding, the platform companies do not disclose the workforce static in detailed form, company structure, or retention rates. This could limit the ability to use evidence-based assessments for HRM strategies, specifically regarding the classification of gig works and the effectiveness of the existing HR policy. In addition, much of the existing literature is on regional sepsis, making it difficult to generalise the findings across digital platforms. While the chapter has compared the global best practices, the transferability to the Indian gig economy, given its labour laws and socio-economic aspects, could remain an aspect for further exploration.

Secondly, the chapter focuses towards the HRM process, such as recruitment, skill development, performance management, and retention strategies. However, it does not cover the other criteria, such as well-being and work-life balance, which are necessary for holistic talent management strategies. Moreover, the policy formwork is limited to the existing regulator frameworks, and the recommendations for the future are processed. Finally, the informal gig workforce, like daily wage workers, hired with unrelated digital platforms, leaving scope for further research into the adaptation for protecting the gig workers outside the platforms could be formalised.

With the gig economy evolving, AI-driven recruitment is essential for future research, especially regarding the ethical implications. With artificial intelligence improving efficiencies in the hiring process, automating the candidate with screening and matching concerns regarding biases, transparency, and fairness exist, algorithm decision-making in recruitment refining the worker demographics' inequalities established on the historical biases in the training data. Adding to this, future research shall explore the HRM practices which can responsibly integrate AI, ensuring the hiring models are adaptable and inclusive of the needs of gig workers. Regulatory frameworks must be assessed to determine whether the AI requirements align with the labour laws and hiring principles, specifically for the emergence of markets in India.

Another critical area is the future of collective bargaining for the gig economy in India and the development of the structure to enable workforce stability. Given the transient nature of gig work, gig workers lack collective bargaining power, leading to income volatility and job insecurity. The research shall focus on tailored HRM models with long-term job satisfaction and access to pensions and healthcare. The development of a new HRM framework is a pressing need to iterate the elements to create a more suitable and equitable dynamic gig workforce.

DECLARATION OF CONFLICTING INTEREST

The authors declare no potential conflicts of interest with respect to the research, authorship and/or publication of this chapter

FUNDING

The authors received no financial support for the research, authorship, and/or publication of this chapter.

REFERENCES

Aayog, N. I. T. I. (2022). Policy brief: India's booming gig and platform economy. National Institution for Transforming India. https://www.niti.gov.in/sites/default/files/2022-06/Policy_Brief_India%27s_Booming_Gig_and_Platform_Economy_27062022.pdf

Abraham, K. G., Haltiwanger, J., Sandusky, K., & Spletzer, J. (2019). The rise of the gig economy: Fact or fiction? *AEA Papers and Proceedings. American Economic Association, 109*, 357–361. DOI: 10.1257/pandp.20191039

Ali, K. T. M., & Sivasubramanian, R. C. (2024). *Understanding the Nexus Between Techno-Stress, Psychological Well-Being, and the Moderating Role of Job Resources in the Gig Economy*. Employ Respons Rights J., DOI: 10.1007/s10672-024-09505-5

Aloisi, A. (2019). Negotiating the digital transformation of work: non-standard workers' voice, collective rights and mobilization practices in the platform economy. https://cadmus.eui.eu/bitstream/handle/1814/63264/MWP_Aloisi_2019_03.pdf?sequence=1&isAl

Ashford, S. J., Caza, B. B., & Reid, E. M. (2018). From surviving to thriving in the gig economy: A research agenda for individuals in the new world of work. *Research in Organizational Behavior, 38*, 23–41. DOI: 10.1016/j.riob.2018.11.001

Atlantis Press. (2024). Gig workers in the digital era in Indonesia: Development, vulnerability, and welfare.DOI: 10.2991/978-94-6463-525-6_6

Banik, N., & Padalkar, M. (2021). The spread of the gig economy: Trends and effects. *Форсайт, 15*(1, 1 (eng)), 19–29. DOI: 10.17323/2500-2597.2021.1.19.29

Barbu, E., & Song, X. (2016). The effects of offshoring on employer-provided training. *The Journal of International Trade & Economic Development*, *25*(4), 479–503. https://doi.org/https://doi.org/ 10.1080/09638199.2015.1068838. DOI: 10.1080/09638199.2015.1068838

Bathini, D. R. (2021). GIG Workers in The Platform Economy: The Case of App-Based Cab Companies In India.

Batmunkh, A., Fekete-Farkas, M., & Lakner, Z. (2022). Bibliometric analysis of gig economy. *Administrative Sciences*, *12*(2), 1–15. https://doi.org/https://doi.org/ 10.3390/admsci12020051. DOI: 10.3390/admsci12020051

BCG. (2021). Unlocking the potential of the gig economy in India. https://www.bcg .com/en-in/unlocking-gigeconomy-in-india

Behl, A., Rajagopal, K., Sheorey, P., & Mahendra, A. (2022). Barriers to entry of gig workers in the gig platforms: Exploring the dark side of the gig economy. *Aslib Journal of Information Management*, *74*(5), 818–839. DOI: 10.1108/AJIM-08-2021-0235

Berger, T., Frey, C. B., Levin, G., & Danda, S. R. (2019). Is Uber happy? Work and well-being in the 'Gig Economy'. *Economic Policy*, *34*(99), 429–477. Advance online publication. DOI: 10.1093/epolic/eiz007

Bhandari, B., Das, G. K., Gupta, S., Sahu, A. K., Urs, K. S., Pal, N., & Raj, K. (2023). Socio-economic impact assessment of food delivery platform workers.DOI: 10.13140/RG.2.2.14642.17605

Bricka, T., & Schroeder, A. (2019). What's the gig deal? Examining contemporary work issues in the gig economy. *Industrial and Organizational Psychology: Perspectives on Science and Practice*, *12*(4), 491–494. DOI: 10.1017/iop.2019.116

Bricka, T., & Schroeder, A. (2019). What's the gig deal? Examining contemporary work issues in the gig economy. *Industrial and Organizational Psychology: Perspectives on Science and Practice*, *12*(4), 491–494. DOI: 10.1017/iop.2019.116

Bush, J. T., & Balven, R. M. (2019). Catering to the crowd: An HRM perspective on crowd worker engagement. Human Resource Management Review.110.1016/j. hrmr.2018.10.003

Cameron, L. D. (2024, April 3). How gig work pits customers against workers. *Harvard Business Review*.https://hbr.org/2024/04/how-gig-work-pits-customers -against-workers0.1111/ntwe.12310

Cao, J. (2021, December). Research on Development and Optimization of Human Resources in Gig Economy. In 2021 4th International Conference on Humanities Education and Social Sciences (ICHESS 2021) (pp. 1288-1298). Atlantis Press.

Cropanzano, R., Keplinger, K., Lambert, B. K., Caza, B., & Ashford, S. J. (2023). The organizational psychology of gig work: An integrative conceptual review. *The Journal of Applied Psychology*, *108*(3), 492–519. DOI: 10.1037/apl0001029 PMID: 36222635

Cropanzano, R., Keplinger, K., Lambert, B. K., Caza, B., & Ashford, S. J. (2023). The organizational psychology of gig work: An integrative conceptual review. *The Journal of Applied Psychology*, *108*(3), 492–519. https://doi.org/https://doi.org/10.1037/apl0001029. DOI: 10.1037/apl0001029 PMID: 36222635

Debgupta, I., & Bhattacharyya, S. (2024). Talent Acquisition and Retention in the Gig Economy: Exploring Innovative HRM Practices for the Modern Workforce. *Journal of Research in Business and Management*, *12*(1), 84–90. www.questjournals.org. DOI: 10.1108/S0742-730120210000039001

Deloitte. (2024). Gig workforce: Talent management strategy. Deloitte. Retrieved from https://www2.deloitte.com/content/dam/Deloitte/in/Documents/human-capital/in-hc-gig-workforce-talent-management-strategy-noexp.pdf

Duggan, J., Sherman, U., Carbery, R., & McDonnell, A. (2020). Algorithmic management and app-work in the gig economy: A research agenda for employment relations and HRM. *Human Resource Management Journal*, *30*(1), 114–132. DOI: 10.1111/1748-8583.12258

Dunn, M. (2020). Making gigs work: Digital platforms, job quality and worker motivations. *New Technology, Work and Employment*, *35*(2), 232–249. https://doi.org/https://doi.org/10.1111/ntwe.12167. DOI: 10.1111/ntwe.12167

Dwivedi, P., Chaturvedi, V., & Vashist, J. K. (2023). Innovation for organizational sustainability: The role of HR practices and theories. *The International Journal of Organizational Analysis*, *31*(3), 759–776. DOI: 10.1108/IJOA-07-2021-2859

Elayan, M. B. (2022). Transformation of Human Resources Management Solutions as a strategic tool for GIG workers contracting. In *IGI Global eBooks* (pp. 790–813). DOI: 10.4018/978-1-6684-4503-7.ch039

European Parliament. (2019, April 4). Gig economy: How the EU improves platform workers' rights. European Parliament. https://www.europarl.europa.eu/topics/en/article/20190404STO35070/gig-economy-how-the-eu-improves-platform-workers-rights

Fair Work Ombudsman. (n.d.). Employee-like workers. Fair Work Ombudsman. Retrieved from https://www.fairwork.gov.au/find-help-for/independent-contractors/regulated-workers/employee-like-workers

Flynn, C. (2023, March 23). How Assembly Bill 5 (AB5) affects independent contractors in 2022. Hackler Flynn & Associates. https://hacklerflynnlaw.com/how-assembly-bill-5-ab5-will-affect-independent-contractors/

Fulmer, I. S., Gerhart, B., & Kim, J. H. (2023). Compensation and performance: A review and recommendations for the future. *Personnel Psychology*, *76*(2), 687–718. DOI: 10.1111/peps.12583

Ganesh, A. (2020). The Gig Economy: An HR Perspective to Managing Platform Workers.https://www.researchgate.net/publication/338987209_The_Gig_Economy_An_HR_Perspective_to_Managing_Platform_Workers

Gautam, V., Mishra, A. A., & Maheshwari, M. (2024). Examining the relevance of Human Resource Management in gig work: A systematic literature review & research agenda. *German Journal of Human Resource Management*, *23970022241231536*(4), 375–412. Advance online publication. DOI: 10.1177/23970022241231536

Gokhale Institute of Politics and Economics. (n.d.). Gig economy workers' livelihood: A qualitative study of ride-hailing platforms in Bangalore city, India. Retrieved from https://gipe.ac.in/gig-economy-workers-livelihood-a-qualitative-study-of-ride-hailing-platforms-in-bangalore-city-india/

Hagiu, A., & Wright, J. (2019). The status of workers and platforms in the sharing economy. *Journal of Economics & Management Strategy*, *28*(1), 97–108. DOI: 10.1111/jems.12299

Hall, J. V., & Krueger, A. B. (2018). An analysis of the labor market for Uber's driver-partners in the United States. *Industrial & Labor Relations Review*, *71*(3), 705–734. DOI: 10.1177/0019793917717222

Hara, H. (2014). The impact of firm-provided training on productivity, wages, and transition to regular employment for workers in flexible arrangements. *Journal of the Japanese and International Economies*, *34*, 336–359. DOI: 10.1016/j.jjie.2014.10.002

Harms, P. D., & Han, G. (2019). Algorithmic leadership: The future is now. *Journal of Leadership Studies*, *12*(4), 74–75. DOI: 10.1002/jls.21615

Harpur, P., & Blanck, P. (2020). Gig workers with disabilities: Opportunities, challenges, and regulatory response. *Journal of Occupational Rehabilitation*, *30*(4), 511–520. DOI: 10.1007/s10926-020-09937-4 PMID: 33146784

Indian Institute of Technology Delhi. (2024). IIT Delhi study on gig workers. Retrieved from https://home.iitd.ac.in/show.php?id=209&in_sections=Press

Kalli, N. K. A., Abba, N. Y. B., & Bukar, N. G. (2023). An assessment of the effect of training and development on employee performance: A review perspective. *World Journal of Advanced Research and Reviews*, *18*(2), 258–270. DOI: 10.30574/wjarr.2023.18.2.0748

Keegan, A., & Meijerink, J. (2022). HRM practices for value creation and value capture in online labor platform ecosystems: towards an integrative perspective. In *A Research Agenda for Strategic Human Resource Management* (pp. 167–194). Edward Elgar Publishing., https://www.masi-journal.com/journal/article/view/26 10.1108/JMP-07-2018-0277 DOI: 10.4337/9781800883802.00017

Kost, D., Fieseler, C., & Wong, S. I. (2020). Boundaryless careers in the gig economy: An oxymoron? *Human Resource Management Journal*, *30*(1), 100–113. DOI: 10.1111/1748-8583.12265

Krishnan, A., & Mishra, S. WORK AND WELL-BEING IN THE SHARING ECONOMY: EVIDENCE FROM INDIA. https://www.ippapublicpolicy.org/file/paper/60c21bc482342.pdf

Kuhn, K. M., Meijerink, J., & Keegan, A. (2021). Human resource management and the gig economy: Challenges and opportunities at the intersection between organizational HR decision-makers and digital labor platforms. *Research in Personnel and Human Resources Management*, *39*, 1–46. DOI: 10.1108/S0742-730120210000039001

Lehdonvirta, V. (2018). Flexibility in the gig economy: Managing time on three online piecework platforms. *New Technology, Work and Employment*, *33*(1), 13–29. DOI: 10.1111/ntwe.12102

Lehdonvirta, V., Kässi, O., Hjorth, I., Barnard, H., & Graham, M. (2019). The global platform economy: A new offshoring institution enabling emerging-economy micro providers. *Journal of Management*, *45*(2), 567–599. DOI: 10.1177/0149206318786781 PMID: 30774168

Lin, P. M., Peng, K. L., Au, W. C., & Baum, T. (2023). Food-delivery workers in the sharing economy: Supply-side human resource transformation. *International Journal of Hospitality & Tourism Administration*, *24*(4), 491–516. DOI: 10.1080/15256480.2021.2015042

Livemint. (2024, January 18). Swiggy introduces ambulance service for delivery executives, dependents. Livemint. Retrieved from https://www.livemint.com/news/india/swiggy-introduces-ambulance-service-for-delivery-executives-dependents-11673877855361.html

Malhotra, P., & Ganghas, S. (2023). HUMAN RESOURCE MANAGEMENT IN THE GIG ECONOMY. *MANAGEMENT METAMORPHOSIS: NAVIGATING THE CHANGING LANDSCAPE*, 113.

Malik, A., Budhwar, P., & Srikanth, N. R. (2020). Gig economy, 4IR and artificial intelligence: Rethinking strategic HRM. In Human & technological resource management (HTRM): New insights into revolution 4.0 (pp. 75-88). Emerald Publishing Limited.DOI:DOI: 10.1108/978-1-83867-223-220201005

Masta, R., & Kaushiva, P. (2024), "Work in the platform economy: a systematic literature review", *Employee Relations*, Vol. ahead-of-print No. ahead-of-print. DOI: 10.1108/ER-12-2023-0638

McKinsey Global Institute. (2016). Independent work: Choice, necessity and the Gig economy.https://www.mckinsey.com/~/media/mckinsey/featured%20insights/employment%20and%20 growth/independent%20work%20choice%20 necessity%20 and%20the%20 gig%20economy/independent-work- choice-necessity-and-the-gig economy-full

Meijerink, J., & Keegan, A. (2019). Conceptualizing human resource management in the gig economy: Toward a platform ecosystem perspective. *Journal of Managerial Psychology*, *34*(4), 214–232. DOI: 10.1108/JMP-07-2018-0277

Mezmir, E. A. (2020). Qualitative data analysis: An overview of data reduction, data display, and interpretation. Research on humanities and social sciences, 10(21), 15-27. https://iiste.org/Journals/index.php/RHSS/article/viewFile/54898/56707

Ola Institute. (2020). Ola COVID-19 report. Retrieved from https://olawebcdn.com/ola-institute/covid19-report.pdf

Outlook Business. (2024). Swiggy announces initiative to provide career growth opportunities to delivery partners. Outlook Business. Retrieved from https://www.outlookbusiness.com/corporate/swiggy-announces-initiative-to-provide-career-growth-opportunities-to-delivery-partners

Oviedo-Trespalacios, O. (2022). Factors influencing road safety compliance among food delivery riders: An extension of the job demands-resources (JD-R) model. *Transportation Research Part A, Policy and Practice*, *166*, 541–556. https://doi.org/https://doi.org/10.1016/j.tra.2022.11.002. DOI: 10.1016/j.tra.2022.11.002

Panda, P. C., Pathak, K., & Panda, R. (2023). Gig Economy: Potential and Challenges for Human Resources in Urban India. Reimagining Management in the post VUCA World, 1.

Pandey, N. D. R. K., & Sarangi, N. S. (2023). A case study on talent acquisition at Organisations. *International Journal of Engineering and Management Research, 13*(1), 6–11. DOI: 10.31033/ijemr.13.1.2

Patil, B. S., & Priya, M. R. S. R. (2024). Human Resource Frontiers: Pioneering Humane Innovations for Fair Treatment of Workers in the Gig Economy. In Ogunyemi, K. (Ed.), *Humanistic Management in the Gig Economy*. Humanism in Business Series. Palgrave Macmillan., DOI: 10.1007/978-3-031-59944-6_4

Rahman, S. U., Sultan, M. S., & Tabassam, A. (2024). The Impact of the Gig economy on the Traditional Employment and the Necessity for Revised Business. *HR and Legal Strategies Pakistan Journal of International Affairs, 7*(1). Advance online publication. DOI: 10.52337/pjia.v7i1.1013

Ray, C., Nyberg, A. J., & Maltarich, M. A. (2023). Human capital resources emergence theory: The role of social capital. *Academy of Management Review, 48*(2), 313–335. DOI: 10.5465/amr.2020.0186

Riordan, T., Robinson, R. N. S., & Hoffstaedter, G. (2023). Seeking justice beyond the platform economy: Migrant workers navigating precarious lives. *Journal of Sustainable Tourism, 31*(12), 2734–2751. https://doi.org/https://doi.org/10.1080/09669582.2022.2136189. DOI: 10.1080/09669582.2022.2136189

Roy, G., & Shrivastava, A. K. (2020). Future of gig economy: opportunities and challenges. Imi Konnect, 9(1), 14-27.https://www.researchgate.net/profile/Gobinda-Roy-2/publication/340253836_Future_of_Gig_Economy_Opportunities_and_Challenges/links/5e7f62bea6fdcc139c0f752b/Future-of-Gig-Economy-Opportunities-and-Challenges.pdf

Singh, G., & Shastri, R. K. (2023). Opportunities and Challenges in Digital Human Resource Management with special reference to gig economy workers.

Spurk, D., & Straub, C. (2020). Flexible employment relationships and careers in times of the COVID-19 pandemic. *Journal of Vocational Behavior, 119*, 103435. Advance online publication. DOI: 10.1016/j.jvb.2020.103435 PMID: 32382161

Stanford, J. (2017). The resurgence of gig work: Historical and theoretical perspectives. *Economic and Labour Relations Review, 28*(3), 382–401. DOI: 10.1177/1035304617724303

Stewart, A., & Stanford, J. (2017). Regulating work in the gig economy: What are the options? *Economic and Labour Relations Review*, *28*(3), 1–18. DOI: 10.1177/1035304617722461

Sung, S. Y., & Choi, J. N. (2023). What drives firms to invest in training and developing employees? Time-dependent effects of firm internal and external contingencies. *The International Journal of Human Resource Management,* 34(2), 223–252. https://doi.org/https://doi.org/10.1080/ 09585192.2021.1965007.

Swiggy. (2024). Swiggy launches Project NEXT, creating a career path for delivery partners. Swiggy Corporate Press Release. Retrieved from https://www.swiggy.com/corporate/press-release/swiggy-launches-project-next-creating-a-career-path-for-delivery-partners/

Talukder, M. B., Chowdhury, S. A., & Khan, M. R. (2025). The Gig Economy: Economic Innovations and Technological Advancements in Human Resource Management. In Economic Innovations and Technological Developments in HRM (pp. 381-404). IGI Global.

Times of India. (2024, January 2). Only three online companies offer minimum wage: Study. The Times of India. Retrieved from https://timesofindia.indiatimes.com/business/india-business/only-three-online-companies-offer-minimum-wage-study/articleshow/104835291.cms

Transformational Upskilling. (n.d.). Uber: Transformational upskilling initiatives. Retrieved from https://www.transformationalupskilling.org/uber

Tripathi, M. A., Tripathi, R., Yadav, U. S., & Shastri, R. K. (2022). Gig economy: Reshaping strategic HRM in the era of industry 4.0 and artificial intelligence. *Journal of Positive School Psychology*, •••, 3569–3579.

Valente, E., Patrus, R., & Córdova Guimarães, R. (2019). Sharing economy: Becoming an Uber driver in a developing country. *Revista De Gestão*, *26*(2), 143–160. DOI: 10.1108/REGE-08-2018-0088

Waldkirch, M., Bucher, E., Schou, P. K., & Grünwald, E. (2021). Controlled by the algorithm, coached by the crowd—How HRM activities take shape on digital work platforms in the gig economy. *International Journal of Human Resource Management*, *32*(12), 2643–2682. DOI: 10.1080/09585192.2021.1914129

Watson, G. P., Kistler, L. D., Graham, B. A., & Sinclair, R. R. (2021). Looking at the Gig Picture: Defining Gig Work and Explaining Profile Differences in Gig Workers' Job Demands and Resources. *Group & Organization Management*, *46*(2), 327–361. DOI: 10.1177/1059601121996548

Wiener, M., Cram, W., & Benlian, A. (2021). Algorithmic control and gig workers: A legitimacy perspective of Uber drivers. *European Journal of Information Systems*. Advance online publication. DOI: 10.1080/0960085X.2021.1977729

Wiener, M., Cram, W., & Benlian, A. (2021). Algorithmic control and gig workers: A legitimacy perspective of Uber drivers. *European Journal of Information Systems*. Advance online publication. DOI: 10.1080/0960085X.2021.1977729

Williams, P., McDonald, P., & Mayes, R. (2023). Recruitment in the gig economy: Attraction and selection on digital platforms. In *Technologically Mediated Human Resource Management* (pp. 142–168). Routledge. DOI: 10.4324/9781003388203-6

Woodside, J., Vinodrai, T., & Moos, M. (2021). Bottom-up strategies, platform worker power and local action: Learning from ride hailing drivers. Local Economy. *Local Economy, 36*(4), 325–343. https://doi.org/https://doi.org/10.1177/02690942211040170. DOI: 10.1177/02690942211040170

Xuan, Z. (2022). The innovation and value pursuit of the compensation system in the gig economy. *Acad. J. Bus Manag, 4*, 50.

Yablonsky, S. (2020). A multidimensional platform ecosystem framework. *Kybernetes, 49*(7), 2003–2035. DOI: 10.1108/K-07-2019-0447

Chapter 8
Market Mobility Effect on Gig Economy Adaptability by Mediation of Talent Management in the Horn of Africa

Wako Jio
https://orcid.org/0009-0003-6192-459X
Bule Hora University, Ethiopia

Shashi Kant
https://orcid.org/0000-0003-4722-5736
Bule Hora University, Ethiopia

ABSTRACT

This chapter examines how mobility of the market affects the flexibility of gig economies for the Horn of Africa, with emphasis on the part played by talent management. The study uses sample size of 390 respondents, and uses Kaiser Meyer Olkin (KMO) measure to test for data adequacy to do factor analysis, and gets a KMO value that deemed it appropriate for factor analysis. CFA is conducted to verify the specification of the measurement model that measures the constructs adequately. Exploratory analysis of the dynamics between MM, TM, and GE-Adapt is conducted using Structural Equation Modeling (SEM) through AMOS software. In all the antecedents, the study concludes that rising market mobility improves the flexibility of gig economies consistently, with talent management as a moderator. Talent management best practices for these gig platforms include recruitment, development, engagement, and rewards, which enhance the platform's capability to

DOI: 10.4018/979-8-3693-9385-7.ch008

quickly address market forces and customer needs.

INTRODUCTION

This chapter examines how mobility of the market affects the flexibility of gig economies for the Horn of Africa, with emphasis on the part played by talent management (Kravariti et al., 2023). The investigation uses sample size of 390 respondents, and uses Kaiser Meyer Olkin (KMO) measure to test for data adequacy to do factor analysis, and gets a KMO value that deemed it appropriate for factor analysis (Civelek, 2018). CFA is conducted to verify the specification of the measurement model that measures the constructs adequately. Exploratory analysis of the dynamics among MM, TM, and GE-Adapt is conducted using Structural Equation Modeling (SEM) through AMOS software (Civelek, 2018). In all the antecedents, the investigation concludes that rising market mobility improves the flexibility of gig economies consistently, with talent management as a moderator (Norwani et al., 2022).

The investigation of market mobility's influence on the flexibility of gig economies in the Horn of Africa has a number of obstacles. For starters, the region's different political and economic landscapes might lead to data gathering discrepancies due to major variations in local rules and market conditions (Kravariti et al., 2023). This diversity complicates determining how market mobility affects gig economies and their capacity to adjust. Furthermore, the gig economy in the Horn of Africa is frequently devoid of official frameworks, making it difficult to track talent management practices and outcomes efficiently (Giousmpasoglou et al., 2024). Cultural considerations may influence views of gig labor and talent management techniques, leading to data biases. Furthermore, restricted access to technology and the internet in some locations impedes efficient communication and data collection, making it difficult to assess the entire range of personnel management techniques in gig economies (Thomas & Baddipudi, 2022). Finally, the dynamic nature of both the gig economy and market needs necessitates a flexible research methodology, which can be challenging to adopt consistently across different contexts in the area (Kravariti et al., 2023).

Talent management best practices for these gig platforms include recruitment, development, engagement, and rewards, which enhance the platform's capability to quickly address market forces and customer needs. Leveraging the concept of market mobility, this chapter stresses the importance of talent management the key stakeholders in the gig economy (Parey & Waldinger, 2023). Altogether, the investigation reveals the channels by which market mobility affects flexibility, which will help policymakers and business executives who want to make the gig economy more sustainable for the Horn of Africa (Norwani et al., 2022). Therefore, this work concludes that there is a need to pursue effective talent management to enable the development of a robust gig economy capable of sustaining the quest of people and corporates in the economic stressors in the market (Kravariti et al., 2023).

BACKGROUND OF INVESTIGATION

The Horn of Africa which includes countries like Ethiopia, Kenya, Somalia and Uganda has been through social and economic changes mainly due to emergence of gig economy (Norwani et al., 2022). These economies are flexible and are defined by working arrangements that allow workers to participate in short term arrangements that are subscription based tasking, where information technology platforms are involved. The general challenges which affect the effectiveness of implementation of gig economies are as follows: One clear example is Ethiopia, where the adoption of mobile technology is rapidly growing, giving rise to different gig sites. However, a lot of gig workers experience real-life problems (Nwaobi, 2024), for example, many have no reliable access to the internet connection, which limits them in participation in such opportunities. Moreover, regulatory provisions in Ethiopia are time-bound and do not suit gig work platforms and their organizational structure. It leads to the fact that workers have no legal rights to protect and can be easily exploited and have instable income (Giousmpasoglou et al., 2024).

In Kenya, the use of ride hailing services such as Uber and Bolt among others has brought to light the same. Despite the fact that these platforms have generated additional employment opportunities for many, drivers' concerns include issues such as erratic income, fixed costs such as vehicle maintenance and fuels. Moreover, the recent talent management practices in these platforms help the workers in developing their skills and expertise for the market needs and improve employability but here point noticed that the structured talent management practices in these platforms are not present for the worker's skills developments (Kravariti et al., 2023). Somalia again manifests another example, where people engage a lot in the informal economy activities. Mobile Money Agents and online delivery services among others have been key sources of income through gig economy. However, the absence of an official status, and lack of state support means that workers often remain in conditions of extreme poverty and have no access to basic needs such as affordable healthcare or training or social security (Norwani et al., 2022).

The foregoing case studies illustrate complex issues related to the application of gig economies in the Horn of Africa. They call attention to the fact that they require integrated solutions that concern regulatory impediments, acquisition of recourse, and talent management systems (Kravariti et al., 2023). Understanding these challenges, this work seeks to identify *"how MNEs might promote market mobility and talent management to encourage adaptability within gig economies and pave the way to more sustainable economic development within the country and, consequently, in the region?"*

STATEMENT OF PROBLEM

While there is an increasing appreciation of gig economies as essential parts of the labor market in the Horn of Africa today, there is a substantial shortfall among the actual challenges faced by gig workers and the potential for effective portable labor markets (Norwani et al., 2022). Ideally, such economies should incorporate FWAs effectively with strong talent management that would lead to stabilization of employments and the economies in question with better position to rebound from extreme shocks (Kravariti et al., 2023). But primary evidence is found in other research showing that most gig service manifestrs are paid irregularly, are denied basic needs necessity, and receive insufficient legal protection. Such disparity invites intense discussion about the relevance of existing paradigms, as well as the practical usability of theoretical concepts.

Also, prior research gives mixed findings about the correlation among the market mobility and the readiness of gig economy (Norwani et al., 2022). Some studies argue that higher market mobility improves gig worker productivity but others demonstrate the lack of effective talent management practices to support this (Kravariti et al., 2023). This theoretical lack calls for a deeper understanding of how these constructs operate in the context of the Horn of Africa, which is characterized by qualitatively higher levels of socio-economic development than the African countries more widely (Parey & Waldinger, 2023). Further, the literature gaps make this terrain challenging due to a lack of empirical studies on the mediating role of TM in adapting gig economies (Thomas & Baddipudi, 2022). This is manifested in the Horn of Africa particularly where social cultural and economic setting creates an existing employment model that does not align with the gig employment type. Further, there are fundamental practical issues that affect the expansion and resiliency of the gig work model including infrastructural constraints, regulatory ambiguities, and lack of access to technology which have not received enough research attention (Norwani et al., 2022).

This research seeks to address these gaps through an expansive investigation of the influence of market mobility on the flexibility of gig economies using talent management lens. In doing so, the research will apply qualitative and quantitative data to theories that may help policymakers and practitioners. More importantly, all these challenges addressed in this work will be closed with practical suggestions for future references to upcoming researchers and policy makers that will help to enhance and promote a sustainable and harmonized gig economy in the Horn of Africa .

THEORETICAL FOUNDATION

Human Capital Theory: Human capital theory argues that undertaking education, training and accumulating skills will improve the number of man hours an individual can produce as well as having a higher economic value than physical capital (Griffen, 2024). This theory by itself would prove rather handy when applied to gig economy since the flexibility in the change of market forces is a substantial aspect of the model. In the Horn of Africa, gig work is generally opaque and highly atomized and the focus on talent management does, therefore, fit with human capital theory in prescribing constant skills acquisition and training (Norwani et al., 2022). Adopting best practices for talent management can help improve the skills of gig workers and therefore improve their ability to negotiate the formal employment relations climate. Thus, the work under discussion pays great attention to the strengthening of human capital the proficiency of which is critical to attain flexibility within gig economies (Griffen, 2024).

Resource-Based View (RBV) Theory: The Resource-Based View (RBV) theory concentrates on analyzing resources and capabilities owned by the organization and which may result in gaining competitive advantages. (Murtiningrum & Aligarh, 2024) Applying this theory in the context of gig economies allows for analyzing how gig platforms maximize their value from human capital the gig workers and their talents in order to create corporates that are responsive to change (Norwani et al., 2022). With talent management being a strategic resource, gig platforms can develop a contingent workforce that supplements notional variations. This theory helps in establishing an understanding of how positive management of human resources brings about success and sustainability of gig economies within Horn of Africa (Norwani et al., 2022).

Institutional Theory: The focus of Institutional Theory is on institutional structures, rules, regulations, norms, and policies as antecedents to organizational activities (Jonas, 2024). Looking at the horn of Africa's gig economies, this theory is essential when explaining the effects of regulations on gig workers and business models. Research on institutional pressures can help us understand why some talent management practices are implemented or not promoted in the gig economy. In the following research, it is thus possible to explore the institutional drivers at work in moderating the effects of market mobility on flexibility of work arrangements in gig economies (Parey & Waldinger, 2023).

Dynamic Resources Theory: Development of Dynamic Capabilities Theory centers on the organization capacity to coordinate create and modify internal and external assets that enable the organization to adapt to evolving environments (Bakker & Demerouti, 2024). This theory makes most sense in gig economies because they are characterized by high levels of dynamism and thus, flexibility offers an edge. While the performance of the gig economy in the Horn of Africa is contextualized by macroeconomic challenges that are rarely stable, this chapter has argued for the need for dynamic ness in response to performance volatility. In this context, there is the need to adopt talent management integration as this creates organizational workforce that is adaptable (Kravariti et al., 2023).

Hence, the major theoretical framework for this investigation is "Human Capital Theory". This decision is based on the perspective of understanding the extent to which talent management investment can improve the skill and productivity of the gig workers to allow them to cope with a dynamic market environment (Kravariti et al., 2023). Through the analysis of human capital, the investigation will offer a broad analysis for the future of gig economical demands in organized and underdeveloped countries of the Horn of Africa. This perspective does not only dovetail with the two primary themes of market mobility and flexibility but also highlighted the overall organizational theme of the challenges related to human capital development in a volatile economic climate (Parey & Waldinger, 2023).

EMPIRICAL LITERATURE REVIEW

Market Mobility and Gig Economies Flexibility

The link among MM and applicability of gig economies has therefore featured prominently in latest empirical literature mainly because gig economies are continuously changing in response to advances in technologies and shifting market conditions. Previous studies also indicate that achieving market mobility is crucial for the improvement of flexibility of gig workers and platforms (Parey & Waldinger, 2023). For instance, it has been found out that a higher degree of market malleability enhance opportunities for gig workers to transfer from one job to the other; and from one sector to the other thus enhancing their employment security and income variability (Norwani et al., 2022). This is essential in nature because it allows flexibility especially within the economic field where job prospects may from time to time; especially within the Horn of Africa region where establishment turbulence due to factors such as political influence or market forces is evident.

Many chapters have pointed out specific features of the relationship among these variables. For instance, manifests out that the survey showed gig platform workers with higher flow mobility observed higher levels of job satisfaction and commitment as compared to their counterparts with limited mobility in choosing the jobs and platforms. The fluidity also serves their need for work-life adjustment and contributes positively to a flexible workforce that is a boon for gig companies that can access a more extensive pool of talents (Norwani et al., 2022). The same observe that open and permeable labor markets especially supported by favorable regulatory measures boost mobility of workers from job to another and indeed flexibility of the workers to cope with shocks in the market. Besides, talent management has a significant part to play in shaping flexibility prevalent across the gig economies. Research analysis manifests that traditional talent management solutions including training, coaching, and enabling promotions enhance gig workers for market requirements (Norwani et al., 2022). It was suggested that while human capital development improves individual work adaptability, it also taps organizational performance improvement. This means that the gig platforms that seek to build sustainable talent management strategies that are consistent with the principles of the market mobility need to go beyond the basic tenets of omni-channel talent management (Parey & Waldinger, 2023).

However, despite the existing literature, there is still a lacuna regarding the specific pathways by which market mobility affects adaptability in Gig economies, in the context of the Horn of Africa's socio-economic environment (Norwani et al., 2022) . Most chapters have been done with samples drawn mainly from developed economy countries because institutions governing such economies and particularly the structures of their labor markets are dissimilar to those of emerging economy countries. hence, there is a need to do more empirical research that explores these dynamics in the context of the Horn of Africa taking into consideration other contextual factors such as; inadequate infrastructure, bounded regulatory environment and socio-cultural factors that may influence both market mobility and talent management (Norwani et al., 2022) . In sum, the conceptual and empirical literature reviewed in this chapter highlights the essential link among market mobility and flexibility of gig markets. These relationships will remain important to understand as gig work brings on to increase in various countries around the world and in the paths that are especially more challenging for the resilience of gig workers and its platforms(Thomas & Baddipudi, 2022) . Further research should focus on how such context-specific factors can be effectively addressed, and how frameworks that have proven successful in other countries have been translated appropriately to African countries with an eye toward effectively incorporating the strategies of market mobility for enhanced flexibility in delivering gig services (Parey & Waldinger, 2023) .

H1: Market Mobility and Gig Economies flexibility have empirical association.

Market Mobility and Talent Management

Suds walking the literature related to market mobility and talent management these two concepts are inseparable in explaining the relationship among market mobility and organizational performance as well as talent management in regards to workforce flexibility (Parey & Waldinger, 2023). Data manifests that increased marketability mobility makes it easier for workers to change jobs and therefore improves acquisition of skills besides satisfaction. Research has also pointed out that corporates with strong talent management processes inclusive of specialized recruitment, training and development, and skills enhancement can influence of employee mobility and retention greatly (Kravariti et al., 2023). Additionally, research evidence manifests evidence that the talent management process moderates the relationship among market mobility and organizational effectiveness by allowing for a workforce flexible enough to meet new mobility challenges (Parey & Waldinger, 2023).

For instance, in a investigation done by Kravariti et al., (2023), it was established that firms with sound talent management policies ensure that they attract talent and retain them while at the same time ensuring that employees frequently swap from one position to another, thus implying high organizational flexibility.. Surveys also have revealed that talent management disparities in the workplace may be addressed through talent management equality: Lastly, there is evidence for the belief that since corporates promoting equity and diversity remain well-equipped to compete for talent within fluid labor markets, (Kravariti et al., 2023). All in all, this pool of literature demonstrates how market mobility together with the management of talent is valuable for organizational buoyancy as well as employee satisfaction (Parey & Waldinger, 2023).

H2: Market Mobility and Talent Management have empirical association.

Talent Management and Gig Economies Adaptability

From this empirical investigation of talent management and adaptability in gig economies, there is a mutual relationship among the workforce and the corporates' overall performance (Kravariti et al., 2023). It has been ascertained that talent management activities such as skill building and flexibility as well as working arrangements are helpful for raising adaptability in a company's gig workers (Ahmad & Norzaidi, 2024) established that corporates that support gig workers' training have a higher chance of enhancing effectiveness in responding to market forces due to the dynamics of gigs. In addition, research findings reveal that talent management practices that are more equitable and diverse yield more satisfied employee's retention of gig work positions (Kravariti et al., 2023). For example, workers noted that availability of supply- and career-enhancing resources and programs keeps gig workers committed to platform and more resilient. Also, from the empirical perspective, it can be stated that technology enhances communication and collaboration in talent management processes, which would in turn help gig workers handle various tasks and projects, (Norwani et al., 2022). In total, the objective of the present article highlights the need to have effective talent management strategies that would facilitate adaptability of corporates in the gig economy, in relation to the setting and dynamism of the labor market (Ahmad & Norzaidi, 2021).

However, issues regarding how each of these dynamics unfolds in various contexts, especially emerging economies remain partially understood. A significant amount of prior research has been conducted in the developed context and hence is not easily generalizable for the electronic labor markets in the developing contexts such as the Horn of Africa. Therefore, further research at micro-level is required towards understanding how and to what extent cultural, economic as well as institutional factors moderate the process of talent management mediation among market mobility and the flexibility of gig economies (Parey & Waldinger, 2023). It can help explain why gig workers in such regions face certain debilities and offer how ground breaking talent management strategies can foster mobility to the market while synchronizing for flexibility (Kravariti et al., 2023).

H3: Talent Management and Gig Economies Adaptability have empirical association.

Market Mobility, Gig Economies Adaptability and Talent Management

It has given rise to a valuable line of research regarding shifts in market mobility, flexibility of gig economy and their influence of talent management as new association will emerge in an ever shifting and globalized talent marketplace (Norwani et al., 2022). Labor market flexibility is a concept categorized as two main forms, firstly, the ability of workers to move from one job to another frequently in order to meet clients' need in the gig economy. This idea is closely related to flexibility of the gig workers who on one hand bargain with changing working conditions, demands of the clients and with on the other hand development of technology. Both market mobility and adaptability are moderated by talent management as the panel indicates through designing and implementing strategic workforce development practices (Parey & Waldinger, 2023) .

The literature has shown that talent management moderates market mobility of gig workers more effectively than past research (Norwani et al., 2022). For example, Cappelli notes that companies that established investments in education and training also manifest avenues for the movement across firm career lines to occur more fluidly. Consequently, talent management investments of this sort are particularly essential in asserting conditions of gig economy where guarantee of stable income may be turbulent (Kravariti et al., 2023). In this way, one can turn the world of work in gig employment and corporates can to develop skills and knowledge to enable gig worker to effectively handle different tasks with a view of improving their market mobility whenever new opportunities come up (Parey & Waldinger, 2023) . This connection means that talent management practices can work as an enabler that leads to the enhancement of the market mobility of gig workers and hence enhance the flexibility of gig workers (Norwani et al., 2022).

In addition, the literature also supports the proposition linking talent management and gig economy's flexibility. In their investigation of the gig economy (Norwani et al., 2022) identify organizational investment in training and development as beneficial to both the individual worker and the general resilience of the gig economy. While having access to quality and continuous skills upgrading and training, gig service manifestrs are in a better position put up with market forces challenges and dynamism. It is also becoming essential across any freelance marketplaces since the changes in volatility rates can be very unpredictable, and flexibility in adapting to such changes is often the key to success.

Market mobility and adaptability have attracted interest in current research in which talent management is postulated to play a mediation role. According to Kravariti et al., (2023), talent management studies suggest that talent management has the potential to greatly support the flexibility of the gig workers for new roles and responsibilities. For instance if companies adopt structures such as mentorship, and career progression options, gig workers are known to have better job satisfaction and productivity. These lead to increased flexibility because the workers now have the feeling that they are quite capable of handling different tasks. From the evidence, it can be seen that talent management not only enable to achieve the market mobility but also to ensure that the gig workers are ready to accept the market mobility that comes with It (Parey & Waldinger, 2023). Therefore, with the help of the findings of the empirical literature, one can analysis the combinational relationships among the agencies of market mobility, the ability of the gig economies to evolve, and the role of talent management (Kravariti et al., 2023). These relationships become important to understand as gig work continues to grow worldwide and ideally, for the creation of frameworks tailored to support these freelancers. From the research gaps highlighted above, the following areas are suggested for future research: The focus should be continued on gathering micro level data about talent management approaches to understand how gig employment can be made less vulnerable to the risks of a new environment (Kravariti et al., 2023).

> H4: Market Mobility, Gig Economies Adaptability and Talent Management mediation have empirical association.

Figure 1. Conceptual Framework

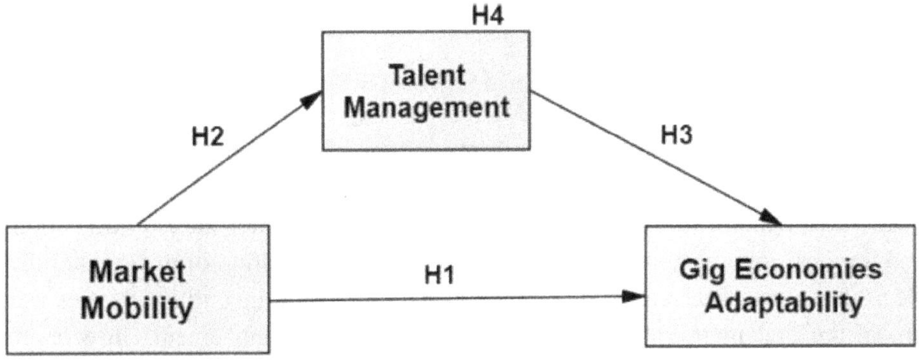

RESEARCH METHODOLOGY

This investigation used a quantitative research technique and examined the connection among personnel management, market mobility, and gig economy adaptation. To guarantee that the outcomes were representative, a sample of 390 respondents was carefully chosen (Stadtländer, 2009). A structured questionnaire with a number of items intended to measure the relevant components was distributed as part of the data gathering procedure. The Kaiser-Meyer-Olkin (KMO) metric was used to evaluate if the data was sufficient for factor analysis. The sample was deemed appropriate for exploratory factor analysis (EFA) when the KMO value was higher than the suggested cutoff of 0.60. EFA was conducted to determine the underlying dimensions of the constructs in the questionnaire after the KMO evaluation. This statistical method made it possible to identify the key components of talent management, market mobility, and gig economy adaptation. By identifying which items loaded strongly on their respective factors, the EFA outcomes helped refine the scale and eventually led to the removal of elements that did not significantly contribute to the constructs (Civelek, 2018).

Confirmatory Factor Analysis (CFA) was performed using AMOS software to evaluate the measurement model after the dimensions were determined using EFA. By using CFA, the researchers were able to confirm that the components they had found fit the theoretical framework proposed in the literature. The scale effectively assessed the relevant constructs, as the analysis verified the model's fit. Cronbach's alpha was used to evaluate the scale's overall reliability; outcomes greater than 0.70 indicated that the items' internal consistency was satisfactory (Stadtländer, 2009).

Scale Development

A comprehensive examination of related literature served as the foundation for the scale creation process and offered a strong conceptual framework for the components being studied. Using current ideas and actual data, the first stage was to define the concepts of talent management, market mobility, and gig economy adaptation. Dimensions including employment mobility, inter-industry transitions, and regional flexibility were included in the operationalization of market mobility. Recruitment, staff development, engagement tactics, and incentive schemes were among the fundamental techniques that constituted talent management. Gig economy adaptation was defined as gig workers' and corporates' capacity to successfully react to shifting market conditions. This conceptual framework served as a guide for item creation. To make sure the things were thorough and pertinent, researchers created pieces that represented the different facets of each build. For example, statements like "I regularly switch jobs to improve my career opportunities" were included in items assessing market mobility, and statements like "My organization offers opportunities for skill development" were included in items measuring talent management.

To assess the items' relevance and intelligibility, a smaller sample of respondents participated in pilot testing. Revisions were made in response to feedback from this step, guaranteeing that the scale appropriately represented the constructions. The completed scale was given to the entire sample of 390 responders after the pilot test. Through statistical analysis, the scale's validity and reliability were thoroughly evaluated. Internal consistency was verified by reliability testing using Cronbach's alpha, and the construct structure was validated by component analysis (Stadtländer, 2009). The scale's thorough measurement of the targeted constructs was guaranteed by the combination of EFA and CFA, which closely matched the theoretical underpinnings outlined in the literature.

DATA ANALYSIS

Table 1. KMO and Bartlett's Test

Kaiser-Meyer-Olkin Measure of Sampling Adequacy.		**.850**
Bartlett's Test of Sphericity	Approx. Chi-Square	1419.738
	Df	91
	Sig.	.000

Source: Authors

In the table 1, the KMO measure is calculated at 0.850, which manifests evidence of sampling adequacy. Any value greater than 0.70 is manifested to be acceptable and values closer to 1.00 mean that the sample used is ideal for factor analysis. This result also suggests that the variables included in the investigation have enough correlations to warrant factor analysis. Also, Bartlett's Test of Sphericity test result is Approx. Chi-square = 1419.738 df = 91 p = 0.000. This result is used to reject the null hypothesis that the correlation matrix is an identity matrix which will imply the variables are unlikely to be useful in factor analysis. The p-value is below 0.05, which is sufficiently small to dismiss this null hypothesis, which means that there are actually quite a few connections among the variables. In aggregate, these findings suggest that the data is appropriate for conducting a second stage of analysis, specifically Exploratory Factor Analysis (EFA) to determine the factor structure of the constructs associated with market mobility, the gig economy's flexibility, and talent management.

Table 2. Total Variance Explained

Component	**Initial Eigenvalues**			**Extraction Sums of Squared Loadings**			**Rotation Sums of Squared Loadings**		
	Total	**% of Variance**	**Cumulative %**	**Total**	**% of Variance**	**Cumulative %**	**Total**	**% of Variance**	**Cumulative %**
1	4.51	32.235	32.235	4.51	32.235	32.235	3.00	21.451	21.451
2	1.37	9.787	42.022	1.37	9.787	42.022	2.16	15.491	36.942
3	1.27	9.087	51.110	1.27	9.087	51.110	1.98	14.168	51.110
4	.949	6.782	57.892						
5	.871	6.223	64.115						
6	.773	5.519	69.634						

Extraction Method: Principal Component Analysis.
Source: Authors

Table 2 manifests the first component which is the first component of the principal component analysis reflects an initial eigenvalue of 4.51 with variance percentage of 32.235%. This means that this component has captured a rather significant variance in the dataset which underlines its importance in explaining the underlying constructs. The second component has an eigenvalue of 1.37, and contribution 9.787% thus giving a cumulative 42.022%. The third component follows closely with an eigenvalue of 1.27, it accounts for 9.087%of the total variance, and the cumulative percentage is 51.110%. Combined, these three components explain over 50 percent of the variance in the data thereby providing robust support to their roles in capturing the constructs under investigation. The next components despite being significant in variance explanation are below one: the 4th one equals to 0.949, the 5th one equals to 0.871 and the 6th one equals to 0.773. These components account for 6,782 percent, 6,223 percent and 5,519 percent of the variance respectively but are not as large in terms of this measure of variance. The type of extraction method used was Principal Component Analysis is widely used in finding the principal components. Taken together these findings suggest that the first three factors might be the most valuable with respect to the constructs of market mobility, the adaptability of gig economies, and the management of talent.

Confirmatory Factor Examination

The actual plan of a set of directed proxies is checked by sorts of statistics called confirmatory principle component assessment. As a result of frame job and the correlative among observed proxy, conjectures can be examined with CFA. As a way to test the hypothesized relationship among the proxies that are being driven and the implicit notions that inform them, the inquiry used CFA based on Table 3.

Table 3. Covariance

Covariance			**Estimate**	**S.E.**	**C.R.**	**P**	**Hy.**
Talent Management	**<-->**	**Market Mobility**	**.242**	**.021**	**8.231**	**.00**	**H2**
Talent Management	<-->	Gig Economies Adaptability	.303	.032	7.692	.00	**H3**
Market Mobility	<-->	Gig Economies Adaptability	.254	.24	7.831	.00	**H1**

Source: Authors

Table 3 manifests the covariance's found that the covariance of "Talent Management" and "Market Mobility" is equal to 0.242 with S.E. equal to 0.021 and C.R. equal to 8.231. This substantial C.R., marked with asterisks (.00), demonstrates a positive association, thus providing empirical support for H2. This indicates that first, talent management practices have an appreciable correlation with improved market fluidity of the gig workers, and second, investing in structured talent management benefits organizational mobility of the workforce. Also, the covariance among "Talent Management" and "Gig Economies Adaptability" is 0.303 and an S.E. of 0.032, which has C.R of 7.692. This also manifests to a high positive correlation which supports H3 Hypothesis. These findings suggest that talent management practices enhance gig worker flexibility because the practices manifest skills and resources to help gig workers succeed in highly flexible work environments. Finally the covariance among "Market Mobility" and "Gig Economies Adaptability" is found to be 0.254; S.E. 0.24, C.R. value is 7.831. This significant association upholds H1, suggesting that more market mobility is related to increased adaptability of gig workers. The positive covariance values indicate that when gig workers encounter more mobility in terms of tasks assignments, their flexibility to new tasks and contexts also rises. In total, the covariance's identified in this table suggest how talent management, market mobility, and flexibility are related in gig work and how SWP has potential to improve the tenacity and efficacy of gig workers.

Table 4. Validity Concern

	CR	AVE	MSV	MaxR(H)	MM	TM	GEA
MM	0.732	0.643	0.219	0.852	**0.654**		
TM	0.758	0.657	0.132	0.763	0.171	**0.665**	
GEA	0.793	0.603	0.274	0.797	0.383	0.193	**0.684**

Note: MM= Market Mobility; TM= Talent Management; GEA= Gig Economies Adaptability
Source: Authors

Table 4 manifests an overview of the validity metrics. Coefficient alphas Composite reliability levels all reveal acceptable levels of internal consistency and completeness of the constructs, as presented in the table below: MM = 0.732; TM = 0.758; GEA = 0.793. In broad, an average CR above 0.70 is deemed reasonably acceptable and this meant that all the items under each construct effectively captured the requisite concepts of the investigation. The following Table 4 manifests the Average Variance Extracted (AVE) figures, which entrenches the validity of the constructs; MM equals 0.643; TM equals 0.657; and GEA equal 0.603. AVE values of above 0.50 suggest that the constructs have a considerable degree of explanation on the variance of their items. To assure that all three constructs indeed target the intended dimensions of market mobility, talent management, and flexibility, all three of them surpass this figure. The MSV which depicts the maximum communality of constructs are 0.219 for MM and TM, for TM and GEA are 0.132 and for MM and GEA are 0.274. These values imply that the correlations among the inter-constructs are moderate, meaning that it self-constructs bear low similarity, hence eliminating any issues of multicollinearity as regards the constructs being used. Finally, the actual reliability level, as captured by the MaxR(H), ranges from 0.852 for MM to 0.763 for TM and 0.797 for GEA. These values also support the reliability of constructs; these findings also suggest that these measurements are consistent. Therefore, based on the measures highlighted in Table 4 below, all the constructs used in this investigation are valid and reliable. The outcomes therefore imply that Market Mobility, Talent Management, and Gig Economies Adaptability are distinct yet interrelated constructs, providing a solid foundation for further analysis and interpretation of the relationships among these variables in the context of gig economies.

Figure 2. Structure Equation Model

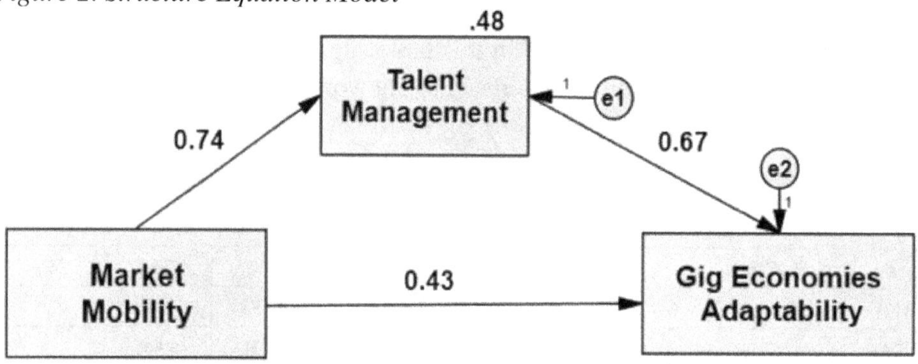

Model Fit Indices

Table 5. indices for Model Fit

Sig.	Chi-Sq	RMR	Fitness Goodness	Fitness Confirmatory	TLI	RMSEA
0.004	1.954	.036	0.930	0.912	0.911	.028

Source: Authors

Table 5 manifests the indices for model fit. The level of significance (Sig.) estimated is 0.004 showing that the chi-square test of the model is both statistically significant. This implies that the covariance matrices of the observed and expected are never the same; which is common in structural equation modeling. The chi-square is recorded as 1.954 to act as a reference in evaluating the fitness of the proposed model. Chi-square which is used here is a measure of goodness-of-fit and a lower chi-square indicating higher goodness of fit but should be manifested in light of other indices listed in the table. The Root Mean Square Residual (RMR) estimated is 0.036, which is fairly good going by the widely accepted standard that an RMR Cut off of less than 0.05 is good enough especially when used in conjunction with the IFI. In addition, the goodness of fit indices of the total test model and the confirmatory test are presented, where Fitness Goodness = 0.930 and Fitness Confirmatory = 0.912. Both estimates are above the conventionally accepted level of 0.90, which confirms the overall goodness-of-fit of the model. The Tucker–Lewis Index (TLI), equal to 0.911 also manifested evidence of an adequate model since this values is greater than 0.90. Last, the Root Mean Square Error of Estimate (RMSEA=0.028) is also less than 0.06, which is a conventionally acceptable estimate. Such a low RMSEA indicates that the theoretically derived model is a good representation of the population covariance matrix. Altogether, the indices of table 5 confirm that the structural model is a good fit of the data and elevate the credibility of the proposed relationships among the constructs of market mobility, talent management on the one hand and, the adaptability of gig economy on the other hand. These outcomes suggest that, therefore, the proposed model is sound and that its theoretical postulations apply to the gig economy environment.

Table 6. Regression Examination

Relative			**Approx.**	**S.E.**	**C.R.**	**P**	**Ass.**
Talent Management	**<---**	**Market Mobility**	**.864**	**.143**	**7.583**	**.00**	**H2**
Gig Economies Adaptability	<---	Talent Management	.328	.131	2.853	.00	H3
Gig Economies Adaptability	<---	Market Mobility	.957	.192	7.958	.00	H1

Source: Authors

Table 6, the regression coefficient for the relationship among market mobility and talent management equals 0.864, SE = 0.143, C.R.= 7.583. This strong positive relationship is statistically significant the p value tend to be ".00" indicating that level of market mobility is likely to improve talent management practices. The second part of the analysis reveals that talent management has a significant direct effect on gig economies' adaptability with coefficients of 0.328, SE of 0.131, and a CR of 2.853. This relationship is also statistically significant, further supporting our argument that talent management positively influences adaptability of freelance markets. Last but not the least, the result also pointed out that market mobility has a strong and positive direct influence on the adaptability of gig economies; the corresponding coefficient, standard error, and critical ratio being 0.957, 0.192 and 7.958 respectively, making it significant too. They stated that this manifests that high levels of Market Mobility greatly improve the flexibility of gig economies signifying a rather positive correlation. Thus, research hypotheses H1, H2, and H3 proposed in this investigation are supported, indicating market mobility and talent management as the major drivers of adaptable gig economies. This underlines the need to promote these elements in the attainment of economic elasticity and flexibility in current employment relations.

Table 7. Mediating role Effect

	Influence	Worth	Path Influence
Market Mobility → Gig Economies Adaptability	Direct Influence	.43	Direct influence stated
Market Mobility → Talent Management → Workplace asymmetries	Indirect Influence	.74*.67=.48	Indirect Influence Ensued
	Whole influence	.91	Partial mediation

Source: Authors

In Table 7, Market mobility has a direct influence on gig economies adaptability and is estimated to be 0.43, which is a higher positive rating. This direct positive connection indicates they found out that greater market mobility is a leading factor that improves the flexibility of gig economies. Regarding the indirect effect, when the path coefficients are multiplied by the alpha coefficient, the index of 0.48 is obtained by multiplying 0.74 of the path from market mobility to talent management, and 0.67 of the path from talent management to workplace asymmetries. This serves to support the object of this chapter that talent management assumes a central intermediary position in defining how the dynamics of the workplace interacts with market mobility. Summing up all the effects, which directly and indirectly compare these variables, gives the total influence value of 0.91. The term "partial mediation" means that although talent management can be seen as mitigating some of the effects of market mobility on workplace relations of asymmetry, certain direct effects are still pronounced. This also underscored the ways in which direct and indirect pathways interact to shape how market mobility influences gig economy flexibility and work environment.

DISCUSSION

The outcomes of this investigation manifest important light on the complex connections among personnel management, market mobility, and gig economy adaptation, especially in light of workplace inequalities. Market mobility has a significant direct influence on gig economies' ability to adapt, which emphasizes how crucial flexible labor markets are to creating an atmosphere in which gig economies may flourish. Employers and employees alike must be able to adjust when market conditions change, indicating that measures intended to promote market mobility may have significant effects on economic resilience. Additionally, the mediation function of talent management emphasizes how important good HR practices are to closing the gap among workplace outcomes and market realities. Corporates that place a high priority on talent management can reduce differences in employment possibilities and working conditions, according to the indirect influence of talent management on workplace asymmetries. The outcomes manifested in Table 7 demonstrate the complex dynamics of market mobility, gig economy flexibility, and human management, notably in terms of workplace imbalances. The direct effect of markct mobility on gig economy adaptation is 0.43, demonstrating a significant and straightforward relationship in which increased market mobility promotes gig economy adaptability. On the other hand, the indirect influence route, which links market mobility to talent management and then to workplace inequalities, manifests a more complex interplay. The calculated indirect influence value of 0.48 (derived from expanding the coefficients of market mobility with talent management at 0.74 as well as talent management to workplace asymmetries at 0.67) suggests that market mobility also has a significant influence on the methods used for talent management, which in turn affect workplace asymmetries. In general, the total influence of market mobility on workplace outcomes is 0.91, indicating a significant effect. This manifests that, though there is a direct influence, talent management plays an important mediation function, leading to the conclusion that this connection is partially mediated. These findings highlight the significance of understanding both direct and indirect paths in organizational dynamics, especially in the context of gig economies and talent management techniques.

The investigation's conclusions have important management ramifications that might help organizational leaders negotiate the challenges of the modern labor market. First and foremost, the close connection among market mobility and adaptability in gig economies implies that managers have to give top priority to creating an atmosphere that promotes responsiveness and flexibility. Corporates can enable their workforce to better adjust to shifting needs and economic situations by putting in place policies that promote market mobility, such as remote work choices, flexible scheduling, and open communication channels. Also, the crucial function that talent management plays as a mediator emphasizes how important it is for managers to make significant investments in talent development plans. This entails offering ongoing training and development opportunities that correspond with the changing demands of the industry in addition to luring and keeping talented employees. Employers may better prepare their staff to succeed in gig economies by fostering a culture of learning and adaptation, which will eventually improve output and lessen workplace disparities. Managers should also think about how their talent management strategies may affect employee engagement and business culture more broadly. Corporates may reduce inequalities and establish a more peaceful workplace by promoting inclusion and fairness in talent management, which is crucial for preserving morale and output. The investigation's practical implications manifest firms looking to improve their agility in the gig economy useful information. First off, the obvious connection among market mobility and the flexibility of gig economies highlights how crucial it is to have flexible work schedules. Companies have to think about putting in place rules that permit project-based assignments, flexible scheduling, and remote employment. In addition to drawing in a varied talent pool, this flexibility helps staff members react swiftly to shifts in the market, which improves overall adaptability. The survey also emphasizes how important it is for businesses to fund thorough personnel management initiatives. This entails creating training that is in line with market trends, creating a culture of continual learning, and setting clear paths for staff growth. Employers can guarantee that their workforce stays competitive and flexible by providing workers with the abilities and information required to successfully negotiate the changing gig economy scenario. Corporates should also concentrate on resolving workplace inequalities that can result from varying degrees of opportunity access. A fairer workplace may be achieved by doable actions including establishing mentorship programs, asking employees for input, and regularly evaluating talent management procedures. These programs improve employee retention and happiness while simultaneously advancing equity. In conclusion, companies may successfully negotiate the difficulties of the gig economy by implementing flexible work arrangements, making investments in the training of employees, and resolving workplace inequalities.

The investigation's theoretical ramifications advance our knowledge of labor market dynamics generally and gig economies and talent management specifically. The outcomes support current views on market mobility, indicating that greater labor market fluidity is not only advantageous for individual workers but also essential for the flexibility of whole economic systems. This supports the view that market mobility is a major factor in fostering economic resilience and is consistent with the premise that a responsive labor market may improve organizational agility. Additionally, the recognized mediating function of talent management broadens theoretical frameworks that investigation how market circumstances and human resource practices interact. The significance of incorporating HR methods into more comprehensive economic theories is shown by this investigation, which manifests how efficient personnel management may close the gap among market mobility and workplace outcomes. It implies that talent management should be seen as a crucial element that affects external market adaptation rather than only as an internal organizational function. The outcomes also call for a reassessment of current workplace asymmetries models. The investigation emphasizes how talent management strategies may lessen gaps in opportunity access, highlighting the necessity of theories that take equality and inclusion in workforce dynamics into account. This enhances the theoretical discussion of labor market fairness by urging more investigation into the factors influencing workplace equity. Several suggestions for businesses and legislators looking to improve flexibility in the gig economy may be made in light of the investigation's findings. First and foremost, companies want to give top priority to creating flexible work schedules that meet the various demands of their employees. Employee engagement and happiness may be greatly increased by implementing choices like project-based jobs, flexible scheduling, and remote work. This will eventually increase flexibility in a market that is changing quickly. Corporates must also make investments in thorough personnel management plans that emphasize ongoing education and skill improvement. In addition to giving workers the skills they need to succeed, offering training programs that follow new market trends will promote an innovative and resilient culture. To encourage employee growth and retention, corporates should think about setting up professional development routes and mentorship programs. Promoting market mobility also requires the active participation of policymakers. Policies that make it simpler to move among industries and positions can improve the flexibility of the labor market generally, which is advantageous to businesses and employees alike. This might involve actions like better access to training materials, portable benefits, and assistance for gig workers in resolving the intricacies of their job status. Last but not least, companies can aggressively combat workplace inequalities by routinely evaluating their personnel management procedures and getting input from staff members. In addition to lowering inequities, putting policies in place that support fairness and diversity will make employees more motivated and cohesive.

The investigation on market mobility's influence on gig economy adaptation through talent management in the Horn of Africa has various limitations. One notable restriction is the dependence on quantitative data, which, while rich in context, may lack the complete qualitative analysis required generalizing findings throughout the area. Furthermore, the frequently changing nature of the gig economy and market circumstances might result in temporal biases, with findings soon becoming obsolete. Geographic constraints may further restrict the investigation's breadth, since concentrating on certain nations or localities may not represent the complete range of experiences throughout the Horn of Africa. In addition, access to accurate data sources can be difficult due to the informal nature of many gig work and differing degrees of recordkeeping and reporting across industries. Finally, significant biases in participant answers, driven by cultural views regarding gig labor and talent management, may undermine the outcomes' validity, making it difficult to make firm conclusions concerning the overall influence of market mobility in this setting.

Future studies in this field should concentrate on delving further into the complex connections among gig economies, personnel management, and market mobility. Examining the precise processes by which market mobility affects adaptation in a variety of industries outside of gig economies is one interesting direction. Gaining knowledge about how various industries react to changes in the market might help develop sector-specific resilience-boosting tactics. Future research might also look at how technology influences people management strategies and market mobility. Examining how these technology developments influence employee adaptability and business tactics will be essential as digital platforms make gig labor and remote employment more accessible. The effects of automation and artificial intelligence on market dynamics and talent management, particularly with regard to job displacement and the development of new positions, might also be studied. Also, longitudinal research may offer a more thorough comprehension of the long-term effects of talent management strategies on employee outcomes and workplace inequalities. By monitoring changes over time, researchers can spot patterns and causal links that might help guide best practices for companies looking to promote inclusion and equity in their workforce. Finally, by exploring how various cultural, economic, and legal settings influence the interaction among market mobility, talent management, and gig economies, cross-cultural comparisons might enhance the conversation. By expanding the investigation's focus to encompass a variety of geographical locations, researchers might find patterns that emphasize effective practices and possible difficulties particular to particular contexts.

CONCLUSION

In summary, this investigation reveals significant implications for theory and practice by highlighting the crucial relationships among personnel management, market mobility, and gig economy adaptation. The requirement for flexible labor regulations that allow people and corporates to react quickly to shifting economic conditions is highlighted by the substantial direct effect of market mobility on the adaptability of gig economies. Policymakers can foster innovation and growth in gig economies by promoting market mobility, which will eventually increase economic resilience. Also, talent management's mediating function emphasizes how important it is for influencing workplace dynamics and reducing disparities. Businesses may more effectively handle the difficulties presented by shifting market conditions by investing in talent management strategies that keep their personnel flexible and ready to adjust to changing needs. Businesses are urged by this conclusion to give talent development first priority and to put policies in place that take into account the changing labor market. Last but not least, the discovery of partial mediation raises the possibility that there are other variables affecting the connection among market mobility and gig economy adaptation, which calls for more research. In order to better grasp the complexity of this connection, future investigation should try to identify these elements. All things manifested, this investigation adds to the conversation on economic adaptability by providing insightful information that may help company executives and legislators create a more resilient and inclusive economic climate.

COMPETING INTERESTS

Authors don't have any competing interests.

FUNDING STATEMENTS

No external funding was used to conduct this study.

REFERENCES

Adula, M., Kant, S., Badi, S., & Kumari, M. (2025). Abusive Work Environment Effect on Female Entrepreneurs' Emotional Wellbeing by Mediation of Social and Moral Values in the Horn of Africa. In *Supporting Psychological and Emotional Wellbeing Among Entrepreneurs* (pp. 1-22). IGI Global. DOI: DOI: 10.4018/979-8-3693-3673-1.ch001

Ahmad, A. A., & Norzaidi, N. H. R. (2024). Adapting to Technological Transformations: Jobs and Skills in Malaysia's Evolving Work Landscape. In *Islamic Finance: New Trends in Law and Regulation* (pp. 527–538). Springer. DOI: 10.1007/978-3-031-48770-5_42

Bakker, A. B., & Demerouti, E. (2024). Job demands–resources theory: Frequently asked questions. *Journal of Occupational Health Psychology*, *29*(3), 188–200. DOI: 10.1037/ocp0000376 PMID: 38913705

Caligiuri, M. D., & Jolly, P. M. (2023). Workforce diversity and management in the hospitality industry: An equal employment opportunity and affirmative action perspective. In *The Routledge Handbook of Diversity, Equity, and Inclusion Management in the Hospitality Industry* (pp. 157–165). Routledge. ISSN 9781000963007

Civelek, M. E. (2018). Essentials of Structural Equation Modeling. In *Zea Books*. Issue March., DOI: 10.13014/K2SJ1HR5

Giousmpasoglou, C., Ladkin, A., & Marinakou, E. (2024). Worker exploitation in the gig economy: The case of dark kitchens. *Journal of Hospitality and Tourism Insights*, *7*(1), 414–435. DOI: 10.1108/JHTI-10-2022-0477

Griffen, Z. W. (2024). The economization of early life: Human capital theory, biology, and social policy. *Science, Technology & Human Values*, *49*(1), 175–205. . DOI: 10.1177/01622439221147701

Jonas Frödin, O. (2024). Cognitive microfoundations and social interaction dynamics. The implications of complexity for institutional theory. *Theory and Society*, *53*(5), 1019–1047. DOI: 10.1007/s11186-024-09574-3

Kravariti, F., Tasoulis, K., Scullion, H., & Alali, M. K. (2023). Talent management and performance in the public sector: The role of organisational and line managerial support for development. *International Journal of Human Resource Management*, *34*(9), 1782–1807. DOI: 10.1080/09585192.2022.2032265

Murtiningrum, V. A., & Aligarh, F. (2024). Adoption of Digital Technology in Micro, Small, and Medium Enterprises (MSMEs): Integration of Innovation Diffusion Theory and Resource Based View (RBV) Theory (A Case Investigation on MSMEs in Surakarta City). *International Conference on Islamic Economics (ICIE)*, *1*, 415–420. ISSN: 3064-2043

Niguse, T., Kant, S., & Adula, M. (2025). Mediation Effect of Customer Loyalty in Relationship Among Market Orientation, Entrepreneurial Orientation, and Firm Performance in Ethiopia. In *Leveraging AI for Effective Digital Relationship Marketing* (pp. 419–458). IGI Global., DOI: 10.4018/979-8-3693-5340-0.ch014

Norwani, N. M., Ismail, Z., Nasir, N. N. A., Yusof, R., & Jamaluddin, N. S. (2022). The Influence of Gender, Age, Academic Level and Motivation on Satisfaction Toward Benefits Received by Gig Economy Workers in Malaysia. *Archives of Business Research*, *10*(12), 89–105. DOI: 10.14738/abr.1012.13602

Nwaobi, G. C. (2024). Gig Sector in the African Economy: Frameworks, Challenges and Prospects. *Challenges and Prospects*. DOI: 10.2139/ssrn.4769988

Parey, M., & Waldinger, F. (2011). Investigationing abroad and the effect on international labour market mobility: Evidence from the introduction of ERASMUS. *Economic Journal (London)*, *121*(551), 194–222. DOI: 10.1111/j.1468-0297.2010.02369.x

Roberto, R., Penna, M., Felici, B., & Rao, M. (2023). Smart working and flexible work arrangements: opportunities and risks for sustainable communities. In *Intelligent Environments* (pp. 243–283). Elsevier., DOI: 10.1016/B978-0-12-820247-0.00001-1

Stadtländer, C. T. K.-H. (2009). Qualitative, Quantitative, and Mixed-Methods Research. *Microbe (Washington, D.C.)*, *4*(11), 485–485. DOI: 10.1128/microbe.4.485.1

Thomas, S. M., & Baddipudi, V. (2022). Changing nature of work and employment in the gig economy: The role of culture building and leadership in sustaining commitment and job satisfaction. *NHRD Network Journal*, *15*(1), 100–113. DOI: 10.1177/26314541211064735

KEY TERMS AND DEFINITIONS

Adaptability: the ability of people or corporates to successfully adapt to changes in their surroundings, such as shifting labor demands, market conditions, and technology breakthroughs. Being highly adaptive is necessary to be competitive in ever-changing economic environments (Ahmad & Norzaidi, 2024).

Employment Equity: ensuring that all workers have equal access to opportunities regardless of their circumstances, identity, or history through the application of the fairness principle in hiring, promotion, and workplace procedures. Reducing workplace asymmetries is facilitated by promoting equity (Caligiuri & Jolly, 2023).

Gig Economy: a work market where flexible, short-term employment is common and frequently made possible by internet platforms. Because they are usually categorized as independent contractors rather than regular employees, workers in the gig economy have less job security and access to benefits (Norwani et al., 2022) .

Market Mobility: the ease with which employees can switch among occupations, industries, or regions in reaction to shifts in the labor market Increased market mobility is frequently linked to an economy that is more flexible and dynamic (Parey & Waldinger, 2023).

Talent Management: a calculated strategy for drawing in, training, and keeping talented workers in a company. It includes a number of procedures like hiring, training, performance reviews, and succession planning (Kravariti et al., 2023).

Workplace Asymmetry: disparities in an employee's access to opportunities, resources, or support at work that may cause them to perform differently. Career progression, work happiness, and overall company success may all be influenceed by these inequalities.

Chapter 9
Diversity, Inclusion, and Equity in Gig Economies

Iris-Panagiota Efthymiou
https://orcid.org/0000-0001-9656-8378
University of Greenwich, UK

ABSTRACT

Diversity, inclusion, and equity (DIE) in gig economies are critical for fostering sustainable, fair, and innovative labour markets. This study examines the structural challenges and opportunities inherent in gig work, emphasizing disparities in access, pay equity, and career progression across gender, race, age, and socioeconomic backgrounds. It explores strategies for promoting inclusive policies, equitable algorithmic practices, and diversified leadership to ensure that gig economies do not perpetuate systemic inequalities. By integrating behavioural economic insights and policy analysis, this research provides actionable recommendations for policymakers, platforms, and stakeholders to create a more equitable gig ecosystem that benefits workers and society at large.

BACKGROUND

The gig economy has grown into a global phenomenon, reshaping traditional employment models and creating new opportunities and challenges. Digital platforms now connect millions of independent workers with clients across industries, offering flexibility and autonomy but also raising concerns about fairness, security, and sustainability. As the gig workforce expands, understanding its structure and

DOI: 10.4018/979-8-3693-9385-7.ch009

impact is essential for developing policies that ensure inclusivity and equitable access to opportunities.

This chapter explores the critical issues of diversity, inclusion, and sustainability within gig economies. These factors determine whether gig work remains a viable and fair employment option or deepens existing inequalities. Marginalized groups often face barriers to entry and lower wages, while companies struggle to implement inclusive policies. Addressing these challenges is essential for making gig economies more sustainable and adaptable in the evolving global business landscape.

By situating these discussions within the broader theme of sustainability and adaptability in global business, this chapter contributes to a deeper understanding of how gig economies can evolve to support diverse workforces. The aim is to highlight both the opportunities and the systemic issues that need to be addressed for gig work to be a sustainable, inclusive, and equitable form of employment.

One of the unique attractions of the gig economy is that it provides flexible, independent work options. Success in tier-one markets has resulted in gig work's transformation from a piecemeal opportunity into a full-time career for many. With this shift comes the need for a keen understanding of who the gig workforce is and the dynamics that structure it. Gig economies are grounded in the leveraging of digital platforms to facilitate transactions between independent workers and consumers of their services. However, as the work continues to increase and become more specialized, marginalized groups consistently face the prospect of poverty and discrimination. From a bottom-up perspective, not having a diverse and inclusive workforce can also have significant financial repercussions, particularly for older employees who do not have the same employment opportunities as younger generations. Companies with diversity and inclusion in their DNA are better poised to tap into new, larger markets with a variety of consumers.

Currently, companies often struggle to maintain inclusivity in their policies, practices, and reporting and are unsure of where to start. This means that progress towards equity promotion in the gig economy is slow, if not inconsistent and uncertain. Individuals looking to further equity in the gig economy often have similarly minimal support structures and often find themselves working independently to ensure diversity promotion.

Diversity, inclusion, and equity in gig economies are essential for fair work practices and global adaptability. A varied workforce enables gig platforms to adjust swiftly to market changes. Inclusive policies are crucial for sustainable growth in global business

INTRODUCTION

In the gig economy, specific services or products are exchanged instead of traditional employment relationships. This means that instead of being tied to a single company or employer, workers have the freedom to offer their skills and services to multiple clients or customers. This flexibility is made possible by digital platforms and various forms of freelancing.

One of the key features of gig work is the use of digital platforms. These platforms act as intermediaries, connecting individuals who need a particular service or product with those who can provide it. By leveraging the power of the internet, these platforms can efficiently match supply and demand, making it easier for people to access the services they need when they need them.

The rise of gig work has had a profound impact on the economy, particularly in relation to the provision of immediate and affordable services. Thanks to the internet, platforms can offer access to a wide range of goods, both tangible and intangible, as well as peer-to-peer services. Whether it's web work, crowd work, online work, digital labour, online labour, micro work, or click working, there is a rapidly growing range of concepts and terms used to describe the various forms of gig work that have emerged.

However, alongside the benefits of flexibility and freedom, the organization of gig labour and the question of employment classification have become hotly debated issues. As more and more people rely on gig work as their primary source of income, there is a need to consider how these workers should be classified and protected. Should they be considered independent contractors or employees? This question has significant implications for issues such as benefits, job security, and legal protections.

Another thing the different terms for digital gig work share is their lack of precision and consistency. For example, the use of the term gig working may be confused with temporary agency work. Furthermore, particularly in the Anglo-Saxon sector, the term gig work is used to encompass other parts of precarious employment relationships as well. These include flexible work that is limited in time, work under atypical contracts, work for intermediaries such as third-party employment services, and temporary employment contracts changed by length of time or tasks. Also, some workers may have fixed-term contracts, zero-hour work contracts, and day tickets. Even though these various forms of work are more or less precarious, there are significant legal implications between these differences, and also in terms of workers' rights.

Gig work, or online digital gig work, means the substitution of paid labour activity for traditional employment relationships through the use of a digital platform specifically designed to connect such labour supply and demand. Such a link can be established using digital networking. But the questions of how supply and demand are coordinated and whether an algorithm for working is used make a difference in struggling to authorize atypical workers for social protection in identical or at least semantically equivalent ways.

In summary, the gig economy has revolutionized the way services and products are exchanged, providing individuals with greater flexibility and opportunities for work. However, it has also raised important questions about the organization of gig labour and the rights and protections afforded to workers in this new sector. As the gig economy continues to evolve, it is crucial that we find ways to support and empower gig workers while ensuring fair and equitable working conditions.

The Impact of Gig Platforms on the Labor Market

Over the last decade, digitization and global connectivity have transformed traditional businesses and led to the creation of entirely new types of business processes. The rise of the Second Machine Age has led to the emergence of new business models that rely on technology to turn idle resources or surplus capacity into profit, and to the birth of entirely new economic sectors that employ an increasingly diverse mix of workers. (Kumar et al., 2021; Langley et al., 2021) From a recruitment and employment perspective, these developments represent just as significant a transformation in the nature of work as the first industrial revolution did, threatening to define the distribution of economic opportunities, wealth creation, and the meaning of community in fundamentally unequal ways. (Boulding, 2021; Hanelt et al., 2021)

A variety of terms are used to describe the phenomenon of online labour, which is defined as paid activities that are mediated through online platforms which connect buyers and sellers with each other under a service contract. (Stephany et al.2021; Dunn; Rani & Furrer, 2021) In some cases, the intended service is made available to the platform or cloud network for any interested customer, who accesses it using modern remote technology and other resources. If this is the case, then the general pattern of employment is called a gig. All independent work arrangements to perform specific projects or piecework are also called temporary jobs, as these individuals are not bound to the organization through employment, and are thus allowed to do other jobs simultaneously.

The rise of gig platforms such as Uber, Upwork, TaskRabbit, Fiverr, and many others, has massively and irrevocably transformed the landscape of the labour market, in ways that were never thought possible before. (Altenried, 2024) With these innovative platforms, workers from all walks of life now have access to a plethora of exciting new opportunities, enabling them to truly take control of their own destinies and flourish in ways they never could have imagined. (Jones, 2021; Woldoff & Litchfield, 2021) However, with these new vistas of possibilities, also come a host of challenges and complexities for the conventional employment structures that have long been firmly entrenched in society.

In this era of gig economies and freelancing, the very foundations on which the traditional workforce was built are being relentlessly reshaped and questioned, leading to a profound shift in the very fabric of our economic existence (Schor, 2020; Bansal et al., 2020; Bruckner & Forman, 2021; Popov, 2023). It is clear that we are standing at the precipice of a monumental juncture, where the old paradigms are being upended, and new ones are being forged, as the gig economy continues to evolve and redefine the way we work and live.

The Attraction of Gig Work: Flexibility, Autonomy and Income Potential

Gig work, with its inherent emphasis on personal freedom and adaptability, offers a vast array of possibilities for individuals hailing from diverse professional backgrounds, possessing an eclectic array of expertise, and originating from various social and cultural contexts, making their mark in the labour market and contributing to economic growth and development. (Myhill et al.2023; Abkhezr and McMahon, 2024; Warren, 2021)

Social limitations are often the primary and fundamental motivating factors for transitioning individuals who are not currently part of the labour force into a diverse and expansive range of gig economic activities. (Bates et al., 2020; Scuotto et al., 2022) The intricate and interconnected nature of the gig economy serves as a catalyst in breaking down the formidable barriers that exist between job seekers and the often elusive notion of a work-life balance. By venturing into gig employment, individuals are granted a newfound sense of autonomy and agency, allowing them to transcend the confines of traditional employment and embark upon a boundless journey towards financial prosperity and personal fulfilment. (Efthymiou, et al., 2025).

In sharp contrast to the limitations imposed by part-time employment in traditional work models, individuals in the gig economy have a unique opportunity to take on extra work that can result in significant financial gains. These individuals are no longer encumbered by their employers' rigid and inflexible time arrangements. Rather, they are bestowed with the liberty to allocate their time and effort in a manner that best aligns with their personal needs and aspirations. This newfound flexibility imparts upon them the ability to seize lucrative opportunities, undertake multiple gigs concurrently, and maximize their earning potential to unprecedented heights. (Kuhn et al., 2021)

Furthermore, the gig economy acts as a conducive platform for fostering innovation, creativity, and professional growth. (Behera & Gaur, 2022) It serves as an empowering domain where individuals can explore their interests, sharpen their skills, and cultivate uncharted talents. The absence of conventional work structures and hierarchies allows gig workers to forge their own path, charting a trajectory that is uniquely tailored to their individual strengths and aspirations. Through engaging in a variety of gig economic activities, these individuals not only diversify their skills but also broaden their horizons, expanding their repertoire of experience and knowledge.

The gig economy represents a paradigm shift in the world of work, transcending barriers and redefining the very essence of employment. It offers a plethora of opportunities for individuals not in the labour force to overcome the shackles of societal limitations and embrace a life characterized by self-determination and financial independence. (Raval, 2020; Masera, 2024) By undertaking this transformative experience, individuals have the ability to break free from the restrictions of conventional employment and venture into a journey that ultimately leads to personal satisfaction and limitless accomplishments. (Efthymiou, 2024) Thus, the gig economy emerges as a beacon of hope, bridging the gap between job seekers and workplace mismatch, and fostering a society that thrives on the limitless potential hidden within every individual.

Gig work remedies part of the extra earning constraints on part-time work by providing flexible working hours and a platform that functions as a transparent extra working time marketplace, thus offering individuals the opportunity to supplement their income without affecting their primary employment status. (Karanovic et al., 2023) Through gig work, individuals can leverage their skills and expertise to engage in various short-term projects, freelance assignments, and on-demand tasks. (Watson et al., 2021) This not only allows them to explore different opportunities and expand their professional network but also provides them with the flexibility to work according to their own schedule and availability.

Moreover, with this level of autonomy, individuals are not only able to effectively manage their own time but also prioritize tasks based on their personal preferences, professional commitments, and overall work-life balance. This aspect of being in control of one's own schedule and responsibilities is highly appealing to numerous individuals who strive for a more harmonious equilibrium between their work and personal life. By having the ability to determine the order and importance of tasks, individuals can optimize their productivity and satisfaction in both areas, leading to enhanced performance and fulfilment. This sense of autonomy empowers individuals to achieve a greater sense of balance, enabling them to fully experience the benefits of a flexible and self-directed work environment. (Wan et al., 2024; Shibata, 2020; Mohsin et al., 2022; Christiaens, 2022) Overall, gig work has emerged as a viable solution for individuals seeking to supplement their income while maintaining the stability and security of their primary employment.

Economic Impact

Gig economies are about work. Work represents the first and most direct benefit of gig economies, where humans are rewarded for the skills they possess and if they are able to deploy them to the benefit of those who require those skills. Earning income, being independent, and being valued are all human experiences associated with work. (Killingsworth, 2021; Jaffe, 2021; Finch & Groves, 2022) Enabling such experiences for large numbers of people is a profoundly impactful human condition. Countries that fail to provide adequate work opportunities through self-employment have very negative social and economic trajectories because the preference for gig over formal work is increasing. Indeed, it is gig economies that are today responsible for taking a workforce into work for several types of more informal jobs, including ride-hailing, food delivery, marketplace sales, freelancing, errands, cleaning, handiwork, trades, and micro-employment. Gig economies are thus directly accountable for the earning and self-employment of millions. (Tyc, 2022; Hernandez et al., 2024; Drahokoupil et al., 2022)

Indirectly, gig economies, as providers of goods and services, ensure more inclusive access to products and services than are available otherwise because prices adjust to the fact that there is more on offer in gig economies. Gig economies also contribute to reducing the severity of under-exploited social divisions as a consequence of providing more equalizing incomes than business models in traditional employment can offer. (Banik & Padalkar, 2021; Tan et al., 2021) As a platform that facilitates microtransactions, it is possible that gig economies can provide further reductions in underlying social tension and divisions. Gig economies should act as engines for more inclusive access (Loganathan, 2022) Output from these sectors should be structured in order to meet the identified market—physical or virtual—including private and public sector funding. Gig economies represent work evolution. Gig economies are not the problem; they are the solution.

CHALLENGES IN DIVERSITY AND INCLUSION

One of the few challenges of the gig economy, in particular for micro giggers, is the lack of diversity in this new type of employment. The selection of micro workers also displays gender, racial, and possibly age biases. (Tubaro et al., 2022; Franklin, 2022; Axelrad et al., 2024) Microwork supply seems to penetrate nations with low overall diversity indices and high levels of sexism. It is important to address the issues of professionalism, as well as diversity and inclusion, given that microwork is being increasingly used for performing a variety of online tasks. (Muldoon et al., 2020; Ness et al., 2023) Unfortunately, marginalized people experience work and other forms of discrimination every day, which impacts their access to opportunities (Efthymiou, et al., 2025). There are a few exceptions to that. Participation in some digital gig ecosystem platforms that provide a range of services will at least provide them with some level of income. The concepts of race and privilege need to be accounted for in addressing these issues within the management and organization studies literature. (Nkomo, 2021; Fitzgerald, 2023; Agyemang et al., 2024) In particular, there is an unjust application of the participative model specifically with marginal groups. Also, many do not get treated equally after having a funded, secure job.

In more practical terms, when faced with costs or financial distress, marginal job groups seek some form of aid, like support for medical treatment, mental health assistance, and educational support for children. (Huang et al., 2020; Healy et al., 2020) These marginalized groups are also victims of corruption. In many cases, marginalized employees also face violence from regulation enforcement officers in addition to bad employer conduct. In many wealthy countries, systemic barriers prevent women from joining the gig economy. (Behl et al., 2022) Women feel left out of the digital economy, without adequate training and experience in computing, programming, and other digital skills. (Shukla et al., 2021; Arroyo, 2020) As a result, these domestic servants struggle to make a good living. This very personal work often involves taking care of an employer's family or residence while the employer is outside of town. In a gig economy that focuses on cashless transactions, being a domestic servant is not viable in the absence of a bank account. So how does all that make the gig economy good and efficient for all parties?

Bias and Discrimination

Discrimination can be worded as favouritism or inclination towards or against someone or something. (Kite et al., 2022; Bunel & Tovar, 2021) Although on theoretical grounds, a variety of reasons may contribute to biases, some of these reasons are based on personal belief systems such as gender and racial prejudice. (Ayala-López & Beeghly, 2020; Fibbi et al., 2021; Phillips et al., 2022). Discrimination in platform work is nothing new. Paid online communities for small tasks have existed at least since the 1900s. Research shows prior digital gamified labour markets are no different.

There is a concern with gig work, which has a direct impact on the labour market because of the kind of exposure it receives. If a job seeker, who is initially facing racial or gender bias in a job application, is fortunate enough to get the job, their ongoing experience is still likely to be negative. A survey shows that women earn less than men on five of the world's biggest crowdsource labour platforms. (Litman L., 2020) They are also more likely to experience bias and be refused payment on completion of a task. Research informs us that these negative responses are more psychological and impact the workers' work satisfaction, and work effort, and in some instances, act as exclusion. Some customers believe women are less knowledgeable about technical or business issues. The rub is that, in most cases forced by regulations, the platforms frown upon such discriminatory work environments, but their policies may circumvent such discrimination.

Access and Opportunity

Besides how workers from underrepresented groups are treated once they are on a platform, there are also issues related to access and opportunity to be on that platform to begin with in gig economies. Although hyperbolic to a point, not all members within societies have equal access to gig work. (Caza et al., 2022; Kost et al., 2020) Socioeconomic barriers and the related opportunity costs are significant. As the fourth industrial revolution increasingly digitizes the global economy, new barriers are emerging. (Li, 2022; Ochillo, 2022)

The lack of equal access to pursue gig work, and the reality that gig workers are not very diverse despite corporate rhetoric dismissing the need for proactive approaches toward diversity, is alarming. Generating opportunities for those who do the work is essential. (Kirton, 2020; Janssens & Zanoni, 2021; Schor & Vallas, 2021) Gig workers make up 16.4% of the American labor force. At some stage, gig work has brought in income for 30% of younger US individuals, aged 18 to 29. As of January 2023, the US has 9.94 million individuals who are self-employed. Approximately 47% of gig workers in the US are employed full-time. On average, US-based 1099-MISC contractors earned $6,810 per month, compared to $6,340 for W-2 employees. One of the main reasons people choose gig work is for the flexibility it offers and the opportunity to earn extra income. 24% of freelancers do not have health insurance, and 29% make less than the minimum wage in their state.

Workers frequently find themselves without crucial benefits and protections. (Smith, R., 2023) African American managers only had a workforce that was 12% African American for their gig economy workers. Efforts for inclusion need to compel change and should amend the economics and society that the gig platforms touch. People are trying to access gig platforms. In the Louisville, Kentucky region, those facing barriers to technology access and digital literacy are busy accessing an estimated 300 online gig platforms. Economic mobility and community health are handling these issues.

Barriers to Entry

Gig workers often face significant barriers to entry, including a myriad of challenges that impede their journey. These encompass a lack of access to the essential technology required to thrive in this digital era, along with limited skills that hinder their ability to secure lucrative opportunities. Additionally, it is disheartening to see that an increasingly alarming and pervasive issue continues to persist within society. The unfortunate reality is that discrimination, in all its ugliness, raises its head in various forms, targeting individuals based on fundamental aspects of their identity such as age, gender, race, and ethnicity. (Kite et al., 2022)

This pervasive issue not only undermines the principles of equality and justice but also perpetuates a climate of prejudice and inequality that must be addressed urgently. It is essential that we actively challenge and dismantle discriminatory systems and attitudes, fostering an inclusive and harmonious society that values and respects every individual, regardless of their age, gender, race, or ethnicity. (Kelkar, 2022; Ness et al., 2023) Only by confronting and overcoming discrimination can we truly progress towards a fair and equitable future for all. This amalgamation of obstacles creates an arduous path for gig workers, placing them at a distinct disadvantage as they strive to build sustainable careers in the modern workforce.

The dramatic increase in freelance and flexible work arrangements, the shifting of talent strategies to focus on gig workers, and the growing trend of emerging enterprising freelancers, popularly known as freelance professionals, are raising new questions for diversity, inclusion, and equity in the future workforce. These trends are changing the nature, variety, and impact of interconnected global labour markets. The ability of workers to participate actively in and benefit from the evolving landscape of work through access to fair and decent work at an individual and collective level, and our readiness to prepare our evolving next generations of gig workers to transition between many different forms of work and enterprising freelancers, remain fundamental responsibilities of companies, educators, and policymakers.

Economic, informational, and workplace social and technological barriers to harnessing diverse talents and to communicating and promoting diversity, inclusion, equity, and participation by the workforce as a whole, the strategic drivers of diversity, are still significant. These barriers undermine the financial and reputational performance drivers of diversity and the long-term sustainability of future talent strategies in an age of diversity-driven skills gaps and worsening employee retention and engagement shortfalls. Our corporate and academic institutions also face a significant continuing issue with corporate and sector diversity and inclusion claims in widespread materials. Examples of such claims include the use of images of disabled and LGBTQ+ people, ethnic minorities, and women in leadership roles, the percentage of women in the workforce, or figures on how much the company spends on diversity and inclusion activities.

Isolation and Social Exclusion

Loneliness results from the actual quantity and quality of social encounters not matching individual social expectations and can lead to feelings of disconnection and disengagement. It is associated with various physical and mental health problems and reduced productivity at work. Isolation, the objective lack of social contact, is seen as one cause of loneliness (Mann et al.2022; Lim et al., 2020). At the same time, it is argued that feeling isolated does not necessarily require having no social contacts, but it suffices that these contacts do not fulfil social needs or are perceived as less satisfying than desired. (Emerson et al., 2021) In the context of gig work, different sources of social connection have to be considered because gig workers cannot necessarily rely on employer-employee relationships for their social needs. (Watson et al., 2021; Koutsimpogiorgos et al., 2020)

The ways in which they have to self-organize their work require them to engage with their colleagues and collaborators, but especially with their customers. At the extreme, however, gig work can mean dispatching and delivering items in isolated work environments, also called 'lonesome work.' It is argued that variety in social connection is important for mitigating feelings of isolation and loneliness. (Wigfield et al., 2022; Della Longa et al., 2022)

Gig workers contact customers for a wide variety of reasons, and it is this variation in reason that they particularly value about customer relationships. For example, compared to other forms of customer contact such as in sales and marketing, delivery drivers are particularly fond of their supportive relationships with others, and mental connection with customers might be just as important to these drivers as the tangible tasks of pick-up, transport, and delivery. Then again, person-to-person interactions different from the exchange of goods can also be a source of subjective value for gig workers, for example, when they think of their role in society. (Uzir et al., 2021; Nadeem et al., 2020; Ostrom et al., 2021)

While personal customer contact is one way to reduce isolation and build social connections, another mode of customer relationship building engaged in by gig workers can be storing delivery boxes or recipient neighbours and talking to employees working at the delivery sorting centre. Gig workers can also meet other gig workers in sorting centres and gather information about planned encounters in busy locations or buildings to potentially meet other workers. According to these empirical insights, positive relations with other workers can also lower feelings of dissatisfaction with gig activity, while quarrels overwork and a colleague taking the work slower than desired are variables that can potentially increase feelings of isolation. Because interaction with either customers or fellow gig workers can positively impact feelings of isolation, gig workers may in fact use their flexibility to select work that offers more of these interactions.

Lack of Protections

Independent contractors and freelancers, who often work in non-traditional employment structures and operate under unique contractual agreements, may not have the same comprehensive level of legal protection as those in traditional jobs. This disparity in legal safeguards can make gig workers significantly more susceptible to various forms of exploitation, unjust treatment, and discrimination within their work environments. Consequently, it becomes essential to address and rectify these disparities, ensuring that all individuals within the workforce are afforded equal and fair protection under the law. (Tan et al., 2021)

The Standard Employment Relationship paradigm has not withstood the test of time. While many regular workers still enjoy the securities – social insurance, employment protection, and so forth – included in the package, an increasing number do not. Insecurity and precariousness, long the trademark of a colonial enterprise that replaced displaced self-employment and crafts, have penetrated the core, the standard, the primary form of employment. (Russell, 2021; Nonini & Susser, 2020; Shukaitis & Figiel, 2024) Still, some of the novel relationships show some resemblances to the standard one. Others do not. A common characteristic of people engaged in most novel relationships is that they do not get any of the securities, rights, and benefits available to many employees. This might bring home some major perceived advantages of the SED relations. Yet, it ignores the inequalities between those who have and those who have not, making normal employment lose the inclusive potential it has actually been expected to have.

Besides the wide variety of formats of independent and non-standard jobs, the plight of workers engaged in traditional relationships is not limited to their widening vulnerability. Over the last two decades, the issue of undeclared work in industrialized countries has received a great deal of attention and has moved from the underworld of industrial relations research to the centre of attention of policymakers. Although there can be various reasons for not being declared, legal protection of employment plays a considerable role in its attractiveness. In many countries, fixed-term, temporary, and part-time employment have been expanding as well. Although several countries establish in terms of law the same protection regime for both part-timers and full-timers, in practice, part-time workers far more frequently are on a kind of inferior track, with less social protection, lower hourly wages, and benefits. Temporary-help work has been the single largest piece of the labour market growth in a number of countries. These workers too often are, or feel, excluded from the labour market.

BEST PRACTICES FOR PROMOTING DIVERSITY, INCLUSION AND EQUITY

As companies that connect, serve, and employ gig workers, the platforms have a responsibility to make their workplaces and communities inclusive and equitable by actively interrupting bias and discrimination. Companies can take the following steps to build inclusive, diverse, and respectful gig platforms:

1. Adopt and implement comprehensive bias-reduction training programs that specifically address ageism, racism, and sexism, aiming to enhance the crucial understanding of intersectionality among the workforce. (Stephens et al., 2020; Costa, 2024) This training initiative should commence with senior leadership and be extended to involve all employees, fostering an inclusive environment. It is vital to emphasize that training should not be a one-time event but an ongoing process. It is equally important for companies to extend these training programs to the broader community and provide them to workers, ensuring that they are easily accessible, readily available, and can be undertaken repeatedly and on demand.
2. Create ongoing partnerships with local, national, and international organizations that are connected to and can actively engage their communities, thereby fostering valuable relationships. (Ansell et al., 2022) Make efforts to establish a strong bond with community organizations such as non-profit organizations, arts organizations, chambers of commerce, and labour unions, building a collaborative network that allows for mutual support and growth (Spade, 2020; Emery & Flora, 2020).
3. During the hiring process, it is essential to explicitly and definitively communicate in the provided information that the platform, company, and employer firmly reject any potential instances of discrimination and bias (Asad et al., 2020; Tushev et al., 2022; Asad et al., 2023). By ardently articulating this noble stance, all potential candidates shall be made aware that the sublime establishment in question accomplishes its indispensable duties with the utmost integrity and ardour, forsaking any vestige of prejudice or partiality.
4. It is essential for companies in gig economies to implement fair hiring practices to ensure diversity, inclusion, and equity in the workplace. Implementing open and transparent communication systems is crucial in mitigating the potential risk associated with favouritism and various other forms of discrimination.

(Mahato et al., 2021) By fostering an environment that encourages honesty, fairness, and equality, organizations can effectively address these concerns. This not only ensures a level playing field for all individuals but also promotes a more inclusive and harmonious work culture. Through robust communication channels, such as regular team meetings, transparent feedback mechanisms, and accessible reporting procedures, organizations can proactively identify and address any biases or discriminatory practices that may arise.

Emphasizing the importance of open dialogue and active engagement encourages individuals to voice their concerns, fostering a sense of trust and promoting a fair and equitable work environment for everyone involved. (Le et al., 2021; Aguilar, 2020) Additionally, creating clear policies and guidelines that outline appropriate behaviour and expectations helps establish a framework for preventing favouritism and discrimination while providing a supportive structure for employees to navigate any issues that may arise.

5. It is highly recommended that resources be devoted to the recruitment, comprehensive training, and continued professional development of a dedicated team of internal diversity and inclusion personnel. By doing so, organizations can ensure that they have a capable and knowledgeable workforce that is fully equipped to foster an environment where diversity and inclusion thrive. (Royall et al., 2022; Coplan et al., 2021) These staff members play a crucial role in implementing effective strategies, conducting insightful assessments, and driving positive change within the workplace. Through their expertise and commitment, they can contribute to building a more inclusive and equitable organization, one that celebrates differences, appreciates unique perspectives, and embraces diversity in all its forms.

Once diversity at the tactical and strategic levels is achieved, companies can cease referring to research and case studies when explaining their commitment to 'real' diversity and inclusion. In other words, the steps listed above should be more than merely acting upon research or case studies (Dobbin & Kalev, 2022; Triana et al.2021; Rozentale & van Baalen, 2021). These activities should become a starting point for systemic change that permeates every aspect of the organization. By creating a culture that embraces diversity and inclusion, companies hold the promise of not only a more inclusive future but also a more successful one. They have already led the way to a more inclusive gig economy, inspiring other companies to follow their transformative examples and implement similar practices. (Montgomery and Baglioni, 2021; Khan et al., 2024) It is through this collective effort that we can foster an environment where every individual feels valued and empowered, paving the way for innovation, productivity, and long-lasting positive impact. (Khan, 2021; Stavros et al., 2021)

Company Policies and Practices

How can companies promote diversity, inclusion, and equity (DEI) in gig economies? One key answer is through policies and practices. Just as guiding principles and management structures are necessary to resolve power dynamics between labour supply chain actors, they are also necessary to foster values of DEI in organizations. Company commitment is demonstrated through the development and implementation of DEI policies and mechanisms.

One of the key forms this commitment and implementation can take is formal declarations and statements published by organizations, which help to assert the value of DEI to the firm, attract new workers who share these values, and create tangible expectations for DEI ideology that, when broken, might legally rectify worker grievances. (Lingras et al., 2021; Brummer & Strine Jr, 2022; Baker et al., 2022) These documents should articulate support for equitable relations as both a point of principle and an incentive for workers to vet out organizations that neither share nor intend to uphold those principles. While these are intentionally nonbinding on the company, they are strategic communication tools that can confer credibility and seriousness to demonstrate support for DEI.

Once companies commit to DEI, they can provide training and education for employees on behavioural and attitudinal equality goals and outcomes. These tools for consciousness-raising, employee awareness, knowledge, skills, and self-efficacy in diversity are visible across the domains of employment, recruitment, training, development, and progress. By increasing awareness of these noncompliant behaviours, employees learn to unsee differences and to act as if all individuals were afforded equality. Increasingly, companies are incorporating unconditional pay equity policies into their structural commitment to the values of DEI. (Rothwell et al., 2022; Smeyers & Iruemiobe, 2023; Walters, 2023) Reports indicate that pay equity analysis is conducted globally every two years, measuring pay fairness between salaried male and female employees and adjusting pay based on compensation philosophy. Other companies also publicly report their progress in reducing payroll disparities between demographic groups.

Harmful behaviours in the form of statements and discriminatory actions can also be made illegal. Anti-discrimination laws make it unlawful to prejudice individual decision-making because of associative identity characteristics. However, in practice, incorporating a proactive, technological, data-first orientation devoted to real equitable representation in company operations in these realms is in its very beginning stages. Regularly measuring progress in creating a culture of inclusion, where the legitimacy and value of having diverse ideas and opinions are recognized, is an additional mechanism for signalling transparency and accountability. (Malhotra, 2024; Francisco et al., 2020; Kuknor and Bhattacharya. 2022) Leaders play an outsized role in shaping in-house attitudes and driving genuine resources into DEI initiatives that conduce diversity to thrive.

Community Engagement

Community engagement is essential in promoting diversity, inclusion, and equity in gig economies. Businesses engaging the communities adjacent to or affected by gig work will help them learn about its challenges and develop solutions that work. Community engagement enables companies to understand the barriers involved in gig work and gain a firsthand account of life through the lens of these workers (Zanoni and Pitts, 2022) Companies that form strategic relationships with communities can also tap into the diversity of thought that is inherent when dealing with various stakeholders – an invaluable asset when looking to make a meaningful change. (Waldman & Sparr, 2023; Freeman et al., 2021; Dauth et al., 2023)

Today, several companies invest in adjacent community programs that go beyond pure community engagement and focus on facilitating the inclusion of various underrepresented groups, supporting them in realizing alternative pathways into work and the empowerment of workers involved in gig economies. Providing all equipment, training, and support at an affordable rate, they receive further training to prepare them for work. Interaction with community leaders or organizations actively involved in these communities lends authenticity and credibility to these programs and can ensure that organizations remain informed of developments that benefit them and their workers. (Lansing et al., 2023; Shulga, 2021) Intermediaries can also work to ensure that training and mentoring programs are culturally sensitive and have language support built in, thus providing a more effective and reliable service to the organizations themselves. Hence, community engagement provides a new understanding of the diversity of workers in the gig economy. It underlines the solution focus that will minimize alienation in the gig economy and help embed diversity. (Byrne, 2022)

Policy and Regulatory Approaches

Despite the absence of employment agencies or regulations and of formal status for the job takers, the gig economy requires some kind of regulations. Without such minimum standards, there is a danger of a race to the bottom that will progressively erode the rights and social security of groups of workers who are already in a notoriously weak labour market position. This chapter will argue that a rights-based approach is required to define a minimum standard for policy and regulation that recognizes the diversity, inclusion, and equity of gig economy workers. Gig workers are more likely to be from minority or ethnic communities, low-income families, and in deprived areas. They are usually employed in labour market segments where national and international regulations are not respected. They are usually in a vulnerable legal and social protection status. Misclassification and co-entrepreneurship are the main strategies to reduce unfamiliar labour costs by enabling digital platforms.

The content of the contract and the conditions of work are often personalized, with different parameters for different workers. Training and protections are highly segmented, often based on competencies and previous experiences. This new form of segmentation is a key political priority as it will reduce the possibilities for extensive inclusiveness for society at large. (Lutfiyya and Bartlett, 2020) These predictions show that we need to think of a series of policy interventions that will simultaneously respect and take advantage of the heterogeneity of the workers in the gig economy while limiting potential segments that could hinder economic and social conflicts. The implications of platform work for the political, social, and technical dimensions of representative democracy are often ambiguous. The development of the digital economy contributes to defining new demands for political and social representations by providing economic agents.

Workers in the sector are extremely diverse, often employed under terms personalized to them as individuals, and many say they would not want standard jobs. Policies must respond to this diversity and provide security but also support. One key to this shift is to support the growing potential for platforms to provide universal benefits to all workers, portable between employers. It may be tempting to prioritize direct regulations and protections for workers in the gig economy, but it is better to focus on ensuring that they have access to the supports and benefits that everyone would like, so long as they have the freedom to negotiate a variety of terms with their employers. (Tirapani & Willmott, 2023)

CONCLUSION AND FUTURE DIRECTIONS

This chapter has critically analysed existing barriers and challenges that inhibit the development of a more diverse, inclusive, and equitable gig economy. It has been suggested that the predominant focus of gig economy critique lacks the nuance required to properly address the myriad of complex problems outlined in this analysis, with the contention that greater academic and associated practical efforts should be made to foster a more inclusive gig economy. Even in its current nascent form, the gig economy is characterized by myriad demonstrations of toxic workplace culture and inequality, primarily based on matters of race, gender, ability, and class. Rather than viewing such phenomena as innate or as part of the core makeup of contemporary gig work, concerted efforts should be made by companies, policymakers, and members of oppressed communities to collaborate in order to develop better, more inclusive work practices and intervene in existing toxic culture (Memon, et al., 2025)

The key to this approach will be rooting these strategies in the material realities of structural inequality. As such, despite the multifaceted nature of the barriers and challenges presented in this chapter, they should all be addressed in service of disrupting and deconstructing white supremacist heteronormative patriarchy and its myriad iterations. With this in mind, even as companies and grassroots organizations begin to take steps to foster more inclusive gig environments, future academic research could be undertaken to explore the interconnections of such barriers and their traversal across or through already existing systemic inequalities. (Efthymiou, I., 2024). Indeed, we may also ask how such research might be integrated into more granular advocacy and activist efforts, to further disrupt the structural status quo.

Similarly, conversations should also be advanced to conceptualize the role of technology and the potential for it to afford participation in the gig economy. In doing so, one will also have to pay proper attention to the limits and latent potential risks associated with this approach. Nonetheless, this chapter contends that a sustained commitment to the furthering of these ideas is necessary if we have any hope of seeing them realized. Thus, it is important for all stakeholders, including corporations, governments, and communities, to collaborate and work together to dismantle the existing barriers and overcome the challenges that hinder the realization of a more diverse, inclusive, and equitable gig economy. This requires a comprehensive approach that not only addresses the overt manifestations of inequality but also addresses the underlying systemic issues that perpetuate these inequalities. It is crucial to recognize the interconnectedness of various forms of discrimination and oppression and actively dismantle the structures that uphold them.

In order to create a more inclusive gig economy, companies must adopt inclusive policies and practices that promote diversity and equal opportunities. This includes implementing fair hiring practices, providing equal pay for equal work, and ensuring a safe and harassment-free work environment. It is also important for policymakers to enact legislation that protects the rights and interests of gig workers, such as fair labour standards, access to benefits, and avenues for recourse in cases of discrimination or mistreatment. At the grassroots level, it is essential for members of oppressed communities to organize and advocate for their rights and interests. This can be done through forming unions, joining advocacy groups, and participating in social movements that aim to challenge the dominant power structures. By amplifying marginalized voices and demanding change, oppressed communities can play a crucial role in shaping a more inclusive and equitable gig economy.

In addition to these efforts, it is necessary to critically examine the role of technology in the gig economy. While technology has the potential to expand access and opportunities for gig workers, it also presents risks and challenges. Issues such as algorithmic bias, data privacy, and worker exploitation need to be carefully addressed to ensure that technology does not perpetuate or deepen existing inequalities. This requires a holistic approach that involves continuous monitoring, regulation, and accountability.

By undertaking these collective efforts, we can begin to dismantle the barriers and challenges that hinder a more inclusive gig economy. However, it is important to recognize that this is an ongoing process that requires sustained commitment and collaboration. Companies, policymakers, and communities must continue to advocate for change, challenge discriminatory norms, and actively work towards creating a gig economy that is truly diverse, inclusive, and equitable. Only by doing so can we create a future where everyone has equal opportunities and fair treatment in the world of work.

COMPETING INTERESTS

The authors of this publication declare there are no competing interests.

FUNDING

This research received no specific grant from any funding agency in the public, commercial, or not-for-profit sectors. Funding for this research was covered by the author(s) of the article.

REFERENCES

Abkhezr, P., & McMahon, M. (2024). The intersections of migration, app-based gig work, and career development: Implications for career practice and research. *International Journal for Educational and Vocational Guidance*, *24*(1), 39–57. DOI: 10.1007/s10775-022-09556-w PMID: 35755081

Agyemang, G., Dhanani, A., Ejiogu, A. R., & Perkiss, S. (2024). Researching race, accounting and accountability: Past, present and future. *Accounting, Auditing & Accountability Journal*, *37*(7/8), 1637–1664. DOI: 10.1108/AAAJ-03-2024-6976

Altenried, M. (2024). Mobile workers, contingent labour: Migration, the gig economy and the multiplication of labour. *Environment and Planning A. Economy and Space*, *56*(4), 1113–1128. DOI: 10.1177/0308518X23121071234

Ansell, C., Sørensen, E., & Torfing, J. (2022). *Co-creation for sustainability: The UN SDGs and the power of local partnerships*. Emerald Publishing.

Arroyo, L. (2020). Implications of digital inclusion: Digitalization in terms of time use from a gender perspective. *Social Inclusion (Lisboa)*, *8*(2), 180–189. Advance online publication. DOI: 10.17645/si.v8i2.2546

Asad, S. A., Banerjee, R., & Bhattacharya, J. (2023). Do workers discriminate against their out-group employers? Evidence from an online platform economy. *Journal of Economic Behavior & Organization*, *216*, 221–242. DOI: 10.1016/j.jebo.2023.10.002

Asad, S. A., Banerjee, R., & Bhattacharya, J. (2023). Do workers discriminate against their out-group employers? Evidence from an online platform economy. *Journal of Economic Behavior & Organization*, *216*, 221–242. DOI: 10.1016/j.jebo.2023.10.002

Axelrad, H., Kalev, A., & Lewin-Epstein, N. (2023). Ambivalent Bias at Work: Managers' Perceptions of Older Workers across Organizational Contexts. *Work, Employment and Society*. Advance online publication. DOI: 10.1177/09500170231175790

Ayala-López, S., & Beeghly, E. (2020). Explaining injustice: Structural analysis, bias, and individuals. In *An introduction to implicit bias* (pp. 211–232). Routledge. DOI: 10.4324/9781315107615-11

Baker, A. C., Larcker, D. F., McCLURE, C. G., Saraph, D., & Watts, E. M.BAKER. (2024). Diversity Washing. *Journal of Accounting Research, 62*(5), 1661–1709. DOI: 10.1111/1475-679X.12542

Banik, N., & Padalkar, M. (2021). The spread of gig economy: Trends and effects. *Форсайт*. Retrieved from https://cyberleninka.ru

Bansal, R., Singh, R., & Gandhi, M. (2020). *The emergence of gig economy in India: A paradigm shift*. Parishodh Journal.

Bates, O., Lord, C., Alter, H., & Kirman, B. (2020, June). Let's start talking the walk: Capturing and reflecting on our limits when working with gig economy workers. In *Proceedings of the 7th International Conference on ICT for Sustainability* (pp. 227–235). DOI: 10.1145/3401335.3401364

Behera, B., & Gaur, M. (2022). Skill training for the success of the gig economy. *Journal of Pharmaceutical Negative Results, 13*(5), 2835–2840.

Behl, A., Rajagopal, K., Sheorey, P., & Mahendra, A. (2022). Barriers to entry of gig workers in the gig platforms: Exploring the dark side of the gig economy. *Aslib Journal of Information Management, 74*(5), 818–839. DOI: 10.1108/AJIM-08-2021-0235

Boulding, K. (2021). *The meaning of the twentieth century: The great transition*. Routledge. DOI: 10.4324/9781003256960

Bruckner, C. L., & Forman, J. B. (2021). Women, Retirement, and the Growing Gig Economy Workforce. *Ga. St. UL Rev., 38*, 259.

Brummer, C., & Strine, L. E.Jr. (2022). Duty and diversity. *Vand. L. Rev., 75*, 1.

Bunel, M., & Tovar, E. (2021). Profit, morality and discrimination. *Applied Economics, 53*(40), 4692–4712. DOI: 10.1080/00036846.2021.1907285

Byrne, Z. S. (2022). *Understanding employee engagement: Theory, research, and practice*. Routledge. DOI: 10.4324/9781003171133

Caza, B. B., Reid, E. M., Ashford, S. J., & Granger, S. (2021). Working on my own: Measuring the challenges of gig work. *Human Relations*. Advance online publication. DOI: 10.1177/00187267211030098

Christiaens, T. (2022). *Digital working lives: Worker autonomy and the gig economy*. Rowman & Littlefield. DOI: 10.5771/9781538173749

Coplan, J., Crocker, L., Landin, J., & Stenn, T. (2021). Building supportive, inclusive workplaces where neurodivergent thinkers thrive: Approaches in managing diversity, inclusion, and building entrepreneurship in the workplace. *S.A.M. Advanced Management Journal*, *86*(1), 21–30. DOI: 10.52770/XTBM1097

Costa, E. (2024). Examining the effectiveness of interventions to reduce discriminatory behavior at work: An attitude dimension consistency perspective. *The Journal of Applied Psychology*, *109*(11), 1669–1692. DOI: 10.1037/apl0001215 PMID: 39207374

Dauth, T., Schmid, S., Baldermann, S., & Orban, F. (2023). Attracting talent through diversity at the top: The impact of TMT diversity and firms' efforts to promote diversity on employer attractiveness. *European Management Journal*, *41*(1), 9–20. DOI: 10.1016/j.emj.2021.10.007

Della Longa, L., Valori, I., & Farroni, T. (2022). Interpersonal affective touch in a virtual world: Feeling the social presence of others to overcome loneliness. *Frontiers in Psychology*, *12*, 795283. DOI: 10.3389/fpsyg.2021.795283 PMID: 35087455

Dobbin, F., & Kalev, A. (2022). *Getting to diversity: What works and what doesn't*. Harvard University Press.

Drahokoupil, J., Kahancová, M., & Meszmann, T. T. (2022). Falling through the cracks: Gig economy and platform work in Central and Eastern Europe. In *The Routledge Handbook of the Gig Economy* (pp. 309–323). Routledge. [HTML] DOI: 10.4324/9781003161875-25

Dunn, M. (2020). Making gigs work: Digital platforms, job quality and worker motivations. *New Technology, Work and Employment*, *35*(2), 232–249. DOI: 10.1111/ntwe.12167

Efthymiou, I. (2024). Exploring the frontier: New and future trends in research. In B. Orlando (Ed.), *Innovation capabilities and entrepreneurial opportunities of smart working* (pp. 48–68). IGI Global. DOI: 10.4018/978-1-7998-8797-3.ch003

Efthymiou, I. P., Egleton, T. E., & Psomiadi, A. (2025). The Role of Artificial Intelligence in Humanitarian Aid for Achieving Sustainable Development Goals. In *Cases on AI-Driven Solutions to Environmental Challenges* (pp. 43–72). IGI Global Scientific Publishing., DOI: 10.4018/979-8-3693-7483-2.ch003

Emerson, E., Fortune, N., Llewellyn, G., & Stancliffe, R. (2021). Loneliness, social support, social isolation and wellbeing among working age adults with and without disability: Cross-sectional study. *Disability and Health Journal, 14*(1), 100965. DOI: 10.1016/j.dhjo.2020.100965 PMID: 32843311

Emery, M., & Flora, C. (2020). Spiraling-up: Mapping community transformation with community capitals framework. In *50 Years of Community Development Vol I* (pp. 163-179). Routledge.

Fibbi, R., Midtbøen, A. H., & Simon, P. (2021). *Migration and discrimination: IMISCOE short reader*. Springer Nature. DOI: 10.1007/978-3-030-67281-2

Finch, J., & Groves, D. (Eds.). (2022). *A labour of love: Women, work and caring*. Taylor & Francis. DOI: 10.4324/9781003303930

Fitzgerald, K. J. (2023). *Recognizing race and ethnicity: Power, privilege, and inequality* (4th ed.). Routledge., DOI: 10.4324/9781003359852

Francisco, M. P., Hartman, M., & Wang, Y. (2020). Inclusion and Special Education. *Education Sciences, 10*(9), 238. DOI: 10.3390/educsci10090238

Franklin, R. C. (2021). Black workers in Silicon Valley: Macro and micro boundaries. *Ethnic and Racial Studies, 45*(1), 69–89. DOI: 10.1080/01419870.2020.1866208

Freeman, R. E., Dmytriyev, S. D., & Phillips, R. A. (2021). Stakeholder Theory and the Resource-Based View of the Firm. *Journal of Management, 47*(7), 1757–1770. Advance online publication. DOI: 10.1177/0149206321993576

Hanelt, A., Bohnsack, R., Marz, D., & Marante, C. A. (2021). A Systematic Review of the Literature on Digital Transformation: Insights and Implications for Strategy and Organizational Change. *Journal of Management Studies, 58*(5), 1159–1197. DOI: 10.1111/joms.12639

Healy, J., Pekarek, A., & Vromen, A. (2020). Sceptics or supporters? Consumers' views of work in the gig economy. *New Technology, Work and Employment, 35*(1), 1–19. DOI: 10.1111/ntwe.12157

Hernandez, R. H., Song, Q., Kou, Y., & Gui, X. (2024, May). "At the end of the day, I am accountable": Gig workers' self-tracking for multi-dimensional accountability management. In *Proceedings of the CHI Conference on Human Factors in Computing Systems* (pp. 1–20). DOI: 10.1287/isre.2019.0896

Huang, N., Burtch, G., Hong, Y., & Pavlou, P. A. (2020). Unemployment and worker participation in the gig economy: Evidence from an online labor market. *Information Systems Research, 31*(2), 431–448. DOI: 10.1287/isre.2019.0896

Jaffe, S. (2021). *Work won't love you back: How devotion to our jobs keeps us exploited, exhausted, and alone*. Bold Type Books.

Janssens, M., & Zanoni, P. (2021). Making diversity research matter for social change: New conversations beyond the firm. *Organization Theory*, *2*(2), 26317877211004603.

Jones, P. (2021). *Work without the worker: Labour in the age of platform capitalism*. Verso Books.

Karanovic, J., Altman, E. J., & Cennamo, C. (2023). Who should price a gig? *MIT Sloan Management Review*, *65*(1), 62–67.

Kelkar, G. (2022). *Patriarchal Discrimination and Capitalist Relations: The Gender Question in the Gig Economy*. Institute for Human Development.

Khan, H. (2021). *Leadership, reinvented: How to foster empathy, servitude, diversity, and innovation in the workplace*. Sourcebooks, Inc.

Khan, M. H., Williams, J., Williams, P., & Mayes, R. (2024). Caring in the gig economy: A relational perspective of decent work. *Work, Employment and Society*, *38*(4), 1107–1127.

Killingsworth, M. A. (2021). Experienced well-being rises with income, even above $75,000 per year. *Proceedings of the National Academy of Sciences of the United States of America*, *118*(4), e2016976118. PMID: 33468644

Kirton, G. (2020). Diversity and inclusion in a changing world of work. In *The future of work and employment* (pp. 49–64). Edward Elgar Publishing.

Kite, M. E., Whitley, B. E.Jr, & Wagner, L. S. (2022). *Psychology of prejudice and discrimination*. Routledge.

Kost, D., Fieseler, C., & Wong, S. I. (2020). Boundaryless careers in the gig economy: An oxymoron? *Human Resource Management Journal*, *30*(1), 100–113.

Koutsimpogiorgos, N., Van Slageren, J., Herrmann, A. M., & Frenken, K. (2020). Conceptualizing the gig economy and its regulatory problems. *Policy and Internet, 12*(4), 525–545.

Kuhn, K. M., Meijerink, J., & Keegan, A. (2021). Human resource management and the gig economy: Challenges and opportunities at the intersection between organizational HR decision-makers and digital labor platforms. *Research in Personnel and Human Resources Management, 39*, 1–46.

Kuknor, S. C., & Bhattacharya, S. (2022). Inclusive leadership: New age leadership to foster organizational inclusion. *European Journal of Training and Development, 46*(9), 771–797.

Kumar, V., Ramachandran, D., & Kumar, B. (2021). Influence of new-age technologies on marketing: A research agenda. *Journal of Business Research*. DOI.org/10.1016/j.jbusres.2020.01.007

Langley, D. J., van Doorn, J., Ng, I. C., Stieglitz, S., Lazovik, A., & Boonstra, A. (2021). The Internet of Everything: Smart things and their impact on business models. *Journal of Business Research, 122*, 853–863. DOI: 10.1016/j.jbusres.2019.12.035

Lansing, A. E., Romero, N. J., Siantz, E., Silva, V., Center, K., Casteel, D., & Gilmer, T. (2023). Building trust: Leadership reflections on community empowerment and engagement in a large urban initiative. *BMC Public Health, 23*(1), 1252. DOI: 10.1186/s12889-023-15860-z PMID: 37380973

Lingras, K. A., Alexander, M. E., & Vrieze, D. M. (2023). Diversity, Equity, and Inclusion Efforts at a Departmental Level: Building a Committee as a Vehicle for Advancing Progress. *Journal of Clinical Psychology in Medical Settings, 30*(2), 356–379. DOI: 10.1007/s10880-021-09809-w PMID: 34529234

Litman, L., Robinson, J., Rosen, Z., Rosenzweig, C., Waxman, J., & Bates, L. M. (2020). The persistence of pay inequality: The gender pay gap in an anonymous online labor market. *PLoS One, 15*(2), e0229383. DOI: 10.1371/journal.pone.0229383 PMID: 32084233

Loganathan, M. (2022). Assessing Social Sustainability in the Gig Economy. *The Indian Journal of Labour Economics : the Quarterly Journal of the Indian Society of Labour Economics, 65*(3), 831–843. DOI: 10.1007/s41027-022-00399-1

Lutfiyya, Z., & Bartlett, N. (2020, September 28). Inclusive Societies. *Oxford Research Encyclopedia ofEducation.* oxfordre.com/education/view/10.1093/acrefore/9780190264093.001.0001/acrefore-9780190264093-e-1022..

Mahato, M., Kumar, N., & Jena, L. K. (2021). Re-thinking gig economy in conventional workforce post-COVID-19: A blended approach for upholding fair balance. *Journal of Work-Applied Management, 13*(2), 261–276.

Malhotra, R. T. (2024). *Inclusion on purpose: An intersectional approach to creating a culture of belonging at work*. MIT Press.

Mann, F., Wang, J., Pearce, E., Ma, R., Schlief, M., Lloyd-Evans, B., Ikhtabi, S., & Johnson, S. (2022). Loneliness and the onset of new mental health problems in the general population. *Social Psychiatry and Psychiatric Epidemiology, 57*(11), 2161–2178. DOI: 10.1007/s00127-022-02261-7 PMID: 35583561

Masera, M. L. (2024). Redefining tomorrow: A comprehensive analysis of AI's impact on employment and identity. http://hdl.handle.net/10579/26098

Memon, F. N., & Memon, S. N. (2025). Digital Divide and Equity in Education: Bridging Gaps to Ensure Inclusive Learning. In *Impact of Digitalization on Education and Social Sustainability* (pp. 107-130). IGI Global. DOI: DOI: 10.4018/979-8-3693-1854-6.ch004

Mohsin, F. H., Isa, N. M., Awee, A., & Purhanudin, N. (2022). Growing gigs: A conceptual report on job autonomy and work engagement on gig workers' performance. *International Journal of Advanced Research in Economics and Finance, 4*(1), 144–156.

Montgomery, T., & Baglioni, S. (2021). Defining the gig economy: Platform capitalism and the reinvention of precarious work. *The International Journal of Sociology and Social Policy, 41*(9/10), 1012–1025.

Muldoon, J., Stronge, W., Avila, R., Gebrial, D., Jones, P., Srnicek, N., ... & Wark, M. (2020). Platforming equality: Policy challenges for the digital economy.

Myhill, K., Richards, J., & Sang, K. (2023). Job quality, fair work and gig work: The lived experience of gig workers. In *Technologically Mediated Human Resource Management* (pp. 116–141). Routledge.

Nadeem, W., Juntunen, M., Shirazi, F., & Hajli, N. (2020). Consumers' value co-creation in sharing economy: The role of social support, consumers' ethical perceptions and relationship quality. *Technological Forecasting and Social Change, 151*, 119786. DOI: 10.1016/j.techfore.2019.119786

Ness, I., Ovetz, R., Roque, I., Swidler, E. M., & Zwick, A. (Eds.). (2023). *The Routledge handbook of the gig economy*. Routledge.

Nkomo, S. M. (2021). Reflections on the continuing denial of the centrality of "race" in management and organization studies. *Equality, Diversity and Inclusion*, *40*(2), 212–224. DOI: 10.1108/EDI-01-2021-0011

Ochillo, F. (2022). The economic consequences and generational impact of the digital divide. *Belfer Center for Science and International Affairs, Harvard Kennedy School*.https://issuu. com/belfercenter/docs/tapp-francella_impact_of_the_digital_divide_final_

Ostrom, A. L., Field, J. M., Fotheringham, D., Subramony, M., Gustafsson, A., Lemon, K. N., & McColl-Kennedy, J. R. (2021). Service research priorities: Managing and delivering service in turbulent times. *Journal of Service Research*, *24*(3), 329–353. DOI: 10.1177/1094670521102191

Ozgumus, E., & Rattan, A. (2025). Motivating support for workplace diversity policies: A mindsets framework. *Current Opinion in Psychology*, *62*, 101999. DOI: 10.1016/j.copsyc.2025.101999 PMID: 39893990

Phillips, L. T., Jun, S., & Shakeri, A. (2022). Barriers and boosts: Using inequity frames theory to expand understanding of mechanisms of race and gender inequity. *The Academy of Management Annals*, *16*(2), 547–587. Advance online publication. DOI: 10.5465/annals.2020.0314

Popov, A. (2023). The future of work: Adapting to technological disruptions in the labor market. *Journal of Philosophical Criticism*.

Rani, U., & Furrer, M. (2021). Digital labour platforms and new forms of flexible work in developing countries: Algorithmic management of work and workers. *Competition & Change*, *25*(2), 212–236. Advance online publication. DOI: 10.1177/1024529420905187

Rothwell, W. J., Ealy, P. L., & Campbell, J. (Eds.). (2022). *Rethinking organizational diversity, equity, and inclusion: A step-by-step guide for facilitating effective change*. CRC Press.

Royall, S., McCarthy, V., & Miller, G. J. (2022). Creating an inclusive workplace: The effectiveness of diversity training. *J. Glob. Econ. Trade Int. Bus*, *3*, 39–55.

Rozentale, I., & van Baalen, P. J. (2021). Crafting business models for conflicting goals: Lessons from creative service firms. *Long Range Planning*, *54*(4), 102092. Advance online publication. DOI: 10.1016/j.lrp.2021.102092

Scuotto, V., Lemaire, S. L. L., Magni, D., & Maalaoui, A. (2022). Extending knowledge-based view: Future trends of corporate social entrepreneurship to fight the gig economy challenges. *Journal of Business Research, 139*, 1111–1122. DOI: 10.1016/j.jbusres.2021.10.060

Shibata, S. (2019). Gig Work and the Discourse of Autonomy: Fictitious Freedom in Japan's Digital Economy. *New Political Economy*, *25*(4), 535–551. DOI: 10.1080/13563467.2019.1613351

Shukaitis, S., & Figiel, J. (2024) *The Wages of Dreamwork Class Composition & the Social Reproduction of Cultural Labor.* Minor Compositions. ISBN 9781570274077. Official URL: https://www.minorcompositions.info/?p=1314

Shukla, A., Kushwah, P., Jain, E., & Sharma, S. K. (2021). Role of ICT in emancipation of digital entrepreneurship among new generation women. *Journal of Enterprising Communities: People and Places in the Global Economy*, *15*(1), 137–154.

Shulga, L. V. (2020). Change Management Communication: The Role of Meaningfulness, Leadership Brand Authenticity, and Gender. *Cornell Hospitality Quarterly*. Advance online publication. DOI: 10.1177/1938965520929022

Smeyers, V., & Iruemiobe, B. (2023). Gender diversity in top management teams and employee DEI perception.

Smith, R. (2023, October 4). Gig economy statistics: What you need to know in 2024. *FinMasters.* Retrieved from https://finmasters.com/gig-economy-statistics/

Stephens, N. M., Rivera, L. A., & Townsend, S. S. (2020). What works to reduce bias? A multilevel approach. Unpublished manuscript. Retrieved from https://www.nicolemstephens.com

Tan, Z. M., Aggarwal, N., Cowls, J., Morley, J., Taddeo, M., & Floridi, L. (2021). The ethical debate about the gig economy: A review and critical analysis. *Technology in Society*, *65*, 101594. DOI: 10.1016/j.techsoc.2021.101594

Tirapani, A. N., & Willmott, H. (2022). Revisiting conflict: Neoliberalism at work in the gig economy. *Human Relations.* Advance online publication. DOI: 10.1177/00187267211064596

Triana, C., Gu, P., Chapa, O., Richard, O., & Colella, A. (2021). Sixty years of discrimination and diversity research in human resource management: A review with suggestions for future research directions. *Human Resource Management*, *60*(1), 145–204. DOI: 10.1002/hrm.22052

Triana, M. D. C., Gu, P., Chapa, O., Richard, O., & Colella, A. (2021). Sixty years of discrimination and diversity research in human resource management: A review with suggestions for future research directions. *Human Resource Management, 60*(1), 145–204.

Tubaro, P., Coville, M., Le Ludec, C., & Casilli, A. A. (2022). Hidden inequalities: The gendered labour of women on micro-tasking platforms. *Internet Policy Review, 11*(1). Advance online publication. DOI: 10.14763/2022.1.1623

Tushev, M., Ebrahimi, F., & Mahmoud, A. (2022). A systematic literature review of anti-discrimination design strategies in the digital sharing economy. *IEEE Transactions on Software Engineering, 48*(12), 5148–5157. DOI: 10.1109/TSE.2021.3139961

Tyc, A. (2022). Gig Economy: How to Overcome the Problem of Misclassifying Gig Workers as Self-Employed? *Revue Européenne du Droit Social, 56*(3), 35–45.

Uzir, M. U. H., Al Halbusi, H., Thurasamy, R., Thiam Hock, R. L., Aljaberi, M. A., Hasan, N., & Hamid, M. (2021). The effects of service quality, perceived value and trust in home delivery service personnel on customer satisfaction: Evidence from a developing country. *Journal of Retailing and Consumer Services, 63*, 102721. DOI: 10.1016/j.jretconser.2021.102721

Waldman, D. A., & Sparr, J. L. (2023). Rethinking diversity strategies: An application of paradox and positive organization behavior theories. *The Academy of Management Perspectives, 37*(2), 174–192. DOI: 10.5465/amp.2021.0183

Walters, D. D. D. (2023). *DEI, Here I Come! Five Lessons From Organizational Dynamics For DEI* (Doctoral dissertation, University of Pennsylvania).

Wan, Z., Zhang, L., Wang, L., & Zhang, F. (2024). Navigating autonomy: Unraveling the dual influence of job autonomy on workplace well-being in the gig economy. *Frontiers in Psychology, 15*, 1369495. DOI: 10.3389/fpsyg.2024.1369495 PMID: 39118837

Warren, T. (2021). Work–life balance and gig work: 'Where are we now' and 'where to next' with the work–life balance agenda? *The Journal of Industrial Relations, 63*(4), 522–545. Advance online publication. DOI: 10.1177/00221856211007161

Watson, G. P., Kistler, L. D., Graham, B. A., & Sinclair, R. R. (2021). Looking at the Gig Picture: Defining Gig Work and Explaining Profile Differences in Gig Workers' Job Demands and Resources. *Group & Organization Management, 46*(2), 327–361. Advance online publication. DOI: 10.1177/1059601121996548

Wigfield, A., Turner, R., Alden, S., Green, M., & Karania, V. K. (2022). Developing a New Conceptual Framework of Meaningful Interaction for Understanding Social Isolation and Loneliness. *Social Policy and Society*, *21*(2), 172–193. DOI: 10.1017/S147474642000055X

Woldoff, R. A., Woldoff, R., & Litchfield, R. C. (2021). *Digital nomads: In search of freedom, community, and meaningful work in the new economy*. Oxford University Press.

Zanoni, P., & Pitts, F. H. (2022). Inclusion through the platform economy?: The "diverse" crowd as relative surplus populations and the pauperisation of labour. In *The Routledge Handbook of the Gig Economy* (pp. 33–45). Routledge.

Chapter 10
Building Inclusive and Equitable Gig Economies for Sustainable Global Growth

Razia Nagina
https://orcid.org/0000-0002-0305-8393
Lovely Professional University, India

ABSTRACT

The gig economy has reshaped labor markets by offering flexible work but also presents challenges such as income instability, lack of social protections, digital access barriers, and sustainability concerns. This chapter examines these issues using secondary research and primary data from a survey of 250 gig workers across ride-hailing, food delivery, freelancing, and domestic services. Findings indicate that 70% face income volatility, 60% lack essential benefits, and 55% experience algorithmic bias in job allocation. Digital access limitations further hinder opportunities, especially in rural areas. The chapter explores regulatory frameworks, technological innovations, and sustainability initiatives, proposing solutions like fair wage policies, algorithmic transparency, and improved worker protections. By addressing structural inequities, this research contributes to discussions on labor rights, platform accountability, and the sustainable evolution of the gig economy.

DOI: 10.4018/979-8-3693-9385-7.ch010

INTRODUCTION

The gig economy, which is fueled by globalization, digitalization, and changing economic paradigms, has become a disruptive force in global labor markets. It offers a wide range of workers worldwide flexible, task-based options, marking a break from traditional employment structures (Jain, 2024). According to estimates, gig workers currently make up a sizable percentage of the workforce worldwide, with millions of people depending on these occupations as their main or secondary source of income. Geographical and structural obstacles to labor have been broken down by platforms like Uber, TaskRabbit, Fiverr, and innumerable others, which have completely changed how people work and how businesses function (Kispert, 2021). New opportunities for economic engagement have been made possible by the gig economy, but its rapid expansion has also raised urgent issues with sustainability, equity, and inclusivity.

This chapter focuses on discussing the intricate relationships that exist between sustainability, equity, and inclusion in the dynamic gig economy. As economies throughout the world attempt to achieve the Sustainable Development Goals (SDGs), especially those related to decent work, inequality reduction, and inclusive economic growth, the gig economy needs to change from being a place where a select few can find opportunity to becoming a driving force for equitable and widespread advancement. This chapter's objective is to explore the gig economy's existing situation from the perspectives of equity and inclusivity, while also investigating workable frameworks and tactics for creating more resilient and sustainable systems.

There is much potential in the gig economy, especially in areas where underemployment and unemployment are still persistent problems. Workers, particularly those in poor nations, may now access global markets thanks to digital gig platforms, opening up options that were unthinkable just ten years ago. Gig work offers many employees freedom, flexibility, and the chance to make money outside of the typical job framework. This flexibility is especially helpful for people who need to take care of others, are students, or are looking for extra money (Cropanzano et al., 2023).

Nevertheless, the gig economy is rife with structural injustices in spite of its potential. Wage, opportunity, and resource disparities produce a stratified ecology in which some groups profit disproportionately while others are left out or taken advantage of. Due to social conventions, safety concerns, and structural hurdles on digital platforms, women frequently face limited prospects and lower compensation, perpetuating gender inequality. Even for comparable work, workers in lower-income countries are paid much less than their counterparts in developed countries. Because these trends perpetuate or worsen already-existing disparities, they jeopardize the gig economy's ability to be an equalizing force (Sachan, 2024).

Additionally, precariousness and a lack of official protections are common characteristics of gig work. Many gig workers are susceptible to economic shocks since they may not have access to benefits like social security, paid time off, or health insurance. Their capacity to push for improved conditions is further weakened by the lack of collective bargaining procedures (Celestin & Vanitha, 2021). These difficulties highlight the necessity of rethinking gig economies in a way that puts justice and inclusion first while making sure that expansion complies with the rules of social and economic sustainability.

For sustainability and resilience, it is both strategically and morally necessary to establish inclusive and equitable gig economies. While equity addresses systemic inequities and allows for meaningful engagement from everyone, inclusivity guarantees equitable access to opportunities (Novitz, 2021). Geographical barriers can be overcome by digital platforms, which can improve socioeconomic mobility, especially for marginalized groups like the disabled or those living in rural areas. However, addressing inequities necessitates giving livable salaries, workplace safety, and benefits equivalent to those of regular employment first priority. Gig platforms need to make sure that job access and pay are transparent and less biased by algorithms. Reducing inequality and attaining sustained global growth depend on addressing these fundamental problems (Liang et al., 2023).

Sustainability is a crucial aspect of the development of the gig economy. Sustainability in this sense encompasses social and economic aspects in addition to environmental ones. The gig economy must minimize negative effects on the environment and society while improving the livelihoods of its workers if it is to be considered genuinely sustainable (Tan et al., 2021). To do this, platforms and policies must be created with long-term worker wellbeing, equitable remuneration, and ethical resource use as top priorities.

Furthermore, gig labor models need to change to meet the demands of a changing world. Due to interrupted demand, millions of gig workers experienced financial volatility during the COVID-19 epidemic, exposing the fragility of gig employment (Yasih, 2024). The significance of developing flexible systems that can endure economic fluctuations and offer strong worker safety nets was emphasized by this. The COVID-19 pandemic significantly disrupted the gig economy, exposing its fragility. A global survey in March 2020 found that 52% of gig workers lost their jobs due to the pandemic (Statista, 2020). In the U.S., the number of workers earning from digital gig platforms increased by 3.1 million between 2020 and 2021, with food delivery and transportation sectors seeing the largest surge (National Bureau of Economic Research [NBER], 2023).

Despite demand increases in certain sectors, gig workers lacked essential social protections. The International Labour Organization (ILO) reported that gig workers were among the most vulnerable, as many lacked access to unemployment benefits, health insurance, and stable income sources (ILO, 2021). This highlighted the need for portable benefits and income security mechanisms to protect gig workers during economic shocks.

Governments, corporations, employees, and civil society organizations must work together to create a gig economy that is inclusive, egalitarian, and sustainable. Legislators must actively participate in creating rules that safeguard gig workers while encouraging innovation and fair competition. By putting fair processes into place, providing perks to employees, and funding training and development initiatives, businesses may demonstrate their commitment to social responsibility. In order to guarantee that workers' interests and concerns are given priority during decision-making processes, their voices must be amplified concurrently through advocacy and collective action (Koh, 2023).

International organizations have the potential to significantly influence global norms for fair gig work. Through knowledge-sharing and technical support, these groups can aid nations in creating flexible frameworks for gig economy regulation and support. Additionally, by encouraging solutions that remove structural hurdles and improve sustainability, cross-sector cooperation can promote diversity and creativity (Heeks et al., 2021).

The gig economy presents both opportunities and challenges, necessitating a critical examination of its structural dynamics to ensure sustainability, inclusivity, and equity. This chapter seeks to analyze the complex interplay between these factors, focusing on the disparities in income, access, and working conditions that disproportionately impact marginalized groups such as women, rural workers, and those in lower-income countries. The research aims to explore how digital platforms, regulatory frameworks, and labor policies shape these inequalities while assessing potential interventions that could foster a more just and sustainable gig economy. Additionally, it investigates the role of technological advancements, such as AI-driven work allocation and algorithmic transparency, in mitigating or exacerbating these disparities.

A comprehensive roadmap is adopted to achieve these research objectives, combining secondary research with primary data from a survey of 250 gig workers across ride-hailing, food delivery, freelancing, and domestic services. First, the chapter outlines the global landscape of the gig economy, emphasizing its rapid expansion and its implications for labor markets. The discussion then shifts to examining the structural inequalities embedded in gig work, including wage gaps, employment instability, algorithmic biases, and the absence of worker protections. A critical review of international and national regulatory efforts follows, analyzing policies such as the European Union's Platform Work Directive and India's Social Security Code (2020) to evaluate their effectiveness in safeguarding gig workers' rights. Furthermore, the chapter explores technological innovations and sustainability measures within gig platforms, such as the adoption of electric vehicles and biodegradable packaging, to assess their role in reducing environmental impact. The survey findings reinforce these discussions by providing insights into gig workers' financial instability, lack of social protections, challenges in digital access, and experiences with algorithmic fairness.

The concluding section synthesizes these insights, integrating both secondary research and primary survey data to advocate for a collaborative approach among policymakers, businesses, and civil society. It proposes solutions for improving labor protections, enhancing digital inclusion, and advancing sustainability within the gig economy. This chapter aims to serve as a foundational resource for academics, policymakers, and industry leaders committed to shaping a more inclusive and sustainable future for the gig economy.

EXAMINING THE GLOBAL INEQUITIES IN THE GIG ECONOMY

Short-term, task-based work that is usually mediated through digital platforms is what defines the gig economy, which has grown to be a key component of contemporary labor markets across the globe. Because of its flexible form, the gig economy gives people the chance to make money without being dependent on traditional, long-term job arrangements. However, despite its many benefits, including freedom and flexibility, the gig economy also has serious drawbacks, especially when it comes to global inequality. There are serious problems with differences in income distribution, working conditions, and access, particularly for marginalized and vulnerable groups. A more sustainable and inclusive future for gig workers worldwide depends on examining these disparities (Moghavvemi et al., 2023).

The global inequalities that exist in the gig economy are identified and examined in this section using secondary data, with an emphasis on marginalized and vulnerable group. These demographics include women, members of ethnic minorities, low-wage workers, people residing in developing nations, and people with restricted access to education and technology. This analysis highlights the fundamental disparities that influence the dynamics of the gig economy and makes recommendations for reform by examining previous studies, publications, and databases (Behl et al., 2022).

Disparities in Access to the Gig Economy

Geographical location, educational background, and technological infrastructure are some of the characteristics that greatly affect access to the gig economy. A well-established online payment infrastructure, increased internet usage, and increased digital literacy make gig work more accessible to people in developed economies.

However, a number of reasons frequently hinder access to gig platforms for persons living in rural or undeveloped areas (Bérastégui, 2021).

The gig economy is inaccessible to vast segments of the population in many regions of the Global South due to the digital divide. Although internet penetration has been rising, the International Telecommunication Union (ITU) reports that many low-income and rural communities continue to confront challenges such limited access to technology, high data charges, and unreliable internet connections (Teja, 2023). In sub-Saharan Africa, for example, internet penetration rates are still far lower than in North America or Europe, which limits people's capacity to engage in gig employment.

The substantial obstacles that women have in obtaining gig work are clearly evident from the available data. According to a McKinsey Global Institute study, women in poor nations are less likely than men to have access to the networks and technology needed for gig work. Women find it more difficult to access digital platforms due to a number of issues, such as social expectations, educational differences, and economic discrepancies (Mehta & Mehta, 2021).

Additionally, systemic hurdles to gig employment also affect underprivileged communities, especially migrant workers and ethnic minorities. These workers face additional challenges due to biases in platform algorithms, discrimination, and a lack of social capital. Ethnic minorities have unequal access to gig platforms, according to OECD research, and biases frequently impact algorithmic suggestions in addition to recruiting (De Angelis et al., 2023). For instance, some groups have fewer chances of being suggested for specialized jobs or receiving high-paying work offers, which restricts their ability to move up the economic ladder in the gig economy.

Disparities in Working Conditions

Gig workers frequently experience difficulties with job security, safety, and support due to the very unpredictable nature of working conditions in the gig economy and the absence of traditional labor laws. Since many gig workers are categorized as independent contractors rather than employees, they frequently aren't eligible for fundamental labor protections like paid time off, unemployment insurance, or health benefits (Salleh et al., 2023).

Job instability is one of the main injustices in the gig economy. Because gig work is typically project-based, employees frequently have downtime in between jobs. This range in income can be especially detrimental to low-wage workers. In the United States, gig workers report much higher levels of job insecurity than those in traditional employment, per Gallup secondary data. Workers in other areas, especially in developing nations, may experience extended periods of underemployment or unemployment as a result of an excessive dependence on erratic gig-based income (Bruckner & Forman, 2021).

The lack of protection from exploitation is another problem that affects working conditions in the gig economy. Workers may be under pressure to take positions that pay poorly, and working hours in the gig economy might be long. A report by the World Economic Forum focuses on the experiences of gig workers in the transportation industry, especially drivers for services like Uber and Lyft, who frequently put in long hours in search of unpredictable pay (Sannon & Cosley, 2022). The absence of labor regulations that protect workers in places like Southeast Asia and Africa makes these vulnerabilities much worse. Many gig workers face financial instability, physical and mental health problems, and fatigue if they are not protected from mistreatment and unfair treatment.

Another important concern is workplace safety, particularly in industries like delivery services and ridesharing where gig workers carry out physically taxing or dangerous jobs. Because they often lack insurance or access to social safety nets, gig workers in these industries are particularly susceptible to accidents, injuries, and exploitation, according to secondary data from the International Labour Organization (ILO). While typical workers might have insurance or safety gear given by their company, gig workers frequently have to pay for it themselves.

Disparities in Income Distribution

Among the most significant disparities in the gig economy is income inequality. Many gig workers get minimal wages with no opportunity for advancement, while some, especially those performing high-skilled work, might make a sizable income. According to secondary data, gig workers in developing countries typically earn far less than their counterparts in more developed countries.

According to World Bank data, there are still persisting salary differences in the gig economy between high- and low-income nations (Liu et al., 2022). Even when they work the same hours and complete comparable activities, people in lower-income nations can receive lesser pay. In addition to pay fixing on the platforms, exchange rates and international financial systems that penalize workers in less affluent areas are also major contributors to this inequality. Due to localized currency depreciation or low cost of living adjustments, workers from impoverished locations typically experience a downward pull in earnings that does not correspond with the global expectations of fair compensation.

Furthermore, a sizable fraction of gig workers does not generate consistent or predictable incomes. Workers who perform lower-level gig work, including manual labor or micro tasking, frequently get far less than the minimum wage, which prevents them from achieving a respectable quality of living. The gig economy has a "gender pay gap" that disproportionately affects women and is greatly impacted by the kinds of gigs they take on. In the gig economy, women typically hold lower-paying jobs, and gender-based pay disparities still exist in industries including caregiving, delivery, and cleaning (Vyas, 2021).

Empirical evidence highlights significant disparities within the gig economy. A study analyzing over a million Uber drivers in the United States found a 7% gender earnings gap, attributed to factors such as experience on the platform, driving speed, and preferences for work location and timing (Cook et al., 2018). Similarly, research on Amazon's Mechanical Turk platform revealed that women earn approximately 10.5% less per hour than men, primarily because they select lower-paying tasks (Litman et al., 2020). Geographical disparities are also evident; for instance, gig workers in some African countries earn as little as $1.25 per hour, significantly below minimum wage standards in developed nations (Masekesa, 2021). Moreover, while women constitute about 42% of online gig workers—exceeding their 31.8% participation in traditional labor markets—they continue to face challenges such as internet access disparities and unequal earnings (World Bank, 2022).

Solutions and Future Directions for addressing the issue of Disparity

Governments, companies, and gig platforms must all work together to address these disparities in the gig economy today. To guarantee that gig workers obtain fair compensation, workplace safeguards, and sufficient benefits, governments must pass legislation (Tan et al., 2021). Classifying gig workers as employees rather than independent contractors has already allowed several nations, like the UK and Spain, to make progress in providing them with greater access to social safety. To prevent workers from being exploited, governments in developing nations with quickly expanding gig economy ought to implement comparable regulations (Cini et al., 2022).

In addition, gig platforms must acknowledge their part in maintaining inequality and take action to lessen it. Transparency in wage-setting procedures should be given top priority by platforms, which should also aim to eradicate algorithmic biases and give employees easy means to contest unfair ratings or compensation policies. Furthermore, platforms ought to make investments in initiatives that broaden access to gig possibilities, such fostering digital literacy and extending internet connectivity in underprivileged regions.

Global corporations and advocacy groups must keep an eye on the gig economy and establish international norms that safeguard workers' rights and promote fair income distribution. In order to enhance working conditions for employees worldwide, initiatives such as the Global Gig Economy Coalition seek to strengthen ties amongst important players (Niebler, 2023).

ANALYZING POLICIES FOR INCLUSIVITY

The gig economy has the unquestionable potential to change the nature of work in the future as it grows around the world. Gig platforms like Uber, Airbnb, TaskRabbit, and Fiverr have given millions of people flexible work options, changing the face of labor relations completely. But along with its expansion have come a number of difficult problems, mostly related to sustainability, equity, and inclusivity. Inequality, job insecurity, and exclusion from benefits usually associated with traditional employment are significant issues for gig workers, who are frequently categorized as independent contractors. As a result, improving fairness and inclusivity in the gig economy has emerged as a pressing concern that calls for strong legislative action (Prassl, 2018). This objective examines how existing regulatory and policy frameworks can influence inclusivity and equity within the gig economy and how these frameworks can be adapted to foster more sustainable growth in global business.

Understanding the Challenges of Inclusivity and Equity in the Gig Economy

The gig economy is frequently hailed as a source of freedom and flexibility. However, these same qualities pose serious obstacles to equity and inclusivity. Unlike their counterparts in regular employment, gig workers are usually not covered by important workplace safeguards including unemployment insurance, paid leave, social benefits (healthcare, pensions), and minimum pay guarantees. Vulnerable and marginalized groups, such as women, racial minorities, migrants, and people from lower socioeconomic origins, are disproportionately impacted by these exclusions (Carter, 2021).

Additionally, platform-based gig employment usually prevents individuals from establishing stable, long-term jobs, which increases income volatility. Lower-skilled jobs, like food delivery or ride-sharing, frequently result in low, unpredictable earnings, exposing workers to financial instability, whereas high-skill gig labor, like software development or consulting, may offer flexibility with appealing pay (Irwin, 2022). These problems can be more severe in nations where gig work accounts for a sizable percentage of all employment, placing workers in vulnerable circumstances that are made worse by a dearth of labor rights and legal protections.

Numerous countries and regions are investigating legislative and policy solutions to enhance equity and inclusivity in gig economies in order to solve these gaps. An understanding of how legal and regulatory frameworks might change to accommodate the particular needs of this quickly expanding industry can be obtained by evaluating the various approaches to gig economy regulation around the world.

Regulatory and Policy Approaches to Gig Worker Inclusivity

Having regulations that permit workers to engage fully and equitably is essential to attaining equity in the gig economy. In order to do this, labor laws must be modified to take gig workers' interests and rights into account while simultaneously promoting economic expansion that benefits both individuals and enterprises. To increase inclusivity in gig employment, some economies have suggested or enacted regulatory measures in recent years. The following list includes some of the most notable regulatory trends:

United Kingdom: Worker Classification and Benefits Protection

When it comes to worker classification, the UK has taken the lead in regulating gig economy activities. In the historic decision of Uber v. Aslam, the UK Supreme Court in 2018 gave Uber drivers the status of "workers" instead of "independent contractors." Gig workers were granted fundamental job rights as a result of this reclassification, including the national minimum wage, holiday pay, and protection from wrongful termination (Jain, 2024). A precedent for resolving the categorization issue in other industries was established by the ruling, which was viewed as a major victory for worker rights.

In response to this decision, the UK government launched a consultation on gig economy workers' rights, looking at how current labor rules might be modified to offer more extensive safeguards. To close the gap between the benefits of employees and independent contractors, legislators have proposed extending social safeguards for gig workers, such as insurance plans and paid sick leave.

There are still issues in spite of these advancements, particularly in fields where low-skilled labor is a major component of the gig economy. The gig economy's emphasis on flexibility, according to many supporters, shouldn't come at the price of employees' rights to social security and just compensation (Woodcook, 2021). Due to these worries, there have been suggestions for a more nuanced strategy that gives gig workers a status that falls somewhere between that of an independent contractor and a regular employee.

United States: State-Level Responses and Calls for Federal Intervention

In the US, the gig economy is governed by a complicated web of federal and state laws, with different jurisdictions taking different stances. Gig workers frequently operate in legal limbo, and regulatory monitoring has lagged behind the growth of gig platforms in the United States.

California has been among the most active states in attempting to modify laws to accommodate gig economy workers. Assembly Bill 5 (AB 5) was approved in California in 2019 with the goal of reclassifying many independent contractors as employees in order to impose stronger employment protections for gig workers (Thordarson, 2021). The main goal of this regulation was to provide gig workers with benefits like unemployment insurance, workers' compensation, and the minimum wage. Gig businesses like Uber, Lyft, and DoorDash have been especially vocal in their opposition to the bill, claiming that it jeopardizes their business model and the flexible nature of gig labor.

Uber, Lyft, and other businesses lobbied for Proposition 22, a 2020 ballot initiative that gave gig workers in California an exemption from AB 5's provisions, allowing them to keep their contractor status while receiving certain restricted benefits, in response to the possible harm that AB 5 might cause to the gig economy. When Proposition 22 was passed, it preserved the business structures of gig companies while offering certain benefits to gig workers, like accident coverage and health insurance subsidies. Proposition 22, however, is criticized for failing to adequately protect gig workers and for potentially undoing the gains gained in the direction of more equitable working conditions (Cherry, 2022).

At the federal level, there is still debate about attempts to enact national laws governing gig work. Through the Department of Labor and other organizations, the Biden administration has stated its support for bolstering labor laws, particularly extending rights for gig workers. In order to give gig workers, the entire range of labor protections, for instance, there are increasing conversations about designating them as employees across sectors; nevertheless, these arguments are continuous and influenced by political factors.

European Union: Comprehensive Regulation and Focus on Social Rights

The EU has been more aggressive in its efforts to regulate the gig economy. With the understanding that fairness and equity must be ingrained in platform work, the EU has created a framework of rights for workers in all industries, including gig labor.

In order to give workers on digital platforms (like Uber or Deliveroo) fundamental rights and protections, the European Commission proposed a Directive on Improving the Working Conditions of Platform Workers in December 2021. The plan includes legislation that give platform workers more access to benefits including paid leave, pension contributions, and protection from abuse, as well as clearer guidelines for worker classification and algorithm transparency (Moniz et al., 2021).

The EU's strategy acknowledges the flexibility that many gig workers want while concentrating on social rights and labor regulations. It does, however, recognize that limiting platform employment is not always necessary to increase worker security. Rather, the emphasis is on striking a balance between decent working conditions and flexibility, which might serve as a useful model for other nations.

The Role of the ILO in Shaping Global Gig Economy Policies

The ILO has emphasized the need to establish global labor standards for digital platform workers, acknowledging the challenges posed by the gig economy. In its 2021 report, the ILO recommended cross-border social security systems, dispute resolution mechanisms, and minimum labor protections to ensure fair treatment of gig workers worldwide (ILO, 2021).

A proposed framework could take inspiration from the EU's Platform Work Directive, which shifts the burden of proof onto companies to justify why workers should not be classified as employees (European Commission, 2022). Similarly, the UK Supreme Court's 2021 ruling on Uber granted gig workers minimum wage and paid leave, offering a model for global policy adoption (Jain, 2024). Integrating such measures within the ILO's labor standards would help regulate gig work globally, ensuring fair wages, job security, and social protections across developed and emerging economies.

India: Policy Challenges and Emerging Developments

With one of the world's most active and rapidly expanding gig labor markets, India is a prime example of the gig economy. In India, the gig economy has played a significant role in creating job opportunities, especially for young people and those living in underprivileged areas. However, problems with labor rights, working conditions, and equitable revenue distribution for gig workers have been exacerbated by the absence of defined policy frameworks.

The lack of social safety nets, low pay, and job insecurity are some of the major issues faced by Indian gig workers. Gig workers in India, especially those working for services like food delivery services like Swiggy and Zomato and ride-sharing services like Ola and Uber, are not entitled to benefits like health insurance, paid time off, or retirement plans that come with full-time jobs. Furthermore, workers in this sector have limited access to grievance redressal channels and labor law protection due to the size of the informal labor force.

India's Ministry of Labour and Employment has started to move toward a more official recognition of gig workers after realizing these loopholes (Thomas, 2024). Through the Code on Social Security and the Occupational Safety, Health, and Working Conditions Code, which for the first time contained rules for the welfare of gig and platform workers, the Indian government proposed significant labor reforms in 2020. These codes grant gig workers access to the social security system, maternity benefits, and life and disability insurance, acknowledging them as members of the "unorganised sector." Although these codes are a positive move, there is still work to be done to ensure their full adoption and efficacy.

Furthermore, state-level policy initiatives have aimed to advance gig workers' social protection. States like Karnataka and Kerala are attempting to integrate gig workers into the formal labor market by developing more extensive welfare systems. At the state level, initiatives to support skill development, improved working conditions, and a minimum pay for gig workers are also being considered (Rahman & Pingali, 2024).

Despite this progress, challenges remain regarding enforcement, consistency in the provision of social benefits, and access to fair pay. One major barrier to full inclusivity is the need to address the digital divide that limits access to gig work in rural areas and among disadvantaged groups, particularly women and lower-income communities. Furthermore, platform companies face resistance to the proposed changes, especially regarding their business model and the financial implications of classifying gig workers as employees.

In analyzing the evolving regulatory landscape, several key insights emerge regarding inclusivity and equity within gig economies:

Classifying gig workers remains one of the most debated issues in labor regulations. Recognizing gig workers as "employees" rather than independent contractors provides them with greater access to benefits, labor rights, and protections. However, many gig platforms resist this classification due to its potential financial and operational implications. Achieving a balance between labor rights and business flexibility requires legal frameworks that promote equitable treatment while accommodating the nature of gig work. One potential solution is hybrid worker status models, which establish a middle ground between independent contracting and traditional employment. These models ensure that gig workers retain their flexibility while benefiting from job security and essential protections.

Regulatory frameworks should also focus on transparency and algorithmic fairness to prevent discrimination and bias in gig platforms. Governments must push for policies requiring platforms to disclose how their algorithms function, particularly regarding task allocation and wage determination. Ensuring algorithmic transparency can help protect underrepresented workers from systemic biases and unfair labor practices. Additionally, because gig platforms operate globally, cross-border collaboration is essential. Coordinating international regulations will help protect gig workers' rights while fostering innovation and digital economy expansion.

Addressing disparities in gig work also requires bridging the digital divide in developing economies, particularly in rural and marginalized regions. Countries such as India face significant challenges in digital access, which limits gig workers' opportunities. Implementing inclusive technologies and providing digital literacy training can expand earning potential and enable greater participation in platform-based employment. By addressing these challenges through targeted policies and global cooperation, the gig economy can evolve into a more equitable and sustainable employment model.

EVALUATING THE ROLE OF TECHNOLOGY IN PROMOTING EQUITY IN THE GIG ECONOMY

Technology has been a key component of the gig economy, allowing platforms to expand their operations internationally, diversify economic participation, and seamlessly connect workers and clients (Brailovskaya, 2023). Artificial intelligence (AI) and sophisticated data analytics are used by digital platforms, such as freelancing job boards and ride-hailing apps, to increase operational efficiency. Although more people can now access flexible employment options thanks to technological breakthroughs, there are serious concerns about how these developments may affect fairness in gig labor (Khang et al., 2024). This chapter examines how technology either helps or hurts inequality around the world and evaluates its effects on the world's largest economies, including India.

Technology as an Equalizer: Bridging Inequities in the Gig Economy

Access to Work Opportunities: People from a wide range of socioeconomic backgrounds and geographic locations can now join the global workforce because to technology, which has democratized access to employment. Platforms like Fiverr, Upwork, and Freelancer have made it possible for independent contractors all over the world to work on global projects without having to move around physically.

Global Examples: Platforms such as Upwork and Toptal have made it possible for skilled professionals, such as software developers and graphic designers, to interact with clients from around the world in developing nations like Bangladesh and the Philippines. Access to the internet and a basic understanding of digital literacy are the sole requirements, narrowing the divide between workers in rural and urban areas (Graham & Ferrari, 2022).

Indian Context: Platforms such as Urban Company and WorkIndia have made it possible for people in India with no formal education to find employment in a variety of fields, including specialized trades and domestic services. Furthermore, platforms like iMerit promote inclusivity by using technology to train and involve underserved communities in data annotation tasks for AI projects (Ghosh et al., 2021).

Algorithmic Efficiency and Transparency: AI-powered matching has simplified the process of connecting employees and customers. In order to provide more equitable access to employment possibilities, algorithms evaluate the abilities, prior performance, and preferences of gig workers.

Enabling Remote Work: Technology has made it possible for workers to overcome the limitations of the local labor market as remote employment becomes more common. For underprivileged populations, who can experience prejudice or lack access to conventional employment opportunities, this is especially advantageous.

Challenges Posed by Technology: Exacerbating Inequities

Technology has a lot of promise to lessen inequality in the gig economy, but it also has drawbacks that could make things worse.

Algorithmic Bias AI: Most gig platforms are built on algorithms and artificial intelligence. But because these systems rely on historical data and opaque processes, they could unintentionally perpetuate societal biases.

Instances of discrimination and inequality within the gig economy have been widely documented across various digital platforms. Ride-sharing services such as Uber and Lyft have faced allegations of racial bias, where drivers have been found more likely to cancel rides for passengers with names perceived as ethnically diverse or belonging to minority groups. Research indicates that such biases create barriers to equal access and service reliability, reinforcing systemic discrimination within gig-based transportation networks (Cobb et al., 2024).

Similarly, skill-based inequality is prevalent in online freelance marketplaces such as Fiverr and Upwork. Workers from developing countries often receive significantly lower compensation for performing the same tasks as their counterparts in wealthier nations. Platform algorithms may contribute to this disparity by prioritizing profiles from high-income regions or favoring freelancers with extensive client reviews. This cycle makes it increasingly difficult for workers from less affluent areas to compete fairly, as they struggle to gain visibility and secure better-paying opportunities (Ravenelle & Kowalski, 2022). These issues highlight the structural challenges within the gig economy that demand regulatory oversight and policy interventions to promote fairness and inclusivity.

Unequal Access to Technology: One of the biggest obstacles to equity in the gig economy is still the digital divide. The exclusion of people without cellphones, high-speed internet, or rudimentary digital literacy from platform-based labor exacerbates already-existing disparities.

The global digital divide presents a significant challenge to inclusivity in the gig economy, particularly in low-income regions. A World Bank report highlights that limited internet connectivity remains a major barrier for gig workers in sub-Saharan Africa, where only 28% of households in low-income areas have internet access, compared to 84% in high-income nations. This stark contrast restricts economic participation and creates structural disadvantages for workers in developing regions, limiting their ability to compete in digital labor markets (Cilliers, 2021).

In India, digital accessibility is similarly uneven, with urban areas benefiting from strong infrastructure while rural populations face significant barriers to gig work participation. Many rural residents struggle to access digital platforms due to limited broadband penetration, high data costs, and lower levels of digital literacy. Rural women remain particularly underrepresented in the gig economy due to sociocultural constraints, gender norms, and lack of technological access. These disparities emphasize the need for targeted policies and investments to improve digital infrastructure and promote inclusive economic opportunities in underprivileged regions.

Algorithm-Driven Gig Economy Challenges: The efficiency brought by technology in the gig economy is often accompanied by challenges where platform profitability is prioritized over worker well-being. AI-driven systems, designed to enhance customer satisfaction, can sometimes lead to the exploitation of gig workers by imposing unfair working conditions. One prominent issue is the misuse of AI in dynamic pricing mechanisms, particularly in food delivery services such as Deliveroo in the UK and Swiggy in India. These platforms utilize algorithmic pricing models that fluctuate based on demand and competition, often leading to reduced earnings for workers during periods of intense competition. Additionally, gig workers face the risk of being deactivated from platforms due to algorithmically managed rating systems. These systems, which assess worker performance based on customer feedback and other automated metrics, may lead to unjust penalties due to factors beyond workers' control, such as biased customer reviews or technical glitches in the platform.

Regulatory Gaps in Tackling Technological Inequities

Lack of Worker Representation in Platform Design: Worker representation is not involved in the design of many gig platforms' technological systems, such as algorithmic management tools. This leads to systems like erratic wage payments or exploitative shifts that could make unfair practices worse.

Global Regulatory Responses: To increase the transparency of algorithmic decision-making in the gig economy, the European Union has implemented measures. A directive from the European Commission in 2022 requires platforms to provide an explanation of how algorithmic systems affect employee compensation and job distribution (De Stefano & Taes, 2023).

Inadequate Data Privacy Protections: In order to increase the openness of algorithmic decision-making in the gig economy, the European Union has implemented measures. Platforms must disclose how algorithmic techniques affect workers' compensation and employment distributions in accordance with a 2022 European Commission directive.

In India, Swiggy and Ola have been criticized for their intrusive data collection methods, sparking debates about ethical technology practices.

Technology-Driven Solutions to Promote Equity: Technology, when utilized responsibly, can serve as a powerful tool to address inequities in the gig economy. One significant application is AI-driven skill development, where platforms like Coursera and Khan Academy offer personalized learning opportunities. Indian gig workers, for instance, have enhanced their earning potential on platforms such as Upwork by completing cost-effective certification programs in fields like AI and digital marketing. Another promising solution is the integration of blockchain technology to improve payment transparency. By ensuring immutable and accurate payment tracking, blockchain-based platforms mitigate risks related to wage disputes and delayed compensation. Projects such as Origin Protocol are actively working to enhance trust and accountability in gig transactions (Biegon, 2023).

Governments worldwide have also initiated digital inclusion programs to bridge technological access gaps. In India, the Digital India Mission has introduced schemes like PMGDISHA (Pradhan Mantri Gramin Digital Saksharta Abhiyan), which aims to equip 60 million rural individuals with digital literacy skills, enabling their broader participation in the gig economy (Kumari et al., 2024). Furthermore, ethical

AI design practices play a crucial role in promoting fairness within gig platforms. Technology companies bear the responsibility of developing algorithms that minimize bias and ensure equitable treatment for workers, fostering a more inclusive and sustainable gig economy.

UNDERSTANDING THE SUSTAINABILITY IMPACTS OF GIG WORK

The gig economy has become a paradigm shift in the global economy, offering millions of people flexible work options and changing the way that traditional employment arrangements are structured. However, there are serious concerns regarding the sustainability of gig employment given its explosive growth. This goal examines how the gig economy's social and environmental aspects relate to international sustainability objectives. Using examples, real-world cases, and secondary sources, this analysis aims to present a fair assessment of gig work's effects on sustainability in major economies, including India.

Environmental Sustainability of Gig Economy Models

Gig platforms, particularly those in the logistics and transportation sectors, have environmental footprints that demand scrutiny.

Carbon Emissions from Gig-Based Transport

The environmental impact of gig platforms, particularly in the transportation and logistics sectors, remains a pressing concern. One of the most significant issues is the carbon footprint resulting from increased vehicle usage. Companies such as DoorDash, Ola in India, and Uber contribute to rising emissions, primarily due to "dead miles," which refer to distances traveled by drivers without passengers or deliveries (Krechetova, 2021). Research conducted by the International Council on Clean Transportation (ICCT) indicates that ride-hailing trips generate approximately 69% more carbon dioxide emissions than the transportation methods they replace, largely due to additional miles driven between passenger pick-ups (Blanco et al., 2022). Although companies like Uber and Lyft have committed to transitioning to electric vehicle (EV) fleets to mitigate this problem, the implementation of such initiatives remains inconsistent. In India, platforms such as Zomato and Swiggy are also facing scrutiny for emissions linked to their delivery operations. While the adoption of EVs in the country is increasing, several barriers, including inadequate charging infrastructure and high initial investment costs, hinder widespread implementation.

In addition to transportation-related emissions, waste management presents another environmental challenge in the gig economy, particularly in food delivery services. Packaging waste is a major concern, with companies such as Deliveroo in Europe and Meituan in China generating significant amounts of disposable materials. In India, Swiggy has taken steps to promote sustainable packaging by collaborating with local organizations and non-governmental entities, yet adoption remains limited due to logistical and cost-related challenges (Zhuo et al., 2023). Furthermore, gig platforms contribute to resource consumption and electronic waste through their reliance on large-scale server infrastructures. A Greenpeace study highlights that data centers supporting gig platforms account for a notable share of global energy consumption, estimated at around 2% of total electricity usage worldwide. Addressing these environmental issues requires a multifaceted approach, including regulatory measures,

Waste Management Concerns

Indirect waste management problems are exacerbated by the gig economy, especially when it comes to food delivery services' packing materials.

Case: Businesses like Deliveroo in Europe and Meituan in China generate a lot of packaging waste. Swiggy has collaborated with regional and non-governmental organizations in India to support eco-friendly packaging options, but uptake is still slow (Zhuo et al., 2023).

Technology and Resource Consumption

Digital gig platforms contribute to energy consumption and e-waste because they rely on large server infrastructures. According to a Greenpeace analysis, gig platforms contribute significantly to the 2% global electricity consumption of data centers.

Despite the environmental challenges associated with the gig economy, there are significant opportunities for progress and innovation that contribute to sustainability. One such initiative is the integration of e-bikes into delivery services, as seen with Gojek in Southeast Asia. By promoting the use of electric bicycles, these platforms actively work toward reducing carbon emissions and fostering carbon-neutral deliveries (ESCAP, 2021). Similarly, in India, companies like EVage are developing affordable electric vehicles designed to meet the specific needs of gig workers. These innovations align with the country's broader sustainability objectives outlined in the Paris Agreement, helping to transition the gig economy toward a more environmentally responsible model. As technological advancements and policy support continue to grow, the gig economy has the potential to evolve into a more sustainable sector while maintaining efficiency and economic viability.

Socioeconomic Sustainability of Gig Economy Models

Beyond its effects on the environment, the gig economy's socioeconomic viability merits careful consideration, especially in relation to social protection, employment quality, and income security.

Income Volatility and Job Insecurity

While gig employment offers flexibility, its unpredictable income and lack of essential benefits raise serious concerns about its long-term socioeconomic viability. Studies indicate that income instability and job insecurity are persistent issues for gig workers across different regions. Pew Research surveys highlight that a significant number of gig workers in the United States struggle with inconsistent earnings, often relying on borrowing or seeking supplementary employment to afford their basic necessities. To address these financial uncertainties, several European nations, including France, have taken legislative measures to introduce minimum wage guarantees for gig workers, ensuring a more stable income structure (Syrovatka, 2021).

In India, gig workers associated with platforms such as Amazon Flex and Urban Company encounter similar financial challenges (Kshatriya & Kurien, 2022). A study conducted by the Observer Research Foundation reveals that income inconsistency forces many Indian gig workers to juggle multiple platforms to sustain their livelihoods. This financial instability is further worsened by the lack of retirement benefits, leaving workers vulnerable to long-term economic insecurity. Without adequate policy interventions, the gig economy's promise of flexible work risks being overshadowed by the persistent struggle for financial stability and job security.

Social Protection and Worker Rights

Gig workers often face heightened vulnerability due to inadequate social safety nets, leaving them exposed to risks such as illness, workplace accidents, and economic downturns. Several international efforts have been made to address these concerns. The European Union's "Platform Work Directive" seeks to extend social security benefits to gig workers while also granting them the right to unionize, aiming to provide greater labor protections. In the United States, California introduced Assembly Bill 5 (AB5) with the objective of reclassifying gig workers as employees rather than independent contractors, thereby granting them employment benefits.

However, subsequent legislative amendments have weakened these protections, limiting the bill's intended impact.

In India, a significant policy advancement was made with the introduction of the Social Security Code (2020), which officially recognized gig workers and mandated that platforms contribute to a social security fund. This framework includes provisions for health insurance and accident protection, marking an important step toward securing gig workers' welfare. However, the effectiveness of this initiative has been hindered by challenges in implementation, particularly due to limited awareness among workers regarding their entitlements and the operational complexities of enforcing these provisions. Without stronger enforcement mechanisms and better outreach efforts, the intended benefits of such policies may remain largely inaccessible to the workers they aim to protect.

3. Skill Development and Career Growth

The gig economy offers opportunities for skill development, yet many platforms prioritize low-skill jobs, restricting long-term career growth. Platforms like Upwork and Fiverr enable skilled professionals to access global markets, fostering upward mobility. In contrast, workers in ride-hailing and food delivery sectors face minimal skill enhancement, limiting socioeconomic progress. In India, initiatives such as the Pradhan Mantri Kaushal Vikas Yojana (PMKVY) aim to upskill gig workers and align their careers with market demands. Additionally, collaborations with platforms like Teamlease support micro-certifications, helping workers acquire industry-relevant skills and improve their employment prospects in an evolving digital economy.

Alignment with Global Sustainability Goals

The gig economy aligns with several United Nations Sustainable Development Goals (SDGs), presenting both opportunities and challenges. In terms of positive contributions, it supports SDG 8 (Decent Work and Economic Growth) by generating employment for millions and fostering entrepreneurship (Kreinin & Aigner, 2022). Additionally, it advances SDG 5 (Gender Equality) by promoting female workforce participation through flexible work models. In India, platforms like UrbanClap actively recruit women for homecare and beauty services (Huđek & Širec, 2024). However, challenges remain, such as exacerbating regional and income disparities, impacting SDG 10 (Reduced Inequalities), and contributing to carbon emissions, affecting SDG 13 (Climate Action).

ENVIRONMENTAL INNOVATIONS, SOCIOECONOMIC REFORMS, AND TECHNOLOGICAL LEVERAGE FOR SUSTAINABLE GIG ECONOMIES

The gig economy presents enormous opportunities for employment, flexibility, and creativity. But in order for this paradigm to be sustainable, urgent environmental, social, and technological issues must be resolved. To meet global sustainability goals, the gig economy must change, from utilizing cutting-edge technology to enhancing workers' rights and investing in green logistics. With examples from the actual world and ramifications for significant economies like India, this part offers a thorough examination of workable ways to promote sustainability in gig economy models.

Environmental Innovations

The gig economy's environmental challenges stem primarily from resource consumption, waste generation, and carbon emissions. Addressing these issues requires innovative, technology-driven strategies to minimize ecological impact. One significant approach is investing in EV infrastructure and promoting green logistics. Transitioning to electric vehicles (EVs) can drastically reduce emissions, with global platforms taking proactive steps. Uber, for example, has pledged to achieve a zero-emissions platform by 2040 through extensive EV adoption in collaboration with automakers. Similarly, Deliveroo in Europe encourages delivery partners to utilize electric scooters and bicycles, demonstrating a commitment to sustainable mobility (Roychowdhury et al., 2023). In India, companies like Zomato and Swiggy have initiated EV adoption in their delivery fleets, but growth remains slow due to high costs and inadequate charging infrastructure. To address these barriers, the Indian Government's Faster Adoption and Manufacturing of Hybrid and Electric Vehicles (FAME) program provides subsidies and infrastructure support to accelerate the transition.

Beyond transportation, waste reduction is another pressing concern, particularly regarding single-use plastics and non-biodegradable packaging in food delivery and e-commerce. Collaboration between platforms, suppliers, and regulatory agencies is essential to standardizing sustainable packaging practices. In response to mounting environmental concerns and regulatory pressure, Deliveroo has integrated biodegradable packaging into its food delivery services in Europe. The company partners with suppliers to procure recyclable and compostable materials while offering financial incentives and guidance to restaurants transitioning away from single-use plastics. This initiative aligns with growing consumer expectations for environmentally responsible business practices. Similarly, Swiggy in India has introduced plastic-free delivery services in select cities, promoting sustainable alternatives such as paper containers, cloth bags, and reusable cutlery. Partnering with NGOs and the United Nations Environment Programme (UNEP), Swiggy provides training programs to assist restaurants in adopting eco-friendly packaging. While these efforts demonstrate progress, widespread implementation requires standardized policies. Governments and platforms must collaborate to develop industry-wide packaging standards, encourage cost-effective sustainable materials, and support small-scale suppliers in adopting green production practices.

Socioeconomic Reforms

The gig economy generates employment opportunities but faces criticism for job instability, lack of social security, and limited career growth. Socioeconomic reforms are essential to ensuring fairness and inclusivity. Strengthening social safety nets and formalizing employment status can provide much-needed financial security for gig workers, who often lack access to basic protections such as healthcare, insurance, and retirement benefits. Comprehensive social security measures are crucial for long-term sustainability (Samsudin et al., 2024). Globally, the European Union has introduced the Platform Work Directive, which aims to guarantee equal access to rights such as collective bargaining and employment benefits. In the U.S., California's Assembly Bill 5 (AB5) attempted to reclassify gig workers as employees, mandating platforms to provide paid leave and health insurance. However, subsequent amendments and resistance from corporations have raised concerns about its effectiveness.

India has made strides in this area with the Social Security Code (2020), requiring platforms to contribute to a social security fund for gig workers. However, low awareness among workers and poor compliance by platforms hinder its effectiveness. Expanding enforcement mechanisms and offering financial incentives could enhance participation and implementation.

Another critical aspect is promoting skill development to facilitate career growth. The gig economy remains largely centered on low-skilled jobs like ride-hailing and food delivery, limiting long-term professional advancement. Upskilling is essential to aligning gig work with evolving labor market demands. Successful examples include platforms like Upwork and Freelancer, which enable skilled professionals to access high-value global projects, promoting economic mobility. In India, initiatives such as the Pradhan Mantri Kaushal Vikas Yojana (PMKVY) focus on digital and entrepreneurial skill development to empower gig workers (Patnaik & Baral, 2023). Training programs tailored for gig workers, such as electric vehicle (EV) management and vehicle maintenance for ride-hailing drivers, can enhance their career prospects. Collaboration between gig platforms, governments, and educational institutions can establish certification programs and mentorship opportunities, fostering sustainable career pathways.

Leveraging Technology

Leveraging technology in gig platforms offers significant potential to address socioeconomic and environmental challenges. AI-powered route optimization plays a crucial role in reducing emissions and fuel consumption by ensuring efficient delivery routes. These systems analyze various factors such as traffic patterns, time constraints, and distance to determine the most sustainable paths for gig workers. Globally, companies like Amazon and Instacart have implemented real-time data analytics to enhance last-mile delivery efficiency, minimizing unnecessary travel and reducing operational costs (Pourrahmani & Jaller, 2021). In India, Flipkart has integrated AI-driven logistics management to improve its delivery network. Additionally, as part of the Climate Group's EV100 initiative, the company has committed to transitioning to a fully electric fleet by 2030. However, the expansion of such advancements across gig platforms requires improved accessibility to data analytics and training programs for workers (Sarkar, 2023).

The rating systems within gig platforms significantly influence workers' earnings and job security, yet their lack of transparency often results in biased assessments and unfair treatment. Ensuring fairness in these rating mechanisms is essential to promoting equity. Uber has recognized the disproportionate impact of its rating system on driver income and job stability. To address this, the company has adjusted its algorithm to minimize the effect of occasional low ratings caused by factors beyond drivers' control, such as traffic congestion or technical glitches. Furthermore, Uber has introduced an appeal mechanism, allowing drivers to contest unfair ratings, thereby ensuring a more just evaluation process. Similarly, Urban Company, a prominent Indian service platform, has enhanced its dispute-resolution framework, enabling workers to challenge low ratings through an integrated review mechanism. This system allows service providers to justify poor ratings due to factors such as inadequate tools or unexpected customer demands, fostering a fairer assessment process. To further enhance accountability, some platforms collaborate with independent auditors to assess their rating systems for potential biases or discrepancies. Regulatory bodies in regions like the European Union have also mandated gig platforms to disclose the impact of ratings on compensation and job allocation, reinforcing transparency in algorithm-driven decisions. Such measures establish necessary safeguards to promote fairness and uphold workers' rights within the gig economy.

SURVEY ON GIG WORKERS' EXPERIENCES AND CHALLENGES

To analyze the disparities in the gig economy, a primary survey was conducted among 250 gig workers across different sectors, including ride-hailing, food delivery, freelancing, and domestic services. The survey aimed to assess income stability, access to worker protections, digital inclusion, and overall working conditions. The respondents were selected from urban and semi-urban regions to ensure diverse representation. A structured questionnaire was administered, combining multiple-choice, Likert-scale, and ranking-based questions to capture both qualitative and quantitative insights.

The collected data highlights the financial insecurity, technological challenges, and workplace inequalities that gig workers experience. Below is a detailed analysis of key findings:

Income Stability and Financial Security

Table 1. How consistent is your monthly income from gig work?

Income Consistency Level	Percentage of Respondents
Highly stable (earnings do not fluctuate)	8%
Moderately stable (minor fluctuations)	22%
Unstable (significant variations)	44%
Highly unstable (frequent income gaps)	26%

Source: Author's Survey Results

As per Table 1 statistics, a significant proportion of gig workers (70%) reported unstable or highly unstable incomes. Only 8% experienced consistent earnings, indicating that income volatility remains a major concern. Workers in food delivery and ride-hailing services reported the highest fluctuations due to unpredictable demand and algorithm-driven job allocations.

Access to Worker Benefits and Protections

Table 2. Which of the following benefits do you receive from the gig platform? (Multiple selections allowed)

Worker Benefits	Percentage of Respondents
Health Insurance	15%
Paid Leave	5%
Social Security Contributions	9%
Accident Coverage	12%
None of the above	59%

Source: Author's Survey Results

The data given in Table 2 reveals that nearly 60% of gig workers receive no formal benefits from platforms, reinforcing concerns over lack of social security. Health insurance and accident coverage were available to a small percentage, primarily for workers in ride-hailing services where safety risks are higher. However, paid leave and retirement benefits remain largely absent.

Digital Inclusion and Technological Barriers

Table 3. What are the biggest challenges you face in using digital platforms for gig work? (Ranking-based)

Challenges	Average Rank (1 = Most Difficult, 5 = Least Difficult)
High Data Cost	1.8
Limited Access to Digital Devices	2.2
Lack of Digital Literacy	2.7
Inconsistent Internet Connectivity	1.6
Platform Algorithm Bias	2.4

Source: Author's Survey Results

Table 3 shows Inconsistent internet access (ranked 1.6) and high data costs (ranked 1.8) emerged as the most significant digital challenges for gig workers. These issues disproportionately affect workers from rural and semi-urban areas, restricting their access to online opportunities. Platform algorithm bias (ranked 2.4) was also noted as a concern, particularly in work distribution and job visibility on freelancing platforms.

Gender-Based Disparities in Gig Work

Table 4. Do you feel there is a gender-based earnings gap in gig work?

Response	Percentage of Respondents
Yes, women earn significantly less	47%
Yes, but only in certain sectors	31%
No, pay is equal for all	22%

Source: Author's Survey Results

Table 4 implies a majority of respondents (78%) acknowledged a gender pay gap, with 47% stating that women earn significantly less. The disparity was more pronounced in lower-wage sectors such as domestic services and ride-hailing, where male workers have better access to high-earning tasks.

Algorithmic Transparency and Work Allocation

Table 5. Do you think gig platforms' rating systems and work allocation algorithms are fair?

Response	Percentage of Respondents
Yes, entirely fair	11%
Somewhat fair, but needs improvement	34%
Not fair, often biased	55%

Source: Author's Survey Results

Table 5 shows that more than half of gig workers (55%) expressed concerns over algorithmic biases, indicating that opaque rating and job allocation systems may reinforce inequities. Workers in food delivery and freelancing services reported frequent instances of job denials due to automated ratings, often without clear justification.

FINDINGS AND IMPLICATIONS

The gig economy has reshaped labor markets worldwide, creating new employment opportunities and flexibility. However, findings from the survey indicate persistent inequalities in income stability, worker protections, digital access, gender-based disparities, and algorithmic fairness. Addressing these challenges is essential to ensuring that the benefits of gig work contribute to inclusive and sustainable growth. Businesses operating within this framework must adopt managerial strategies that enhance efficiency while prioritizing fairness, transparency, and long-term sustainability. Likewise, policy frameworks must align with broader global objectives, such as reducing income disparities, promoting decent work conditions, and ensuring economic and environmental stability.

From a managerial standpoint, companies must address the disparities affecting marginalized communities, including women, rural workers, and individuals from low-income backgrounds. Survey findings revealed that 70% of gig workers experience income instability, with significant fluctuations in earnings, particularly in food delivery and ride-hailing sectors. To mitigate this, businesses should invest in financial security measures such as fair payment structures and minimum earnings guarantees. Additionally, given that nearly 60% of workers lack health insurance or social protections, platforms must extend benefits like accident coverage, social security contributions, and paid leave to improve worker well-being and align business models with equity and inclusivity.

Technology plays a critical role in shaping gig work experiences, yet 55% of respondents perceive platform rating systems and job allocation algorithms as unfair. To counteract this, businesses must implement transparent algorithmic systems that minimize biases in work distribution, wage determination, and performance evaluations. Regular audits and independent oversight can ensure that employment opportunities, ratings, and remuneration remain equitable. Furthermore, digital access remains a significant barrier, with high data costs and inconsistent internet connectivity ranking as the most pressing issues for gig workers, particularly in rural and semi-urban areas. Addressing these challenges requires targeted investments in digital literacy and infrastructure, enabling broader participation in the gig economy.

Environmental responsibility should also be a key focus. While some platforms, such as Flipkart, have committed to electric vehicle integration, broader adoption remains slow due to cost barriers and infrastructure limitations. To reduce the gig economy's carbon footprint, companies must accelerate sustainable initiatives, including adopting electric fleets, offering subsidies for vehicle upgrades, and implementing eco-friendly packaging solutions. Such measures can enhance corporate reputations while contributing to long-term sustainability goals.

From a policy perspective, governments must establish robust regulations that protect gig workers' rights while maintaining job flexibility. Findings show that gig workers often lack employment security, requiring policymakers to develop hybrid employment models that provide stability while preserving flexibility. Strengthening social safety nets is crucial, with financial incentives needed to encourage platform compliance in offering social security, health benefits, and unemployment insurance. Addressing gender-based disparities is equally important, as 78% of respondents acknowledged pay gaps, particularly in lower-wage sectors. Governments and industry regulators must enforce fair pay structures, ensuring equitable compensation across gig work platforms.

Global wage disparities must also be tackled through international collaboration to create standardized compensation mechanisms. Additionally, sustainability initiatives should be incentivized through policies such as tax benefits for platforms adopting electric vehicles and eco-friendly waste management practices. To improve digital access, targeted investments in internet infrastructure and digital literacy programs, particularly in underserved communities, will enable broader participation in the gig economy.

The sustainable and equitable growth of the gig economy requires a coordinated effort from businesses, policymakers, and civil society. By integrating inclusive policies with responsible management strategies, the gig economy can become a powerful force for economic resilience and global sustainability. Addressing systemic inequalities, enhancing financial security, improving digital access, and promoting sustainability will ensure that gig workers receive fair opportunities while aligning the sector with broader developmental goals.

CONCLUSION

The gig economy holds immense potential for global economic growth, yet it remains fraught with disparities in income stability, worker protections, and access to opportunities. These inequities, particularly affecting marginalized communities and lower-income regions, highlight the urgency of adopting an inclusive and sustainable approach. Findings from this study confirm that 70% of gig workers experience income instability, with ride-hailing and food delivery workers facing the highest fluctuations. Additionally, 60% of respondents lack essential social protections such as health insurance and paid leave, reinforcing the need for regulatory frameworks that balance job flexibility with economic security. Establishing fair wage structures, ensuring minimum earnings, and strengthening social safety nets are crucial for addressing these gaps.

Technology, while a critical driver of efficiency, must be governed responsibly to prevent the reinforcement of systemic inequalities. The survey revealed that 55% of gig workers perceive job allocation and rating systems as biased, demonstrating the need for greater transparency and oversight in algorithmic decision-making. Platforms must implement fair AI-driven mechanisms, conduct regular audits, and establish worker appeal processes to ensure equitable treatment. Digital inclusion remains another pressing concern, as high data costs and poor connectivity limit access to gig work, particularly in rural areas. Expanding internet infrastructure and launching targeted digital literacy programs will be essential to bridging this gap and fostering equitable participation.

Sustainability must be integrated into the gig economy's evolution, both in social and environmental dimensions. While some platforms have initiated eco-friendly measures such as electric vehicle adoption and sustainable packaging, broader implementation is hindered by cost barriers and infrastructure limitations. Policy incentives, such as subsidies for electric fleets and mandatory sustainability reporting, can accelerate the transition to environmentally responsible gig work. Collaborative efforts between governments, platforms, and industry stakeholders will be essential in ensuring that economic growth does not come at the cost of environmental degradation.

The future of the gig economy depends on a coordinated effort among policymakers, businesses, and civil society to create a fair and resilient labor system. Strengthening labor rights, implementing transparent and ethical technological solutions, promoting digital accessibility, and advancing sustainability initiatives are key steps in addressing systemic inequities. By prioritizing inclusivity and long-term worker welfare, the gig economy can transform into a model that benefits workers, businesses, and economies alike. A commitment to fair practices, regulatory innovation, and international cooperation will ensure its viability as a sustainable and equitable force in the global labor market.

COMPETING INTERESTS AND FUNDING STATEMENTS

The author declares no competing interests related to this chapter. This research received no specific grant from any funding agency in the public, commercial, or not-for-profit sectors.

REFERENCES

Behl, A., Rajagopal, K., Sheorey, P., & Mahendra, A. (2022). Barriers to entry of gig workers in the gig platforms: Exploring the dark side of the gig economy. *Aslib Journal of Information Management*, *74*(5), 818–839. DOI: 10.1108/AJIM-08-2021-0235

Bérastégui, P. (2021). Exposure to psychosocial risk factors in the gig economy: a systematic review. *ETUI Research Paper-Report*.

Biegon, C. K. (2023). *Blockchain-based Ride-sharing Model With Decentralized Governance* (Doctoral dissertation, University of Nairobi).

Blanco, J. P., Windisch, E., Perkins, S., Ito, A., & Leape, J. (2022). Decarbonising Transport in Latin American Cities: A Review of Policies and Key Challenges. DOI: 10.18235/0003987

Brailovskaya, V. (2023). Digital Labor Gig Economy from the Worker's Perspective: A Literature.

Bruckner, C. L., & Forman, J. B. (2021). Women, Retirement, and the Growing Gig Economy Workforce. *Ga. St. UL Rev.*, *38*, 259.

Carter, B. (2021). Impact of social inequalities and discrimination on vulnerability to crises. DOI: 10.19088/K4D.2021.049

Celestin, M., & Vanitha, N. (2021). The gig economy and its effects on personal finance. *Indo American Journal of Multidisciplinary Research and Review*, *5*(2), 39–46.

Cherry, M. A. (2022). Employee Status for" Essential Workers": The Case for Gig Worker Parity. *Loy. LAL Rev.*, *55*, 683.

Cilliers, J. (2021). The future of work in Africa. *The Future of Africa: Challenges and Opportunities*, 195-219. DOI: 10.1007/978-3-030-46590-2_9

Cini, L., Maccarrone, V., & Tassinari, A. (2022). With or without U(nions)? Understanding the diversity of gig workers' organizing practices in Italy and the UK. *European Journal of Industrial Relations*, *28*(3), 341–362. DOI: 10.1177/09596801211052531

Cobb, A., Mohan, A., Harper, C. D., Nock, D., & Michalek, J. (2024). Ride-hailing technology mitigates effects of driver racial discrimination, but effects of residential segregation persist. *Proceedings of the National Academy of Sciences of the United States of America*, *121*(41), e2408936121. DOI: 10.1073/pnas.2408936121 PMID: 39348538

Cook, C., Diamond, R., Hall, J. V., List, J. A., & Oyer, P. (2021). The gender earnings gap in the gig economy: Evidence from over a million rideshare drivers. *The Review of Economic Studies*, *88*(5), 2210–2238. DOI: 10.1093/restud/rdaa081

Cropanzano, R., Keplinger, K., Lambert, B. K., Caza, B., & Ashford, S. J. (2023). The organizational psychology of gig work: An integrative conceptual review. *The Journal of Applied Psychology*, *108*(3), 492–519. DOI: 10.1037/apl0001029 PMID: 36222635

De Angelis, M., Donà, S., & Bergamante, F. (2023). Algorithmic Discriminations and New Forms of Protections: An Analysis of the Italian Case. *Social Sciences (Basel, Switzerland)*, *12*(9), 503. DOI: 10.3390/socsci12090503

De Stefano, V., & Taes, S. (2023). Algorithmic management and collective bargaining. *Transfer: European Review of Labour and Research*, *29*(1), 21–36. DOI: 10.1177/10242589221141055

ESCAP, U. (2021). Review of developments in transport in Asia and the Pacific 2021: towards sustainable, inclusive and resilient urban passenger transport in Asian cities.

European Commission. (2021, December 9). *Commission proposes measures to improve working conditions of people working through digital labour platforms*. https://ec.europa.eu/commission/presscorner/detail/en/ip_21_6605

Ghosh, A., Ramachandran, R., & Zaidi, M. (2021). Women workers in the gig economy in India: An exploratory study. *Available atSSRN* 3944205. DOI: 10.2139/ssrn.3944205

Gonzalez, B. N. (2021). Employment Classification and Human Dignity in the Gig Economy. *Thomas L. Rev.*, *34*, 52.

Graham, M., & Ferrari, F. (Eds.). (2022). *Digital work in the planetary market*. Mit Press. DOI: 10.7551/mitpress/13835.001.0001

Heeks, R., Graham, M., Mungai, P., Van Belle, J. P., & Woodcock, J. (2021). Systematic evaluation of gig work against decent work standards: The development and application of the Fairwork framework. *The Information Society*, *37*(5), 267–286. DOI: 10.1080/01972243.2021.1942356

Huđek, I., & Širec, K. (2024). Unveiling the Impact of the Gig Economy on Sustainable Development. In *International Scientific Conference ERAZ–Knowledge Based Sustainable Development* (pp. 125-133).

International Labour Organization. (2021). *World employment and social outlook: The role of digital labor platforms in transforming the world of work*.https://www.ilo.org/wcmsp5/groups/public/---dgreports/ dcomm/ publ/documents/publication/ wcms_771749.pdf

Irwin, J. L. (2022). *Leveraging Local Workforce Systems to Better Serve Workers and Improve Job Quality A Case Study and Complex Systems Analysis* (Doctoral dissertation, The Pardee RAND Graduate School).

Jain, A. (2024). The Gig Economy: Disruption, Innovation, and Economic Evolution. *Educational Administration: Theory and Practice*, *30*(5), 5133–5140.

Jain, M. (2024). In Context of Uber BV v. Aslam in London ([2021] WLR (D) 108): Do Uber Drivers Work for Uber as Employees or as Independent Contractors? *Justice and Law Bulletin, 3*(1), 7-19.

Khang, A., Dave, T., Jadhav, B., Katore, D., & Dave, D. (2024). Gig Financial Economy: Big Data and Analytics. In *Synergy of AI and Fintech in the Digital Gig Economy* (pp. 244-267). CRC Press.

Kispert, M. (2021). *Clouds of discontent: art, work, solidarity and digital platform labour* (Doctoral dissertation, University of Westminster). DOI: 10.34737/vqx44

Koh, J. M. (2023). *Cooperative Firms and the Sustainable Development Goals: Pursuing Decent Work and Reducing Inequality*. Taylor & Francis. DOI: 10.4324/9781003457596

Krechetova, V. (2021). Green and sustainable logistics network: micro mobility in the first-last mile.

Kreinin, H., & Aigner, E. (2022). From "Decent work and economic growth" to "Sustainable work and economic degrowth": A new framework for SDG 8. *Empirica*, *49*(2), 281–311. DOI: 10.1007/s10663-021-09526-5

Kshatriya, N., & Kurien, D. (2022). Gig Workers in India: Emerging Opportunities in the New Economy. *Liberal Stud.*, *7*, 78.

Kumari, B. S. S., Lavanya, P., & Padmambika, P. (2024). Bridging The Digital Divide: Addressing Inequality and Access Disparities. *International Journal of Indian Psychology, 12*(3). Advance online publication. DOI: 10.25215/1203.111

Liang, C., Peng, J., Hong, Y., & Gu, B. (2023). The hidden costs and benefits of monitoring in the gig economy. *Information Systems Research, 34*(1), 297–318. DOI: 10.1287/isre.2022.1130

Litman, L., Robinson, J., & Abberbock, T. (2020). *Gender-based pay gaps in the gig economy*. Harvard Journal of Law & Gender. https://journals.law.harvard.edu/jlg/2020/02/gender-based-pay-gaps-in-the-gig-economy/

Liu, H., Fernandez, F., & Dutz, G. (2022). Educational attainment, use of numeracy at work, and gender wage gaps: Evidence from 12 middle-income countries. *International Journal of Educational Development, 92*, 102625. DOI: 10.1016/j.ijedudev.2022.102625

Masekesa, T. (2021). *The gig economy, the digital divide, and developing countries*. Maseconomics. https://maseconomics.com/the-gig-economy-the-digital-divide-and-developing-countries/

Mehta, B. S., Awasthi, I., & Mehta, N. (2021). Women's employment and digital technology: A regional analysis in India. *Indian Journal of Human Development, 15*(3), 427–442. DOI: 10.1177/09737030211064138

Moghavvemi, S., Teng, L. S., & Mahmoud, H. (2023). The Future of Work, A Knowledge-based Gig Economy. In *Reshaping the Future: The Phenomenon of Gig Workers and Knowledge-Economy* (pp. 61–71). Emerald Publishing Limited., DOI: 10.1108/978-1-83753-350-320231005

Moniz, A. B., Boavida, N., Makó, C., Krings, B. J., & de Miguel, P. S. (Eds.). (2021). *Digital Labour Platforms: Representing Workers in Europe*. Húmus.

National Bureau of Economic Research (NBER). (2023). *The evolving role of gig work during the COVID-19 pandemic.*https://www.nber.org/digest/20238/evolving-role-gig-work-during-covid-19-pandemic

Niebler, V. (2023). *Coalitional Power in the Digital Economy: Alliances of Gig and Tech Workers*. Humboldt-Universität zu Berlin.

Novitz, T. (2021). Gig work as a manifestation of short-termism: Crafting a sustainable regulatory agenda. *Industrial Law Journal, 50*(4), 636–661. DOI: 10.1093/indlaw/dwab027

Patnaik, R., & Baral, S. K. (2023). The Post-pandemic Perspective of Rejigging the Gig Economy in India and the Issues of Returnees to Homeland. In *Industry 4.0 and the Digital Transformation of International Business* (pp. 273–285). Springer Nature Singapore. DOI: 10.1007/978-981-19-7880-7_16

Pourrahmani, E., & Jaller, M. (2021). Crowdshipping in last mile deliveries: Operational challenges and research opportunities. *Socio-Economic Planning Sciences, 78*, 101063. DOI: 10.1016/j.seps.2021.101063

Prassl, J. (2018). *Humans as a service: The promise and perils of work in the gig economy*. Oxford University Press. DOI: 10.1093/oso/9780198797012.001.0001

Rahman, A., & Pingali, P. (2024). Social Welfare 'Schemes' to an Economic Security 'System. In *The Future of India's Social Safety Nets: Focus, Form, and Scope* (pp. 357–425). Springer International Publishing. DOI: 10.1007/978-3-031-50747-2_10

Ravenelle, A. J., & Kowalski, K. C. (2022). Working at the Nexus of Global Markets and Gig Work: US Gig Workers, Credential Capitalization, and Wealthy International Clientele. In *Economies, Institutions and Territories* (pp. 199-214). Routledge.

Roychowdhury, A., Chattopadhyaya, V., & Tripathi, M. (2023). *Policy brief on Zero emission vehicle (ZEV) mandate policy: Scaling up electric vehicle markets*. Centre for Science.

Sachan, B. (2024). A Sociological Investigation of the Theoretical Underpinnings and Applied Consequences of Social Stratification. *International Journal of Multidisciplinary Research in Arts. Science and Technology, 2*(8), 51–61. DOI: 10.61778/ijmrast.v2i8.61

Salleh, N. M., Shukry, S. N. M., Maylyn, V., & Jokinol, C. (2023). Analyzing the Challenges, Effects, and Motivations of Gig Economy Workers. *International Journal of Academic Research in Business & Social Sciences, 13*(6), 2125–2142. DOI: 10.6007/IJARBSS/v13-i6/17514

Samsudin, S., Khan, S. J. M., Hasan, J., Daud, S. N. M., & Jia, N. J. (2024). Financial Vulnerability of Gig Workers: Insights and Implications for Social Protection Schemes. [IJSPS]. *International Journal of Social Policy and Society, 20*, 27–44.

Sannon, S., & Cosley, D. (2022). Toward a more inclusive gig economy: Risks and opportunities for workers with disabilities. *Proceedings of the ACM on Human-Computer Interaction, 6*(CSCW2), 1-31. DOI: 10.1145/3555755

Sarkar, M. (2023). Last-Mile Carbon Emission under E-Commerce: Environmental Perspective. *Open Journal of Social Sciences, 11*(12), 277–292. DOI: 10.4236/jss.2023.1112020

Statista. (2020). *Percentage of gig workers worldwide affected by the COVID-19 pandemic.*https://www.statista.com/statistics/1128298/gig-workers-worldwide-effect-covid-19

Syrovatka, F. (2021). Labour market policy under the new European economic governance: France in the focus of the new European labour market policy. *Capital and Class*, *45*(2), 283–309. DOI: 10.1177/0309816820943177

Tan, Z. M., Aggarwal, N., Cowls, J., Morley, J., Taddeo, M., & Floridi, L. (2021). The ethical debate about the gig economy: A review and critical analysis. *Technology in Society*, *65*, 101594. DOI: 10.1016/j.techsoc.2021.101594

Teja, U. S. K. (2023). *Policy*. Regulation, Community Wireless Networks.

Thomas, P. N. (2024). *The Gig Economy in India: Start-Ups, Infrastructure and Resistance*. Taylor & Francis. DOI: 10.4324/9781003491705

Thordarson, K. (2021). AB-5 and drive: Worker classification in the gig economy. *Hastings Bus. LJ*, *17*, 137.

Vyas, N. (2021). 'Gender inequality-now available on digital platform': An interplay between gender equality and the gig economy in the European Union. *European Labour Law Journal*, *12*(1), 37–51. DOI: 10.1177/2031952520953856

Woodcock, J. (2021). *The fight against platform capitalism: an inquiry into the global struggles of the gig economy*. University of Westminster Press. DOI: 10.2307/j.ctv1ktbdrm

World Bank. (2022). *Spotlight on gender gaps in online hourly rates*. https://documents1.worldbank.org/curated/en/099022224194519519/pdf/P1773021be8b0701d1a8e7167a651768f63.pdf

Yasih, D. W. P. (2024). Precarious Workers in the Gig Economy.

Zhuo, Y., He, J., Li, W., Deng, J., & Lin, Q. (2023). A review on takeaway packaging waste: Types, ecological impact, and disposal route. *Environmental Pollution*, *122518*, 122518. Advance online publication. DOI: 10.1016/j.envpol.2023.122518 PMID: 37678737

Chapter 11
Social Sustainability in the Gig Economy: Rethinking Social Protection Systems for Platform Workers

Zyed Achour
https://orcid.org/0000-0002-1578-9062
National Institute of Labor and Social Studies, University of Carthage, Tunisia

ABSTRACT

The platform economy is reshaping labor markets, offering flexibility but increasing worker precarity through income instability, algorithmic management, and limited social protections. This chapter examines social sustainability in platform work, focusing on social capital, digital solidarity networks, and social innovation as resilience mechanisms. It explores regulatory gaps and the role of platform cooperativism and hybrid support systems in addressing labor vulnerabilities. By proposing an integrated framework that balances economic flexibility with institutional protections, the chapter advocates for sustainable policies ensuring fair conditions, worker empowerment, and inclusive social security in the gig economy.

INTRODUCTION

In a context of accelerated digital transformation, the platform economy is emerging as a major economic model, profoundly redefining employment relations and modes of social protection. While this model offers unprecedented flexibility and economic opportunities, it also raises crucial questions about its social sustainability. Indeed, the growing precariousness of platform workers, characterized by income instability, limited social protection, and professional isolation, highlights

DOI: 10.4018/979-8-3693-9385-7.ch011

the adaptation challenges faced by traditional social protection systems. While the existing literature has largely focused on the economic and regulatory aspects of the platform economy (Belleflamme & Peitz, 2021; Graham et al. 2017; De Stefano, 2016), the question of how to adapt social protection systems to these new realities remains insufficiently explored. This gap is particularly problematic in a context where the sustainability and adaptability of the platform economy closely depend on its ability to reconcile economic flexibility and social security. Social sustainability in the context of platform workers refers to the necessity of ensuring equitable working conditions and protections for individuals engaged in gig economy activities. This concept emphasizes the importance of creating a framework that addresses the precarious nature of platform work, where many individuals operate without the benefits associated with traditional employment contracts. Jean-Michel Servais (2018) highlights that these workers often lack clear legal protections, leading to instability in their social relations and economic security. Furthermore, the challenges posed by algorithmic management and the ambiguous status of these workers necessitate a nuanced regulatory approach that balances economic opportunities with adequate social safeguards. The International Labour Organization (ILO, 2021) underscores the need for extending social protections to platform workers, advocating for frameworks that recognize their unique circumstances and promote decent work standards. Thus, social sustainability in this context is fundamentally about fostering an inclusive labor market that protects the rights and welfare of all workers, particularly those who are most vulnerable in the gig economy. This chapter aims to answer the following question: How can we design and implement sustainable social protection systems to ensure the sustainability of the platform economy while effectively protecting its workers? To answer this question, we develop an innovative conceptual framework that integrates three key dimensions: social sustainability as a central objective, social networks as vectors of solidarity, and social innovation as a driver of systemic transformation. Our analysis is structured in four parts. First, we explore the theoretical foundations necessary for understanding social dynamics in the platform economy. Second, we analyze the new forms of precarity specific to this economic model. Third, we examine the limits of current approaches to social protection. Finally, we propose an innovative conceptual framework for developing sustainable and adaptable support systems in the platform economy. This research contributes to the debate on the sustainability and adaptability of the platform economy by proposing concrete avenues to strengthen its social dimension. It is part of a social innovation perspective, aiming to reconcile economic performance and worker protection in the digital economy of the 21st century.

THEORETICAL FRAMEWORK

In a context of accelerated digital transformation, the platform economy – also called the "gig economy" – is emerging as a major economic model, profoundly redefining employment relations and modes of social protection. This model is characterized by temporary or short-term employment, where independent workers or freelancers carry out specific missions via digital platforms, rather than occupying permanent positions (Woodcock & Graham, 2020). While this system offers increased flexibility and unprecedented economic opportunities, it also raises crucial questions about its social sustainability, particularly in terms of job security and social protection (De Stefano, 2016). The increasing precariousness of platform workers, marked by income instability, limited access to traditional social protections, and professional isolation, highlights the adaptation challenges faced by traditional social intervention systems (Ravenelle, 2019). For example, drivers and delivery workers working through platforms such as Uber or Deliveroo often report work experiences marked by economic insecurity and a reliance on algorithms to manage their income (Schor et al. 2020). These challenges are exacerbated by a lack of clear regulation, making it difficult to protect these workers in increasingly competitive environments (Johnston & Land-Kazlauskas, 2018). While the existing literature has largely focused on the economic and regulatory aspects of the platform economy (Graham et al. 2017), the question of how social protection systems can adapt to these new realities remains underexplored (Spasova et al. 2017). This gap is particularly worrying, as the sustainability and adaptability of the platform economy closely depend on its ability to reconcile economic flexibility and social security for its workers. This section aims to establish a theoretical framework that analyzes these transformations and proposes ways to rethink social protection in this evolving economic model. By mobilizing three key concepts – social capital, social networks, and social innovation – we seek to shed light on how these levers can contribute to the social sustainability of the platform economy and strengthen the resilience of its workers (figure 1).

Figure 1. Rethinking social protection in the platform economy

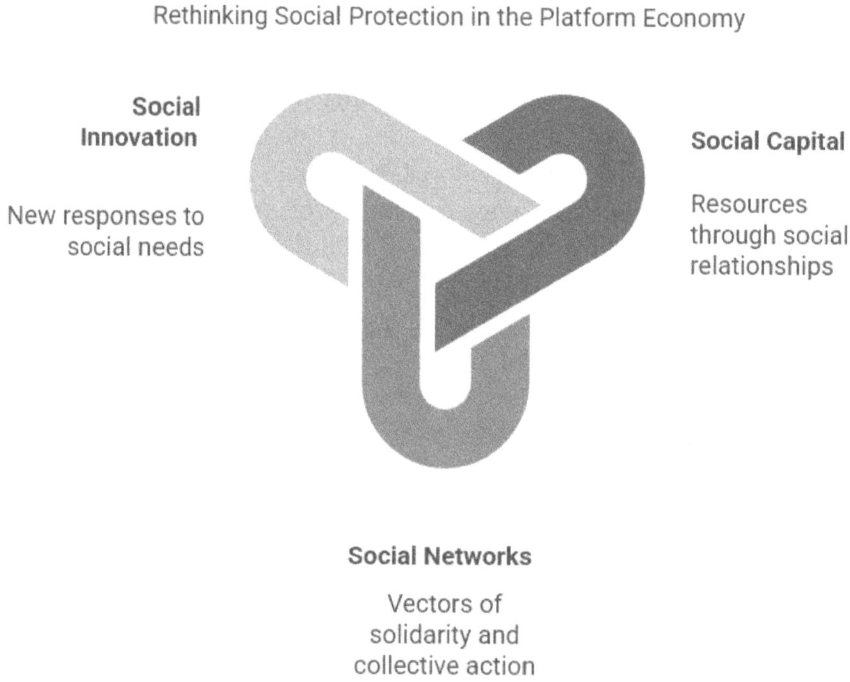

Social Capital: A Strategic Resource for Platform Worker Resilience

Social capital, defined as the resources accessible through social relationships (Bourdieu, 2018), represents a crucial intangible asset in the contemporary digital economy. In the specific context of the platform economy, this concept takes on a particularly strategic dimension, acting as an informal safety net in the face of the uncertainties of digital work. Recent research demonstrates that workers' ability to mobilize and maintain this social capital becomes a determining factor in their professional resilience (Di Gangi et al. 2024; Pilatti et al. 2024). Social capital contributes to occupational risk mitigation, professional development, and emotional support before examining how social networks enable solidarity and collective action.

Mitigation of Occupational Risks

Platform workers actively mobilize their social capital as a protection mechanism against the vagaries of their activity. Empirical research by Schor et al. (2020) demonstrates that these workers develop sophisticated networking strategies, notably via WhatsApp and Facebook groups, to share critical information in real time on working conditions, algorithmic changes, and emerging opportunities. As documented by Lehdonvirta (2016) and Chen (2018), these digital communities have become crucial spaces where workers exchange tactical knowledge about platform dynamics and develop collective responses to managerial control. Studies by Tassinari & Maccarrone (2020) specifically highlight how food delivery workers in European cities use these networks to coordinate spontaneous work stoppages and build solidarity. This collective mobilization not only helps to reduce information asymmetry with platforms but also to create mutual aid mechanisms in the face of down periods or unilateral changes in working conditions. These informal networks often serve as incubators for more structured forms of worker organization, including unions and cooperatives (Cant, 2019; Woodcock, 2021).

Professional Development

Social capital plays a crucial role in acquiring skills and accessing better opportunities within the platform economy, as strong networks and community engagement can significantly enhance workers' earnings and career prospects (Graham & Woodcock, 2018). In this context, initiatives like Fairwork Foundation, based at the University of Oxford, play a pivotal role by assessing labor conditions on digital platforms and advocating for fairer work standards, thus helping to mitigate the precariousness inherent to gig work (Katta et al., 2020). Developing connections between workers and fostering collective initiatives not only strengthens their bargaining power but also creates an environment where social skills and mutual support become essential levers for professional growth and resilience in the online labor market.

Emotional and Practical Support

Support networks among workers are a fundamental pillar of psychosocial resilience in the platform economy. As demonstrated by Ray & Sam (2023) in their longitudinal study of food delivery workers during the COVID-19 pandemic, these informal networks have played a crucial role in transmitting good health practices and managing work-related stress. Beyond simply sharing information, these support communities develop sophisticated mutual aid mechanisms, ranging from informal mentoring to pooling resources, thus creating a real "social safety net" in a professional environment often characterized by its individualism (Rosenblat, 2018).

Social Networks: Vectors of Solidarity and Collective Action

Social network theory (Granovetter, 1973) provides a relevant framework for analyzing how platform workers organize themselves and develop collective protection mechanisms. This theoretical approach highlights the importance of weak ties and relational structures in social mobilization. In this context, social networks play a crucial role in three key areas: facilitating collective organization, enabling the exchange of strategic information, and fostering grassroots social innovation. First, they allow platform workers to build collective organizations that counteract power imbalances in the gig economy. Second, they serve as a space for sharing information on working conditions, negotiation strategies, and best practices. Finally, they act as catalysts for worker-led social innovations, such as platform cooperatives and mutual aid systems, which offer alternative models of economic organization.

Collective Organization

Social media facilitates the emergence of forms of collective organization adapted to the platform economy. For example, recent studies explore how gig economy workers use social media to mitigate power imbalances and strengthen their autonomy (Graham et al. 2017). These networks notably allow the creation of instant discussion groups and dedicated forums where workers can coordinate their actions and share their experiences. Lehdonvirta et al. (2019) demonstrate how these virtual spaces become privileged places for professional identity construction and collective mobilization.

Sharing Information

Digital networks allow workers to share crucial information about working conditions and negotiation strategies with platforms. Research shows that workers can increase their income by developing social skills and participating in online communities (Ravenelle, 2019). These information exchanges include tips on time management, optimizing income, and navigating platform algorithms. Wood et al. (2019) also highlight how these networks facilitate the sharing of good practices related to safety and social protection.

Bottom-Up Social Innovation

Social networks catalyze the emergence of worker-led social innovations, such as platform cooperatives or mutual aid systems. A recent study highlights the importance of off-platform social networks in supporting workers. These bottom-up initiatives allow workers to develop alternatives to the dominant models of the platform economy, creating more equitable and democratic structures. Scholz's (2016) research on "platform cooperativism" shows how these social innovations can emerge from networked interactions between workers.

Social Innovation: Driving the Transformation of Protection Systems

Social innovation, understood as the development of new responses to social needs (Moulaert et al. 2013), offers a framework for rethinking social protection in the platform economy. Social innovation contributes to transforming protection systems in three key ways: by creating new forms of social security adapted to platform work, by promoting the co-construction of solutions involving workers, and by encouraging institutional experimentation. First, it allows for the development of protection mechanisms that address the unique challenges of gig work, such as risk mutualization and the portability of social rights. Second, it fosters participatory approaches where workers take an active role in designing protection systems, ensuring their relevance and sustainability. Finally, it supports experimental initiatives, such as innovation labs, that test and refine new institutional models before wider implementation.

New Forms of Protection

Social innovation allows us to imagine protection systems adapted to the specificities of platform work. For example, recent research analyzes the evolution and models of the gig economy, highlighting the need for new approaches to social protection (Forde et al. 2017). These innovations include systems for mutualizing risks between workers and mechanisms for the portability of social rights. Berg et al. (2018)'s work shows how these new forms of protection can adapt to the flexibility inherent in platform work while ensuring adequate social security.

Co-Construction of Solutions

It involves actively involving workers in the design of social protection systems to ensure their relevance, effectiveness, and sustainability. This approach is based on the idea that workers, as end users, are best placed to identify their needs and the gaps in existing systems. Furthermore, Kilhoffer et al. (2017), in their study for the Centre for European Policy Studies, highlight that involving workers in the platform economy is essential to develop social protection frameworks adapted to the new realities of work. A concrete example can be found in France, where the "Loi El Khomri" (Légifrance, 2016) required platforms to cover accident insurance for independent workers and introduced a right to form unions (Daugareilh et al. 2019). In addition, tools such as social network analysis, mentioned by Sundararajan (2017), can identify collaborative dynamics between workers and help design innovative solutions, such as mutual aid funds or mutual support mechanisms. These participatory approaches enable the development of more resilient and adaptable social protection systems that reflect the diverse needs of platform workers. By directly involving workers, co-construction makes it possible to develop systems that are truly adapted to their needs while promoting their sustainability.

Institutional Experimentation

Social innovation encourages experimentation with new institutional models, such as "social innovation labs" (Wascher et al. 2019). Dedicated to the platform economy, these experimental spaces serve as crucial intermediaries for developing novel approaches to social protection in the digital economy. These labs convene and facilitate cross-sector stakeholder working groups, providing a physical space and/or process to support collaboration between different actors in order to develop new projects, processes, models, products, and regulations. Through structured methodologies, including co-creation and design thinking, these labs enable systematic experimentation with institutional frameworks while ensuring multi-stakeholder engagement. A recent systematic review (Howcroft & Bergvall-Kåreborn, 2019) explores power dynamics, worker autonomy, and the role of social networks in the gig economy, offering perspectives for future institutional experimentation. Such experimentation allows for testing and refining new models of social protection before their deployment on a larger scale.

ANALYSIS OF NEW FORMS OF PRECARITY IN THE PLATFORM ECONOMY

This section examines the multiple dimensions of precarity that emerge in the platform economy. It highlights the implications of these vulnerabilities for the social and economic sustainability of the model while highlighting the need for institutional and social adaptations to address them.

Precariousness of Labor Relations and Fragility of Statuses

The platform economy is profoundly transforming working relationships, introducing forms of precariousness that are often difficult to integrate into traditional legal and social frameworks:

Ambiguity of Professional Status

Platforms exploit legal gray areas, classifying workers as independent contractors while exercising significant control over their activity. This allows platforms to circumvent certain social and tax obligations (De Stefano, 2016). For example, an analysis by the International Labour Organization (ILO, 2018) showed that this ambiguity often deprives workers of fundamental rights such as paid leave and access to health coverage.

Fragmentation of Working Time

Flexibility, presented as an asset by platforms, often translates into unpredictable schedules and permanent availability. This leads to an alternation between periods of high activity and unpaid periods, aggravating the financial instability of workers (Schor et al. 2020).

Income Instability

Platform workers' incomes are subject to significant fluctuations, influenced by demand and algorithmic adjustments. This instability compromises their ability to plan financially in the medium to long term (Wood et al. 2019; Eurofound, 2018).

Vulnerability to Algorithmic Management Systems

Algorithmic management, which is a central pillar of the functioning of platforms, introduces new forms of vulnerability:

Opacity of Decisions

Algorithmic management, which is a central pillar of the functioning of platforms, introduces new forms of vulnerability for gig economy workers. Algorithms that assign tasks or evaluate workers' performance often lack transparency, making it difficult for workers to understand the reasoning behind decisions that affect their work. This lack of clarity complicates challenges to decisions perceived as unfair, such as a deactivated account or an undeserved rating. The opacity surrounding these decisions exacerbates the power asymmetry between platforms and workers, where the latter have little recourse or understanding of how their performance is evaluated. For instance, Uber drivers, without being provided any clear explanation, can be penalized or even banned based on algorithmic judgments (Rosenblat, 2018). Similarly, Deliveroo riders have reported sudden drops in their priority access to shifts without understanding the algorithmic criteria behind these changes (Gregory, 2020). Another striking example comes from Amazon Flex delivery drivers, who can be automatically terminated if their "reliability rating" falls below a certain threshold, yet the exact calculation of this rating remains obscure (Griesbach et al. 2019). As a result, workers are left powerless to challenge or appeal decisions that significantly impact their livelihood (Mateescu & Nguyen, 2019).

Pressure on Working Conditions

Rating and reputation systems, essential to platform-based employment, exert continuous pressure on workers to take underpaid assignments or tolerate precarious conditions to preserve their ratings and reputation. These systems drive workers to perform in ways that prioritize meeting algorithmic expectations over their well-being. For example, delivery drivers for platforms often feel compelled to work under unfavorable conditions—long hours, harsh weather, and high stress—just to keep up with their ratings. The fear of receiving a poor rating can deter workers from rejecting low-paying jobs, even when the working conditions are unsafe or exploitative (Lee et al. 2015). This constant pressure can lead to mental and physical exhaustion, contributing to a vicious cycle of precarious employment (Ravenelle, 2019).

Dehumanization of Relationships

The automation of interactions between employers and workers through algorithmic management also contributes to the dehumanization of relationships in the gig economy. By replacing direct communication and social dialogue with automated systems, platforms reduce opportunities for workers to negotiate their terms of employment, express concerns, or resolve conflicts. This lack of human interaction can create a sense of professional isolation, as workers are treated more like units of labor to be optimized rather than individuals with needs and rights. For example, an Uber driver with a problem related to a fare or a passenger may find it difficult to contact a human representative, relying instead on a faceless system or algorithmic support. Over time, this process of automation and depersonalization contributes to feelings of alienation and decreased job satisfaction, as workers are reduced to mere data points in the system (Graham et al. 2017).

Impacts on Social and Professional Capital

The changes brought about by the platform economy are not limited to income or working conditions; they also affect the development of workers' social and professional capital:

Professional Isolation

The platform economy has led to a fundamental shift in how workers interact with one another, contributing to professional isolation. The geographical dispersion of workers—often scattered across various regions or even countries—combined with their limited connection through digital platforms, significantly restricts opportunities for professional networking and collaboration. Workers who perform tasks through apps rarely meet their colleagues in person, which limits the exchange of knowledge, peer support, and the development of collective solidarities. This lack of social cohesion can result in feelings of isolation and alienation, as workers do not have a shared workspace or communal environment where they can form bonds with others in the same profession (Eurofound, 2018). Moreover, without traditional office settings, workers lose out on informal learning and mentorship opportunities that often contribute to career growth and skill development.

Disqualification

The tasks offered by platforms are often standardized and highly routinized, which can lead to a form of "disqualification" or skill degradation for workers. As workers repeatedly perform the same simple tasks—whether it's driving for delivering food or assembling products—there is little room for the acquisition of new, more advanced skills. This can limit workers' professional development and reduce their opportunities to advance in their careers. For example, a delivery driver working for a platform may be able to improve their efficiency, but they are unlikely to gain new skills that would translate to a higher-paying or more complex role within or outside of the platform. This phenomenon can lead to workers becoming "stuck" in low-skill, low-wage positions, making it more difficult to transition into more skilled or better-paid work in the future. In the long term, this disqualification may result in a workforce that is increasingly vulnerable to economic shifts and automation (Eurofound, 2018).

Weakening of Professional Networks

The weakening of professional networks is another significant impact of the platform economy. Unlike traditional employment, where workers can form strong connections with colleagues, supervisors, and mentors within a physical workspace, platform-based work often lacks these opportunities for relationship-building. In a traditional job, colleagues may become valuable sources of professional support, advice, and opportunities for career advancement. However, platform workers, who often operate independently and remotely, have limited chances to cultivate meaningful professional relationships. As a result, they miss out on the informal networks that are crucial for career development, such as gaining referrals, recommendations, or learning about new job opportunities (Berg et al. 2018). In the absence of such networks, platform workers may struggle to find new career pathways or even seek advice on how to improve their work conditions or secure better pay.

Challenges for Social Protection

Traditional social protection systems, which were built around the model of full-time, long-term employment with a single employer, are often ill-suited to the realities of platform workers._Several key factors explain this inadequacy:

The Mismatch Between Social Protection and Gig Work

Traditional social protection systems, which were designed for stable, full-time employment relationships, are often ill-equipped to address the realities faced by platform workers. These systems typically assume continuous, stable work with a single employer, making them inadequate for workers who experience intermittent, project-based employment or hybrid statuses (where they juggle multiple gigs and non-gig work). As a result, many platform workers are excluded from basic social protections, such as health insurance, paid sick leave, and retirement benefits. For instance, while gig economy workers may work for multiple platforms, they often fall outside the scope of national welfare systems that are primarily structured around conventional employment (International Labour Organization, 2021). This leaves workers vulnerable to economic shocks, such as periods of unemployment or illness, without the safety nets that traditional employees benefit from (Forde et al. 2017).

Discontinuity of Rights

One of the primary challenges for platform workers is the discontinuity of rights, which arises from the nature of gig work that involves mobility between platforms and irregular income. As workers frequently switch between platforms or fluctuate between periods of high and low demand, there are interruptions in the accumulation of social rights such as pensions, unemployment benefits, or healthcare coverage. Workers in the gig economy often face difficulties in maintaining a consistent and continuous record of employment that is necessary for qualifying for these benefits. For example, a delivery driver who works for several different platforms over a year may struggle to accumulate enough contributions to be eligible for social benefits, including paid leave or unemployment insurance (Florisson & Mandl, 2018). These breaks in coverage often leave workers in precarious positions without the necessary support when transitioning between jobs or during periods of low income.

Inequalities of Access

Inequalities of access to social protection are another significant challenge within the platform economy, as workers from marginalized or disadvantaged socio-economic backgrounds are often the least covered by existing systems. Minority groups, lower-income workers, and those with less formal education are overrepresented in the gig economy and are more likely to experience gaps in social protection coverage. These groups often face additional barriers to accessing social welfare programs, such as lack of awareness about available protections, language barriers, or limited digital literacy, which further reinforces existing inequalities (International Labour Organization, 2021). In many cases, these workers are not only excluded from traditional social benefits but may also be less likely to have the flexibility or financial resources to participate in voluntary, alternative social insurance schemes, thus leaving them more vulnerable to financial hardship.

SUSTAINABILITY CHALLENGES OF THE PLATFORM ECONOMY AND RESPONSES THROUGH SOCIAL INNOVATION

Limitations of Current Models of the Platform Economy

Protection and Rights of Workers

Platform workers operate in a legal gray area where their rights are not clearly defined. As De Stefano (2016) points out, this ambiguity limits their access to social protection mechanisms. For example, in the European Union, significant disparities exist in social rights between member states, amplifying structural inequalities (Hauben et al. 2020). For instance, while Denmark ensures that platform workers can unionize and negotiate collectively, countries like Poland lack clear legal frameworks for such actions. This imbalance creates a patchwork system that fails to address the broader challenges faced by workers in the gig economy.

Some policy initiatives are considering the creation of hybrid classifications for platform workers to ensure their inclusion in appropriate legal frameworks (ILO, 2021). A notable example is California's Assembly Bill 5 (AB5), which initially aimed to reclassify gig workers as employees to provide them with greater labor protections (Lake, 2023). However, this reform has faced resistance and has been partially overturned, illustrating the challenges of implementing such policies in dynamic economies.

Income Security

Platform workers are often exposed to unstable and unpredictable incomes. Algorithms that determine task allocation and evaluate performance exacerbate this precarity by introducing algorithmic dependency (Wood et al. 2019). This volatility prevents workers from planning financially or accessing traditional credit or insurance systems. For example, drivers for Uber in India reported significant income fluctuations during the COVID-19 pandemic, with earnings dropping by up to 50% in some cases (Ray & Sam, 2023). These sudden shifts highlight the fragile economic position of many platform workers.

Professional Development

The platform model favors standardized and repetitive tasks, limiting opportunities for acquiring transferable skills. According to Graham et al. (2020), these circumstances make it difficult for workers to advance in their careers, especially young ones who are frequently stuck in positions with few opportunities. For instance, food delivery workers in Brazil, surveyed by Scholz (2016), expressed concerns that their work offered little opportunity for skill enhancement, leaving them vulnerable to future technological disruptions such as autonomous delivery systems.

Strategies for a Sustainable Platform Economy

Platform Cooperativism

Platform cooperativism represents a viable and sustainable alternative to traditional centralized models by prioritizing worker ownership and self-governance. According to Scholz (2016), this approach fosters fairness and democratic decision-making, ensuring that workers actively participate in managing the platform rather than being subjected to unilateral corporate control. A notable example is CoopCycle, a French cooperative that brings together delivery workers under a solidarity-based structure, allowing them to collectively organize their activities while benefiting from a system that safeguards their economic and social interests (Mannan & Pek, 2024). By adopting this model, CoopCycle promotes democratic governance, ensures a more equitable distribution of profits, and integrates collective social protection mechanisms that offer workers greater financial security.

Similarly, Smart.coop, a European cooperative dedicated to supporting freelancers, provides a comprehensive framework that enhances workers' social security and administrative support (European Commission, 2022). Through resource pooling, this initiative enables gig workers to mitigate income instability and better anticipate their financial future. By offering access to essential protections such as social insurance and professional development opportunities, Smart.coop exemplifies how platform cooperativism can empower workers, creating a more resilient and equitable labor ecosystem.

Hybrid Support Systems

A growing number of initiatives are integrating digital tools with physical resources to provide comprehensive support for platform workers. Johnston & Land-Kazlauskas (2018) highlight several key strategies that have proven effective in addressing the challenges faced by gig workers. One such approach involves the creation of virtual communities that help mitigate professional isolation by fostering real-time communication and knowledge sharing. For instance, social media groups have become essential tools for ride-hailing drivers to exchange critical information about safety and trip optimization. For example, a survey by Bernard (2023) found that Uber drivers in Paris, London, and Montreal use these platforms to share tips and strategies, helping them better navigate the demands of their jobs.

Bernard notes that these exchanges help drivers anticipate peak demand periods and schedule accordingly, increasing their chances of getting premium rides while minimizing wait times.

Additionally, mutual aid networks have emerged as a vital mechanism for strengthening workers' resilience by facilitating the sharing of logistical and professional resources. In Spain, the Riders x Derechos movement has pioneered the establishment of collective funds aimed at supporting platform workers during periods of economic uncertainty, demonstrating the potential of solidarity-based initiatives to provide financial security and stability (Eurofound, 2024). By combining digital connectivity with collaborative action, these initiatives contribute to a more inclusive and sustainable platform economy.

Policy Innovation and Regulatory Frameworks

Regulatory frameworks play a fundamental role in fostering a more equitable platform economy by ensuring that workers benefit from fair labor protections and transparent employment conditions. Prassl (2018) outlines several key reforms aimed at addressing the vulnerabilities inherent in gig work. One such reform involves the creation of hybrid employment statuses that bridge the gap between traditional employee protections and the flexibility associated with self-employment. A notable example of evolving labor legislation is Italy's 2019 reform, which reclassifies food delivery riders as "collaborators," granting them access to essential social protections such as accident insurance while maintaining a degree of work autonomy (Ogletree Deakins, 2019). This approach reflects broader efforts to address the precarity of platform work and emphasizes the need for hybrid frameworks that balance flexibility with worker protections. While this legislative framework marks a significant step forward, its long-term impact on both workers' rights and the sustainability of platform business models remains to be fully assessed.

Another crucial regulatory measure focuses on establishing minimum remuneration thresholds and enforcing algorithmic transparency. Portugal has taken significant steps in this direction by implementing new gig economy laws that require platforms to disclose how their algorithms influence worker evaluations and task allocations (Arruda, 2021). These initiatives aim to reduce information asymmetry and ensure fairer working conditions by preventing arbitrary decision-making that disadvantages workers. The legislation reflects a broader commitment to improving labor standards within the gig economy, acknowledging the need for protections that align with modern work practices.

Additionally, ensuring the portability of social rights has emerged as a key policy priority to provide gig workers with continuous access to social protections, regardless of the platforms they engage with. The French "Compte Personnel d'Activité" (CPA) serves as a pioneering model, allowing workers to retain accrued rights and benefits as they transition between different jobs and work arrangements (Valenti, 2021).

By combining these regulatory approaches with coordinated efforts among national governments and international organizations, policymakers can develop more resilient and inclusive frameworks that address the structural challenges of the gig economy, ultimately fostering greater labor security and economic sustainability.

FRAMEWORK AND IMPLEMENTATION OF SUSTAINABLE SUPPORT SYSTEMS IN PLATFORM ECONOMIES: FROM THEORY TO PRACTICE

Foundations of an Integrated System for Sustainable Platform Work

Sustainability in the platform economy relies on effective coordination among various stakeholders. According to the COLLEEM survey, over 11% of working-age Europeans have provided services through digital platforms (Pesole et al. 2018). This trend underscores the growing importance of developing inclusive and adaptive frameworks to support these workers, particularly in ensuring equitable access to social protection mechanisms.

Innovative regulatory frameworks are emerging, such as the “Charter of Fundamental Rights for Digital Labour” in Bologna, exemplifying this integrated approach. The Charter, signed in May 2018, sets standards for platform workers, including a fixed hourly rate at least equal to the sectoral minimum wage, compensation for overtime, public holidays, and adverse weather conditions, as well as insurance covering accidents and occupational illnesses (Eurofound, 2024). This initiative inspired Italy's Legislative Decree No. 101/2019, granting specific rights to platform workers at the national level (EU-OSHA, 2022).

Internationally, the development of global guidelines inspired by decent work principles is leading to the creation of cross-border frameworks for portable benefits, particularly in health insurance and pensions. These initiatives highlight the importance of cross-border collaboration and standardization to address the transnational nature of platform work. For instance, the ILO convened a meeting of experts in October 2022 to discuss ways to ensure decent work in the platform economy (ILO, 2022).

These collective efforts, both local and international, are crucial to ensuring that platform economy workers benefit from fair working conditions and adequate social protection, reflecting a coordinated and sustainable approach to the challenges posed by the digitization of work.

Adaptive Social Protection Mechanisms and Platform Accountability

Data from Kilhoffer et al. (2020) reveal that 43% of platform workers do not have access to adequate social protection. In response, several innovative initiatives have emerged. France, with the El Khomri law (Légifrance, 2016), introduced the portability of social rights, while Spain, with the "Ley Rider" (Gobierno de España, 2021), established a specific framework for delivery workers. These legislative efforts demonstrate a commitment to bridging gaps in protection but face challenges in enforcement and worker compliance. These reforms are accompanied by algorithmic transparency requirements and new pricing models that integrate social protection costs. For example, platforms like Glovo and Deliveroo are now required to disclose how algorithmic evaluations affect worker status, enabling better accountability. The creation of emergency funds and the integration of social benefits into platforms' pricing structures reinforce this protective approach.

Social Innovation and Technological Infrastructure

Social innovation is manifested through alternative governance models. According to Pesole et al. (2018), CoopCycle and Smart.coop demonstrate that 7.2% of workers are involved in cooperative models. These cooperatives not only offer financial stability but also empower workers by granting them decision-making authority within the organization. These initiatives rely on advanced technological solutions, including blockchain-based portable social benefit systems and integrated platforms for benefit management. Blockchain technology, for example, enables secure and transparent tracking of workers' contributions to social funds, ensuring that benefits remain accessible regardless of platform changes. Establishing secure data-sharing protocols between platforms and public authorities facilitates the monitoring and evaluation of social impacts, promoting greater accountability.

Collaborative Governance and Capacity Building

Effective multi-stakeholder governance is essential to the success of support systems. 68% of platform workers operate in a transnational environment, according to research by Kilhoffer et al. (2020), which calls for cooperation among local and international actors. This complexity requires multi-level advisory committees that incorporate worker representatives, platform executives, and policymakers to create balanced and inclusive strategies. To support this governance framework, continuous training and awareness-raising programs on sustainable practices are implemented. The EU Observatory on the Online Platform Economy, as described by the European

Commission (2021), monitors these developments and contributes to understanding the evolving dynamics of digital labor markets. This initiative is part of a broader effort to address the complexities of the platform economy, ensuring that workers are informed and prepared to engage effectively with digital platforms.

Assessment, Adaptation, and Roadmap for Sustainability

Achieving sustainable development in the platform economy requires a comprehensive evaluation system capable of assessing progress and guiding policy adaptations. The COLLEEM study has established a set of key indicators, now widely utilized by the International Labour Organization and the European Platform Work Observatory, to monitor the evolving landscape of platform work and inform regulatory decisions. This evaluative approach is embedded within a structured roadmap designed to ensure both immediate worker protections and long-term structural reforms.

In the short term, the focus is on implementing fundamental labor protections, such as access to health insurance and basic income guarantees, to provide immediate relief for the most vulnerable platform workers. These measures serve as a foundation for ensuring minimum social security standards and reducing economic precarity.

In the medium term, efforts shift toward developing integrated digital social protection systems that facilitate the portability of benefits across different platforms and geographic regions. By streamlining access to social rights and ensuring continuity in workers' protections, these systems enhance labor security and reduce administrative barriers for gig workers.

In the long term, the goal is to establish autonomous labor ecosystems that promote innovation and resilience. This includes fostering worker-owned platforms that incorporate social protections directly into their business models, ensuring fairer working conditions and greater economic stability for platform workers.

This progressive roadmap underscores the importance of iterative adaptation, allowing social protection mechanisms and labor policies to evolve alongside technological and economic transformations. By striking a balance between economic flexibility and social security, these strategic measures aim to build a platform economy that is both dynamic and equitable, benefiting all stakeholders involved.

CONCLUSION AND FUTURE PERSPECTIVES

This chapter has explored the challenges posed by new forms of precarity, particularly those emerging in the platform economy, and has proposed a comprehensive, integrated, and proactive conceptual framework to enhance social intervention. By combining coordinated strategies among stakeholders, adaptive social protection policies, and increased support for social innovation, this framework aims to provide more sustainable and inclusive solutions to contemporary socio-economic challenges.

The findings underscore that current intervention models remain fragmented and insufficient, necessitating a fundamental rethinking of both public policies and civil society initiatives. Public policies must evolve to better reflect the realities of precarious populations, while civil society efforts, though promising, require enhanced institutional and financial backing to maximize their impact. The proposed framework contributes to this reflection by introducing mechanisms for improved coordination, the development of more inclusive and adaptive policies, and the reinforcement of community-driven initiatives.

A crucial aspect of this approach lies in rethinking how social protection systems address the needs of precarious workers, particularly those engaged in platform-based employment. The integration of tailored employment policies, coupled with digital tools that facilitate worker support networks, legal assistance, and financial inclusion, could foster greater stability for vulnerable populations. Additionally, fostering a culture of cross-sector partnerships—uniting governments, private enterprises, social organizations, and research institutions—will be key to implementing truly innovative and resilient solutions.

Looking ahead, several directions merit further exploration. Empirical studies should assess the real-world effectiveness of these proposed strategies, identifying best practices and potential areas of improvement. Experimental initiatives, such as pilot projects in collaborative housing or digital platforms designed to support gig workers, could provide valuable insights into scalable intervention models. Moreover, reinforcing international and interdisciplinary collaborations can help accelerate the diffusion of successful social intervention mechanisms across different contexts.

Finally, policy frameworks must remain adaptable and forward-thinking, capable of evolving in response to emerging socio-economic shifts. This requires ongoing dialogue between researchers, policymakers, and practitioners to anticipate future vulnerabilities and craft agile, data-driven response strategies. By embracing these principles, it is possible to construct a more cohesive, equitable, and effective approach to addressing the complexities of modern precarity—one that prioritizes coordination, prevention, and innovation as pillars of sustainable social intervention.

FUNDING SUPPORT

This research received no external funding

CONFLICTS OF INTEREST

The author declares that he have no conflicts of interest to this work.

REFERENCES

Arruda, M. D. S. (2023). Pro-immigrant digital platforms in Portugal: An overview. *E-Journal of International and Comparative Labour Studies*, *12*(1), 1–17.

Belleflamme, P., & Peitz, M. (2021). *The economics of platforms*. Cambridge University Press. DOI: 10.1017/9781108696913

Berg, J., Furrer, M., Harmon, E., Rani, U., & Silberman, M. S. (2018). Digital labour platforms and the future of work. *Towards decent work in the online world. Rapport de l'OIT*. https://www.ilo.org/publications/digital-labour-platforms-and-future-work-towards-decent-work-online-world

Bernard, S. (2023). *UberUsés: Le capitalisme racial de plateforme à Paris*. Puf.

Bourdieu, P. (2018). The forms of capital. In *The sociology of economic life* (pp. 78–92). Routledge., DOI: 10.4324/9780429494338-6

Cant, C. (2019). *Riding for Deliveroo: Resistance in the New Economy*. Polity.

Chen, J. Y. (2018). Thrown under the bus and outrunning it! The logic of Didi and taxi drivers' labour and activism in the on-demand economy. *New Media & Society*, *20*(8), 2691–2711. DOI: 10.1177/1461444817729149

Daugareilh, I., Degryse, C., & Pochet, P. (Eds.). (2019). *The platform economy and social law: Key issues in comparative perspective* (ETUI Working Paper 2019.10). ETUI.

De Stefano, V. M. (2016). The rise of the 'just-in-time workforce': On-demand work, crowd work and labour protection in the 'gig-economy'. *SSRN*, *37*(3), 471–504. DOI: 10.2139/ssrn.2682602

Deakins, O. (2019, October 24). New legislation in Italy to boost delivery riders' rights. International Employment Update. https://ogletree.com/international-employment-update/articles/november-2019/italy/2019-10-24/new-legislation-in-italy-to-boost-delivery-riders-rights/

Di Gangi, P. M., Howard, J. L., McAllister, C. P., & Thatcher, J. B. (2024). The Influence of Political Skill and Community Capabilities on Microtask Worker Hourly Wage: A Mixed Methods Study of Mechanical Turk. *Journal of the Association for Information Systems*, *25*(4), 890–935. DOI: 10.17705/1jais.00858

EU-OSHA. (2022). *Italy: A national and local answer to the challenges of the platform economy*. Retrieved from https://osha.europa.eu/sites/default/files/2022-02/A_national_local_answer_challenges_platform_economy_Italy.pdf

Eurofound. (2018). Employment and working conditions of selected types of platform work. Publications Office of the European Union. https://www.eurofound.europa.eu/en/publications/2018/employment-and-working-conditions-selected-types-platform-work

Eurofound. (2024, December). *Riders x Derechos (Riders for Rights)*. Platform Economy Database. Retrieved from https://apps.eurofound.europa.eu/platformeconomydb/riders-x-derechos-riders-for-rights-103036

Eurofound. (2024). Riders Union Bologna. https://apps.eurofound.europa.eu/platformeconomydb/riders-union-bologna-103125

European Commission. Directorate-General for Communications Networks, Content and Technology, *Study on "Support to the observatory for the online platform economy" – Final report*, Publications Office, 2021, https://data.europa.eu/doi/10.2759/801457

European Commission. (2022, May 11). Smart Coop. European Social Fund Plus. https://european-social-fund-plus.ec.europa.eu/en/social-innovation-match/case-study/smart-coop

Florisson, R., & Mandl, I. (2018). Platform work: Types and implications for work and employment—Literature review. Eurofound. https://apo.org.au/node/201491

Forde, C., Stuart, M., Joyce, S., Oliver, L., Valizade, D., Alberti, G., . . . Carson, C. (2017). The social protection of workers in the platform economy. Retrieved from https://www.europarl.europa.eu/RegData/etudes/STUD/2017/614184/IPOL_STU(2017)614184_EN.pdf

Gobierno de España. (2021). *Ley 12/2021, de 28 de septiembre, de medidas urgentes para la regulación del trabajo en plataformas digitales. Boletín Oficial del Estado.* https://www.boe.es/buscar/doc.php?id=BOE-A-2021-15548

Graham, M., Hjorth, I., & Lehdonvirta, V. (2017). Digital labour and development: Impacts of global digital labour platforms and the gig economy on worker livelihoods. *Transfer: European Review of Labour and Research, 23*(2), 135–162. DOI: 10.1177/1024258916687250 PMID: 28781494

Graham, M., & Woodcock, J. (2018). Towards a fairer platform economy: Introducing the Fairwork Foundation. *Alternate Routes*, *29*, 242–253.

Granovetter, M. S. (1973). The strength of weak ties. *American Journal of Sociology*, *78*(6), 1360–1380. DOI: 10.1086/225469

Gregory, K. (2021). 'My Life Is More Valuable Than This': Understanding Risk among On-Demand Food Couriers in Edinburgh. *Work, Employment and Society*, *35*(2), 316–331. DOI: 10.1177/0950017020969593

Griesbach, K., Reich, A., Elliott-Negri, L., & Milkman, R. (2019). Algorithmic Control in Platform Food Delivery Work. *Socius: Sociological Research for a Dynamic World*, *5*, 1–15. DOI: 10.1177/2378023119870041

Hauben, H., Lenaerts, K., & Waeyaert, W. (2020). *The platform economy and precarious work.* Publication for the Committee on Employment and Social Affairs, Policy Department for Economic, Scientific and Quality of Life Policies, European Parliament.

Howcroft, D., & Bergvall-Kåreborn, B. (2019). A typology of crowdwork platforms. *Work, Employment and Society*, *33*(1), 21–38. DOI: 10.1177/0950017018760136

International Labour Organization. (2018). *Digital labour platforms and the future of work: Towards decent work in the online world.* Retrieved from https://www.ilo.org/sites/default/files/wcmsp5/groups/public/%40dgreports/%40dcomm/%40publ/documents/publication/wcms_645337.pdf

International Labour Organization. (2021). *The role of digital labour platforms in transforming the world of work.* https://www.ilo.org/publications/flagship-reports/role-digital-labour-platforms-transforming-world-work

International Labour Organization (ILO). (2022). *Meeting of experts on decent work in the platform economy.* Retrieved from https://www.ilo.org/meetings-and-events/meeting-experts-decent-work-platform-economy

Johnston, H., & Land-Kazlauskas, C. (2018). *Organizing On-Demand Representation, Voice, and Collective Bargaining in the Gig Economy*. International Labour Organization.

Katta, S., Howson, K., & Graham, M. (2020). The Fairwork Foundation: Action research on the gig economy. *Global Dialogue, 10*(1), 44–46.

Kilhoffer, Z., De Groen, W. P., Lenaerts, K., Smits, I., Hauben, H., Waeyaert, W., & Robin-Olivier, S. (2020). *Study to gather evidence on the working conditions of platform workers* (VT/2018/032). https://www.ceps.eu/ceps-publications/study-to-gather-evidence-on-the-working-conditions-of-platform-workers/

Kilhoffer, Z., Lenaerts, K., & Beblavý, M. (2017). The platform economy and industrial relations: Applying the old framework to the new reality (CEPS Research Report No. 2017/12). Centre for European Policy Studies.

Lake, R. (2023). *California Assembly Bill 5 (AB5): What's in it and what it means.* Investopedia. Retrieved September 23, 2023, from https://www.investopedia.com/california-assembly-bill-5-ab5-4773201

Lee, M. K., Kusbit, D., Metsky, E., & Dabbish, L. (2015). Working with machines: The impact of algorithmic and data-driven management on human workers. In *Proceedings of the 33rd Annual ACM Conference on Human Factors in Computing Systems (CHI '15)* (pp. 1603–1612). Association for Computing Machinery. DOI: 10.1145/2702123.2702548

Légifrance. (2016). *Loi n° 2016-1088 du 8 août 2016 relative au travail, à la modernisation du dialogue social et à la sécurisation des parcours professionnels.* https://www.legifrance.gouv.fr/jorf/id/JORFTEXT000032983213

Lehdonvirta, V. (2016). Algorithms that Divide and Unite: Delocalisation, Identity and Collective Action in 'Microwork. In Flecker, J. (Ed.), *Space, Place and Global Digital Work. Dynamics of Virtual Work.* Palgrave Macmillan., DOI: 10.1057/978-1-137-48087-3_4

Lehdonvirta, V., Kässi, O., Hjorth, I., Barnard, H., & Graham, M. (2019). The global platform economy: A new offshoring institution enabling emerging-economy microproviders. *Journal of Management, 45*(2), 567–599. DOI: 10.1177/0149206318786781 PMID: 30774168

Mannan, M., & Pek, S. (2024). Platform cooperatives and the dilemmas of platform worker-member participation. *New Technology, Work and Employment, 39*(2), 219–237. DOI: 10.1111/ntwe.12273

Mateescu, A., & Nguyen, A. (2019). *Explainer: Workplace monitoring and surveillance.* Data & Society. Retrieved May 15, 2021, from https://datasociety.net/wp-content/uploads/2019/02/DS_Workplace_Monitoring_Surveillance_Explainer.pdf

Moulaert, F. (Ed.). (2013). *The international handbook on social innovation: collective action, social learning and transdisciplinary research.* Edward Elgar Publishing. DOI: 10.4337/9781849809993

Pesole, A., Urzi Brancati, M. C., Fernandez Macias, E., Biagi, F., & Gonzalez Vazquez, I. (2018). *Platform workers in Europe: Evidence from the COLLEEM survey* (EUR 29275 EN). Publications Office of the European Union. DOI: 10.2760/742789

Pilatti, G. R., Pinheiro, F. L., & Montini, A. A. (2024). Systematic Literature Review on Gig Economy: Power Dynamics, Worker Autonomy, and the Role of Social Networks. *Administrative Sciences, 14*(10), 267. DOI: 10.3390/admsci14100267

Prassl, J. (2018). *Humans as a service: The promise and perils of work in the gig economy.* Oxford University Press. DOI: 10.1093/oso/9780198797012.001.0001

Ravenelle, A. J. (2019). "We're not uber:" control, autonomy, and entrepreneurship in the gig economy. *Journal of Managerial Psychology, 34*(4), 269–285. DOI: 10.1108/JMP-06-2018-0256

Ray, R., & Sam, J. S. (2023). Off-platform Social Networks and Gig Work During the COVID-19 Pandemic in India. *Journal of South Asian Development, 18*(3), 359–382. DOI: 10.1177/09731741231191876

Rosenblat, A. (2018). *Uberland: How algorithms are rewriting the rules of work.* Univ of California Press. DOI: 10.1525/9780520970632

Scholz, T. (2016). *Platform cooperativism: Challenging the corporate sharing economy.* Rosa Luxemburg Stiftung. https://www.rosalux-nyc.org/wp-content/files_mf/scholz_platformcoop_5.9.201650.pdf

Schor, J. B., Attwood-Charles, W., Cansoy, M., & Lee, D. (2020). Dependence and precarity in the platform economy. *Theory and Society, 49*(5-6), 833–861. DOI: 10.1007/s11186-020-09408-y PMID: 32836676

Servais, J.-M. (2018). Digital service platform workers: What social guarantees? [Travailleurs des plateformes numériques de services: quelles garanties sociales?]. Revue Interventions économiques, 60. DOI: 10.4000/interventionseconomiques.4785

Spasova, S., Bouget, D., Ghailani, D., & Vanhercke, B. (2017). *Access to social protection for people working on non-standard contracts and as self-employed in Europe: A study of national policies. European Commission, European Social Policy Network*. ESPN.

Sundararajan, A. (2017). *The sharing economy: The end of employment and the rise of crowd-based capitalism*. MIT press.

Tassinari, A., & Maccarrone, V. (2020). Riders on the Storm: Workplace Solidarity among Gig Economy Couriers in Italy and the UK. *Work, Employment and Society, 34*(1), 35–54. DOI: 10.1177/0950017019862954

Valenti, C. (2021). The individual right to continuous training of workers: an analysis of best practices in the international framework. *Labour & Law Issues, 7*(1), 54-88. DOI: 10.6092/issn.2421-2695/12922

Wascher, E., Kaletka, C., & Schultze, J. (2019). SI-Labs: A Seedbed for Social Innovation. In J. Howaldt, C. Kaletka, A. Schröder, & M. Zirngiebl (Eds.), Atlas of Social Innovation – 2nd Volume: A World of New Practices (pp. 22-25). oekom verlag GmbH. https://www.socialinnovationatlas.net/articles/

Wood, A. J., Graham, M., Lehdonvirta, V., & Hjorth, I. (2019). Good gig, bad gig: Autonomy and algorithmic control in the global gig economy. *Work, Employment and Society, 33*(1), 56–75. DOI: 10.1177/0950017018785616 PMID: 30886460

Woodcock, J. (2021). *The fight against platform capitalism: An inquiry into the global struggles of the gig economy*. University of Westminster Press., DOI: 10.2307/j.ctv1ktbdrm

Woodcock, J., & Graham, M. (2020). *The gig economy: A critical introduction*. Polity.

Chapter 12
Balancing Flexibility and Precarity:
Ethical Implications and Sustainable Practices in Global Gig Economies

Muhammad Usman Tariq
https://orcid.org/0000-0002-7605-3040
Abu Dhabi University, UAE & University College Cork, Ireland

ABSTRACT

The transformed traditional form of labor markets is what defines gig economies across the globe, wherein workers have more flexibility and freedom than ever before. The innovation that comes with digital platforms and technology powers gig work in creating opportunities for income, entrepreneurship, and economic growth. This flexibility usually comes at precarity because a gig worker has an unstable income, little access to benefits, and little legal protection. Gig work has significant ethical issues, such as work's dual nature. This chapter will discuss the ethical implications of gig economies regarding flexibility. The experiences of different gig workers, such as delivery drivers, freelancers, and virtual assistants, will be defined by their mode of employment and the relationship between that experience and the practice that determines the transformation of short-term contracts into job and life security. It also underscores the need to promote diversity, inclusion, and equity in gig economies to address systemic barriers against women, migrants, and marginalized communities.

DOI: 10.4018/979-8-3693-9385-7.ch012

INTRODUCTION

The emergence of gig economies is perhaps one of the most momentous changes in the global workforce over the last few decades, transforming old employment models and connections between workers and those who hire them. Work in gig economies is short-term, flexible, and often task-based work arranged worldwide. It allows individuals to work independently outside the boundaries of standard employment contracts. Such modern needs changed aspirations of workers, and quick technological development that has created digital platforms have created and perpetuated the gig economy. Therefore, the gig economy spans several industries, such as transport, hospitality, technology, and creative services, to name just a few. Their importance for businesses worldwide lies in providing flexible work options and promoting entrepreneurship while at the same time developing an agile workforce able to adjust to changing market needs (Huđek & Širec, 2024). One of the primary attractions of gig work is that it allows you to be flexible with your boss. Unlike traditional jobs with standard office hours and stereotypical managerial control, gig work hands over the work to the person who works it regarding the time and place. Such a benefit is directed towards work-life balancers, caregivers, students, retirees, multipotentiality, or anyone keen on side hustles. The autonomy that the gig work gives also enables people to take much greater control over their work lives. People can now more strongly realign their work based on their skills, interests, and goals in life at large, thus offering them a sense of fulfillment. For many more people, gig work is associated with escape from the confinements of standard employment. It supports them in forming their economic destinies. Moreover, it further democratizes access to income-generating opportunities for diverse populations— typically even the marginalized traditional labor market— to participate and earn a living (Ness et al., 2023).

BACKGROUND

Gig economies would not be in the position known today without that significant transformative effect on digital platforms and the integration of Industry 4.0 technologies. Companies such as Uber, Airbnb, Upwork, and TaskRabbit are likely to make relatively simple transaction intermediation between workers and consumers on a large scale available by collecting these data. They use advanced algorithms, analytics, and user-friendly interfaces to match tasks to workers to optimize efficiency and convenience efficiently. Gig work dynamics further flourish through Industry 4.0 technologies that include IoT, AI, and blockchain because it is all about transparency, trust, and efficiency of operations. Some examples are blockchain-based smart contracts that ensure that gig workers receive payment fairly and in due time. At the same time, IoT devices in logistics and creative service work enable remote and real-time monitoring work. These technological developments have further lowered barriers to entry, stimulated creativity, and extended the reach of the gig economy into new, previously untouched markets (Tariq, 2024). Besides, the gig economy fits the more significant digital transformation across the business world. The attractive development of smartphones, high-speed internet, and mobile applications make an environment ripe for gig platforms to flourish. Such tools allow gig workers to access jobs at any time and from anywhere in the world, thus promoting a culture of immediacy and ease. Workers can benefit, and consumers can get instantaneous quality services without negotiating labyrinthine bureaucracies. Because of this, the gig economy is now mainstream in the global business environment and shapes consumer behavior, labor markets, and opportunities for economic growth worldwide. Businesses are, for instance, increasingly turning to independent workers for just-in-time talent, reducing fixed labor costs and enabling efficient scaling. This increasing reliance on independent workers to meet immediate business needs underscores the symbiotic linkage between the gig economies and the broader digital revolution (Tariq, 2025). Besides, the gig economy fits the more significant digital transformation across the business world. The attractive development of smartphones, high-speed internet, and mobile applications make an environment ripe for gig platforms to flourish. Such tools allow gig workers to access jobs at any time and from anywhere in the world, thus promoting a culture of immediacy and ease. Workers can benefit, and consumers can get instantaneous quality services without negotiating labyrinthine bureaucracies. Because of this, the gig economy is now mainstream in the global business environment and shapes consumer behavior, labor markets, and opportunities for economic growth worldwide. Businesses are, for instance, increasingly turning to independent workers for just-in-time talent, reducing fixed labor costs and enabling efficient scaling. This increasing reliance on independent workers to meet immediate business needs underscores the symbiotic linkage between the gig economies and the broader digital revolution (Abbas, 2024).

Flexibility vs. Precarity: The Dual Nature of Gig Work

The flexibility/precariat dualism is perhaps the most critical feature that captures the tension within gig work between its flexibility and precarity. On one hand, gig work provides workers with high levels of autonomy over their working hours, locations, and types of work. Indeed, these flexible arrangements can meet various needs and preferences and, for this reason, can be quite popular for work-life balance or to provide extra income. On the other hand, it is often the same attractive features of gig work that create precarious conditions, which now raise concerns about the very low security of jobs, the instability of incomes, and the absence of other benefits associated with traditional employment. This duality affects different categories of workers differently and to different extents (Tariq, 2024). One of the most apparent benefits of gig work is flexibility (Ahmed & Lee, 2023). Unlike traditional jobs, it allows workers to choose when they want to work, often hampered by rigid schedules and other geographic constraints. For instance, a freelance graphic designer might opt to do the bulk of her work during her most productive hours, in the early morning or late at night. In the same vein, drivers can now set their hours to sign into various platforms, including Uber Eats or DoorDash; this variation can also appeal to students and other categories of caregivers seeking flexibility based on their routines. For instance, virtual assistants can provide administrative support to a business at the other end of the world and benefit from the time difference in enhanced productivity (Tariq, 2025). Precarity is a significant characteristic of gig work, which does not have long-term contracts or an old-fashioned employer-employee relationship, thus making any worker very vulnerable to large fluctuations in income and economic conditions. For instance, the delivery driver for Instacart or Grubhub may face unpredictable earnings because demand may be variable, assignments are made through algorithmic tasking, and there is a competition effect amongst workers. For instance, freelance creative and technical professionals can go through feast-famine cycles, with weeks or months of too much work followed by a similar period of no work. It can often mean that virtual assistants, whose work is dependent on retaining good relationships with clients, find that their income stream is cut if the client abruptly terminates a contract. Such instability typically undermines any financial security and long-term planning many independent workers have (Anwar & Graham, 2021). Depending on the sector, the experiences of gig workers can simultaneously highlight the tenuous link between flexibility and precarity. For drivers, the appeal of the gig economy lies in quick earning opportunities that sometimes require very little upfront investment. It changed when some companies began to deduct certain costs, such as fuel, from their pay. For drivers, insurance and maintenance costs take a chunk from their earnings, and typically, no employer in this space provides health insurance or leaves with pay. Freelancers also have an average better income and a diversity of projects. Yet they encounter problems like unfavorable bargaining for fair rates, managing unrealistic deliveries, and prompt payment. Therefore, the short-term contract's effect on job security and worker welfare is the dominant concern of gig work. Since gig workers are not regular employees but are independent contractors, they are generally not eligible for the benefits and protections offered by the employer to an ordinary worker. In that regard, these workers are not entitled to unemployment benefits, workers' compensation, or retirement plans that expose them entirely to most of the significant risks. For example, a delivery driver injured while working may lack employer-provided insurance and be unable to meet high medical expenses. For example, an independent worker might not immediately replace a large lost client's business, putting the individual's financial stability at risk. This lack of a safety net perpetuates chronic stress for many gig workers and affects their mental and physical well-being (Tariq, 2024).

It undermines workers' traditional avenues and processes to build careers, develop skills, and navigate upward mobility. Many find it difficult to pursue long-term personal or professional development because it requires some planning and investment—it sees more immediate needs. For example, the gig economy often erases the boundaries between work and life, creating burnout and fatigue. Consider a virtual assistant serving an international clientele; such a worker may feel compelled to answer emails at 3 am. The delivery driver may end up working irregular and extended shifts to hit the peak hours that allow earnings to be maximized (Asfahani et al., 2023). Before long, they hardly find time to rest, alone recover from their tired bodies. Nonetheless, the gig economy continues to grow as demand for flexibility from workers and consumers surges. For many workers, the gig economy is a means to an end, whether as a bridge to other opportunities, a way to gain experience, a source of supplementary income during a transition towards self-employment, or anything else. As a matter of fact, for some individuals, gig work has increasingly become a long-term lifestyle choice that fits with their values and aspirations. Different actors- governments, platforms, and workers- are currently looking for solutions to enhance security with respect to the dual nature of gig work and preserve its flexibility. Workers could include provisions like health insurance benefits or paid leave. For example, legislators discuss reclassifying some of them into another category that would afford more protection. Such measures will go a long way in crafting a more sustainable and fair gig economy that balances the rewards of flexibility against the desire for stability and security (Bieber and Moggia, 2021). The tension between flexibility and precarity in gig work speaks to the complex realities of this employment model. On the one hand, gig work provides unprecedented freedom and flexibility. However, on the other, it greatly exposes the workforce to risks and vulnerabilities. Stories of deliverymen, freelance writers, and virtual assistants articulate how these dynamics work across very different sectors. The challenges of precarity demand many voices and, thus, a regulatory redesign with a view to platform obligations and workers' rights. Properly developed, the push will bear more fruit as the gig economy matures and balances flexibility with safety in the critical long-run interest of all participants (Abbas, 2024).

Ethical Concerns In Gig Economies

The gig economy has received accolades due to its flexibility and dynamism; however, it has also attracted attention to systemic challenges it poses to workers regarding exploitation, labor rights, and social protection. The development of regulations in the gig economy, essentially designed as safeguards for workers' rights, has often lagged behind the lightning pace at which gig work has expanded. It leaves millions of people exposed to unfavorable practices and precarious conditions. Gig workers do not have an explicit service contract; thus, there is no provision for fundamental protections. One is the guarantee of minimum wages, health coverage, or secure employment. This apparent structural lacuna justifies much anxiety regarding the ethical dimensions of gig work, particularly regarding wage differentials, job insecurity, and working conditions (Griep et al., 2023). That would make labor regulation, legislation, and trade unions more vital as they re-balance innovation, fairness, and equality in the gig economy. It has become so common in the gig economy because, most of the time, power mainly falls into the hands of the platforms rather than the workers. Gig workers are typically categorized as independent contractors, a designation that absolves platforms of traditional employer responsibilities. While this classification allows platforms to offer flexible work arrangements, it also enables them to sidestep obligations such as providing minimum wages, overtime pay, or contributions to social security. It has led to workers earning far below the minimum wage after accounting for vehicle maintenance, fuel, and equipment expenses. For example, many delivery drivers and rideshare operators report net earnings that barely cover their costs, particularly in regions with high operational expenses. This dynamic creates a cycle of dependence, where workers must work longer hours to achieve subsistence-level earnings, effectively trapping them in a state of economic vulnerability (Sankararaman et al., 2024).

Labor rights within the gig economy further disenfranchise workers due to the non-existence of collective bargaining infrastructures. In most jurisdictions, ICs are not regarded as employees and, therefore, are not allowed to unionize under the narrow definitions established by standard labor laws in many jurisdictions. Consequently, with no organized representation, gig workers have limited ability to negotiate fair pay, hours of work, and improved conditions (Hadi and Pratono, 2024)). The platform typically deploys algorithms for task allocations, computation of earnings, and even exit from work, thus further exacerbating power asymmetry. Generally, these algorithms are opaque, making it difficult for workers to understand or contest decisions affecting their livelihoods. For instance, a worker may have several penalties because their ratings have been low, or their assignments have been canceled without a clear explanation. It harms workers and their households because they lose income and labor market attachment. Such practices underscore the urgent need for more transparency and accountability in the governance of platforms (Ahmed & Lee, 2023). Another significant issue is the absence of social protection for gig workers, especially in matters relating to health and safety. In traditional models, employment covers provisions where perks such as health insurance, compensated sick leave, and pension plans are provided as a cushion against illness, loss of work due to injury, or economic slowdown. However, the first pushed-in delivery workers are excluded from most of these provisions and are most exposed to risk. For example, if injured in an accident, a food delivery driver would have to pay a hefty medical bill without the safety coverage of employer-provided insurance. Similarly, gig workers during the COVID-19 pandemic did not qualify for unemployment compensation in many parts of the world because they were out of the normal relief program due to their status as independent contractors. Such programs are essential for low-income gig workers who depend on rideshare and related businesses for their income. However, the ethical challenges in the gig economy go further than exploitation and social protection. They also include disparities in pay, job insecurity, and poor working conditions. For example, pay disparities are starkly visible within the global gig platforms as workers from lower-income countries earn much less than their counterparts in wealthier regions for the same work. The inequality is further exacerbated because there are no standardized pay structures to ensure that rates are related to the actual cost of living where the workers reside. There are periods of prolonged inactivity where no income is gained, yet fixed expenses are supposed to be incurred. Many gig workers also operate in hazardous or physically demanding work, such as delivery drivers in highly dense urban localities or warehouse contractors handling bulky materials without proper safety precautions (Hadi et al., 2024).

One of the most pertinent ways to address these ethical challenges is through strong labor regulation and legislation fashioned to the unique dynamics of the gig economy. Governments have been posed with a classification of gig workers that balances flexibility with fairness in labor laws. In some jurisdictions like California, such an approach has been tried through the highly contested Assembly Bill 5 (AB5) to reclassify gig workers as employees and make them eligible for traditional labor laws. While this is well-intentioned, it meets some form of resistance from platforms and some workers who would instead maintain the status that allows them more autonomy (Ishcuk et al., 2024). Other approaches are hybrid models that maintain gig work's flexibility but give some basic guarantees, such as ensuring minimum wage contributions to social insurance and protections against arbitrary deactivation by not having the same level of innovation with equity. These models preserve gig work as a decent and well-balanced opportunity for everyone. The place of trade unions and worker organizations in the gig workers' rights is increasingly important. Where there is no formal union representation, grassroots movements and digital advocacy claim to have come to unite the workers and campaign for fair treatment. They have successfully pushed for higher wages, better working conditions, and greater platform accountability in both the Independent Workers of Great Britain (IWGB) and the Gig Workers Rising movement in the United States. Such actions are specific manifestations of the importance of collective action in addressing systemic challenges within the gig economy. Furthermore, technology is providing gig workers with new tools, as all of these rely increasingly on mobile applications and online forums through which information can be shared and dissent organized toward change-demanding methods.

International labor organizations have also started looking at the global dimensions of the gig economy. A case in point is that the International Labour Organization (ILO) has called for universal labor standards that will be applied to every worker category irrespective of their job. Some of these standards could involve essential factors like fair pay, working in a safe environment, and social security to enable gig workers not to be left behind when the world attempts to make work decent (Jan, 2024). In addition to this, the burden of ensuring that welfare laws for employees extend a good deal beyond differences in the region rests with multinational platforms that want to reach transparent pay structures and uniform benefits for all markets upon which platforms can answer those priorities with a more sustainable gig economy, one that lives up to their interests on the one hand and their social responsibility on the other hand (Rahman et al., 2024). The rapid growth of the gig economy has brought critical issues of worker exploitation, labor rights, and social protection to the fore. Indeed, many advantages of gig work—working from home, designing one's schedule, and general flexibility and independence— must be balanced with less job security, unfair pay, and poor working conditions. Such ethical dilemmas, like unequal compensation and lack of safety nets, reveal the need for more comprehensive solutions that governments, labor organizations, and indeed platforms might work out collaboratively in terms of regulations and standards to ensure equity and dignity for gig workers while preserving the innovation forcing the gig economy forward.

Diversity, Inclusion, and Equity in Gig Economies

The gig economy is increasingly popular across the globe for being a flexible and more inclusive work model. Yet, the promises of diversity, inclusion, and equity are often at odds with the disparities and systemic inequities they mask. Structural biases present in gig work are gender inequality, women's underrepresentation, challenges of marginalized groups, and barriers to accessing underserved communities. Therefore, all the disparities require understanding their root causes with specific strategies to make things fair and inclusive. Therefore, creating a fair gig economy is a complex but indispensable goal, from eliminating gender imbalances to uplifting migrant labor (Jain, 2024). While the gig economy mainly advantages women by giving them opportunities under flexible working conditions that would accommodate caregiving and work-balanced responsibilities, it is laden with gendered disparities wherein most women find themselves in low-wage and insecure parts of the gig economy. It is, for example, domestic work caregiving, among other administrative roles. A case in point is the platforms TaskRabbit and Care.com, which often attract far more women to the workforce doing tasks that have been traditionally undervalued and underpaid. On-demand sectors such as ridesharing and package delivery, which are male-dominated, generally have higher earning potential, though not without their risks and challenges. Moreover, gender discrimination and harassment continue to pervade the gig economy. Females rideshare drivers often feel threatened at work because of the dangers of harassment by their passengers. It is then the freelancers or virtual assistants who are women who have their work quality assumed to be of a lower quality than that of a man because the women will likely be "subordinate" and thus learn the tasks much worse than the men. Such experiences compromise not only the safety and dignity of women but also their capacity to compete with men on equal terms. The underrepresented females in higher-paying gig work are further undercut by systemic barriers—like the digital divide and limited access to capital. Many platforms require the worker to own or lease expensive equipment, such as vehicles or special tools— a barrier for women and even more so for low-income women. Furthermore, social norms and cultural expectations tend not to align women with certain types of gig work, further decelerating change in gendered economies and their attendant inequalities (Kuhn et al., 2021).

People with disabilities and other marginalized and underserved communities face many unique challenges in the gig economy. Some migrant workers are also particularly vulnerable because most of them depend on gig work for income, and their legal status does not grant them full access to protective labor laws. Platforms can use this by charging exorbitant fees, keeping back earnings, or not offering adequate safety measures. For instance, in migrant communities, drivers could be working long hours in risky conditions with no assurance of being well paid or having health benefits (Atmaca, 2023). In most cases, tech and infrastructural challenges bar the underserved from accessing gig work. For instance, many are left out of the gig economy in places with poor internet connectivity or where smartphones are expensive. Even when such disparities are overcome, and gig work is availed, algorithms for matching supply with demand— used by gig platforms— can further reinforce several such biases, such as placing higher-valued workers in better-resourced neighborhoods relative to those in economically disadvantaged neighborhoods. Hence, systemic inequities constantly perpetuate algorithmic biases at the cost of the gig economy's potential for marginalized people to enhance their economic prospects (Griep et al., 2023).

For example, workers with disabilities face giant extra barriers in the gig economy, ranging from the inaccessibility of platform interfaces to the nature of tasks, which are either physically taxing or poorly adapted to their needs. Although there are examples of some platforms making such efforts to accommodate their disabled workers, like enabling remote work or work-from-home options, the efforts are spotty and not enough. Consequently, people living with disabilities continue not to be well represented in the gig workforce, often left out of the fruits of its development (Kuhn et al., 2021). Diversity, inclusion, and equity in the gig economy can happen with a concerted effort from various stakeholders such as government, platforms, and worker advocacy groups. One crucial factor is the implementation of policies and practices that include everyone and work to eliminate systemic biases, creating opportunities for multiple workers. For example, they could launch algorithms to support equal work loading and safety features specifically for female workers, such as rejecting unsafe tasks without repercussions (Silva & Nyobe, 2023). Platforms must also invest in initiatives that lower the barriers and support worker development to enable the marginalized. Subsidies in equipment provision, perhaps even microloans or direct training programs, may further encourage gig work participation, especially for those from underserved communities, and support the creation of sustainable careers. Moreover, making platform interfaces accessible to people with disabilities is incredibly important for fostering inclusion. Features like screen reader compatibility, voice commands, and flexible tasks can make gig work more accessible and equitable (Warren, 2021).

Governments must institute more work regulations and social protection to ensure equity in this gig economy. Governments should implement policies that ensure every worker is paid equally, provide opportunities to all, and offer benefits like health coverage and parental leave to everybody. More specifically, taxing in favor of those platforms that promote diversity or community-based gig initiatives through grants would attract more platforms to develop diverse ecosystems (Mahato et al., 2021). Trade unions and worker advocacy groups can help lift those voices to press for systemic change. These organizations can challenge exploitative practices by organizing gig workers and lobbying for their rights, which, in turn, could foster fair treatment. For instance, some campaigns on wage transparency, standard contracts, and mechanisms for grievance redresses have successfully reduced some of the disparities already noted in gig work. Further, encouraging cross-border collaboration between worker organizations can help address the global nature of gig platforms and the need for uniform standards of equity and inclusion. Another essential factor is closing the gendered disparities in the digital divide. Enabling greater participation in an expanded gig economy offers the ability to access affordable internet, digital literacy programs, and technology infrastructure on which gig work relies. Partnerships among government agencies, non-profit-making institutions, and private-sector stakeholders will bridge that gap and ensure that the digital landscape is more inclusive (Sihela & Paulse, 2024).

The platforms need to act by developing a more inclusive environment for all with policies and constant checks to root out any inequalities. An example would be using demographic data to check if the representation of women and underrepresented groups is adequate and take necessary steps where it is not. Platform transparency on earnings, how tasks are allocated, and mechanisms for dispute resolution are critical for trust-building purposes and accountability. Moreover, they can use their platforms to give visibility to social impact initiatives that benefit the most under served communities. Programs focused on hiring from economically disadvantaged neighborhoods or supporting worker cooperatives can help redistribute wealth and create equal opportunities for everyone. In return, by making a business model that supports a more just economy, they help build an innovative but also inclusive and equitable gig economy (Li et al., 2023). The gig economy allows greater diversity, inclusion, and equity. However, it will not achieve these ends unless systemic problems and the attendant biases are addressed. Present gender disparities, underrepresentation of other marginalized constituencies, as well as disparities in access and opportunity all point to the need for transformational change. It will be achievable through active policy interventions that empower the underserved community and further enhance platforms' responsibilities to ensure the gig economy welcomes and benefits everyone. It is a vision that calls for collaboration, innovation, and commitment to social justice in making the gig economy work as a driver of empowerment and equality in the world of work (Szostak, 2024).

Sustainability and Adaptability of Gig Economies

The gig economy has become one of the most significant forces in the labor market worldwide, completely changing the old work models and adding to economic energy. Its durability and flexibility depend on more significant perspectives related to regional economic conditions, the potential for job creation, entrepreneurial opportunities, and the strength of digital infrastructure (Longoni et al., 2024). Although the gig economy promises innovation, economic growth, and resilience in the short run, the long-term prospects rest on how well challenges concerning worker welfare, regulatory frameworks, and access on an equitable ground are handled. The dynamics between these elements would lay out healthy and robust gig economies in any context. The economic sustainability of gig economies varies across regions because of market size, labor supply, technological penetration, and regulatory environment variations. The gig economy, in many cases, especially in developed countries, thrives in some urban centers where there is high consumer demand, and a digital ecosystem is quite advanced. For example, in cities like New York, London, and Tokyo, companies like Uber, Airbnb, and Upwork find solid markets for their app-based services. In these regions, the availability of skilled workers, the internet, and high levels of digital literacy make it possible for the gig economy to thrive and be sustained in the long term. Conversely, gig economy sustainability in developing countries is usually constrained due to socioeconomic factors. Limited technology access, low digital literacy, and inadequate internet coverage do not help to build up gig platforms. The gig economy in areas with high unemployment and no formal opportunities is an ad hoc rather than sustainable employment model. The workers in these areas may depend on gig work for survival rather than for their long-term economic advancement, leading to aspirations mismatching the opportunities provided by platforms (Webb, 2022).

However, the gig economy has shown flexibility by adjusting the models to fit the contexts. In the case of Southeast Asia, for example, the likes of Gojek and Grab platforms diversify their services beyond transportation into food deliveries, financial services, and e-commerce, thereby creating a multi-faceted ecosystem that meets local needs. In Africa, companies like SweepSouth and Lynk have created marketplaces for domestic services and artisanal trades, connecting workers with demand and thus filling specific gaps in the regional labor markets. Such examples show how gig economies can be sustainable, given that they dovetail with regional economic and social dynamics (Ogunyemi, 2024). The gig economy has become a significant impetus in creating jobs in sectors that previously could not create traditional employment opportunities. They reduce barriers to entry and make work flexible; in this sense, gig platforms make it possible for all kinds of workers to enter the labor market, including delivery drivers, independent contractors for ride-hailing services, freelance writers, and software developers. Therefore, gig work has the potential to broaden the group of people who can be engaged in economic activities—to include students, retirees, and other people who would typically be excluded from formal employment (Mahato et al., 2021). Apart from job creation, the gig economy nurtures entrepreneurship by allowing workers to own businesses. For instance, independent professionals could advertise their services to a global clientele with great prospects of becoming self-employed entrepreneurs. Equally important, small independent service providers like cleaners and tutors can use platforms to access much broader clientele bases, automate their operations, and grow their businesses. This entrepreneurial feature within the gig economy not only boosts the potential for earnings at the individual level but also exerts innovation by eliciting the impetus to create new skills and services. The gig economy also does its part in fueling economic growth by enhancing productivity and efficiency. Digital platforms reduce the costs of bringing service providers together with consumers, and this optimizes resource allocation. For instance, ride-hailing platforms increase their utilization by providing a market for idle vehicles. At the same time, freelance marketplaces enable efficient matching of talent to work. This efficiency — which also raises economic value, conduces to competition, and hence brings with it the adoption of new business models — is what destroys jobs in the gig economy. All this, in turn, raises the demand for other related services, such as app development, digital marketing, and even data analytics, creating still more layers of economic activity (Ishchuk et al., 2024).

With all these pluses, the contribution of the gig economy toward creating jobs and economic growth is not without minuses. The composition of low-paid and insecure jobs in specific sectors of the gig economy points to the quality of employment that this new form of work can generate. Since many of these gig platforms are based in cities, they generate an urban bias, which may worsen regional disparities and leave rural populations underserved (Malik et al., 2021). To address these problems, more effort is needed from all stakeholders to ensure that the gig economy's growth is also inclusive. The gig economy relies heavily on digital infrastructure since this allows the platforms to connect the workers to the consumer, manage transactions, and deliver services, among other things. Therefore, investments in digital infrastructure are investments in the resilience and adaptability of gig economies. Improved internet connectivity, more widespread smartphone usage, and accessible data plans are just a few conditions for this model to maximize its potential. Equally important are digital payment systems, cloud computing, and cybersecurity measures that guarantee the functioning of gig platforms (Asfahani et al., 2023). Gig economies have enjoyed outstanding dynamism in areas with a more mature digital infrastructure. For instance, gig platforms in developed nations quickly reoriented their services toward changing demand patterns. In the process, the gig economy supported nations as they adapted to the "new normal." All of these were made possible by advanced tools and technologies in the digital space, whereby platforms could channel their operations towards the provision of such services. Hence, business continuity was sustained (Yadav, 2022). However, the gig economy's promise does not always materialize in regions hamstrung by weak digital infrastructures. For example, in areas with poor internet access or frequent power outages, the promise of workers willing to take up gigs to be done digitally cannot be realized since they would be unable to complete tasks or communicate with clients consistently. Such inefficiency, coupled with the absence of a digital mode of payment, steers away from gig platforms that could have been attractive to both consumers and producers on the platform. The way forward for governments and private sector players is to increase investments in digital infrastructure, mainly focusing on increasing broadband coverage, improving mobile network capacity, and pushing for digital literacy (Smith et al., 2021).

Partnerships between the public and private sector governments raise the primary method through which affordable Internet access can be extended to all and foster gig economies that are more robust and stress resilient. A government-tech company-non-profit collaboration may inject funds to initiate a project that provides inexpensive internet access to underserved areas or places cheap smartphones in the hands of many, supported by locally developed digital tools. The other includes the creation of regulatory environments that promote competition and innovation not only among telecommunications companies but also in the Internet Service Provider (ISP) ecosystem to drive infrastructure quality and affordability, facilitated through enhanced user experience (Longoni et al., 2024). Examples of other emerging technologies include artificial intelligence, blockchain, and the Internet of Things, enabling the gig economy to be more resilient and adaptive. Algorithms optimized with AI can improve task assignments and improve the personalization of user experiences; blockchain can bring transparency and trust to transactions made on the platform. IoT gadgets, like GPS trackers and smart sensors, render the monitoring and coordination of gig service real-time and efficient. Gig platforms should look into these technologies to create more robust and sustainable ecosystems that benefit workers, consumers, and businesses simultaneously (Sutherland et al., 2020). The long-term viability and resilience of gig economies can only be ensured if a more integrated solution between the opportunities and the challenges is achieved where policymakers create a regulatory environment that balances innovation and worker protection so that gig workers can access proper wages plus benefits and social protections. Platforms should ensure the implementation of transparent algorithms, fair pay structures, and measures to combat worker exploitation (Bieber & Moggia, 2021). Education and skills development investments are crucial for preparing workers to adjust to the gig economy. The programs include digital literacy, technical skills, and entrepreneurship, allowing employees to seize these emerging opportunities and respond to the market's changing demands. A much broader culture of learning at all ages will be essential for gig workers and how they keep up with the rapid changes in a labor market increasingly driven by technology (Abbas, 2024).

Stakeholder collaboration is critical in building resilient gig economies. Governments, platforms, worker organizations, and civil society must come together to work on systemic challenges and create inclusive gig economy ecosystems. Through stakeholder coordination to foster a structured dialogue, best practice exchange, and alignment of goals, it can be ensured that gig work continues contributing towards economic growth and social welfare (Anwar & Graham, 2021). Innovation and inclusivity must balance flexibility, fairness, and growth with equity to sustain and make gig economies adaptable. Although the gig economy has proven capable of creating jobs and being a channel for entrepreneurship while enhancing economic growth in the short run, many systemic issues regarding worker welfare, regional imbalances, and digital infrastructure must be addressed. Inclusive policy measures, significant investment in strong digital ecosystems, and more technological takeup can make gig economies fragile but also sustainable and equitable with the collective vision of this transformative force that empowers the gig economy to work for and transform global labor markets (Szostak, 2024).

THE FUTURE OF GIG ECONOMIES: OPPORTUNITIES AND CHALLENGES

The gig economy, one of the hallmarks of 21st-century labor markets, is rapidly changing. In the process, it continuously molds the global business landscape and employment parameters. Innovation and inclusivity must balance flexibility, fairness, and growth with equity to sustain and make gig economies adaptable. Although the gig economy has proven capable of creating jobs and being a channel for entrepreneurship while enhancing economic growth in the short run, many systemic issues regarding worker welfare, regional imbalances, and digital infrastructure must be addressed. Inclusive policy measures, significant investment in strong digital ecosystems, and more technological takeup can make gig economies fragile but also sustainable and equitable with the collective vision of this transformative force that empowers the gig economy to work for and transform global labor markets (Ness et al., 2023). The gig economy, one of the hallmarks of 21st-century labor markets, is rapidly changing. In the process, it continuously molds the global business landscape and employment parameters. Artificial intelligence, machine learning, and robotics will be the prime movers for developing gig platforms with increased productivity, personalization, and scalability. AI-powered systems will make it much easier to match people to tasks by breaking them down into micro-tasks. At the same time, automation will simplify the administration-related work on payments and performance ratings. These will cut the cost of operations for the platform, which can bring down consumer prices while raising the take-home pay of labor. It will slowly seep into sectors beyond those already profoundly entrenched - transportation, delivery, and freelancing. Healthcare, education, and professional services will be some sectors that are increasingly adopting gig work models. For instance, patients might increasingly find their way to freelance healthcare professionals through telemedicine platforms, and e-learning platforms might provide gig-based opportunities for tutors and educators (Ogunyemi, 2024). This diversification will open new channels for workers to commercialize their knowledge and skills, opening more active and interrelated cross-border labor markets (Li et al., 2023). The internationalization of gig economies is another long-awaited trend. As digital platforms solidify their existence on the international stage, workers worldwide will participate in the race for tasks, which will provide cross-border opportunities but also reveal conflicting perspectives of wage inequalities and unequal access to opportunities. The increase of digital nomadism and remote work is to erase more and more geographical limits by which workers may participate in gig economies from virtually any place on Earth. Such a globalized nature of gig work would drive cultural exchange and innovation while requiring a harmonized regulation package on taxation, labor standards, or data protection.

However, the increased reliance on technology and data will raise new ethical and practical questions. Algorithmic decision-making, for example, may perpetuate biases through oversight or even exclusion of some groups from opportunities. Building transparency and responsibility into such systems will help build the confidence needed and ensure that participation in the gig economy is done on equal terms. The gig economy can advance sustainable development through its potential contribution to job creation, entrepreneurship, and more inclusive economic growth (Pathiranage, 2024). Gig platforms create flexibility in jobs and provide opportunities for individuals who might face obstacles in being formally employed, such as caretakers, students, retirees, and disabled persons. This inclusiveness can also reduce unemployment and underemployment in areas lagging traditional labor markets in absorption capacities (Malik et al., 2021). In developing economies, gig work can act as the channel through which poverty alleviation is accelerated—more importantly, economic development. By allowing platforms to connect labor to global demand, foreign exchange earnings are enhanced, purchasing power increases, and local economies benefit from the spending. For example, skilled workers in developing countries can use platforms like Upwork and Fiverr to gain high-paying opportunities that may not have been available in their domestic markets. Ridesharing and delivery platforms also create income-generating opportunities for low-skilled workers to attain financial stability. Moreover, the gig economy can stimulate environmental sustainability through resource utilization and waste minimization efficiency. For example, ride-hailing services reduce emissions by promoting carpooling and cutting the number of cars on the road. Gig platforms devoted to recycling, second-hand goods, and sharing economy models also share goals for sustainable development by further promoting the principles of the circular economy. By efficiently linking supply and demand with technology, the gig economy can reduce resource inefficiencies and start-up sustainable consumption patterns (Pathiranage, 2024). Its effect on inequality is mixed. However, the gig economy has immense potential. It creates avenues for economic empowerment but, at the same time, can worsen disparities where sharing is not inclusive. For example, digital literacy and access to the internet and technology are some barriers to entry for gig work. Those living in rural or underserved areas may not have access to work from gig platforms and hence miss out on some of the gig platforms' benefits, thus widening the urban-rural divide. The other is that gig work is global: it races to the bottom, where workers from lower-income areas are offered to do the work at a lower price than their counterparts in higher-income regions. It depresses wages and the quality of jobs everywhere (Griep et al., 2024).

To achieve this potential in reducing inequality through the gig economy, concerted efforts should be channeled towards addressing the systematic barriers. Further investment in digital infrastructure, education, and skills training can cover the gap between advantaged and disadvantaged populations and create equal chances for everybody to participate in the gig economy. Specific redistributive policies, such as subsidies on internet access or programs oriented toward female and minority workers, may boost the benefits of illustrative and positive discrimination regarding inclusivity and equity. The gig economy is the machinic growth of ethical considerations and regulatory frames that will be pivotal to its development trajectory. As worker rights, income security, and social protection storm the debate about the gig economy's sustainability, most gig entrepreneurs—unlike conventional workers—fail to acquire healthcare coverage, paid leave, and an orderly retirement arrangement (Ray et al., 2024). They suffer from any rude economic jolt and uncertainty. What is needed to fill these gaps is the reimagination of labor laws and social safety nets in a manner that can adjust to the peculiarities of gig work. Governments need to balance the interests of promoting innovation and protecting workers. Regulations should guarantee a decent wage, healthy working conditions, and machinery for dispute settlement while allowing the platforms the flexibility that makes gig work attractive. For instance, providing portable benefits systems through which workers can carry their benefits across different gigs and platforms may help provide a safety net without undue harm to flexibility. The other could be setting a minimum wage level for gig workers. It would eliminate overreaching and secure some minimum baseline income security for them. Furthermore, platforms bear immense ethical responsibility in defining the future of gig work. Fair algorithms, fair pay structures, and preemptive measures against discrimination will go a long way in building trust and credibility. Platforms can go beyond mere compliance and take up voluntary standards to prioritize the well-being of workers, offering health insurance packages, training programs, and access to financial planning resources. Ethical leadership within the gig economy will create pleased workers and a strong platform reputation, leading to customer loyalty. Trade unions and worker advocacy groups will continue playing their critical function in amplifying the gig workers' voices. They have the advantage of organizing workers and pushing policymakers to undertake reforms, removing systemic challenges and injecting fairness. Multi-stakeholder initiatives — involving, for example, governments, platforms, and worker organizations — might thereby identify shared solutions that work for everyone (Tan et al., 2021).

Data privacy and security are also additional ethical considerations that will shape the future of gig economies. As platforms accumulate troves of data on workers and consumers, it is equally essential to ensure responsible use of this information. Clearly defined rules regarding ownership, consent, and data protection can shield individual privacy while opening avenues for responsible innovation to the platforms. Ethical artificial intelligence practices, such as transparency in algorithmic decision-making and avenues for redress, will also be vital in preserving fairness and the notion of responsibility (Raval, 2020). The future of gig economies is bright yet fraught—the opportunity for innovation, inclusivity, and economic growth versus risks of inequality, worker welfare, and ethical governance. This juxtaposition only sparks optimism for gig economies. As it happens, the gig economies will only be able to drive sustainable development and reduce disparities in the long run if governments, platforms, and workers take necessary actions to achieve this together with other stakeholders as gig economies evolve. It must be achieved by approaching the gig economy with proactive collaboration to address the challenges and seize the opportunities, turning them into a transformative force for good in the global labor market (Zvavahera et al., 2024; Ray et al., 2024).

CONCLUSION

Flexible and platform work defines the labor market giant in the name of the gig economy. The potential upside from massive economic inclusion and adaptability is enormous. However, it comes with risks, mainly tied to job security and social inequalities. The chapter touches on different angles of the gig economy, from its possibilities to drive sustainable development to the ethics and regulatory frameworks that guarantee fairness and resilience. Navigating towards a fairer gig economy demands knowledge about its dynamics, strong policy efforts, corporate action, and other stakeholders. The gig economy derives its strength from offering flexibility to the worker and convenience to the consumer. It's an avenue for entrepreneurship and innovation where individuals can create ways to monetize their skills and adapt to the changing economic conditions. However, gig work lacks stability since the worker has no benefits and legal protections, coupled with an uneven income. These issues make long-term sustainability quite challenging for this type of employment model. Significant challenges include the absence of social safety nets, disparities in pay, and the exploitation of marginalized groups. While technology gave way to the gig economy, it also led to concerns about algorithmic bias and market power concentration within a few platforms.

COMPETING INTEREST

Author declare no competing interest.

FUNDING STATEMENT

Author did not receive any funding.

REFERENCES

Abbas, H. (2024). The double-edged sword: Exploring the socioeconomic impact of the gig economy. *Social Science Review Archives*, *2*(1), 26–34.

Ahmed, S., & Lee, M. (2023). Human resource management in the gig economy: Challenges and opportunities. *Management Science Research Archives*, *1*(1), 60–69.

Anwar, M. A., & Graham, M. (2021). Between a rock and a hard place: Freedom, flexibility, precarity and vulnerability in the gig economy in Africa. *Competition & Change*, *25*(2), 237–258. DOI: 10.1177/1024529420914473

Asfahani, A. M., Alsobahi, G., & Dahlan, D. A. (2023). Navigating the Saudi gig economy: The role of human resource practices in enhancing job satisfaction and career sustainability. *Sustainability (Basel)*, *15*(23), 16406. DOI: 10.3390/su152316406

Atmaca, M. Ç. (2023). Passionate work ethics: Affective economy of precarity and flexibility.

Bieber, F., & Moggia, J. (2021). Risk shifts in the gig economy: The normative case for an insurance scheme against the effects of precarious work. *Journal of Political Philosophy*, *29*(3), 281–304. DOI: 10.1111/jopp.12233

Griep, Y., Bankins, S., Kraak, J. M., Sherman, U., & Hansen, S. D. (2023). Sustainable psychological contracts: A pathway for addressing precarious employment. In *Tackling precarious work* (pp. 302–324). Routledge. DOI: 10.4324/9781003440444-16

Griep, Y., Hansen, S. D., Kraak, J. M., Sherman, U., & Bankins, S. (2024). Sustainable human resource management: The good, the bad, and making it work. *Organizational Dynamics*, *101112*, 101112. Advance online publication. DOI: 10.1016/j.orgdyn.2024.101112

Hadi, A. A. W. K., & Pratono, A. H. (2024). Ethical predicaments of gig economy: Bibliometric approach. *Optimum: Jurnal Ekonomi dan Pembangunan*, 14(1), 40–48.

Huđek, I., & Širec, K. (2024). Unveiling the impact of the gig economy on sustainable development. In *International Scientific Conference ERAZ–Knowledge Based Sustainable Development* (pp. 125–133).

Ishchuk, M., Diedkov, M., Khrypko, S., Oblova, L., Binkivska, K., Syhyda, H., & Turchyn, M. (2024). Navigating precarity: Political struggles and the impact on the shadow economy. *European Journal of Sustainable Development, 13*(2), 156. DOI: 10.14207/ejsd.2024.v13n2p156

Jain, A. (2024). The gig economy: Disruption, innovation, and economic evolution. *Educational Administration: Theory and Practice, 30*(5), 5133–5140.

Kuhn, K. M., Meijerink, J., & Keegan, A. (2021). Human resource management and the gig economy: Challenges and opportunities at the intersection between organizational HR decision-makers and digital labor platforms. *Research in Personnel and Human Resources Management, 39*, 1–46. DOI: 10.1108/S0742-730120210000039001

Li, Y., Xu, S., Yu, Y., & Meadows, R. (2023). The well-being of gig workers in the sharing economy during COVID-19. *International Journal of Contemporary Hospitality Management, 35*(4), 1470–1489. DOI: 10.1108/IJCHM-01-2022-0064

Longoni, A., Salas, S., Sancha, C., Sierra, V., & Wiengarten, F. (2024). Exploring the implications of working conditions for corporate sustainability in last-mile delivery platform companies. *Journal of Business Ethics*, •••, 1–25. DOI: 10.1007/s10551-024-05840-7

Mahato, M., Kumar, N., & Jena, L. K. (2021). Re-thinking gig economy in conventional workforce post-COVID-19: A blended approach for upholding fair balance. *Journal of Work-Applied Management, 13*(2), 261–276. DOI: 10.1108/JWAM-05-2021-0037

Malik, R., Visvizi, A., & Skrzek-Lubasińska, M. (2021). The gig economy: Current issues, the debate, and the new avenues of research. *Sustainability (Basel), 13*(9), 5023. DOI: 10.3390/su13095023

Ness, I., Ovetz, R., Roque, I., Swidler, E. M., & Zwick, A. (Eds.). (2023). *The Routledge handbook of the gig economy*. Routledge.

Ogunyemi, K. (2024). Humanistic management and the gig economy: Fairness considerations. In *Humanistic management in the gig economy: Dignity, fairness and care* (pp. 1–13). Springer Nature Switzerland. DOI: 10.1007/978-3-031-59944-6_1

Pathiranage, H. S. K. (2024). Precarious employment in the gig economy: Understanding the roles of employed poor. *Open Journal of Business and Management, 12*(4), 2288–2307. DOI: 10.4236/ojbm.2024.124117

Ray, B., Sengupta, A., & Varma, A. (2024). The gig verse: Building a sustainable future. *The International Journal of Organizational Analysis*, *32*(10), 2275–2298. DOI: 10.1108/IJOA-08-2023-3946

Sankararaman, G., Rengaraju, N., Rengarajan, V., Vembu, N. R., & Indhumathi, D. (2024). Gig economy's impact on workforce dynamics and economic resilience. *Educational Administration: Theory and Practice*, *30*(6), 1627–1634.

Sihela, J., & Paulse, M. (2024). Reimagining an Ubuntu-inspired model to address precarity and vulnerability in the African gig economy. In *Humanistic Management in the Gig Economy: Dignity, Fairness and Care* (pp. 129–149). Springer Nature Switzerland. DOI: 10.1007/978-3-031-59944-6_7

Silva, M., & Nyobe, S. (2023). Social sustainability in the gig economy era: Insights from the on-demand delivery sector. *Revue Française de Gestion Industrielle*, *37*(1), 55–69. DOI: 10.53102/2023.37.01.1140

Smith, B., Goods, C., Barratt, T., & Veen, A. (2021). Consumer 'app-etite' for workers' rights in the Australian 'gig' economy. *Journal of Choice Modelling*, *38*, 100254. DOI: 10.1016/j.jocm.2020.100254

Sutherland, W., Jarrahi, M. H., Dunn, M., & Nelson, S. B. (2020). Work precarity and gig literacies in online freelancing. *Work, Employment and Society*, *34*(3), 457–475. DOI: 10.1177/0950017019886511

Szostak, M. (2024a). Balancing fairness and care through aesthetical lens in humanistic management in the gig economy. In *Humanistic Management in the Gig Economy: Dignity, Fairness and Care* (pp. 85–102). Springer Nature Switzerland. DOI: 10.1007/978-3-031-59944-6_5

Szostak, M. (2024b). Balancing fairness and care through. *Humanistic Management in the Gig Economy: Dignity, Fairness and Care*, 85.

Tan, Z. M., Aggarwal, N., Cowls, J., Morley, J., Taddeo, M., & Floridi, L. (2021). The ethical debate about the gig economy: A review and critical analysis. *Technology in Society*, *65*, 101594. DOI: 10.1016/j.techsoc.2021.101594

Tariq, M. U. (2024a). Integrating ESG principles into corporate governance for sustainable ecosystem services. In Castanho, R. (Ed.), *ESG and Ecosystem Services for Sustainability* (pp. 89–118). IGI Global., DOI: 10.4018/979-8-3693-3771-4.ch004

Tariq, M. U. (2024b). Smart transportation systems: Paving the way for sustainable urban mobility. In Munuhwa, S. (Ed.), *Contemporary Solutions for Sustainable Transportation Practices* (pp. 254–283). IGI Global., DOI: 10.4018/979-8-3693-3755-4.ch010

Tariq, M. U. (2024c). Integration of IoMT for enhanced healthcare: Sleep monitoring, body movement detection, and rehabilitation evaluation. In Liu, H., Tripathy, R., & Bhattacharya, P. (Eds.), *Clinical Practice and Unmet Challenges in AI-Enhanced Healthcare Systems* (pp. 70–95). IGI Global., DOI: 10.4018/979-8-3693-2703-6.ch004

Tariq, M. U. (2025a). The Belmont Report: Guiding ethical principles in human research. In Throne, R. (Ed.), *IRB, Human Research Protections, and Data Ethics for Researchers* (pp. 245–268). IGI Global Scientific Publishing., DOI: 10.4018/979-8-3693-3848-3.ch010

Tariq, M. U. (2025b). Africanization of research in higher education: Shaping perspectives and paradigms. In Mdikana, A. (Ed.), *Enhancing Research for Academicians in Higher Education* (pp. 101–124). IGI Global Scientific Publishing., DOI: 10.4018/979-8-3693-4496-5.ch007

Tariq, M. U., & Sergio, R. P. (2025). Ethical considerations and social impact of AI and computational intelligence in Society 5.0. In Pandey, R., Srivastava, N., Prasad, R., Prasad, J., & Garcia, M. (Eds.), *Open AI and Computational Intelligence for Society 5.0* (pp. 225–248). IGI Global Scientific Publishing., DOI: 10.4018/979-8-3693-4326-5.ch010

Warren, T. (2021). Work–life balance and gig work: 'Where are we now' and 'where to next' with the work–life balance agenda? *The Journal of Industrial Relations*, *63*(4), 522–545. DOI: 10.1177/00221856211007161

Webb, A. (2022). A trade between flexibility and security: Examining the evolution of non-standard work arrangements and ways to rebalance the position of platform workers in the labor exchange. In *Platform Labour and Global Logistics* (pp. 89–107). Routledge. DOI: 10.4324/9781003351764-9

Yadav, P. (2022). The gig and labour law reform: Balancing flexibility and workers' rights in changing employment landscape.

Zvavahera, P., Chigora, F., & Aquino, E. (2024). Location-based gig work in emerging economies: A literature review. In Ogunyemi, K. (Ed.), *Humanistic management in the gig economy: Dignity, fairness and care* (pp. 153–182). Springer Nature Switzerland., DOI: 10.1007/978-3-031-59944-6_8

KEY TERMS AND DEFINITIONS

Diversity: The state of being diverse.

Flexibility: The ability of being changed or to change based on the situation.

Gig: A job, mainly one that is not permanent and done on an informal or on-demand base.

Inclusion: The act of including someone.

Compilation of References

Aayog, N. I. T. I. (2022). Policy brief: India's booming gig and platform economy. National Institution for Transforming India. https://www.niti.gov.in/sites/default/files/2022-06/Policy_Brief_India%27s_Booming_Gig_and_Platform_Economy_27062022.pdf

Abbas, H. (2024). The double-edged sword: Exploring the socioeconomic impact of the gig economy. *Social Science Review Archives*, *2*(1), 26–34.

Abdullah, N., Mohd Ismail, M., Huzni Murad, M. S., Jusoff, K., Kurniawan, F., & Salah, M. (2024). Critical Insights into Gig Economy: A Peninsular Malaysia Case Study. *Jambe Law Journal*, *7*(2), 395–427. DOI: 10.22437/home.v7i2.460

Abdulmatin, A. L., Makhija, G., Bhandari, G. B., Raj, H., & Shylashree, N. (2025). Hiring and Keeping Talent in a Time of Transformation and Staff Empowerment. In *Innovative Recruitment and Retention for Employee Empowerment* (pp. 211–242). IGI Global Scientific Publishing., DOI: 10.4018/979-8-3693-6602-8.ch008

Abkhezr, P., & McMahon, M. (2024). The intersections of migration, app-based gig work, and career development: Implications for career practice and research. *International Journal for Educational and Vocational Guidance*, *24*(1), 39–57. DOI: 10.1007/s10775-022-09556-w PMID: 35755081

Abraham, K. G., Haltiwanger, J., Sandusky, K., & Spletzer, J. (2019). The rise of the gig economy: Fact or fiction? *AEA Papers and Proceedings. American Economic Association*, *109*, 357–361. DOI: 10.1257/pandp.20191039

Abraham, M., Kinne, J., Klotz, J., & Winker, P. (2022). The evolution of gig work: From simple tasks to complex professional services. *Labour Economics*, *75*, 102102. DOI: 10.1016/j.labeco.2022.102102

Acemoglu, D., & Restrepo, P. (2019). Automation and new tasks: How technology displaces and reinstates labor. *The Journal of Economic Perspectives*, *33*(2), 3–30. DOI: 10.1257/jep.33.2.3

Acuna-Choque, K., Bazan-Joaquin, B., Malvaceda-Espinoza, E. L., & Monroy-Valasco, I. R. (2023). Social Representations of Migration Among Venezuelan Immigrants Residing in Metropolitan Lima, Peru. *Migraciones Internacionales, 14*(11), 1–21. DOI: 10.33679/rmi.v1i1.2568

Adamovic, M. (2022). How does employee cultural background influence the effects of telework on job stress? The roles of power distance, individualism, and beliefs about telework. *International Journal of Information Management, 62*, 102437. DOI: 10.1016/j.ijinfomgt.2021.102437

Adula, M., Kant, S., Badi, S., & Kumari, M. (2025). Abusive Work Environment Effect on Female Entrepreneurs' Emotional Wellbeing by Mediation of Social and Moral Values in the Horn of Africa. In *Supporting Psychological and Emotional Wellbeing Among Entrepreneurs* (pp. 1-22). IGI Global. DOI: DOI: 10.4018/979-8-3693-3673-1.ch001

Agarwal, R., Kumar, T., Singh, A., & Schutte, D. P. (2025). Empowering Indigenous Economies: Financial and Investment Prediction for Sustainable Development. In Irfan, M., Majeed, M., Kassim, S., & Ofori, K. (Eds.), *The Future of Indigenous Inclusivity: Unlocking Finance for Economic Development* (pp. 63–82). IGI Global Scientific Publishing., DOI: 10.4018/979-8-3693-7924-0.ch004

Agbanyo, G. K., & Shi, M. (2024). The Moderating Effect of Management Polychronicity and Knowledge Sharing on Career Sustainability in the Work-from-Anywhere New Normal—From a Social Exchange Theory Perspective. *Sustainability (Basel), 16*(8), 3302. DOI: 10.3390/su16083302

Agrawal, A., Kumar, T., Agarwal, R., & Gupta, A. (2024), "AI-Driven Personalized Risk Management in the Insurance Sector", Taneja, S., Kumar, P., Reepu, Kukreti, M. and Özen, E. (Ed.) Data Alchemy in the Insurance Industry, Emerald Publishing Limited, Leeds, pp. 27-39. DOI: 10.1108/978-1-83608-582-920241006

Agyemang, G., Dhanani, A., Ejiogu, A. R., & Perkiss, S. (2024). Researching race, accounting and accountability: Past, present and future. *Accounting, Auditing & Accountability Journal, 37*(7/8), 1637–1664. DOI: 10.1108/AAAJ-03-2024-6976

Ahmad, A. A., & Norzaidi, N. H. R. (2024). Adapting to Technological Transformations: Jobs and Skills in Malaysia's Evolving Work Landscape. In *Islamic Finance: New Trends in Law and Regulation* (pp. 527–538). Springer. DOI: 10.1007/978-3-031-48770-5_42

Ahmed, S., & Lee, M. (2023). Human resource management in the gig economy: Challenges and opportunities. *Management Science Research Archives, 1*(1), 60–69.

Airbnb Incorporations. (2022). *Annual Report 2022*.

Alanzi, T. M. (2021). Gig Health vs eHealth: Future Prospects in Saudi Arabian Health-Care System. *Journal of Multidisciplinary Healthcare*, *14*, 1945–1953. DOI: 10.2147/JMDH.S304690 PMID: 34326645

Ali, K. T. M., & Sivasubramanian, R. C. (2024). *Understanding the Nexus Between Techno-Stress, Psychological Well-Being, and the Moderating Role of Job Resources in the Gig Economy*. Employ Respons Rights J., DOI: 10.1007/s10672-024-09505-5

Allen, A. (2010). Neither Rural nor Urban: Service Delivery Options That Work for the Peri-urban Poor. *Peri-Urban Water and Sanitation Services: Policy, Planning and Method*, 27–61. DOI: 10.1007/978-90-481-9425-4_2

allRiDi. (2023a). *allRiDi Fulfilment*.https://af.allridi.com/

allRiDi. (2023b). *Getting a fare estimate*.https://help.allridi.com/support/solutions/articles/47001079281-getting-a-fare-estimate

Aloisi, A. (2019). Negotiating the digital transformation of work: non-standard workers' voice, collective rights and mobilization practices in the platform economy. https://cadmus.eui.eu/bitstream/handle/1814/63264/MWP_Aloisi_2019_03.pdf?sequence=1&isAl

Alsos, K., & Dolvik, J. E. (2021). *The Future of Work in the Nordic Countries: Opportunities and Challenges for the Nordic Model*. Nordic Council of Ministers., https://pub.norden.org/temanord2021-520/temanord2021-520.pdf

Altenried, M. (2020). The platform as a factory: Crowdwork and the hidden labor behind artificial intelligence. *Capital and Class*, *44*(2), 145–158. DOI: 10.1177/0309816819899410

Altenried, M. (2024). Mobile workers, contingent labour: Migration, the gig economy and the multiplication of labour. *Environment & Planning A*, *56*(4), 1113–1128. DOI: 10.1177/0308518X211054846

Altenried, M. (2024). Mobile workers, contingent labour: Migration, the gig economy and the multiplication of labour. *Environment and Planning A. Economy and Space*, *56*(4), 1113–1128. DOI: 10.1177/0308518X23121071234

Anatol, M. (2023). An Examination of the Vulnerable Venezuelan Population in Trinidad and Tobago: Some Considerations. In Wallace, W. C. (Ed.), *The Movement of Venezuelans to the Americas and the Caribbean in the 21st Century* (pp. 271–285). Palgrave Macmillan., DOI: 10.1007/978-3-031-31762-0_14

Anatol, M., Roberts-Kasmally, K. A., & de Gourville, D. (2023). The Impact of Venezuelan Migration on Trinidad and Tobago. In *The Caribbean Social Justice Agenda* (pp. 33–61). Rowman & Littlefield.

Andersen, M., & Spanger, M. (2024). Gig work in transnational spaces: Infrastructures of migration and the simultaneous lives of migrants in the gig economy. *Journal of Ethnic and Migration Studies*, *50*(15), 3751–3767. DOI: 10.1080/1369183X.2024.2379643

Andersen, M., Zampoukos, K., Spanger, M., & Mitchell, D. (2024). At your service: The mobilities, rhythms and everyday lives of migrant labour in the gig economy. *Journal of Ethnic and Migration Studies*, *50*(15), 3733–3750. DOI: 10.1080/1369183X.2024.2379641

Androff, D., & Mathis, C. (2021). Human Rights-Based Social Work Practice with Immigrants and Asylum Seekers in a Legal Service Organization. *Journal of Human Rights and Social Work*, *26*(7), 178–188. DOI: 10.1007/s41134-021-00197-7 PMID: 34722859

Anitha, K., & Amala, J. (2025). Future of Work: Generations and Retaining Talent Focus. In *Modern Trends and Future Innovation in Human Resource Management* (pp. 239–258). IGI Global., DOI: 10.4018/979-8-3693-6402-4.ch008

Annett, M. (2020). Understanding the Homepreneurship Opportunities Afforded by Social Networking and Personal Fabrication Technologies. *Proceedings of the ACM on Human-Computer Interaction*, *4*(CSCW2), 1–48. DOI: 10.1145/3415170

Ansell, C., Sørensen, E., & Torfing, J. (2022). *Co-creation for sustainability: The UN SDGs and the power of local partnerships*. Emerald Publishing.

Anwar, M. A., & Graham, M. (2020). Between a rock and a hard place: Freedom, flexibility, precarity and vulnerability in the gig economy in Africa. *Competition & Change*, *25*(2), 237–258. DOI: 10.1177/1024529420914473

Anwar, M. A., & Graham, M. (2020). Hidden transcripts of the gig economy: Labor agency and the new art of resistance among African gig workers. *Environment and Planning A. Economy and Space*, *52*(7), 1269–1291. DOI: 10.1177/0308518X19894584

Arriagada, A., Bonhomme, M., Ibanez, F., & Leyton, J. (2023). The gig economy in Chile: Examining labor conditions and the nature of gig work in a Global South country. *Digital Geography and Society*, *100063*, 1–6. DOI: 10.1016/j.diggeo.2023.100063

Arroyo, L. (2020). Implications of digital inclusion: Digitalization in terms of time use from a gender perspective. *Social Inclusion (Lisboa)*, *8*(2), 180–189. Advance online publication. DOI: 10.17645/si.v8i2.2546

Arruda, M. D. S. (2023). Pro-immigrant digital platforms in Portugal: An overview. *E-Journal of International and Comparative Labour Studies, 12*(1), 1–17.

Asad, S. A., Banerjee, R., & Bhattacharya, J. (2023). Do workers discriminate against their out-group employers? Evidence from an online platform economy. *Journal of Economic Behavior & Organization, 216*, 221–242. DOI: 10.1016/j.jebo.2023.10.002

Asadullah, M., & Persson, S. (2024). *The Working Conditions of Couriers and Their Performance and Well-being : A Case of Food Delivery Companies in Sweden.* https://urn.kb.se/resolve?urn=urn:nbn:se:sh:diva-54971

Asenjo Cruz, A., Coddou Mc Manus, A., & Dhir, R. K. (2023). *The platform economy and transformations in the world of work: The case of delivery platform workers in Santiago, Chile.* Working Paper, 100: 1-70. Geneva, Switzerland: International Labor Organization (ILO). DOI: 10.54394/JCVG2192

Asfahani, A. M., Alsobahi, G., & Dahlan, D. A. (2023). Navigating the Saudi gig economy: The role of human resource practices in enhancing job satisfaction and career sustainability. *Sustainability (Basel), 15*(23), 16406. DOI: 10.3390/su152316406

Ashford, S. J., Caza, B. B., & Reid, E. M. (2018). From surviving to thriving in the gig economy: A research agenda for individuals in the new world of work. *Research in Organizational Behavior, 38*, 23–41. DOI: 10.1016/j.riob.2018.11.001

Asian Productivity Organization (APO). (2019). *Nepal's Gig Economy and its Implications on Labor Participation and Income Distribution.* APO.

Atlantis Press. (2024). Gig workers in the digital era in Indonesia: Development, vulnerability, and welfare.DOI: 10.2991/978-94-6463-525-6_6

Atmaca, M. Ç. (2023). Passionate work ethics: Affective economy of precarity and flexibility.

Augustinraj, R., Jain, V., & Bansal, S. (2021). *Unlocking the Potential of the Gig Economy in India.*

Autor, D. H. (2015). Why are there still so many jobs? The history and future of workplace automation. *The Journal of Economic Perspectives, 29*(3), 3–30. DOI: 10.1257/jep.29.3.3

Axelrad, H., Kalev, A., & Lewin-Epstein, N. (2023). Ambivalent Bias at Work: Managers' Perceptions of Older Workers across Organizational Contexts. *Work, Employment and Society*. Advance online publication. DOI: 10.1177/09500170231175790

Ayala-López, S., & Beeghly, E. (2020). Explaining injustice: Structural analysis, bias, and individuals. In *An introduction to implicit bias* (pp. 211–232). Routledge. DOI: 10.4324/9781315107615-11

Azevedo, E. S. F., Souza, D. F., & Mendonca, J. R. C. (2023). Algorithmic management on digital labor platforms: A Systematic Literature Review. *Contextus - Contemporary Journal of Economics and Management,* 21 (e83099): 1-14. DOI: 10.19094/contextus.2023.83099

Bajwa, U., Gastaldo, D., Di Ruggiero, E., & Knorr, L. (2018). The health of workers in the global gig economy. *Globalization and Health, 14*(1), 124. Advance online publication. DOI: 10.1186/s12992-018-0444-8 PMID: 30563539

Bajwa, U., Knorr, L., Di Ruggiero, E., Gastaldo, D., & Zendel, A. (2018). Towards an understanding of workers' experiences in the global gig economy. *Globalization and Health, 14*(124), 2–4.

Baker, A. C., Larcker, D. F., McCLURE, C. G., Saraph, D., & Watts, E. M.BAKER. (2024). Diversity Washing. *Journal of Accounting Research, 62*(5), 1661–1709. DOI: 10.1111/1475-679X.12542

Bakker, A. B., & Demerouti, E. (2024). Job demands–resources theory: Frequently asked questions. *Journal of Occupational Health Psychology, 29*(3), 188–200. DOI: 10.1037/ocp0000376 PMID: 38913705

Banerjee, D. (2024). Caste, gig-economy, and youth: The resurgence of a new caste politics in urban Gujarat. *South Asian History and Culture, 15*(2), 1–16. DOI: 10.1080/19472498.2024.2346867

Banik, N., & Padalkar, M. (2021). The spread of gig economy: Trends and effects. *Форсайт.* Retrieved from https://cyberleninka.ru

Banik, N., & Padalkar, M. (2021). The spread of the gig economy: Trends and effects. *Форсайт, 15*(1, 1 (eng)), 19–29. DOI: 10.17323/2500-2597.2021.1.19.29

Bansal, R., Singh, R., & Gandhi, M. (2020). *The emergence of gig economy in India: A paradigm shift.* Parishodh Journal.

Barbu, E., & Song, X. (2016). The effects of offshoring on employer-provided training. *The Journal of International Trade & Economic Development, 25*(4), 479–503. https://doi.org/https://doi.org/ 10.1080/09638199.2015.1068838. DOI: 10.1080/09638199.2015.1068838

Bari, M. W., & Di Virgilio, F. (Eds.). (2025). *Handbook of Talent Management and Learning Organizations: A Post-Pandemic Perspective*. CRC Press., DOI: 10.1201/9781003429890

Bates, O., Lord, C., Alter, H., & Kirman, B. (2020, June). Let's start talking the walk: Capturing and reflecting on our limits when working with gig economy workers. In *Proceedings of the 7th International Conference on ICT for Sustainability* (pp. 227–235). DOI: 10.1145/3401335.3401364

Bathini, D. R. (2021). GIG Workers in The Platform Economy: The Case of App-Based Cab Companies In India.

Batmunkh, A., Fekete-Farkas, M., & Lakner, Z. (2022). Bibliometric analysis of gig economy. *Administrative Sciences*, *12*(2), 1–15. https://doi.org/https://doi.org/10.3390/admsci12020051. DOI: 10.3390/admsci12020051

BCG. (2021). Unlocking the potential of the gig economy in India. https://www.bcg.com/en-in/unlocking-gigeconomy-in-india

Behera, B., & Gaur, M. (2022). Skill training for the success of the gig economy. *Journal of Pharmaceutical Negative Results*, *13*(5), 2835–2840.

Behl, A., Rajagopal, K., Sheorey, P., & Mahendra, A. (2022). Barriers to entry of gig workers in the gig platforms: Exploring the dark side of the gig economy. *Aslib Journal of Information Management*, *74*(5), 818–839. DOI: 10.1108/AJIM-08-2021-0235

Behrendt, C., Nguyen, Q. A., & Rani, U. (2019). Social protection systems and the future of work: Ensuring social security for digital platform workers. *International Social Security Review*, *72*(3), 17–41. DOI: 10.1111/issr.12212

Belleflamme, P., & Peitz, M. (2021). *The economics of platforms*. Cambridge University Press. DOI: 10.1017/9781108696913

Benach, J., & Muntaner, C. (2007). Precarious employment and health: Developing a research agenda. *Journal of Epidemiology and Community Health*, *61*(4), 276–277. DOI: 10.1136/jech.2005.045237 PMID: 17372284

Bérastégui, P. (2021). Exposure to psychosocial risk factors in the gig economy: a systematic review. *ETUI Research Paper-Report*.

Berg, J., Furrer, M., Harmon, E., Rani, U., & Silberman, M. S. (2018). Digital labour platforms and the future of work. *Towards decent work in the online world. Rapport de l'OIT*. https://www.ilo.org/publications/digital-labour-platforms-and-future-work-towards-decent-work-online-world

Berger, T., Frey, C. B., Levin, G., & Danda, S. R. (2019). Is Uber happy? Work and well-being in the 'Gig Economy'. *Economic Policy*, *34*(99), 429–477. Advance online publication. DOI: 10.1093/epolic/eiz007

Berhane, Y. (2024). *Enhancing Social Protection for Migrant Workers: Challenges and Strategies in the East and Horn of Africa*. Geneva, Switzerland: International Labor Organization (ILO).

Bernard, S. (2023). *UberUsés: Le capitalisme racial de plateforme à Paris*. Puf.

Betten, L. (1995). *The Employment Contract in Transforming Labour Relations*. 1–202.

Bhandari, B., Das, G. K., Gupta, S., Sahu, A. K., Urs, K. S., Pal, N., & Raj, K. (2023). Socio-economic impact assessment of food delivery platform workers.DOI: 10.13140/RG.2.2.14642.17605

Bieber, F., & Moggia, J. (2021). Risk shifts in the gig economy: The normative case for an insurance scheme against the effects of precarious work. *Journal of Political Philosophy*, *29*(3), 281–304. DOI: 10.1111/jopp.12233

Biegon, C. K. (2023). *Blockchain-based Ride-sharing Model With Decentralized Governance* (Doctoral dissertation, University of Nairobi).

Blanco, J. P., Windisch, E., Perkins, S., Ito, A., & Leape, J. (2022). Decarbonising Transport in Latin American Cities: A Review of Policies and Key Challenges. DOI: 10.18235/0003987

Bonhomme, M., & Muldoon, J. (2024). Racism and food delivery platforms: Shaping migrants' work experiences and future expectations in the United Kingdom and Chile. *Ethnic and Racial Studies*, •••, 1–24. DOI: 10.1080/01419870.2024.2349268

Bonhomme, M., Ustek-Spilda, F., & Arriagada, A. (2024). Between acceptance and resistance: Conceptualising migrant platform labour agency in Chile. *New Technology, Work and Employment*, •••, 1–19. DOI: 10.1111/ntwe.12308

Borghi, P., & Murgia, A. (2024). Beyond borders: Trans-organisational and transnational alliances among gig workers in the United Kingdom and Italy. *The Journal of Industrial Relations*, *66*(3), 410–433. DOI: 10.1177/00221856241238617

Boulding, K. (2021). *The meaning of the twentieth century: The great transition*. Routledge. DOI: 10.4324/9781003256960

Bourdieu, P. (2018). The forms of capital. In *The sociology of economic life* (pp. 78–92). Routledge., DOI: 10.4324/9780429494338-6

Brailovskaya, V. (2023). Digital Labor Gig Economy from the Worker's Perspective: A Literature.

Brailovskaya, V. (2023). Digital Labor Gig Economy From the Worker's Perspective: A Literature. https://www.idinsight.org/wp-content/uploads/2024/01/PUBLIC-Digital-Labor-Gig-Economy-From-the-Workers-Perspective_-A-Literature-Review-.pdf

Brathwaite, C. (2021). *The gig economy in the Caribbean.* Bridgetown, Barbados: Barbados Today. https://barbadostoday.bb/2021/10/15/btcolumn-the-gig-economy-in-the-caribbean/

Bricka, T. M., & Schroeder, A. N. (2019). What's the gig deal? Examining contemporary work issues in the gig economy. *Industrial and Organizational Psychology: Perspectives on Science and Practice*, *12*(4), 491–494. DOI: 10.1017/iop.2019.116

Bruckner, C. L., & Forman, J. B. (2021). Women, Retirement, and the Growing Gig Economy Workforce. *Ga. St. UL Rev.*, *38*, 259.

Brummer, C., & Strine, L. E.Jr. (2022). Duty and diversity. *Vand. L. Rev.*, *75*, 1.

Buchak, G. (2023). Financing the Gig Economy. *The Journal of Finance*, *79*(1), 219–256. DOI: 10.1111/jofi.13292

Bunel, M., & Tovar, E. (2021). Profit, morality and discrimination. *Applied Economics*, *53*(40), 4692–4712. DOI: 10.1080/00036846.2021.1907285

Bunjack, A., Cerne, M., & Popovic, A. (2021). Absorbed in technology but digitally overloaded: Interplay effects on gig worker's burnout and creativity. *Information & Management,* 58(8-103533):1-12. DOI: 10.1016/j.im.2021.103533

Bush, J. T., & Balven, R. M. (2019). Catering to the crowd: An HRM perspective on crowd worker engagement. Human Resource Management Review.110.1016/j.hrmr.2018.10.003

Bushe, B. (2019). The causes and impact of business failure among small to micro and medium enterprises in South Africa. *Africa's Public Service Delivery and Performance Review*, *7*(1). Advance online publication. DOI: 10.4102/apsdpr.v7i1.210

Bush, J. T., & Balven, R. M. (2021). Catering to the crowd: An HRM perspective on crowd worker engagement. *Human Resource Management Review*, *31*(1), 100670. DOI: 10.1016/j.hrmr.2018.10.003

Byrne, Z. S. (2022). *Understanding employee engagement: Theory, research, and practice*. Routledge. DOI: 10.4324/9781003171133

Cahn, N., Carbone, J., & Levit, N. (2019). Discrimination by Design? *Arizona State Law Journal, 51*(1), 1–70. https://scholarship.law.umn.edu/cgi/viewcontent.cgi?article=1632&context=faculty_articles

Caligiuri, M. D., & Jolly, P. M. (2023). Workforce diversity and management in the hospitality industry: An equal employment opportunity and affirmative action perspective. In *The Routledge Handbook of Diversity, Equity, and Inclusion Management in the Hospitality Industry* (pp. 157–165). Routledge. ISSN 9781000963007

Caligiuri, P. M., & Stroh, L. K. (1995). Multinational corporation management strategies and international human resources practices: Bringing IHRM to the bottom line. *International Journal of Human Resource Management, 6*(3), 494–507. DOI: 10.1080/09585199500000032

Cameron, L. D. (2024, April 3). How gig work pits customers against workers. *Harvard Business Review.*https://hbr.org/2024/04/how-gig-work-pits-customers-against-workers0.1111/ntwe.12310

Campana, P. (2022). *Online and technology-facilitated trafficking in human beings.* Council of Europe.

Cant, C. (2019). *Riding for Deliveroo: Resistance in the New Economy.* Polity.

Cao, J. (2021, December). Research on Development and Optimization of Human Resources in Gig Economy. In 2021 4th International Conference on Humanities Education and Social Sciences (ICHESS 2021) (pp. 1288-1298). Atlantis Press.

Caribbean, D. R. O. P. (2024a). *We Are Now Distance and Time Fares.*https://dropcaribbean.com/distance-and-time-fares/

Caribbean, D. R. O. P. (2024b). *More than food delivery.* https://dropcaribbean.com/fooddrop/

Carter, B. (2021). Impact of social inequalities and discrimination on vulnerability to crises. DOI: 10.19088/K4D.2021.049

Cascio, W. F., & Shurygailo, S. (2003). E-leadership and virtual teams. *Organizational Dynamics, 31*(4), 362–376. DOI: 10.1016/S0090-2616(02)00130-4

Cassell, M. K., & Deutsch, A. M. (2023). Urban Challenges and the Gig Economy: How German Cities Cope with the Rise of Airbnb. *German Politics, 32*(2), 319–340. DOI: 10.1080/09644008.2020.1719072

Caza, B. B., Reid, E. M., Ashford, S. J., & Granger, S. (2021). Working on my own: Measuring the challenges of gig work. *Human Relations.* Advance online publication. DOI: 10.1177/00187267211030098

Celestin, M., & Vanitha, N. (2021). The gig economy and its effects on personal finance. *Indo American Journal of Multidisciplinary Research and Review*, *5*(2), 39–46.

Chaffey, D., & Patron, M. (2012). From web analytics to digital marketing optimization: Increasing the commercial value of digital analytics. *Journal of Direct, Data and Digital Marketing Practice*, *14*(1), 30–45. DOI: 10.1057/dddmp.2012.20

Charles, R. N. (2008). *Motivation and job satisfaction: The implications of context and national culture in Grenada, St. Vincent & the Grenadines and St. Lucia.* Nova Southeastern University.https://www.proquest.com/openview/5d7a46f357157 06c2f9673dcd97f6cbe/1?pq-origsite=gscholar&cbl=18750

Charlton, E. (2021). *What is the gig economy and what's the deal for gig workers?* Geneva, Switzerland: World Economic Forum (WEF).

Charlton, E. (2024). *What is the gig economy and what's the deal for gig workers?* Geneva, Switzerland: World Economic Forum (WEF).

Chen, J. (2024). Are we only all by ourselves? A double-level perspective to cope with the insecurity of the nonstandard gig work model. *International Journal of Manpower*, *45*(4), 733–753. DOI: 10.1108/IJM-05-2023-0231

Chen, J. Y. (2018). Thrown under the bus and outrunning it! The logic of Didi and taxi drivers' labour and activism in the on-demand economy. *New Media & Society*, *20*(8), 2691–2711. DOI: 10.1177/1461444817729149

Chen, J. Y., & Qiu, J. L. (2019). Digital utility: Datafication, regulation, labor, and DiDi's Platformization of urban transport in China. *Chinese Journal of Communication*, *12*(3), 274–289. DOI: 10.1080/17544750.2019.1614964

Chen, T., Song, W., Song, J., Ren, Y., Dong, Y., Yang, J., & Zhang, S. (2022). Measuring Well-Being of Migrant Gig Workers: Exampled as Hangzhou City in China. *Behavioral Sciences (Basel, Switzerland)*, *12*(365), 1–29. DOI: 10.3390/bs12100365 PMID: 36285934

Chen, Y. (2018). Blockchain tokens and the potential democratization of entrepreneurship and innovation. *Business Horizons*, *61*(4), 567–575. DOI: 10.1016/j.bushor.2018.03.006

Cherry, M. A. (2022). Employee Status for" Essential Workers": The Case for Gig Worker Parity. *Loy. LAL Rev.*, *55*, 683.

Chigori, D. T. (2024). Worker well-being in the digital economy: Lens through bibliometrics analysis. *SA Journal of Human Resource Management*, 22(0), a2773:1-11. DOI: 10.4102/sajhrm.v22i0.2773

Chitranshi, J., & Chopra, K. (2023). AI Driven Quick delivery services in India and Employee wellbeing challenges. *Proceedings of 2023 IEEE Technology and Engineering Management Conference - Asia Pacific, TEMSCON-ASPAC 2023*. DOI: 10.1109/TEMSCON-ASPAC59527.2023.10531469

Choudhari, R. (2020). COVID 19 pandemic: Mental health challenges of internal migrant workers of India. *Asian Journal of Psychiatry*, *54*, 102254. Advance online publication. DOI: 10.1016/j.ajp.2020.102254 PMID: 32593122

Choudhary, V., & Shireshi, S. S. (2022). Analysing the Gig Economy in India and Exploring Various Effective Regulatory Methods to Improve the Plight of the Workers. *Journal of Asian and African Studies*, *57*(7), 1343–1356. DOI: 10.1177/00219096221082581

Christiaens, T. (2022). *Digital working lives: Worker autonomy and the gig economy*. Rowman & Littlefield. DOI: 10.5771/9781538173749

Cilliers, J. (2021). The future of work in Africa. *The Future of Africa: Challenges and Opportunities*, 195-219. DOI: 10.1007/978-3-030-46590-2_9

Cini, L., Maccarrone, V., & Tassinari, A. (2022). With or without U(nions)? Understanding the diversity of gig workers' organizing practices in Italy and the UK. *European Journal of Industrial Relations*, *28*(3), 341–362. DOI: 10.1177/09596801211052531

Civelek, M. E. (2018). Essentials of Structural Equation Modeling. In *Zea Books*. Issue March., DOI: 10.13014/K2SJ1HR5

Cobb, A., Mohan, A., Harper, C. D., Nock, D., & Michalek, J. (2024). Ride-hailing technology mitigates effects of driver racial discrimination, but effects of residential segregation persist. *Proceedings of the National Academy of Sciences of the United States of America*, *121*(41), e2408936121. DOI: 10.1073/pnas.2408936121 PMID: 39348538

Codagnone, C., Abadie, F., & Biagi, F. (2016). The Future of Work in the 'Sharing Economy'. Market Efficiency and Equitable Opportunities or Unfair Precarisation? SSRN *Electronic Journal*. https://doi.org/DOI: 10.2139/SSRN.2784774

Connelly, B. L., Certo, S. T., Ireland, R. D., & Reutzel, C. R. (2011). Signaling theory: A review and assessment. *Journal of Management*, *37*(1), 39–67. DOI: 10.1177/0149206310388419

Cook, C., Diamond, R., Hall, J. V., List, J. A., & Oyer, P. (2021). The gender earnings gap in the gig economy: Evidence from over a million rideshare drivers. *The Review of Economic Studies*, *88*(5), 2210–2238. DOI: 10.1093/restud/rdaa081

Coplan, J., Crocker, L., Landin, J., & Stenn, T. (2021). Building supportive, inclusive workplaces where neurodivergent thinkers thrive: Approaches in managing diversity, inclusion, and building entrepreneurship in the workplace. *S.A.M. Advanced Management Journal*, *86*(1), 21–30. DOI: 10.52770/XTBM1097

Cornelissen, J. (2016). Editor's Comments: Developing Propositions, a Process Model, or a Typology? Addressing the Challenges of Writing Theory Without a Boilerplate. Https://Doi.Org/10.5465/Amr.2016.0196, *42*(1), 1–9. DOI: 10.5465/amr.2016.0196

Costa, E. (2024). Examining the effectiveness of interventions to reduce discriminatory behavior at work: An attitude dimension consistency perspective. *The Journal of Applied Psychology*, *109*(11), 1669–1692. DOI: 10.1037/apl0001215 PMID: 39207374

Cranston, S., & Duplan, K. (2023). Infrastructures of migration and the ordering of privilege in mobility. *Migration Studies*, *11*(2), 330–348. DOI: 10.1093/migration/mnad001

Cropanzano, R., Keplinger, K., Lambert, B. K., Caza, B., & Ashford, S. J. (2023). The organizational psychology of gig work: An integrative conceptual review. *The Journal of Applied Psychology*, *108*(3), 492–519. DOI: 10.1037/apl0001029 PMID: 36222635

Da Silva, A. N. R., Pitombo, C. S., Junior, J. U. P., Ciriaco, T. G. M., & Costa, C. S. (2023). Changes in mobility and challenges to the transport sector in Brazil due to COVID-19. In Zhang, J., & Hayashi, Y. (Eds.), *Transportation Amid Pandemics* (pp. 105–118). Elsevier., DOI: 10.1016/B978-0-323-99770-6.00010-7

Dargay, J. M., & Clark, S. (2012). The determinants of long-distance travel in Great Britain. *Transportation Research Part A, Policy and Practice*, *46*(3), 578–587. DOI: 10.1016/j.tra.2011.11.016

Datta, N., Rong, C., Singh, S., Stinshoff, C., Iacob, N., Nigatu, N. S., Nxumalo, M., & Klimaviciute, L. (2023). Working Without Borders: The Promise and Peril of Online Gig Work. Washington DC, United States: World Bank (WB).

Datta, N., Rong, C., Singh, S., Stinshoff, C., Iacob, N., Nigatu, N. S., Nxumalo, M., & Klimaviciute, L. (2023). Working Without Borders: The Promise and Peril of Online Gig Work. Washington DC, United States: World Bank (WB). DOI: 10.1596/40066

Daugareilh, I., Degryse, C., & Pochet, P. (Eds.). (2019). *The platform economy and social law: Key issues in comparative perspective* (ETUI Working Paper 2019.10). ETUI.

Dauth, T., Schmid, S., Baldermann, S., & Orban, F. (2023). Attracting talent through diversity at the top: The impact of TMT diversity and firms' efforts to promote diversity on employer attractiveness. *European Management Journal, 41*(1), 9–20. DOI: 10.1016/j.emj.2021.10.007

Davenport, T. H., Guha, A., Grewal, D., & Bressgott, T. (2020). How artificial intelligence will change the future of marketing. *Journal of the Academy of Marketing Science, 48*(1), 24–42. DOI: 10.1007/s11747-019-00696-0

De Angelis, M., Donà, S., & Bergamante, F. (2023). Algorithmic Discriminations and New Forms of Protections: An Analysis of the Italian Case. *Social Sciences (Basel, Switzerland), 12*(9), 503. DOI: 10.3390/socsci12090503

De Stefano, V. (2015). The Rise of the "Just-in-Time Workforce": On-Demand Work, Crowd Work and Labour Protection in the "Gig-Economy." SSRN *Electronic Journal*. DOI: 10.2139/ssrn.2682602

De Stefano, V. (2015). The Rise of the "Just-in-Time Workforce": On-Demand Work, Crowd Work and Labour Protection in the "Gig-Economy." SSRN *Electronic Journal*. https://doi.org/DOI: 10.2139/SSRN.2682602

De Stefano, V., & Taes, S. (2023). Algorithmic management and collective bargaining. *Transfer: European Review of Labour and Research, 29*(1), 21–36. DOI: 10.1177/10242589221141055

Deakins, O. (2019, October 24). New legislation in Italy to boost delivery riders' rights. International Employment Update. https://ogletree.com/international-employment-update/articles/november-2019/italy/2019-10-24/new-legislation-in-italy-to-boost-delivery-riders-rights/

Debgupta, I., & Bhattacharyya, S. (2024). Talent Acquisition and Retention in the Gig Economy: Exploring Innovative HRM Practices for the Modern Workforce. *Journal ofResearch in Business and Management, 12*(1), 84–90. www.questjournals.org. DOI: 10.1108/S0742-730120210000039001

Deci, E. L., & Ryan, R. M. (2013). *Intrinsic motivation and self-determination in human behavior*. Springer Science & Business Media., DOI: 10.1007/978-1-4899-2271-7

Dekker, S. (2021). Compliance capitalism: How free markets have led to unfree, overregulated workers. *Compliance Capitalism: How Free Markets Have Led to Unfree, Overregulated Workers*, 1–190. https://doi.org/DOI: 10.4324/9781003177807/COMPLIANCE-CAPITALISM-SIDNEY-DEKKER/ACCESSIBILITY-INFORMATION

Della Longa, L., Valori, I., & Farroni, T. (2022). Interpersonal affective touch in a virtual world: Feeling the social presence of others to overcome loneliness. *Frontiers in Psychology*, *12*, 795283. DOI: 10.3389/fpsyg.2021.795283 PMID: 35087455

Deloitte. (2024). Gig workforce: Talent management strategy. Deloitte. Retrieved from https://www2.deloitte.com/content/dam/Deloitte/in/Documents/human capital/in-hc-gig-workforce-talent-management-strategy-noexp.pdf

Deming, D. J. (2017). The growing importance of social skills in the labor market. *The Quarterly Journal of Economics*, *132*(4), 1593–1640. DOI: 10.1093/qje/qjx022

Di Gangi, P. M., Howard, J. L., McAllister, C. P., & Thatcher, J. B. (2024). The Influence of Political Skill and Community Capabilities on Microtask Worker Hourly Wage: A Mixed Methods Study of Mechanical Turk. *Journal of the Association for Information Systems*, *25*(4), 890–935. DOI: 10.17705/1jais.00858

Di Tella, R., & Rodrik, D. (2020). Labor Market Shocks and the Demand for Trade Protection: Evidence from Online Surveys. *Economic Journal (London)*, *130*(628), 1008–1030. DOI: 10.1093/ej/ueaa006

Dobbin, F., & Kalev, A. (2022). *Getting to diversity: What works and what doesn't.* Harvard University Press.

Docquier, F. (2014). The brain drain from developing countries. *IZA World of Labor: Evidence-Based Policy Making*, *31*, 1–10. DOI: 10.15185/izawol.31

Doherty, M., & Franca, V. (2020). The (non/) response of trade unions to the "gig" challenge. *Italian Labor Law E-Journal,* 13(1):125-140. DOI: 10.6092/issn.1561-8048/10762

Donovan, S. A., Bradley, D. H., & Shimabukuro, J. O. (2016). *What Does the Gig Economy Mean for Workers?* Dubal, V. (2017). The Drive to Precarity: A Political History of Work, Regulation, & Labor Advocacy in San Francisco's Taxi & Uber Economies. *Berkeley Journal of Employment and Labor Law*, *38*(1), 73–136.

Doon, R. (2023). The Struggle for Venezuelan Migrant Integration into Trinidad and Tobago's Labor Market. In *The Palgrave Handbook of Global Social Problems* (pp. 1–29). Palgrave Macmillan., DOI: 10.1007/978-3-030-68127-2_404-1

Doon, R. (2024). The Impact of Climate Change on the Vulnerability of Venezuelan Migrants to Human Trafficking in Trinidad and Tobago. In *The Palgrave Handbook of Global Social Change* (pp. 1–28). Palgrave Macmillan., DOI: 10.1007/978-3-030-87624-1_413-1

Duffy, B. E., & Schwartz, B. (2018). Digital "women's work?": Job recruitment ads and the feminization of social media employment. *New Media & Society*, *20*(8), 2972–2989. DOI: 10.1177/1461444817738237

Duggan, J., Sherman, U., Carbery, R., & McDonnell, A. (2020). Algorithmic management and app-work in the gig economy: A research agenda for employment relations and HRM. *Human Resource Management Journal*, *30*(1), 114–132. DOI: 10.1111/1748-8583.12258

Dunn, M. (2020). Making gigs work: Digital platforms, job quality and worker motivations. *New Technology, Work and Employment*, *35*(2), 232–249. https://doi.org/https://doi.org/10.1111/ntwe.12167. DOI: 10.1111/ntwe.12167

Dwivedi, P., Chaturvedi, V., & Vashist, J. K. (2023). Innovation for organizational sustainability: The role of HR practices and theories. *The International Journal of Organizational Analysis*, *31*(3), 759–776. DOI: 10.1108/IJOA-07-2021-2859

Earley, P. C., & Ang, S. (2003). *Cultural intelligence: Individual interactions across cultures*. Stanford University Press., DOI: 10.1515/9780804766005

Economic Commission for Latin America and the Caribbean and the International Labor Organization (ECLAC & ILO). (2021). *Employment Situation in Latin America and the Caribbean, Decent Work for Platform Workers in Latin America*. ILO.

Economic Commission for Latin America and the Caribbean and the International Labor Organization (ECLAC-ILO). (2021). *Employment Situation in Latin America and the Caribbean. Decent Work for Platform Workers in Latin America*. ECLAC-ILO.

Efobi, U., Beecroft, I., & Osabuohien, E. (2018). Digital inclusion, financial inclusion and the adoption of mobile money in Nigeria. *Technology in Society*, *55*, 36–46. DOI: 10.1016/j.techsoc.2018.06.010

Efthymiou, I. (2024). Exploring the frontier: New and future trends in research. In B. Orlando (Ed.), *Innovation capabilities and entrepreneurial opportunities of smart working* (pp. 48–68). IGI Global. DOI: 10.4018/978-1-7998-8797-3.ch003

Efthymiou, I. P., Egleton, T. E., & Psomiadi, A. (2025). The Role of Artificial Intelligence in Humanitarian Aid for Achieving Sustainable Development Goals. In *Cases on AI-Driven Solutions to Environmental Challenges* (pp. 43–72). IGI Global Scientific Publishing., DOI: 10.4018/979-8-3693-7483-2.ch003

Elayan, M. B. (2022). Transformation of Human Resources Management Solutions as a strategic tool for GIG workers contracting. In *IGI Global eBooks* (pp. 790–813). DOI: 10.4018/978-1-6684-4503-7.ch039

Emerson, E., Fortune, N., Llewellyn, G., & Stancliffe, R. (2021). Loneliness, social support, social isolation and wellbeing among working age adults with and without disability: Cross-sectional study. *Disability and Health Journal*, *14*(1), 100965. DOI: 10.1016/j.dhjo.2020.100965 PMID: 32843311

Emery, M., & Flora, C. (2020). Spiraling-up: Mapping community transformation with community capitals framework. In *50 Years of Community Development Vol I* (pp. 163-179). Routledge.

Erez, M. (2011). Cross-cultural and global issues in organizational psychology. In S. Zedeck (Ed.), *APA handbook of industrial and organizational psychology, Vol. 3. Maintaining, expanding, and contracting the organization* (pp. 807–854). American Psychological Association. DOI: 10.1037/12171-023

ESCAP, U. (2021). Review of developments in transport in Asia and the Pacific 2021: towards sustainable, inclusive and resilient urban passenger transport in Asian cities.

Estlund, C. (2023). Sectoral Solutions That Work: The Case for Sectoral Co-Regulation. *Chicago-Kent Law Review*, *98*, •••. https://heinonline.org/HOL/Page?handle=hein.journals/chknt98&id=549&div=27&collection=journals

EU-OSHA. (2022). *Italy: A national and local answer to the challenges of the platform economy*. Retrieved from https://osha.europa.eu/sites/default/files/2022-02/A_national_local_answer_challenges_platform_economy_Italy.pdf

Eurofound. (2018). Employment and working conditions of selected types of platform work. Publications Office of the European Union. https://www.eurofound.europa.eu/en/publications/2018/employment-and-working-conditions-selected-types-platform-work

Eurofound. (2024). Riders Union Bologna. https://apps.eurofound.europa.eu/platformeconomydb/riders-union-bologna-103125

Eurofound. (2024, December). *Riders x Derechos (Riders for Rights)*. Platform Economy Database. Retrieved from https://apps.eurofound.europa.eu/platformeconomydb/riders-x-derechos-riders-for-rights-103036

European Commission. (2021, December 9). *Commission proposes measures to improve working conditions of people working through digital labour platforms*. https://ec.europa.eu/commission/presscorner/detail/en/ip_21_6605

European Commission. (2022, May 11). Smart Coop. European Social Fund Plus. https://european-social-fund-plus.ec.europa.eu/en/social-innovation-match/case-study/smart-coop

European Commission. Directorate-General for Communications Networks, Content and Technology, *Study on "Support to the observatory for the online platform economy" – Final report*, Publications Office, 2021, https://data.europa.eu/doi/10.2759/801457

European Parliament. (2019, April 4). Gig economy: How the EU improves platform workers' rights. European Parliament. https://www.europarl.europa.eu/topics/en/article/20190404STO35070/gig-economy-how-the-eu-improves-platform-workers-rights

Fair Work Ombudsman. (n.d.). Employee-like workers. Fair Work Ombudsman. Retrieved from https://www.fairwork.gov.au/find-help-for/independent-contractors/regulated-workers/employee-like-workers

Fairwork. (2023a). *The Mobilities of Gig Work in Colombia, Fairwork Colombia Ratings 2023.* Oxford, United Kingdom: Oxford, Internet Institute.

Fairwork. (2023b). *Labor Standards in the Platform Economy, Fairwork Peru Ratings 2023.* Oxford, United Kingdom: Oxford, Internet Institute.

Fairwork. (2024). *Labour Standards in the Platform Economy, Fairwork Chile Ratings 2024.* Oxford, United Kingdom: Oxford, Internet Institute.

Fan, Z., Wang, Y., & Ying, Z. (2023). Empowerment of Cross-Border E-Commerce Platforms for Small and Medium-Sized Enterprises: Evidence from China. *Journal of Business-To-Business Marketing*, *30*(1), 33–44. DOI: 10.1080/1051712X.2023.2175633

Farbenblum, B., Berg, L., & Kintominas, A. (2018). *Transformative Technology for Migrant Workers - Opportunities, Challenges, and Risks.* https://papers.ssrn.com/abstract=3295430

Fibbi, R., Midtbøen, A. H., & Simon, P. (2021). *Migration and discrimination: IMISCOE short reader.* Springer Nature. DOI: 10.1007/978-3-030-67281-2

Finch, J., & Groves, D. (Eds.). (2022). *A labour of love: Women, work and caring.* Taylor & Francis. DOI: 10.4324/9781003303930

Fitzgerald, K. J. (2023). *Recognizing race and ethnicity: Power, privilege, and inequality* (4th ed.). Routledge., DOI: 10.4324/9781003359852

Fiverr. (2024). *Find the right freelance service, right away.* https://www.fiverr.com/

Fiverr. (2024). *Find the right freelance service, right away.* Tel Aviv, Israel: Fiverr. https://www.fiverr.com/

Flanagan, F. (2018). Theorising the gig economy and home-based service work. Https://Doi.Org/10.1177/0022185618800518, *61*(1), 57–78. DOI: 10.1177/0022185618800518

Florisson, R., & Mandl, I. (2018). Platform work: Types and implications for work and employment—Literature review. Eurofound. https://apo.org.au/node/201491

Flynn, C. (2023, March 23). How Assembly Bill 5 (AB5) affects independent contractors in 2022. Hackler Flynn & Associates. https://hacklerflynnlaw.com/how-assembly-bill-5-ab5-will-affect-independent-contractors/

Food Depot. (2024). *Ordering groceries for delivery from local stores.* https://fooddepottt.com/

Forde, C., Stuart, M., Joyce, S., Oliver, L., Valizade, D., Alberti, G., . . . Carson, C. (2017). The social protection of workers in the platform economy. Retrieved from https://www.europarl.europa.eu/RegData/etudes/STUD/2017/614184/IPOL_STU(2017)614184_EN.pdf

Francisco, M. P., Hartman, M., & Wang, Y. (2020). Inclusion and Special Education. *Education Sciences*, *10*(9), 238. DOI: 10.3390/educsci10090238

Franklin, R. C. (2021). Black workers in Silicon Valley: Macro and micro boundaries. *Ethnic and Racial Studies*, *45*(1), 69–89. DOI: 10.1080/01419870.2020.1866208

Freelance Latin America. (2023). *About Us.* Florida, United States: Freelance Latin America. https://freelancelatam.com/about-us/

Freeman, R. E., Dmytriyev, S. D., & Phillips, R. A. (2021). Stakeholder Theory and the Resource-Based View of the Firm. *Journal of Management*, *47*(7), 1757–1770. Advance online publication. DOI: 10.1177/0149206321993576

Frey, B. (2020). Platform Labor and In/Formality: Organization among Motorcycle Taxi Drivers in Bandung, Indonesia. *Anthropology of Work Review*, *41*(1), 36–49. DOI: 10.1111/awr.12187

Friedman, G. (2014). Workers without employers: Shadow corporations and the rise of the gig economy. *Review of Keynesian Economics*, *2*(2), 171–188. DOI: 10.4337/roke.2014.02.03

Fulmer, I. S., Gerhart, B., & Kim, J. H. (2023). Compensation and performance: A review and recommendations for the future. *Personnel Psychology*, *76*(2), 687–718. DOI: 10.1111/peps.12583

Ganapathy, V., Gupta, C., & Arora, R. (2024). Digital Transformation of Grocery Delivery Services in India. In *Technological Innovations in the Food Service Industry* (pp. 1–22). IGI Global. DOI: 10.4018/979-8-3693-7683-6.ch001

Gandini, A. (2016). *The reputation economy: Understanding knowledge work in digital society*. Palgrave Macmillan., DOI: 10.1057/978-1-137-56107-7

Ganesh, A. (2020). The Gig Economy: An HR Perspective to Managing Platform Workers.https://www.researchgate.net/publication/338987209_The_Gig_Economy_An_HR_Perspective_to_Managing_Platform_Workers

Gautam, V., Mishra, A. A., & Maheshwari, M. (2024). Examining the relevance of Human Resource Management in gig work: A systematic literature review & research agenda. *German Journal of Human Resource Management, 23970022241231536*(4), 375–412. Advance online publication. DOI: 10.1177/23970022241231536

Ghosh, A., Ramachandran, R., & Zaidi, M. (2021). Women Workers in the Gig Economy in India: An Exploratory Study. SSRN *Electronic Journal*. https://doi.org/DOI: 10.2139/SSRN.3944205

Ghosh, A., Maeder, A., Baker, M., & Chandramouli, D. (2019). 5G Evolution: A View on 5G Cellular Technology Beyond 3GPP Release 15. *IEEE Access : Practical Innovations, Open Solutions*, *7*, 127639–127651. DOI: 10.1109/ACCESS.2019.2939938

Ghosh, A., Ramachandran, R., & Zaidi, M. (2021). Women workers in the gig economy in India: An exploratory study. Available at *SSRN* 3944205.

Gillis, K., & Kallenbach, S. R. (2019). Gig Workers. Who are they and What do they Want? *LIMRA Secure Retirement Institute Review*, *2*, 1–11.

Giousmpasoglou, C., Ladkin, A., & Marinakou, E. (2024). Worker exploitation in the gig economy: The case of dark kitchens. *Journal of Hospitality and Tourism Insights*, *7*(1), 414–435. DOI: 10.1108/JHTI-10-2022-0477

Glazer, S., Kożusznik, M. W., & Shargo, I. A. (2012). Global virtual teams: A cure for–or a cause of–stress. In *The role of the economic crisis on occupational stress and well-being* (pp. 213–266). Emerald Group Publishing Limited., DOI: 10.1108/S1479-3555(2012)0000010010

Gobierno de España. (2021). *Ley 12/2021, de 28 de septiembre, de medidas urgentes para la regulación del trabajo en plataformas digitales. Boletín Oficial del Estado.* https://www.boe.es/buscar/doc.php?id=BOE-A-2021-15548

Gojeck, (2023). *About us.* Singapore: Gojeck. https://www.gojek.com/sg/about

Gokhale Institute of Politics and Economics. (n.d.). Gig economy workers' livelihood: A qualitative study of ride-hailing platforms in Bangalore city, India. Retrieved from https://gipe.ac.in/gig-economy-workers-livelihood-a-qualitative-study-of-ride-hailing-platforms-in-bangalore-city-india/

Gonzalez, B. N. (2021). Employment Classification and Human Dignity in the Gig Economy. *Thomas L. Rev.*, *34*, 52.

Grab. (2024). *From essential services to earning opportunities. We're an all-in-one platform.* Singapore: Grab. https://www.grab.com/sg/

Graham, M., & Ferrari, F. (Eds.). (2022). *Digital work in the planetary market.* Mit Press. DOI: 10.7551/mitpress/13835.001.0001

Graham, M., Hjorth, I., & Lehdonvirta, V. (2017). Digital labour and development: Impacts of global digital labour platforms and the gig economy on worker livelihoods. *Transfer: European Review of Labour and Research*, *23*(2), 135–162. DOI: 10.1177/1024258916687250 PMID: 28781494

Graham, M., Lehdonvirta, V., Wood, A., Barnard, H., Hjorth, I., & Simon, D. P. (2017). *The Risks and Rewards of Online Gig Work at the Global Margins.* Oxford Internet Institute, University of Oxford.

Graham, M., & Woodcock, J. (2018). Towards a fairer platform economy: Introducing the Fairwork Foundation. *Alternate Routes*, *29*, 242–253.

Granovetter, M. S. (1973). The strength of weak ties. *American Journal of Sociology*, *78*(6), 1360–1380. DOI: 10.1086/225469

Gregory, K. (2021). 'My Life Is More Valuable Than This': Understanding Risk among On-Demand Food Couriers in Edinburgh. *Work, Employment and Society*, *35*(2), 316–331. DOI: 10.1177/0950017020969593

Griep, Y., Bankins, S., Kraak, J. M., Sherman, U., & Hansen, S. D. (2023). Sustainable psychological contracts: A pathway for addressing precarious employment. In *Tackling precarious work* (pp. 302–324). Routledge. DOI: 10.4324/9781003440444-16

Griep, Y., Hansen, S. D., Kraak, J. M., Sherman, U., & Bankins, S. (2024). Sustainable human resource management: The good, the bad, and making it work. *Organizational Dynamics*, *101112*, 101112. Advance online publication. DOI: 10.1016/j.orgdyn.2024.101112

Griesbach, K., Reich, A., Elliott-Negri, L., & Milkman, R. (2019). Algorithmic Control in Platform Food Delivery Work. *Socius: Sociological Research for a Dynamic World*, *5*, 1–15. DOI: 10.1177/2378023119870041

Griffen, Z. W. (2024). The economization of early life: Human capital theory, biology, and social policy. *Science, Technology & Human Values*, *49*(1), 175–205. . DOI: 10.1177/01622439221147701

Groenewald, E., Groenewald, C. A., Kilag, O. K., Andrin, G., Pernites, M. J., & Macapaz, M. K. (2024). Talent Management in the 21st Century: A Comprehensive Review and Prospects for Innovation. *International Multidisciplinary Journal of Research for Innovation, Sustainability, and Excellence (IMJRISE), 1*(3), 93-99. https://risejournals.org/index.php/imjrise/article/view/188

Hadi, A. A. W. K., & Pratono, A. H. (2024). Ethical predicaments of gig economy: Bibliometric approach. *Optimum: Jurnal Ekonomi dan Pembangunan*, 14(1), 40–48.

Hadiati, D., Budiono, A. R., & Widhiyanti, H. N. (2023). Legal Relationship Between Platform Service Providers and Online Transportation Drivers as Gig Workers (Platform Workers). *International Journal of Islamic Education. Research and Multiculturalism*, *5*(3), 751–771. DOI: 10.47006/ijierm.v5i3.276

Hafeez, S., Gupta, C., & Sprajcer, M. (2022). Stress and the gig economy: It's not all shifts and giggles. *Industrial Health*, *4*(61), 140–150. DOI: 10.2486/indhealth.2021-0217 PMID: 35249894

Hagiu, A., & Wright, J. (2019). The status of workers and platforms in the sharing economy. *Journal of Economics & Management Strategy*, *28*(1), 97–108. DOI: 10.1111/jems.12299

Håkansta, C., Gunn, V., Kreshpaj, B., Matilla-Santander, N., Wegman, D. H., Hogstedt, C., Vignola, E. F., Muntaner, C., Bodin, T., O'Campo, P., & Lewchuk, W. (2024). What is the Role of Minimum Wages in Addressing Precarious Employment in the Informal and Formal Sectors? Findings from a Systematic Review. *International Journal of Social Determinants of Health and Health Services*, 27551938241286463. Advance online publication. DOI: 10.1177/27551938241286463 PMID: 39370929

Hall, E. T. (1976). *Beyond culture*. Anchor Books.

Halliday, D. (2021). On the (mis)classification of paid labor: When should gig workers have employee status? *Politics, Philosophy & Economics*, *20*(3), 229–250. DOI: 10.1177/1470594X211015467

Hall, J. V., & Krueger, A. B. (2018). An analysis of the labor market for Uber's driver-partners in the United States. *Industrial & Labor Relations Review*, *71*(3), 705–734. DOI: 10.1177/0019793917717222

Haneefa, K. V. (2024). Quick Commerce in the Quantum Age. In *The Quantum AI Era of Neuromarketing* (pp. 403–428). IGI Global Scientific Publishing., DOI: 10.4018/979-8-3693-7673-7.ch017

Hanelt, A., Bohnsack, R., Marz, D., & Marante, C. A. (2021). A Systematic Review of the Literature on Digital Transformation: Insights and Implications for Strategy and Organizational Change. *Journal of Management Studies*, *58*(5), 1159–1197. DOI: 10.1111/joms.12639

Haque, F., & Dard, A. R. (2023). New Face of Job Quality Challenge in India: Gig Worker Studies. *Journal of Indonesian Applied Economics*, *11*(1), 101–109. DOI: 10.21776/ub.jiae.2017.011.01.8

Hara, H. (2014). The impact of firm-provided training on productivity, wages, and transition to regular employment for workers in flexible arrangements. *Journal of the Japanese and International Economies*, *34*, 336–359. DOI: 10.1016/j.jjie.2014.10.002

Hardy, T., & McCrystal, S. (2022). The importance of competition and consumer law in regulating gig work and beyond. *The Journal of Industrial Relations*, *64*(5), 785–800. DOI: 10.1177/00221856211068868

Harms, P. D., & Han, G. (2019). Algorithmic leadership: The future is now. *Journal of Leadership Studies*, *12*(4), 74–75. DOI: 10.1002/jls.21615

Harpur, P., & Blanck, P. (2020). Gig Workers with Disabilities: Opportunities, Challenges, and Regulatory Response. *Journal of Occupational Rehabilitation*, *30*(4), 511–520. DOI: 10.1007/s10926-020-09937-4 PMID: 33146784

Hart, J., & Pomponi, F. (2021). A Circular Economy: Where Will It Take Us? *Circular Economy and Sustainability*, *1*(1), 127–141. DOI: 10.1007/s43615-021-00013-4 PMID: 34888551

Hauben, H., Lenaerts, K., & Waeyaert, W. (2020). *The platform economy and precarious work*. Publication for the Committee on Employment and Social Affairs, Policy Department for Economic, Scientific and Quality of Life Policies, European Parliament.

Healy, J., Pekarek, A., & Vromen, A. (2020). Sceptics or supporters? Consumers' views of work in the gig economy. *New Technology, Work and Employment*, *35*(1), 1–19. DOI: 10.1111/ntwe.12157

Heeks, R. (2017). Decent Work and the Digital Gig Economy: A Developing Country Perspective on Employment Impacts and Standards in Online Outsourcing, Crowdwork, Etc. SSRN *Electronic Journal*. DOI: 10.2139/ssrn.3431033

Heeks, R. (2021). *From Digital Divide to Digital Justice in the Global South: Conceptualizing Adverse Digital Incorporation.* 1st Virtual Conference on Implications of Information and Digital Technologies for Development, Conference Proceedings, arXiv preprint arXiv, 776(2108.09783): 1-11. DOI: 10.2139/ssrn.3907633

Heeks, R., Graham, M., Mungai, P., Van Belle, J. P., & Woodcock, J. (2021). Systematic evaluation of gig work against decent work standards: The development and application of the Fairwork framework. *The Information Society*, *37*(5), 267–286. DOI: 10.1080/01972243.2021.1942356

Hernandez, R. H., Song, Q., Kou, Y., & Gui, X. (2024, May). "At the end of the day, I am accountable": Gig workers' self-tracking for multi-dimensional accountability management. In *Proceedings of the CHI Conference on Human Factors in Computing Systems* (pp. 1–20). DOI: 10.1287/isre.2019.0896

Himani Srihita, R., Goli, G., M, R., & Gobinath, R. (2025). Transformative dynamics of the gig economy: Technological impacts, worker well-being and global research trends. *International Journal of Engineering Business Management*, *17*, 18479790241310362. Advance online publication. DOI: 10.1177/18479790241310362

Hobfoll, S. E., Halbesleben, J., Neveu, J. P., & Westman, M. (2018). Conservation of resources in the organizational context: The reality of resources and their consequences. *Annual Review of Organizational Psychology and Organizational Behavior*, *5*(1), 103–128. DOI: 10.1146/annurev-orgpsych-032117-104640

Hofstede, G. (1980). *Culture's consequences: International differences in work-related values.* Sage Publications., DOI: 10.1002/job.4030030208

Hofstede, G., & Bond, M. H. (1988). The Confucius connection: From cultural roots to economic growth. *Organizational Dynamics*, *16*(4), 4–21. DOI: 10.1016/0090-2616(88)90009-5

Hofstede, G., Hofstede, G. J., & Minkov, M. (2010). *Cultures and Organizations: Software of the Mind* (Rev. 3rd ed.). McGraw-Hill., DOI: 10.1002/hrdq.3920040314

Holliman, G., & Rowley, J. (2014). Business to business digital content marketing: Marketers' perceptions of best practice. *Journal of Research in Interactive Marketing*, *8*(4), 269–293. DOI: 10.1108/JRIM-02-2014-0013

Horton, J. J. (2017). The effects of algorithmic labor market recommendations: Evidence from a field experiment. *Journal of Labor Economics*, *35*(2), 345–385. DOI: 10.1086/689213

House, R. J., Hanges, P. J., Javidan, M., Dorfman, P. W., & Gupta, V. (Eds.). (2004). *Culture, leadership, and organizations: The GLOBE study of 62 societies*. Sage., DOI: 10.5465/ame.2005.16965495

Howcroft, D., & Bergvall-Kåreborn, B. (2019). A typology of crowdwork platforms. *Work, Employment and Society*, *33*(1), 21–38. DOI: 10.1177/0950017018760136

Howson, K., Ustek-Spilda, F., Grohmann, R., Salem, N., Carellim, R., Abs, D., Salvagni, J., Graham, M., Balbornoz, M. B., Chavez, H., Arriagada, A., & Bonhomme, M. (2020). 'Just because you don't see your boos, doesn't mean you don't have a boss': Covid-19 and Gig Worker Strikes across Latin America. *International Union Rights*, *27*(3), 20–28. DOI: 10.1353/iur.2020.a838172

Hsieh, J., Adisa, O., Bafna, S., & Zhu, H. (2023, June). *Designing Individualized Policy and Technology Interventions to Improve Gig Work Conditions*. In, *Proceedings of the 2nd Annual Meeting of the Symposium on Human-Computer Interaction for Work*, Oldenburg, Germany, 1-9. DOI: 10.1145/3596671.3598576

Huang, H. (2023). Algorithmic management in food-delivery platform economy in China. *New Technology, Work and Employment*, *38*(2), 185–205. DOI: 10.1111/ntwe.12228

Huang, X., Sun, Z., Li, J., & Li, J. (2024). Will Fun and Care Prevent Gig Workers' Withdrawal? A Moderated Mediation Model. *Asia Pacific Journal of Human Resources*, *62*(4), e12425. Advance online publication. DOI: 10.1111/1744-7941.12425

Huđek, I., & Širec, K. (2024). Unveiling the impact of the gig economy on sustainable development. In *International Scientific Conference ERAZ–Knowledge Based Sustainable Development* (pp. 125–133).

Huđek, I., & Širec, K. (2024). Unveiling the Impact of the Gig Economy on Sustainable Development. In *International Scientific Conference ERAZ–Knowledge Based Sustainable Development* (pp. 125-133).

Hunt, A., & Machingura, F. (2016). A good gig? The rise of on-demand domestic work. [London, UK: Overseas Development Institute] [ODI]. *Working Paper*, *7*, 1–44.

IBEF Report. (2021, May 21). *Emergence of India's Gig Economy*. IBEF. Accessed on Aug 24, 2024

Indian Institute of Technology Delhi. (2024). IIT Delhi study on gig workers. Retrieved from https://home.iitd.ac.in/show.php?id=209&in_sections=Press

Inter-Agency Coordination Platform for Refugees and Migrants from Venezuela. (R4V). (2024c). *RMRP 2025-2026, Regional Refugee and Migrant Response Plan (RMRP).*https://www.r4v.info/sites/g/files/tmzbdl2426/files/2024-12/RMRP_25-26_VF.pdf

Inter-Agency Coordination Platform for Refugees and Migrants. (R4V). (2023). *Regional Refugee and Migrant Response Plan (RMRP) 2024.* https://www.r4v.info/sites/g/files/tmzbdl2426/files/2024-04/RMRP%202024_WEB.pdf

Inter-Agency Coordination Platform for Refugees and Migrants. (R4V). (2024a). *May-June 2024 Situation Report Caribbean Sub Regional Platform.*https://www.r4v.info/sites/g/files/tmzbdl2426/files/2024-10/May-June%20Situation%20Report%20-%20Caribbean.pdf

Inter-Agency Coordination Platform for Refugees and Migrants. (R4V). (2024b). *Refugees and Migrants From Venezuela.*https://www.r4v.info/en/refugeeandmigrants

International Labor Organization (ILO). (2021). *World Employment and Social Outlook. The Role of digital labor platforms in transforming the world of work.* ILO.

International Labor Organization (ILO). (2023). *Digital platforms for domestic and care work in Latin America.* ILO.

International Labor Organization (ILO). International Social Security Association (ISSA), & (OCED). (2023). *Providing adequate and sustainable social protection for workers in the gig and platform economy.* Geneva, Switzerland: ILO.

International Labour Organization (ILO). (2022). *Meeting of experts on decent work in the platform economy.* Retrieved from https://www.ilo.org/meetings-and-events/meeting-experts-decent-work-platform-economy

International Labour Organization. (2018). *Digital labour platforms and the future of work: Towards decent work in the online world.* Retrieved from https://www.ilo.org/sites/default/files/wcmsp5/groups/public/%40dgreports/%40dcomm/%40publ/documents/publication/wcms_645337.pdf

International Labour Organization. (2021). *The role of digital labour platforms in transforming the world of work.* https://www.ilo.org/publications/flagship-reports/role-digital-labour-platforms-transforming-world-work

International Labour Organization. (2021). *World employment and social outlook: The role of digital labor platforms in transforming the world of work.*https://www.ilo.org/wcmsp5/groups/public/---dgreports/---dcomm/---publ/documents/publication/wcms_771749.pdf

International Organization for Migration (IOM). (2019). *Monitoring Migrants Presence: Trinidad and Tobago*. Geneva, Switzerland: United Nations High Commissioner for Refugees (UNHCR). https://data.unhcr.org/ar/documents/download/75687

Irwin, J. L. (2022). *Leveraging Local Workforce Systems to Better Serve Workers and Improve Job Quality A Case Study and Complex Systems Analysis* (Doctoral dissertation, The Pardee RAND Graduate School).

Ishchuk, M., Diedkov, M., Khrypko, S., Oblova, L., Binkivska, K., Syhyda, H., & Turchyn, M. (2024). Navigating precarity: Political struggles and the impact on the shadow economy. *European Journal of Sustainable Development, 13*(2), 156. DOI: 10.14207/ejsd.2024.v13n2p156

Jaakkola, E. (2020). *Designing conceptual articles: four approaches*. DOI: 10.1007/s13162-020-00161-0

Jabłoński, A., & Jabłoński, M. (2020). Social factors as a basic driver of the digitalization of business models. *Sustainability, 12*(9), 3940. DOI: 10.3390/su12093940

Jaffe, S. (2021). *Work won't love you back: How devotion to our jobs keeps us exploited, exhausted, and alone*. Bold Type Books.

Jain, M. (2024). In Context of Uber BV v. Aslam in London ([2021] WLR (D) 108): Do Uber Drivers Work for Uber as Employees or as Independent Contractors? *Justice and Law Bulletin, 3*(1), 7-19.

Jain, A. (2024). The gig economy: Disruption, innovation, and economic evolution. *Educational Administration: Theory and Practice, 30*(5), 5133–5140.

Jain, A. (2024). The Gig Economy: Disruption, Innovation, and Economic Evolution. *Educational Administration: Theory and Practice, 30*(5), 5133–5140.

Janssens, M., & Zanoni, P. (2021). Making diversity research matter for social change: New conversations beyond the firm. *Organization Theory, 2*(2), 26317877211004603.

Jarrahi, M. H., Newlands, G., Lee, M. K., Wolf, C. T., Kinder, E., & Sutherland, W. (2021). Algorithmic management in a work context. *Big Data & Society, 8*(2), 20539517211020332. Advance online publication. DOI: 10.1177/20539517211020332

Jarrahi, M. H., Sutherland, W., Nelson, S. B., & Sawyer, S. (2020). Platformic Management, Boundary Resources for Gig Work, and Worker Autonomy. *Computer Supported Cooperative Work, 29*(1-2), 153–189. DOI: 10.1007/s10606-019-09368-7

Jarvenpaa, S. L., & Leidner, D. E. (1999). Communication and trust in global virtual teams. *Organization Science, 10*(6), 791–815. DOI: 10.1287/orsc.10.6.791

Jiang, Z., & Hu, X. (2016). Knowledge Sharing and Life Satisfaction: The Roles of Colleague Relationships and Gender. *Social Indicators Research, 126*(1), 379–394. DOI: 10.1007/s11205-015-0886-9

Johnston, H., & Land-Kazlauskas, C. (2018). *Organizing On-Demand Representation, Voice, and Collective Bargaining in the Gig Economy*. International Labour Organization.

Jonas Frödin, O. (2024). Cognitive microfoundations and social interaction dynamics. The implications of complexity for institutional theory. *Theory and Society, 53*(5), 1019–1047. DOI: 10.1007/s11186-024-09574-3

Jones, P. (2021). *Work without the worker: Labour in the age of platform capitalism*. Verso Books.

Kadolkar, I., Kepes, S., & Subramony, M. (2024). Algorithmic management in the gig economy: A systemic review and research integration. *Journal of Organizational Behavior*, •••, 1–24. DOI: 10.1002/job.2831

Kalbalia, P., Nath, N. J., & Haneefa, K. V. (2024). Utilisation and Accessibility of Healthcare Services Among Gig Workers: A Systematic Review. *Population. Environmental Disease*, •••, 77–95. DOI: 10.1007/978-3-031-67624-6_5

Kalli, N. K. A., Abba, N. Y. B., & Bukar, N. G. (2023). An assessment of the effect of training and development on employee performance: A review perspective. *World Journal of Advanced Research and Reviews, 18*(2), 258–270. DOI: 10.30574/wjarr.2023.18.2.0748

Kang, H., & Shen, J. (2013). International recruitment and selection practices of South Korean multinationals in China. *International Journal of Human Resource Management, 24*(17), 3325–3342. DOI: 10.1080/09585192.2013.770777

Kant, S., Adula, M., Kumari, M., & Nimbrain, N. (2025). Role of SMEs in Greening the Economy by Mediation of Eco-Innovation in the Horn of Africa. In *Examining Green Human Resources Management and Nascent Entrepreneurship* (pp. 173–200). IGI Global., DOI: 10.4018/979-8-3693-7046-9.ch007

Kaplan, A. M., & Haenlein, M. (2010). Users of the world, unite! The challenges and opportunities of social media. *Business Horizons, 53*(1), 59–68. DOI: 10.1016/j.bushor.2009.09.003

Karanovic, J., Altman, E. J., & Cennamo, C. (2023). Who should price a gig? *MIT Sloan Management Review, 65*(1), 62–67.

Kasliwal, R. (2020). *Gender and the Gig Economy: A Qualitative Study of Gig Platforms for Women Workers INtrODUctION: GIG EcONOMY AND GENDEr IssUEs*.

Kasliwal, R. (2020). Gender and the Gig Economy: A Qualitative Study of Gig Platforms for Women Workers. *ORF. Issue Brief*, *359*, 1–14.

Kässi, O., & Lehdonvirta, V. (2018). Online labour index: Measuring the online gig economy for policy and research. *Technological Forecasting and Social Change*, *137*, 241–248. DOI: 10.1016/j.techfore.2018.07.056

Katta, S., Howson, K., & Graham, M. (2020). The Fairwork Foundation: Action research on the gig economy. *Global Dialogue*, *10*(1), 44–46.

Katz, L. F., & Krueger, A. B. (2019). The Rise and Nature of Alternative Work Arrangements in the United States, 1995–2015. *Industrial & Labor Relations Review*, *72*(2), 382–416. DOI: 10.1177/0019793918820008

Kavese, K., & Mbali, A. (2022). The Gig Economy, Digital Labor Platforms and Independent Employment in the Eastern Cape. Vincent, London: Eastern Cape Socioeconomic Consultative Council (ECSECC).

Keegan, A., & Meijerink, J. (2022). HRM practices for value creation and value capture in online labor platform ecosystems: towards an integrative perspective. In *A Research Agenda for Strategic Human Resource Management* (pp. 167–194). Edward Elgar Publishing., https://www.masi-journal.com/journal/article/view/26 10.1108/JMP-07-2018-0277 DOI: 10.4337/9781800883802.00017

Keith, M. G., Harms, P. D., & Long, A. C. (2020). Worker Health and Well-Being in the Gig Economy: A Proposed Framework and Research Agenda. In Perrewe, P. L., Harms, P. D., Harms, P. D., & Chang, C.-H. (Eds.), Research in Occupational Stress and Well-Being: Vol. 18. *Entrepreneurial and Small Business Stressors, Experienced Stress, and Well-Being* (pp. 1–33). Emerald Publishing., DOI: 10.1108/S1479-355520200000018002

Kelkar, G. (2022). *Patriarchal Discrimination and Capitalist Relations: The Gender Question in the Gig Economy*. Institute for Human Development.

Khang, A., Dave, T., Jadhav, B., Katore, D., & Dave, D. (2024). Gig Financial Economy: Big Data and Analytics. In *Synergy of AI and Fintech in the Digital Gig Economy* (pp. 244-267). CRC Press.

Khan, H. (2021). *Leadership, reinvented: How to foster empathy, servitude, diversity, and innovation in the workplace*. Sourcebooks, Inc.

Khan, M. H., Williams, J., Williams, P., & Mayes, R. (2024). Caring in the gig economy: A relational perspective of decent work. *Work, Employment and Society, 38*(4), 1107–1127.

Khan, M. H., Williams, P., & Mayes, R. (2024). Caring in the Gig Economy: A Relational Perspective of Decent Work. *Work, Employment and Society, 38*(4), 1107–1127. DOI: 10.1177/09500170231173586

Khan, M., & Saqib, Z. (2024). Emerging Voice Mechanisms in Asian Gig Economies: Implications for Gig Workers' Work and Life. In Chan, X. W., Shang, S., & Lu, L. (Eds.), *Work-Life Research in the Asia-Pacific. Palgrave Studies in Equity, Diversity, Inclusion, and Indigenization in Business*. Palgrave Macmillan., DOI: 10.1007/978-3-031-52795-1_3

Kilhoffer, Z., De Groen, W. P., Lenaerts, K., Smits, I., Hauben, H., Waeyaert, W., & Robin-Olivier, S. (2020). *Study to gather evidence on the working conditions of platform workers* (VT/2018/032). https://www.ceps.eu/ceps-publications/study-to-gather-evidence-on-the-working-conditions-of-platform-workers/

Kilhoffer, Z., Lenaerts, K., & Beblavý, M. (2017). The platform economy and industrial relations: Applying the old framework to the new reality (CEPS Research Report No. 2017/12). Centre for European Policy Studies.

Killingsworth, M. A. (2021). Experienced well-being rises with income, even above $75,000 per year. *Proceedings of the National Academy of Sciences of the United States of America, 118*(4), e2016976118. PMID: 33468644

Kirton, G. (2020). Diversity and inclusion in a changing world of work. In *The future of work and employment* (pp. 49–64). Edward Elgar Publishing.

Kispert, M. (2021). *Clouds of discontent: art, work, solidarity and digital platform labour* (Doctoral dissertation, University of Westminster). DOI: 10.34737/vqx44

Kite, M. E., Whitley, B. E.Jr, & Wagner, L. S. (2022). *Psychology of prejudice and discrimination*. Routledge.

Klitmøller, A., & Lauring, J. (2013). When global virtual teams share knowledge: Media richness, cultural difference, and language commonality. *Journal of World Business, 48*(3), 398–406. DOI: 10.1016/j.jwb.2012.07.023

Koh, J. M. (2023). *Cooperative Firms and the Sustainable Development Goals: Pursuing Decent Work and Reducing Inequality*. Taylor & Francis. DOI: 10.4324/9781003457596

Kombe, W. J. (2005). Land use dynamics in peri-urban areas and their implications on the urban growth and form: The case of Dar es Salaam, Tanzania. *Habitat International*, *29*(1), 113–135. DOI: 10.1016/S0197-3975(03)00076-6

Kost, D., Fieseler, C., & Wong, S. I. (2020). Boundaryless careers in the gig economy: An oxymoron? *Human Resource Management Journal*, *30*(1), 100–113. DOI: 10.1111/1748-8583.12265

Koustas, D. K. (2019). What Do Big Data Tell Us About Why People Take Gig Economy Jobs. *AEA Papers and Proceedings. American Economic Association*, *109*, 367–371. DOI: 10.1257/pandp.20191041

Koutsimpogiorgos, N., Frenken, K., & Herrmann, A. M. (2023). Platform adaptation to regulation: The case of domestic cleaning in Europe. *The Journal of Industrial Relations*, *65*(2), 156–184. DOI: 10.1177/00221856221146833

Koutsimpogiorgos, N., Van Slageren, J., Herrmann, A. M., & Frenken, K. (2020). Conceptualizing the gig economy and its regulatory problems. *Policy and Internet*, *12*(4), 525–545.

Koutsimpogiorgos, N., van Slageren, J., Herrmann, A., & Frenken, K. (2020). Conceptualizing the Gig Economy and Its Regulatory Problems. *Policy & Internet*. https://doi.org/DOI: 10.31235/OSF.IO/JMQYT

Kravariti, F., Tasoulis, K., Scullion, H., & Alali, M. K. (2023). Talent management and performance in the public sector: The role of organisational and line managerial support for development. *International Journal of Human Resource Management*, *34*(9), 1782–1807. DOI: 10.1080/09585192.2022.2032265

Krechetova, V. (2021). Green and sustainable logistics network: micro mobility in the first-last mile.

Kreinin, H., & Aigner, E. (2022). From "Decent work and economic growth" to "Sustainable work and economic degrowth": A new framework for SDG 8. *Empirica*, *49*(2), 281–311. DOI: 10.1007/s10663-021-09526-5

Krishnan, A., & Mishra, S. WORK AND WELL-BEING IN THE SHARING ECONOMY: EVIDENCE FROM INDIA. https://www.ippapublicpolicy.org/file/paper/60c21bc482342.pdf

Kshatriya, N., & Kurien, D. (2022). Gig Workers in India: Emerging Opportunities in the New Economy. *Liberal Stud.*, *7*, 78.

Kudyba, S., Fjermestad, J., & Davenport, T. (2020). A research model for identifying factors that drive effective decision-making and the future of work. *Journal of Intellectual Capital, 21*(2), 835–851. DOI: 10.1108/JIC-05-2019-0130

Kuhn, K. M., & Maleki, A. (2017). Micro-entrepreneurs, dependent contractors, and instaserfs: Understanding online labor platform workforces. *The Academy of Management Perspectives, 31*(3), 183–200. DOI: 10.5465/amp.2015.0111

Kuhn, K. M., Meijerink, J., & Keegan, A. (2021). Human resource management and the gig economy: Challenges and opportunities at the intersection between organizational HR decision-makers and digital labor platforms. *Research in Personnel and Human Resources Management, 39*, 1–46.

Kuknor, S. C., & Bhattacharya, S. (2022). Inclusive leadership: New age leadership to foster organizational inclusion. *European Journal of Training and Development, 46*(9), 771–797.

Kumar, T., & Kaur, S. (2022). Cyber Security in Businesses: Challenges and Recovery Modes. In 2022 2nd International Conference on Emerging Smart Technologies and Applications (eSmarTA) (pp. 1-5). IEEE.

Kumari, B. S. S., Lavanya, P., & Padmambika, P. (2024). Bridging The Digital Divide: Addressing Inequality and Access Disparities. *International Journal of Indian Psychology, 12*(3). Advance online publication. DOI: 10.25215/1203.111

Kumar, S., Prasad, K., & Aithal, P. S. (2024). Tech-Business Analytics in GIG Economy-A Futuristic Technology Supported Online Business Model. *Poornaprajna International Journal of Teaching & Research, 1*(1), 1–32. DOI: 10.5281/zenodo.12754703

Kumar, V., Ramachandran, D., & Kumar, B. (2021). Influence of new-age technologies on marketing: A research agenda. *Journal of Business Research*. DOI.org/10.1016/j.jbusres.2020.01.007

Lake, R. (2023). *California Assembly Bill 5 (AB5): What's in it and what it means*. Investopedia. Retrieved September 23, 2023, from https://www.investopedia.com/california-assembly-bill-5-ab5-4773201

Lambert, S. J., Haley-Lock, A., & Henly, J. R. (2012). Schedule flexibility in hourly jobs: Unanticipated consequences and promising directions. *Community Work & Family, 15*(3), 293–315. DOI: 10.1080/13668803.2012.662803

Lam, L., & Triandafyllidou, A. (2021). An unlikely stepping stone? Exploring how platform work shapes newcomer migrant integration. *Transitions: Journal of transient. Migration, 5*(1), 11–29. DOI: 10.1386/tjtm_00029_1

Lam, L., & Triandafyllidou, A. (2024). Road to nowhere or to somewhere? Migrant pathways in platform work in Canada. *Environment & Planning A, 56*(4), 1150–1169. DOI: 10.1177/0308518X221090248

Langaas, M., & Mujtaba, B. G. (2023). Communication across cultures in the workplace: Swimming in Scandinavian waters. *Open Journal of Social Sciences, 11*(4), 174–192. DOI: 10.4236/jss.2023.114014

Langley, D. J., van Doorn, J., Ng, I. C., Stieglitz, S., Lazovik, A., & Boonstra, A. (2021). The Internet of Everything: Smart things and their impact on business models. *Journal of Business Research, 122*, 853–863. DOI: 10.1016/j.jbusres.2019.12.035

Lansing, A. E., Romero, N. J., Siantz, E., Silva, V., Center, K., Casteel, D., & Gilmer, T. (2023). Building trust: Leadership reflections on community empowerment and engagement in a large urban initiative. *BMC Public Health, 23*(1), 1252. DOI: 10.1186/s12889-023-15860-z PMID: 37380973

Lantowa, F. D., & Machmud, J. (2020). Development of Micro, Small and Medium Enterprises (MSMEs) Based on the Creative Economy (EKRAF) and Gig Economy in Gorontaldo Regency. *Journal of Asian Multicultural Research for Economy and Management Study, 1*(2), 43–53. DOI: 10.47616/jamrems.v1i2.61

Lee, J. W. (2014). Labour contracting and changing employment relationships in South Korea. *Development Policy Review, 32*(4), 449–473. DOI: 10.1111/dpr.12063

Lee, M. K., Kusbit, D., Metsky, E., & Dabbish, L. (2015). Working with machines: The impact of algorithmic and data-driven management on human workers. In *Proceedings of the 33rd Annual ACM Conference on Human Factors in Computing Systems (CHI '15)* (pp. 1603–1612). Association for Computing Machinery. DOI: 10.1145/2702123.2702548

Légifrance. (2016). *Loi n° 2016-1088 du 8 août 2016 relative au travail, à la modernisation du dialogue social et à la sécurisation des parcours professionnels.* https://www.legifrance.gouv.fr/jorf/id/JORFTEXT000032983213

Lehdonvirta, V. (2016). Algorithms that Divide and Unite: Delocalisation, Identity and Collective Action in 'Microwork. In Flecker, J. (Ed.), *Space, Place and Global Digital Work. Dynamics of Virtual Work.* Palgrave Macmillan., DOI: 10.1057/978-1-137-48087-3_4

Lehdonvirta, V. (2018). Flexibility in the gig economy: Managing time on three online piecework platforms. *New Technology, Work and Employment, 33*(1), 13–29. DOI: 10.1111/ntwe.12102

Lehdonvirta, V., Kässi, O., Hjorth, I., Barnard, H., & Graham, M. (2019). The global platform economy: A new offshoring institution enabling emerging-economy micro providers. *Journal of Management, 45*(2), 567–599. DOI: 10.1177/0149206318786781 PMID: 30774168

Lesala Khethisa, B., Tsibolane, P., & Van Belle, J. P. (2020). Surviving the Gig Economy in the Global South: How Cape Town Domestic Workers Cope. In: Bandi, R.K., C. R., R., Klein, S., Madon, S., Monteiro, E. (eds.) *The Future of Digital Work: The Challenge of Inequality* (pp.76-85). IFIP Advances in Information and Communication Technology, 601. Springer, Cham. DOI: 10.1007/978-3-030-64697-4_7

Liang, C., Peng, J., Hong, Y., & Gu, B. (2023). The hidden costs and benefits of monitoring in the gig economy. *Information Systems Research, 34*(1), 297–318. DOI: 10.1287/isre.2022.1130

Lingras, K. A., Alexander, M. E., & Vrieze, D. M. (2023). Diversity, Equity, and Inclusion Efforts at a Departmental Level: Building a Committee as a Vehicle for Advancing Progress. *Journal of Clinical Psychology in Medical Settings, 30*(2), 356–379. DOI: 10.1007/s10880-021-09809-w PMID: 34529234

Lin, P. M., Peng, K. L., Au, W. C., & Baum, T. (2023). Food-delivery workers in the sharing economy: Supply-side human resource transformation. *International Journal of Hospitality & Tourism Administration, 24*(4), 491–516. DOI: 10.1080/15256480.2021.2015042

Litman, L., Robinson, J., & Abberbock, T. (2020). *Gender-based pay gaps in the gig economy*. Harvard Journal of Law & Gender. https://journals.law.harvard.edu/jlg/2020/02/gender-based-pay-gaps-in-the-gig-economy/

Litman, L., Robinson, J., Rosen, Z., Rosenzweig, C., Waxman, J., & Bates, L. M. (2020). The persistence of pay inequality: The gender pay gap in an anonymous online labor market. *PLoS One, 15*(2), e0229383. DOI: 10.1371/journal.pone.0229383 PMID: 32084233

Liu, Y., Zhao, X., & Li, X. (2021). The coin of AI has two sides: Matching enhancement and information revelation effects of AI on gig economy platforms. *Social Sciences Research Network,* 1-51.

Liu, H., Fernandez, F., & Dutz, G. (2022). Educational attainment, use of numeracy at work, and gender wage gaps: Evidence from 12 middle-income countries. *International Journal of Educational Development, 92*, 102625. DOI: 10.1016/j.ijedudev.2022.102625

Livemint. (2024, January 18). Swiggy introduces ambulance service for delivery executives, dependents. Livemint. Retrieved from https://www.livemint.com/news/india/swiggy-introduces-ambulance-service-for-delivery-executives-dependents-11673877855361.html

Li, Y., Xu, S., Yu, Y., & Meadows, R. (2023). The well-being of gig workers in the sharing economy during COVID-19. *International Journal of Contemporary Hospitality Management*, *35*(4), 1470–1489. DOI: 10.1108/IJCHM-01-2022-0064

Loganathan, M. (2022). Assessing Social Sustainability in the Gig Economy. *The Indian Journal of Labour Economics : the Quarterly Journal of the Indian Society of Labour Economics*, *65*(3), 831–843. DOI: 10.1007/s41027-022-00399-1

Longoni, A., Salas, S., Sancha, C., Sierra, V., & Wiengarten, F. (2024). Exploring the implications of working conditions for corporate sustainability in last-mile delivery platform companies. *Journal of Business Ethics*, •••, 1–25. DOI: 10.1007/s10551-024-05840-7

Lozano-Paredes, L. H., & Reilly, K. M. (2018). Decent Work for Ride Hailing Workers in the Platform Economy in Cali, Colombia. Urban Transport in the Sharing Economy Era, 92-127. Buenos Aries, Argentina: Centro de Implementacion de Politicas Publicas para la Equidad y el Crecimiento (CIPPEC).

Lutfiyya, Z., & Bartlett, N. (2020, September 28). Inclusive Societies. *Oxford Research Encyclopedia ofEducation.*oxfordre.com/education/view/10.1093/acrefore/9780190264093.001.0001/acrefore-9780190264093-e-1022..

Lux, M., & Chung, C. (2023). *Earned Wage Access: An Innovation in Financial Inclusion?* M-RCBG Associate Working Paper Series, 214: 1-50.

Mahato, M., Kumar, N., & Jena, L. K. (2021). Re-thinking gig economy in conventional workforce post-COVID-19: A blended approach for upholding fair balance. *Journal of Work-Applied Management*, *13*(2), 261–276.

Makridakis, S. (2017). The forthcoming artificial intelligence (AI) revolution: Its impact on society and firms. *Futures*, *90*, 46–60. DOI: 10.1016/j.futures.2017.03.006

Malhotra, P., & Ganghas, S. (2023). HUMAN RESOURCE MANAGEMENT IN THE GIG ECONOMY. *MANAGEMENT METAMORPHOSIS: NAVIGATING THE CHANGING LANDSCAPE*, 113.

Malhotra, R. T. (2024). *Inclusion on purpose: An intersectional approach to creating a culture of belonging at work.* MIT Press.

Malik, A., Budhwar, P., & Srikanth, N. R. (2020). Gig economy, 4IR and artificial intelligence: Rethinking strategic HRM. In Human & technological resource management (HTRM): New insights into revolution 4.0 (pp. 75-88). Emerald Publishing Limited.DOI:DOI: 10.1108/978-1-83867-223-220201005

Malik, R., Visvizi, A., & Skrzek-Lubasińska, M. (2021). The gig economy: Current issues, the debate, and the new avenues of research. *Sustainability (Basel)*, *13*(9), 5023. DOI: 10.3390/su13095023

Mandere, N. M., Ness, B., & Anderberg, S. (2010). Peri-urban development, livelihood change and household income: A case study of peri-urban Nyahururu, Kenya. *Journal of Agricultural Extension and Rural Development*, *2*(5), 73–83.

Mangla, N. (2021). Working in a pandemic and post-pandemic period–Cultural intelligence is the key. *International Journal of Cross Cultural Management*, *21*(1), 53–69. DOI: 10.1177/14705958211002877

Manky, O., & Mogollon, N. (2024). *How DiDi Chuxing Adapts to Latin America's Era of Digital Platforms*. Carnegie Endowment for International Peace.

Mannan, M., & Pek, S. (2024). Platform cooperatives and the dilemmas of platform worker-member participation. *New Technology, Work and Employment*, *39*(2), 219–237. DOI: 10.1111/ntwe.12273

Mann, F., Wang, J., Pearce, E., Ma, R., Schlief, M., Lloyd-Evans, B., Ikhtabi, S., & Johnson, S. (2022). Loneliness and the onset of new mental health problems in the general population. *Social Psychiatry and Psychiatric Epidemiology*, *57*(11), 2161–2178. DOI: 10.1007/s00127-022-02261-7 PMID: 35583561

Mark, K. P., So, J. C. H., Chan, V. C. W., Luk, G. W. T., & Ho, W. T. (2018). Surviving in the Gig Economy: Change of STEM Students' Perceptions on the Generic Skills for the Workplace. In, *2018 IEEE International Conference on Teaching, Assessment, and Learning for Engineering (TALE)*, Wollongong, Australia,1085-1090, DOI: 10.1109/TALE.2018.8615414

Marshall, A. (2024). A new rural digital divide? Taking stock of geographical digital inclusion in Australia. *Media International Australia, Incorporating Culture & Policy*, *190*(1), 68–84. DOI: 10.1177/1329878X231202274

Masekesa, T. (2021). *The gig economy, the digital divide, and developing countries*. Maseconomics. https://maseconomics.com/the-gig-economy-the-digital-divide-and-developing-countries/

Masera, M. L. (2024). Redefining tomorrow: A comprehensive analysis of AI's impact on employment and identity. http://hdl.handle.net/10579/26098

Masta, R., & Kaushiva, P. (2024), "Work in the platform economy: a systematic literature review", *Employee Relations*, Vol. ahead-of-print No. ahead-of-print. DOI: 10.1108/ER-12-2023-0638

Mateescu, A., & Nguyen, A. (2019). *Explainer: Workplace monitoring and surveillance*. Data & Society. Retrieved May 15, 2021, from https://datasociety.net/wp-content/uploads/2019/02/DS_Workplace_Monitoring_Surveillance_Explainer.pdf

Ma, X., & Yang, S. (2018). Airtasker and the Australian freelance worker: The reflections on the gig economy. *International Journal of Advanced and Applied Sciences*, *5*(7), 35–45. DOI: 10.21833/ijaas.2018.07.005

McDowell, L.-B. (2023). *How the gig economy is shaping the landscape of LATAM*. Mauve Group.

McKinsey Global Institute. (2016). Independent work: Choice, necessity and the Gig economy.https://www.mckinsey.com/~/media/mckinsey/featured%20insights/employment%20and%20 growth/independent%20work%20choice%20necessity%20 and%20the%20 gig%20economy/independent-work- choice-necessity-and-the-gig economy-full

Mdhlalose, D. (2024). An examination of employee rewards and work environment on employee creativity and innovation. *SEISENSE Journal of Management*, *7*(1), 21–34. DOI: 10.33215/rewfe541

MEDICAS. (2022). *About US*.https://medicasapp.com/tt/aboutus/

Mehta, B. S., Awasthi, I., & Mehta, N. (2021). Women's employment and digital technology: A regional analysis in India. *Indian Journal of Human Development*, *15*(3), 427–442. DOI: 10.1177/09737030211064138

Meijerink, J., & Keegan, A. (2019). Conceptualizing human resource management in the gig economy: Toward a platform ecosystem perspective. *Journal of Managerial Psychology*, *34*(4), 214–232. DOI: 10.1108/JMP-07-2018-0277

Memon, F. N., & Memon, S. N. (2025). Digital Divide and Equity in Education: Bridging Gaps to Ensure Inclusive Learning. In *Impact of Digitalization on Education and Social Sustainability* (pp. 107-130). IGI Global. DOI: DOI: 10.4018/979-8-3693-1854-6.ch004

Mer, A., Matthew, J., & Arora, S. (2024). Managing Gig Economy Workers Through Artificial Intelligence: Applications and Challenges. In N. Joshi., F. A. Malik, C. Gulati, & A. Dubey (eds), *Fostering Industry-Academia Partnerships for Innovation-Driven Tade*, pp. 17-30. IGI Global. DOI: 10.4018/979-8-3693-3096-8.ch002

Metawala, P. G., Golda-Pongratz, K., & Irazabal, C. (2024). All in a Day's Work: Impact of On-Demand Platform Delivery Work on Immigrant Riders in Barcelona. In Vale, M., Ferreira, D., & Rodrigues, N. (Eds.), *Geographies of the Platform Economy* (pp. 157–172). Springer Cham., DOI: 10.1007/978-3-031-53594-9_11

Meyer, E. (2014). *The culture map: Breaking through the invisible boundaries of global business*. PublicAffairs., DOI: 10.15733/jast.2018.76.243

Mezmir, E. A. (2020). Qualitative data analysis: An overview of data reduction, data display, and interpretation. Research on humanities and social sciences, 10(21), 15-27. https://iiste.org/Journals/index.php/RHSS/article/viewFile/54898/56707

Moghavvemi, S., Teng, L. S., & Mahmoud, H. (2023). The Future of Work, A Knowledge-based Gig Economy. In *Reshaping the Future: The Phenomenon of Gig Workers and Knowledge-Economy* (pp. 61–71). Emerald Publishing Limited., DOI: 10.1108/978-1-83753-350-320231005

Mohd Daud, S. N., Osman, Z., Samsudin, S., & Phang, I. G. (2024). Adapting to the gig economy: Determinants of financial resilience among "Giggers.". *Economic Analysis and Policy*, *81*, 756–771. DOI: 10.1016/j.eap.2024.01.002

Mohsin, F. H., Isa, N. M., Awee, A., & Purhanudin, N. (2022). Growing gigs: A conceptual report on job autonomy and work engagement on gig workers' performance. *International Journal of Advanced Research in Economics and Finance*, *4*(1), 144–156.

Mokhtar, R., & Rohaizat, A. (2024). Cybercrimes and Cyber Security Trends in the New Normal. In Kamaruddin, N., Idris, A., & Fernandez, K. (Eds.), *The New Normal and Its Impact on Society* (pp. 41–60)., DOI: 10.1007/978-981-97-0527-6_4

Moniz, A. B., Boavida, N., Makó, C., Krings, B. J., & de Miguel, P. S. (Eds.). (2021). *Digital Labour Platforms: Representing Workers in Europe*. Húmus.

Montgomery, T., & Baglioni, S. (2021). Defining the gig economy: Platform capitalism and the reinvention of precarious work. *The International Journal of Sociology and Social Policy*, *41*(9/10), 1012–1025.

Mont, O., Palgan, Y. V., Bradley, K., & Zvolska, L. (2020). A decade of the sharing economy: Concepts, users, business and governance perspectives. *Journal of Cleaner Production*, *1*(122215), 1–9. DOI: 10.1016/j.jclepro.2020.122215 PMID: 32542067

Moulaert, F. (Ed.). (2013). *The international handbook on social innovation: collective action, social learning and transdisciplinary research*. Edward Elgar Publishing. DOI: 10.4337/9781849809993

Mourelatos, E., Giannakopoulos, N., & Tzagarakis, M. (2024). Payment schemes in online labour markets. Does incentive and personality matter? *Behaviour & Information Technology*, *43*(11), 2544–2565. DOI: 10.1080/0144929X.2023.2254853

Mousa, M. (2025). Gig work, management education and changes in working conditions: A qualitative study. *Industrial and Commercial Training*, *57*(1), 82–98. DOI: 10.1108/ICT-07-2024-0066

Muldoon, J., Stronge, W., Avila, R., Gebrial, D., Jones, P., Srnicek, N., ... & Wark, M. (2020). Platforming equality: Policy challenges for the digital economy.

Muldoon, J., & Sun, P. (2024). The Global Gig Economy: How Transport Platform Companies Adapt to Regulatory Challenges—A Comparative Analysis of Six Countries. *Industrial Law Journal*, *53*(3), 481–504. DOI: 10.1093/indlaw/dwae010

Mumby, D. K. (2019). Work: What is it good for? (Absolutely nothing)—a critical theorist's perspective. *Industrial and Organizational Psychology: Perspectives on Science and Practice*, *12*(4), 429–443. DOI: 10.1017/iop.2019.69

Murtiningrum, V. A., & Aligarh, F. (2024). Adoption of Digital Technology in Micro, Small, and Medium Enterprises (MSMEs): Integration of Innovation Diffusion Theory and Resource-Based View (RBV) Theory (A Case Investigation on MSMEs in Surakarta City). *International Conference on Islamic Economics (ICIE)*, *1*, 415–420. ISSN: 3064-2043

Nadeem, W., Juntunen, M., Shirazi, F., & Hajli, N. (2020). Consumers' value co-creation in sharing economy: The role of social support, consumers' ethical perceptions and relationship quality. *Technological Forecasting and Social Change*, *151*, 119786. DOI: 10.1016/j.techfore.2019.119786

National Bureau of Economic Research (NBER). (2023). *The evolving role of gig work during the COVID-19 pandemic*.https://www.nber.org/digest/20238/evolving-role-gig-work-during-covid-19-pandemic

Neighbourhood Munchies. (2024). *Welcome to the Neighbourhood. South Trinidad's Premier Food Delivery Service*.https://www.neighbourhoodmunchies.com/

Ness, I., Ovetz, R., Roque, I., Swidler, E. M., & Zwick, A. (Eds.). (2023). *The Routledge handbook of the gig economy*. Routledge.

Newlands, G. (2022). 'This isn't forever for me': Perceived employability and migrant work in Norway and Sweden. Environment and Planning A. *Economy and Space*, *56*(4), 1262–1279. DOI: 10.1177/0308518X221083021

Niebler, V. (2023). *Coalitional Power in the Digital Economy: Alliances of Gig and Tech Workers*. Humboldt-Universität zu Berlin.

Niguse, T., Kant, S., & Adula, M. (2025). Mediation Effect of Customer Loyalty in Relationship Among Market Orientation, Entrepreneurial Orientation, and Firm Performance in Ethiopia. In *Leveraging AI for Effective Digital Relationship Marketing* (pp. 419–458). IGI Global., DOI: 10.4018/979-8-3693-5340-0.ch014

Nkomo, S. M. (2021). Reflections on the continuing denial of the centrality of "race" in management and organization studies. *Equality, Diversity and Inclusion*, *40*(2), 212–224. DOI: 10.1108/EDI-01-2021-0011

Norwani, N. M., Ismail, Z., Nasir, N. N. A., Yusof, R., & Jamaluddin, N. S. (2022). The Influence of Gender, Age, Academic Level and Motivation on Satisfaction Toward Benefits Received by Gig Economy Workers in Malaysia. *Archives of Business Research*, *10*(12), 89–105. DOI: 10.14738/abr.1012.13602

Novitz, T. (2021). Gig work as a manifestation of short-termism: Crafting a sustainable regulatory agenda. *Industrial Law Journal*, *50*(4), 636–661. DOI: 10.1093/indlaw/dwab027

Nwaobi, G. C. (2024). Gig Sector in the African Economy: Frameworks, Challenges and Prospects. *Challenges and Prospects*. DOI: 10.2139/ssrn.4769988

O'Reilly, T. (2005). What is Web 2.0? *O'Reilly Media*. https://www.oreilly.com/pub/a/web2/archive/what-is-web-20.html

Ochillo, F. (2022). The economic consequences and generational impact of the digital divide. *Belfer Center for Science and International Affairs, Harvard Kennedy School*.https://issuu. com/belfercenter/docs/tapp-francella_impact_of_the_digital_divide_final_

Ogunyemi, K. (2024). Humanistic management and the gig economy: Fairness considerations. In *Humanistic management in the gig economy: Dignity, fairness and care* (pp. 1–13). Springer Nature Switzerland. DOI: 10.1007/978-3-031-59944-6_1

Ola Institute. (2020). Ola COVID-19 report. Retrieved from https://olawebcdn.com/ola-institute/covid19-report.pdf

Oranburg, S., & Palagashvili, L. (2018). The Gig Economy, Smart Contracts, and Disruption of Traditional Work Arrangements. *Social Science Research Network*, 1-24. DOI: 10.2139/ssrn.3270867

Organization for Economic Co-operation and Development, International Labor Organization, and the European Union. (OECD, ILO & EU). (2023). *Handbook on Measuring Digital Platform Employment and Work*. Paris, France: OECD Publishing. DOI: 10.1787/0ddcac3b-en

Ostrom, A. L., Field, J. M., Fotheringham, D., Subramony, M., Gustafsson, A., Lemon, K. N., & McColl-Kennedy, J. R. (2021). Service research priorities: Managing and delivering service in turbulent times. *Journal of Service Research, 24*(3), 329–353. DOI: 10.1177/1094670521102191

Outlook Business. (2024). Swiggy announces initiative to provide career growth opportunities to delivery partners. Outlook Business. Retrieved from https://www.outlookbusiness.com/corporate/swiggy-announces-initiative-to-provide-career-growth-opportunities-to-delivery-partners

Oviedo-Trespalacios, O. (2022). Factors influencing road safety compliance among food delivery riders: An extension of the job demands-resources (JD-R) model. *Transportation Research Part A, Policy and Practice, 166*, 541–556. https://doi.org/https://doi.org/10.1016/j.tra.2022.11.002. DOI: 10.1016/j.tra.2022.11.002

Ozgumus, E., & Rattan, A. (2025). Motivating support for workplace diversity policies: A mindsets framework. *Current Opinion in Psychology, 62*, 101999. DOI: 10.1016/j.copsyc.2025.101999 PMID: 39893990

Panda, P. C., Pathak, K., & Panda, R. (2023). Gig Economy: Potential and Challenges for Human Resources in Urban India. Reimagining Management in the post VUCA World, 1.

Pandey, N. D. R. K., & Sarangi, N. S. (2023). A case study on talent acquisition at Organisations. *International Journal of Engineering and Management Research, 13*(1), 6–11. DOI: 10.31033/ijemr.13.1.2

Pant, J. J., & Majumder, M. G. (2022). Themes and Narratives of Gig Economy: An Indian HR Perspective. *NHRD Network Journal, 15*(1), 83–99. DOI: 10.1177/26314541211064751

Parey, M., & Waldinger, F. (2011). Investigationing abroad and the effect on international labour market mobility: Evidence from the introduction of ERASMUS. *Economic Journal (London), 121*(551), 194–222. DOI: 10.1111/j.1468-0297.2010.02369.x

Pathiranage, H. S. K. (2024). Precarious employment in the gig economy: Understanding the roles of employed poor. *Open Journal of Business and Management, 12*(4), 2288–2307. DOI: 10.4236/ojbm.2024.124117

Patil, B. S., & Priya, M. R. S. R. (2024). Human Resource Frontiers: Pioneering Humane Innovations for Fair Treatment of Workers in the Gig Economy. In Ogunyemi, K. (Ed.), *Humanistic Management in the Gig Economy*. Humanism in Business Series. Palgrave Macmillan., DOI: 10.1007/978-3-031-59944-6_4

Patnaik, R., & Baral, S. K. (2023). The Post-pandemic Perspective of Rejigging the Gig Economy in India and the Issues of Returnees to Homeland. In *Industry 4.0 and the Digital Transformation of International Business* (pp. 273–285). Springer Nature Singapore. DOI: 10.1007/978-981-19-7880-7_16

Pesole, A., Urzi Brancati, M. C., Fernandez Macias, E., Biagi, F., & Gonzalez Vazquez, I. (2018). *Platform workers in Europe: Evidence from the COLLEEM survey* (EUR 29275 EN). Publications Office of the European Union. DOI: 10.2760/742789

Phillips, L. T., Jun, S., & Shakeri, A. (2022). Barriers and boosts: Using inequity frames theory to expand understanding of mechanisms of race and gender inequity. *The Academy of Management Annals*, *16*(2), 547–587. Advance online publication. DOI: 10.5465/annals.2020.0314

Piasna, A., & Zwysen, W. (2024). *Migrant labour in the "gig" economy: progress or trap*? Berlin, Germany: Social Europe. https://www.socialeurope.eu/migrant-labour-in-the-gig-economy-progress-or-trap

Pietrogiovanni, V., & Iossa, A. (2022). Don't GIG Up, Never! https://www.dontgigup.eu/

Pilatti, G. R., Pinheiro, F. L., & Montini, A. A. (2024). Systematic Literature Review on Gig Economy: Power Dynamics, Worker Autonomy, and the Role of Social Networks. *Administrative Sciences*, *14*(10), 267. DOI: 10.3390/admsci14100267

Popov, A. (2023). The future of work: Adapting to technological disruptions in the labor market. *Journal of Philosophical Criticism.*

Pourrahmani, E., & Jaller, M. (2021). Crowdshipping in last mile deliveries: Operational challenges and research opportunities. *Socio-Economic Planning Sciences*, *78*, 101063. DOI: 10.1016/j.seps.2021.101063

Prassl, J. (2018). *Humans as a service: The promise and perils of work in the gig economy*. Oxford University Press. DOI: 10.1093/oso/9780198797012.001.0001

Pulignano, V. (2019). Work and Employment under the Gig Economy. *Partecipazione e Conflitto, 12*(3), 629–639. DOI: 10.1285/I20356609V12I3P629

Putnam, L. L., Myers, K. K., & Gailliard, B. M. (2014). Examining the tensions in workplace flexibility and exploring options for new directions. *Human Relations*, *67*(4), 413–440. DOI: 10.1177/0018726713495704

Putzel-Kavanaugh, C., & Benton, M. (2024). *Bridging the Gap between the Gig Economy and Migration Policy*. Migration Policy Institute.

Rahman, A., & Pingali, P. (2024). Social Welfare 'Schemes' to an Economic Security 'System. In *The Future of India's Social Safety Nets: Focus, Form, and Scope* (pp. 357–425). Springer International Publishing. DOI: 10.1007/978-3-031-50747-2_10

Rahman, S. U., Sultan, M. S., & Tabassam, A. (2024). The Impact of the Gig economy on the Traditional Employment and the Necessity for Revised Business. *HR and Legal Strategies Pakistan Journal of International Affairs*, *7*(1). Advance online publication. DOI: 10.52337/pjia.v7i1.1013

Rajendran, L. P., Raúl, L., Chen, M., Guerrero Andrade, J. C., Akhtar, R., Mngumi, L. E., Chander, S., Srinivas, S., & Roy, M. R. (2024). The 'peri-urban turn': A systems thinking approach for a paradigm shift in reconceptualising urban-rural futures in the global South. *Habitat International*, *146*, 103041. DOI: 10.1016/j.habitatint.2024.103041

Ramaswamy, K. V. (2019). Non-standard Employment, Labour Laws and Social Security: Learning from the US Gig Economy Debate. *Globalization, Labour Market Institutions, Processes and Policies in India*, 277–299. DOI: 10.1007/978-981-13-7111-0_11

Rani, U., & Furrer, M. (2021). Digital Labor Platforms and New Forms of Flexible Work in Developing Countries: Algorithmic Management of Work and Workers. *Competition & Change*, *25*(2), 212–236. DOI: 10.1177/1024529420905187

Rao, R. K., Kumar, K., Gupta, R., Khurana, S., Verma, K. N., Chandra, S., Singh, R. R., & Dharap, O. (2022). India's Booming Gig and Platform Economy: Perspectives and Recommendations on the Future of Work. In *Niti Aayog* (Issue June). https://www.niti.gov.in/sites/default/files/2022-06/25th_June_Final_Report_27062022.pdf

Rappi. (2024). *About Us*. Bogota, Colombia: Rappi Inc. https://about.rappi.com/about-us

Ravenelle, A. J., & Kowalski, K. C. (2022). Working at the Nexus of Global Markets and Gig Work: US Gig Workers, Credential Capitalization, and Wealthy International Clientele. In *Economies, Institutions and Territories* (pp. 199-214). Routledge.

Ravenelle, A. J. (2019). "We're not uber:" control, autonomy, and entrepreneurship in the gig economy. *Journal of Managerial Psychology, 34*(4), 269–285. DOI: 10.1108/JMP-06-2018-0256

Ray, A. (2024). Coping with crisis and precarity in the gig economy: 'Digitally organised informality', migration and socio-spatial networks among platform drivers in India. Https://Doi.Org/10.1177/0308518X231220296*, 56*(4), 1227–1244. DOI: 10.1177/0308518X231220296

Ray, B., Sengupta, A., & Varma, A. (2024). The gig verse: Building a sustainable future. *The International Journal of Organizational Analysis, 32*(10), 2275–2298. DOI: 10.1108/IJOA-08-2023-3946

Ray, C., Nyberg, A. J., & Maltarich, M. A. (2023). Human capital resources emergence theory: The role of social capital. *Academy of Management Review, 48*(2), 313–335. DOI: 10.5465/amr.2020.0186

Ray, R., & Sam, J. S. (2023). Off-platform Social Networks and Gig Work During the COVID-19 Pandemic in India. *Journal of South Asian Development, 18*(3), 359–382. DOI: 10.1177/09731741231191876

Ray, S., Herman, N., & Sen, I. (2021). *Disruptive Transformation Fuelling Gig Economies. I.* EEE Technology & Engineering Management Conference-Europe., DOI: 10.1109/TEMSCONEUR52034.2021.9488630

Ray, S., Herman, N., & Sen, I. (2021). *Disruptive Transformation Fuelling Gig Economies.* IEEE Technology & Engineering Management Conference-Europe., DOI: 10.1109/TEMSCON-EUR52034.2021.9488630

Reichenberger, I. (2018). Digital nomads: A quest for holistic freedom in work and leisure. *Annals of Leisure Research, 21*(3), 364–380. DOI: 10.1080/11745398.2017.1358098

Reilly, K. M. A., & Lozano-Paredes, L. H. (2019). Ride Hailing Regulations in Cali, Colombia: Towards Autonomous and Decent Work. In Nielsen, P., & Kimaro, H. C. (Eds.), *Information and Communications Technologies for Development. Strengthening Southern-Driven Cooperation as a Catalyst for ICT4D. IFIP Advances in Information and Communication Technology* (Vol. 551). Springer., DOI: 10.1007/978-3-030-18400-1_35

Riordan, T., Robinson, R. N. S., & Hoffstaedter, G. (2023). Seeking justice beyond the platform economy: Migrant workers navigating precarious lives. *Journal of Sustainable Tourism, 31*(12), 2734–2751. https://doi.org/https://doi.org/10.1080/09669582.2022.2136189. DOI: 10.1080/09669582.2022.2136189

Rivera, L. A., & Tilcsik, A. (2016). Class advantage, commitment penalty: The gendered effect of social class signals in an elite labor market. *American Sociological Review, 81*(6), 1097–1131. DOI: 10.1177/0003122416668154

Roberto, R., Penna, M., Felici, B., & Rao, M. (2023). Smart working and flexible work arrangements: opportunities and risks for sustainable communities. In *Intelligent Environments* (pp. 243–283). Elsevier., DOI: 10.1016/B978-0-12-820247-0.00001-1

Rosenblat, A. (2018). *Uberland: How algorithms are rewriting the rules of work.* Univ of California Press. DOI: 10.1525/9780520970632

Rothwell, W. J., Ealy, P. L., & Campbell, J. (Eds.). (2022). *Rethinking organizational diversity, equity, and inclusion: A step-by-step guide for facilitating effective change.* CRC Press.

Roy, G., & Shrivastava, A. K. (2020). Future of gig economy: opportunities and challenges. Imi Konnect, 9(1), 14-27.https://www.researchgate.net/profile/Gobinda-Roy-2/publication/340253836_Future_of_Gig_Economy_Opportunities_and_Challenges/links/5e7f62bea6fdcc139c0f752b/Future-of-Gig-Economy-Opportunities-and-Challenges.pdf

Royall, S., McCarthy, V., & Miller, G. J. (2022). Creating an inclusive workplace: The effectiveness of diversity training. *J. Glob. Econ. Trade Int. Bus, 3*, 39–55.

Roychowdhury, A., Chattopadhyaya, V., & Tripathi, M. (2023). *Policy brief on Zero emission vehicle (ZEV) mandate policy: Scaling up electric vehicle markets.* Centre for Science.

Rozentale, I., & van Baalen, P. J. (2021). Crafting business models for conflicting goals: Lessons from creative service firms. *Long Range Planning, 54*(4), 102092. Advance online publication. DOI: 10.1016/j.lrp.2021.102092

Sachan, B. (2024). A Sociological Investigation of the Theoretical Underpinnings and Applied Consequences of Social Stratification. *International Journal of Multidisciplinary Research in Arts. Science and Technology, 2*(8), 51–61. DOI: 10.61778/ijmrast.v2i8.61

Saks, A. M. (2006). Antecedents and consequences of employee engagement. *Journal of Managerial Psychology, 21*(7), 600–619. DOI: 10.1108/02683940610690169

Salleh, N. M., Shukry, S. N. M., Maylyn, V., & Jokinol, C. (2023). Analyzing the Challenges, Effects, and Motivations of Gig Economy Workers. *International Journal of Academic Research in Business & Social Sciences, 13*(6), 2125–2142. DOI: 10.6007/IJARBSS/v13-i6/17514

Samsudin, S., Khan, S. J. M., Hasan, J., Daud, S. N. M., & Jia, N. J. (2024). Financial Vulnerability of Gig Workers: Insights and Implications for Social Protection Schemes. [IJSPS]. *International Journal of Social Policy and Society, 20*, 27–44.

Sanghi, N., Chandra Balodi, K., & Gupta, V. (2023). "The emergence of the Indian hyperlocal grocery delivery industry: Dunzo v/s Blinkit." Https://Doi.Org/10.1177/20438869231151449, *14*(1), 119–128. DOI: 10.1177/20438869231151449

Sankararaman, G., Rengaraju, N., Rengarajan, V., Vembu, N. R., & Indhumathi, D. (2024). Gig economy's impact on workforce dynamics and economic resilience. *Educational Administration: Theory and Practice, 30*(6), 1627–1634.

Sannon, S., & Cosley, D. (2022). Toward a more inclusive gig economy: Risks and opportunities for workers with disabilities. *Proceedings of the ACM on Human-Computer Interaction, 6*(CSCW2), 1-31. DOI: 10.1145/3555755

Sarkar, M. (2023). Last-Mile Carbon Emission under E-Commerce: Environmental Perspective. *Open Journal of Social Sciences, 11*(12), 277–292. DOI: 10.4236/jss.2023.1112020

Sarker, M. R., Taj, T. A., Sarkar, M. A. R., Hassan, M. F., McKenzie, A. M., Al Mamun, M. A., Sarker, D., & Bhandari, H. (2024). Gender differences in job satisfaction among gig workers in Bangladesh. *Scientific Reports, 14*(17128), 1–18. DOI: 10.1038/s41598-024-68327-5 PMID: 39054341

Scholz, T. (2016). *Platform cooperativism: Challenging the corporate sharing economy*. Rosa Luxemburg Stiftung. https://www.rosalux-nyc.org/wp-content/files_mf/scholz_platformcoop_5.9.201650.pdf

Schor, J. B., Attwood-Charles, W., Cansoy, M., & Lee, D. (2020). Dependence and precarity in the platform economy. *Theory and Society, 49*(5-6), 833–861. DOI: 10.1007/s11186-020-09408-y PMID: 32836676

Schulze, L., Trenz, M., Cai, Z., & Tan, C.-W. (2022). *Algorithmic Unfairness on Digital Labor Platforms: How Algorithmic Management Practices Disadvantage Workers*. 43rd International Conference on Information Systems, Conference Proceedings, 8, Denmark.

Scuotto, V., Lemaire, S. L. L., Magni, D., & Maalaoui, A. (2022). Extending knowledge-based view: Future trends of corporate social entrepreneurship to fight the gig economy challenges. *Journal of Business Research, 139*, 1111–1122. DOI: 10.1016/j.jbusres.2021.10.060

Seppanen, L., Spinuzzi, C., Poutanen, S., & Alasoini, T. (2021). Co-creation in Macrotask Knowledge takaWork on Online Labor Platforms. *Nordic Journal of Working Life Studies*, *11*(2), 77–98. DOI: 10.18291/njwls.123166

Sequoia Capital. (2024). *Our Companies.*https://www.sequoiacap.com/our-companies/

Servais, J.-M. (2018). Digital service platform workers: What social guarantees? [Travailleurs des plateformes numériques de services: quelles garanties sociales?]. Revue Interventions économiques, 60. DOI: 10.4000/interventionseconomiques.4785

Seshasai, S. J., Raja, R. V., & Kumar, G. (2025). The Two Sides of the Coin: Optimizing Recruitment and Retention for Sustainable Talent Management. In *Innovative Recruitment and Retention for Employee Empowerment* (pp. 309-328). IGI Global Scientific Publishing. DOI: 10.4018/979-8-3693-6602-8.ch012

Sharma, B., Arora, P., Budhiraja, M., Sharma, K., Kumar, S., Gupta, N., & Kumari, S. (2024). " A Systematic Literature Review of Gamification Applications in Human Resource Processes: Insights, Trends, and Future Directions". *Library of Progress-Library Science, Information Technology & Computer, 44*(3). https://bpasjournals.com/library-science/index.php/journal/article/view/2475

Shibata, S. (2019). Gig Work and the Discourse of Autonomy: Fictitious Freedom in Japan's Digital Economy. *New Political Economy*, *25*(4), 535–551. DOI: 10.1080/13563467.2019.1613351

Shukaitis, S., & Figiel, J. (2024) *The Wages of Dreamwork Class Composition & the Social Reproduction of Cultural Labor.* Minor Compositions. ISBN 9781570274077. Official URL: https://www.minorcompositions.info/?p=1314

Shukla, A., Kushwah, P., Jain, E., & Sharma, S. K. (2021). Role of ICT in emancipation of digital entrepreneurship among new generation women. *Journal of Enterprising Communities: People and Places in the Global Economy*, *15*(1), 137–154.

Shulga, L. V. (2020). Change Management Communication: The Role of Meaningfulness, Leadership Brand Authenticity, and Gender. *Cornell Hospitality Quarterly*. Advance online publication. DOI: 10.1177/1938965520929022

Sihela, J., & Paulse, M. (2024). Reimagining an Ubuntu-inspired model to address precarity and vulnerability in the African gig economy. In *Humanistic Management in the Gig Economy: Dignity, Fairness and Care* (pp. 129–149). Springer Nature Switzerland. DOI: 10.1007/978-3-031-59944-6_7

Silva, M. E., & Nyobe, S. (2023). Social sustainability in the gig economy era. *Revue Française de Gestion Industrielle*, *37*(1), 55–69. DOI: 10.53102/2023.37.01.1140

Simon, H. A. (1991). Organizations and Markets. *The Journal of Economic Perspectives*, *5*(2), 25–44. DOI: 10.1257/jep.5.2.25

Singh, G., & Shastri, R. K. (2023). Opportunities and Challenges in Digital Human Resource Management with special reference to gig economy workers.

Singh, G., Walia, J. S., & Singh, A. (2025). Virtual Onboarding: Crafting Immersive Introduction Experiences for New Hires. In *The Future of HRM in a World of Persistent Virtual Reality* (pp. 281-303). Emerald Publishing Limited. DOI: 10.1108/978-1-83662-110-220251012

Singh, R., & Bhushan, V. (2023). UNDERSTANDING THE FUNDAMENTALS AND DYNAMICS OF THE GIG EMPLOYMENT LANDSCAPE IN INDIA. *International Journal of Advanced Research*, *11*(07), 300–315. DOI: 10.21474/IJAR01/17232

SKIPDLINE. (2020). *About US.*https://skipdline.com/en/content/aboutus

Smeyers, V., & Iruemiobe, B. (2023). Gender diversity in top management teams and employee DEI perception.

Smith, R. (2023, October 4). Gig economy statistics: What you need to know in 2024. *FinMasters.* Retrieved from https://finmasters.com/gig-economy-statistics/

Smith, B., Goods, C., Barratt, T., & Veen, A. (2021). Consumer 'app-etite' for workers' rights in the Australian 'gig' economy. *Journal of Choice Modelling*, *38*, 100254. DOI: 10.1016/j.jocm.2020.100254

Smith, E. F., Gilmer, D. O., & Stockdale, M. S. (2019). The Importance of Culture and support for workplace flexibility: An ecological framework for understanding flexibility support structures. *Business Horizons*, *62*(5), 557–566. DOI: 10.1016/j.bushor.2019.04.002

Smit, R., & Rugunanan, P. (2014). From precarious lives to precarious work: The dilemma facing refugees in Gauteng, South Africa. *South African Review of Sociology*, *45*(2), 4–26. DOI: 10.1080/21528586.2014.917876

Song, L., & Jo, S. J. (2023). How job crafting behaviours influence the innovative behaviour of knowledge workers in the gig economy: Based on organismic integration theory. *Frontiers in Psychology*, *14*(1228881), 1–13. DOI: 10.3389/fpsyg.2023.1228881 PMID: 37731880

Sonnentag, S., & Fritz, C. (2015). Recovery from job stress: The stressor-detachment model as an integrative framework. *Journal of Organizational Behavior*, *36*(S1), S72–S103. DOI: 10.1002/job.1924

Spasova, S., Bouget, D., Ghailani, D., & Vanhercke, B. (2017). *Access to social protection for people working on non-standard contracts and as self-employed in Europe: A study of national policies. European Commission, European Social Policy Network*. ESPN.

Spreitzer, G. M., Cameron, L., & Garrett, L. (2017). Alternative work arrangements: Two images of the new world of work. *Annual Review of Organizational Psychology and Organizational Behavior*, *4*(1), 473–499. DOI: 10.1146/annurev-orgpsych-032516-113332

Spurk, D., & Straub, C. (2020). Flexible employment relationships and careers in times of the COVID-19 pandemic. *Journal of Vocational Behavior*, *119*, 103435. Advance online publication. DOI: 10.1016/j.jvb.2020.103435 PMID: 32382161

Stadtländer, C. T. K.-H. (2009). Qualitative, Quantitative, and Mixed-Methods Research. *Microbe (Washington, D.C.)*, *4*(11), 485–485. DOI: 10.1128/microbe.4.485.1

Standing, G. (2011). Labour market policies, poverty and insecurity. *International Journal of Social Welfare*, *20*(3), 260–269. DOI: 10.1111/j.1468-2397.2010.00778.x

Stanford, J. (2017). The resurgence of gig work: Historical and theoretical perspectives. *Economic and Labour Relations Review*, *28*(3), 382–401. DOI: 10.1177/1035304617724303

Statista. (2020). *Percentage of gig workers worldwide affected by the COVID-19 pandemic*.https://www.statista.com/statistics/1128298/gig-workers-worldwide -effect-covid-19

Steinbaum, M. (2019). Antitrust, the Gig Economy, and Labor Market Power. SSRN *Electronic Journal*. DOI: 10.2139/ssrn.3347949

Stephens, N. M., Rivera, L. A., & Townsend, S. S. (2020). What works to reduce bias? A multilevel approach. Unpublished manuscript. Retrieved from https://www .nicolemstephens.com

Stewart, A., & Standford, J. (2017). Regulating work in the gig economy: What are the Options? *Economic and Labour Relations Review*, *28*(3), 420–437. DOI: 10.1177/1035304617722461

Sudirman, L., & Disemadi, H. S. (2023). Gig Economy: Unleashing the Potential of Digital Banking in Indonesia's Employment Regulations. *Human Rights and Economy in the Global South*, *10*(2), 301–330. DOI: 10.19184/ejlh.v10i2.39688

Sundararajan, A. (2016). *The sharing economy: The end of employment and the rise of crowd-based capitalism*. MIT Press., DOI: 10.3917/rimhe.035.0092

Sung, S. Y., & Choi, J. N. (2023). What drives firms to invest in training and developing employees? Time-dependent effects of firm internal and external contingencies. *The International Journal of Human Resource Management,* 34(2), 223–252. https://doi.org/https://doi.org/10.1080/ 09585192.2021.1965007.

Sutherland, W., & Jarrahi, M. H. (2018). The sharing economy and digital platforms: A review and research agenda. *International Journal of Information Management, 43*, 328–341. DOI: 10.1016/j.ijinfomgt.2018.07.004

Sutherland, W., Jarrahi, M. H., Dunn, M., & Nelson, S. B. (2020). Work precarity and gig literacies in online freelancing. *Work, Employment and Society*, *34*(3), 457–475. DOI: 10.1177/0950017019886511

Swiggy. (2024). Swiggy launches Project NEXT, creating a career path for delivery partners. Swiggy Corporate Press Release. Retrieved from https://www.swiggy.com/corporate/press-release/swiggy-launches-project-next-creating-a-career-path-for-delivery-partners/

Syrovatka, F. (2021). Labour market policy under the new European economic governance: France in the focus of the new European labour market policy. *Capital and Class*, *45*(2), 283–309. DOI: 10.1177/0309816820943177

Szostak, M. (2024b). Balancing fairness and care through. *Humanistic Management in the Gig Economy: Dignity, Fairness and Care*, 85.

Takagi, S. (2020). Literature survey on the economic impact of digital platforms. *International Journal of Economic Policy Studies*, *14*(2), 449–464. DOI: 10.1007/s42495-020-00043-0

Talukder, M. B., Chowdhury, S. A., & Khan, M. R. (2025). The Gig Economy: Economic Innovations and Technological Advancements in Human Resource Management. In Economic Innovations and Technological Developments in HRM (pp. 381-404). IGI Global.

Talukder, M. B., Chowdhury, S. A., & Khan, M. R. (2025). The Gig Economy: Economic Innovations and Technological Advancements in Human Resource Management. In *Economic Innovations and Technological Developments in HRM* (pp. 381-404). IGI Global. DOI: 10.4018/979-8-3693-4412-5.ch015

Tandon, N., Basu, P., Krishnan, O., & Bhavani, R. V. (2022). Emerging work trends in Urban India: COVID-19 and beyond. *Emerging Work Trends in Urban India: COVID-19 and Beyond*, 1–208. DOI: 10.4324/9781003264194

Tannen, D. (1990). *You just don't Understand Women and men in conversation.* Ballantine Books., DOI: 10.1017/S0047404500015372

Tanoamchard, W., & Ceienwattanasook, K. (2024). The Future of Work and the Impact of Automation on Jobs in Gig Economy in Thailand: A Review of Literature. *Scholar: Human Sciences,* 16(1), 77-88. DOI: 10.14456/shserj.2024.9

Tan, Z. M., Aggarwal, N., Cowls, J., Morley, J., Taddeo, M., & Floridi, L. (2021). The ethical debate about the gig economy: A review and critical analysis. *Technology in Society*, *65*, 101594. DOI: 10.1016/j.techsoc.2021.101594

Tapscott, D., & Tapscott, A. (2018). *Blockchain revolution: How the technology behind Bitcoin and other cryptocurrencies is changing the world.* Portfolio.

Tariq, M. U. (2024a). Integrating ESG principles into corporate governance for sustainable ecosystem services. In Castanho, R. (Ed.), *ESG and Ecosystem Services for Sustainability* (pp. 89–118). IGI Global., DOI: 10.4018/979-8-3693-3771-4.ch004

Tariq, M. U. (2024b). Smart transportation systems: Paving the way for sustainable urban mobility. In Munuhwa, S. (Ed.), *Contemporary Solutions for Sustainable Transportation Practices* (pp. 254–283). IGI Global., DOI: 10.4018/979-8-3693-3755-4.ch010

Tariq, M. U. (2024c). Integration of IoMT for enhanced healthcare: Sleep monitoring, body movement detection, and rehabilitation evaluation. In Liu, H., Tripathy, R., & Bhattacharya, P. (Eds.), *Clinical Practice and Unmet Challenges in AI-Enhanced Healthcare Systems* (pp. 70–95). IGI Global., DOI: 10.4018/979-8-3693-2703-6.ch004

Tariq, M. U. (2025a). The Belmont Report: Guiding ethical principles in human research. In Throne, R. (Ed.), *IRB, Human Research Protections, and Data Ethics for Researchers* (pp. 245–268). IGI Global Scientific Publishing., DOI: 10.4018/979-8-3693-3848-3.ch010

Tariq, M. U. (2025b). Africanization of research in higher education: Shaping perspectives and paradigms. In Mdikana, A. (Ed.), *Enhancing Research for Academicians in Higher Education* (pp. 101–124). IGI Global Scientific Publishing., DOI: 10.4018/979-8-3693-4496-5.ch007

Tariq, M. U., & Sergio, R. P. (2025). Ethical considerations and social impact of AI and computational intelligence in Society 5.0. In Pandey, R., Srivastava, N., Prasad, R., Prasad, J., & Garcia, M. (Eds.), *Open AI and Computational Intelligence for Society 5.0* (pp. 225–248). IGI Global Scientific Publishing., DOI: 10.4018/979-8-3693-4326-5.ch010

Tassinari, A., & Maccarrone, V. (2020). Riders on the Storm: Workplace Solidarity among Gig Economy Couriers in Italy and the UK. *Work, Employment and Society, 34*(1), 35–54. DOI: 10.1177/0950017019862954

Teja, U. S. K. (2023). *Policy*. Regulation, Community Wireless Networks.

Tenorio, S. L., O'Donnell, C. I., Hernandez, J., Rozjabek, H. M., Lynch, D., & Marcus, P. M. (2014). Culturally sensitive approaches to recruitment and retention of Hispanics in the national lung screening trial. *Journal of Immigrant and Minority Health, 16*(4), 761–764. DOI: 10.1007/s10903-013-9862-0 PMID: 23780349

Thomas, P. N. (2024). *The Gig Economy in India: Start-Ups, Infrastructure and Resistance*. Taylor & Francis. DOI: 10.4324/9781003491705

Thomas, S. M., & Baddipudi, V. (2022). Changing nature of work and employment in the gig economy: The role of culture building and leadership in sustaining commitment and job satisfaction. *NHRD Network Journal, 15*(1), 100–113. DOI: 10.1177/26314541211064735

Thompson, B. Y. (2018). Digital nomads: Employment in the online gig economy. *Glocalism: Journal of Culture. Politics and Innovation, 2018*(1), 1–26. DOI: 10.12893/gjcpi.2018.1.11

Thordarson, K. (2021). AB-5 and drive: Worker classification in the gig economy. *Hastings Bus. LJ, 17*, 137.

Times of India. (2024, January 2). Only three online companies offer minimum wage: Study. The Times of India. Retrieved from https://timesofindia.indiatimes.com/business/india-business/only-three-online-companies-offer-minimum-wage-study/articleshow/104835291.cms

Tirapani, A. N., & Willmott, H. (2022). Revisiting conflict: Neoliberalism at work in the gig economy. *Human Relations*. Advance online publication. DOI: 10.1177/00187267211064596

Tran, M., & Sokas, R. K. (2017). The Gig Economy and Contingent Work. *Journal of Occupational and Environmental Medicine, 59*(4), e63–e66. DOI: 10.1097/JOM.0000000000000977 PMID: 28244887

Transformational Upskilling. (n.d.). Uber: Transformational upskilling initiatives. Retrieved from https://www.transformationalupskilling.org/uber

Transparency International (TI). (2024). *Corruption Perceptions Index*. Berlin, Germany: TI. https://www.transparency.org/en/cpi/2023/index/tto

Triana, C., Gu, P., Chapa, O., Richard, O., & Colella, A. (2021). Sixty years of discrimination and diversity research in human resource management: A review with suggestions for future research directions. *Human Resource Management*, *60*(1), 145–204. DOI: 10.1002/hrm.22052

Triandis, H. C. (1995). *Individualism & collectivism*. Westview Press.

TriniFreelance. (2023). *Services Archive*. San Juan, Trinidad & Tobago. https://trinifreelance.com/services/

Tripathi, M. A., Tripathi, R., Yadav, U. S., & Shastri, R. K. (2022). Gig economy: Reshaping strategic HRM in the era of industry 4.0 and artificial intelligence. *Journal of Positive School Psychology*, •••, 3569–3579.

TT RideShare (TTRS). (2024). *Rider Frequently Asked Questions*. https://ttrideshare.com/rider-faqs/

Tubaro, P., Coville, M., Le Ludec, C., & Casilli, A. A. (2022). Hidden inequalities: The gendered labour of women on micro-tasking platforms. *Internet Policy Review*, *11*(1). Advance online publication. DOI: 10.14763/2022.1.1623

Tug, M. A., & Basar, P. (2023). FUTURE OF THE GIG ECONOMY. *Pressacademia*. DOI: 10.17261/Pressacademia.2023.1796

Tushev, M., Ebrahimi, F., & Mahmoud, A. (2022). A systematic literature review of anti-discrimination design strategies in the digital sharing economy. *IEEE Transactions on Software Engineering*, *48*(12), 5148–5157. DOI: 10.1109/TSE.2021.3139961

Tyc, A. (2022). Gig Economy: How to Overcome the Problem of Misclassifying Gig Workers as Self-Employed? *Revue Européenne du Droit Social*, *56*(3), 35–45.

Uber Technologies Inc. (2022). *Annual Report 2022*.

Upwork. (2024). *Search*. California, United States: Upwork. https://www.upwork.com/nx/search/talent/?nbs=1

Uzir, M. U. H., Al Halbusi, H., Thurasamy, R., Thiam Hock, R. L., Aljaberi, M. A., Hasan, N., & Hamid, M. (2021). The effects of service quality, perceived value and trust in home delivery service personnel on customer satisfaction: Evidence from a developing country. *Journal of Retailing and Consumer Services*, *63*, 102721. DOI: 10.1016/j.jretconser.2021.102721

Vaiman, V., Cascio, W. F., Collings, D. G., & Swider, B. W. (2021). The shifting boundaries of talent management. *Human Resource Management*, *60*(2), 253–257. Advance online publication. DOI: 10.1002/hrm.22050

Valente, E., Patrus, R., & Córdova Guimarães, R. (2019). Sharing economy: Becoming an Uber driver in a developing country. *Revista De Gestão, 26*(2), 143–160. DOI: 10.1108/REGE-08-2018-0088

Valenti, C. (2021). The individual right to continuous training of workers: an analysis of best practices in the international framework. *Labour & Law Issues, 7*(1), 54-88. DOI: 10.6092/issn.2421-2695/12922

Vallas, S. P., & Cummins, E. R. (2015). Personal branding and identity norms in the popular business press: Enterprise culture in an age of precarity. *Organization Studies, 36*(3), 293–319. DOI: 10.1177/0170840614563741

Vallas, S., & Schor, J. B. (2020). What do platforms do? Understanding the gig economy. *Annual Review of Sociology, 46*(1), 273–294. DOI: 10.1146/annurev-soc-121919-054857

Van Doorn, N., Ferrari, F., & Graham, M. (2022). Migration and Migrant Labour in the Gig Economy: An Intervention. *Work, Employment and Society, 5*(37), 1099–1111. DOI: 10.1177/09500170221096581 PMID: 37588943

Van Doorn, N., & Vijay, D. (2021). Gig work as migrant work: The Platformization of migrant infrastructure. *Environment and Planning A. Economy and Space, 56*, 1129–1149. DOI: 10.1177/0308518X211065049

Van Fossen, J. A., Watson, G. P., Schuster, A. M., Baker, N. M., Chang, C., & Cotten, S. R. (2024). Striving for the self: A self-regulation model of positive identity maintenance in platform-based gig drivers. *Journal of Organizational Behavior*, job.2828. Advance online publication. DOI: 10.1002/job.2828

Vandaele, K. (2024). Inevitable, vulnerable, unprofitable: an inquiry into food delivery platforms in Europe. Future of Work Series, 1-46. Brussels, Belgium: European Trade Union Institute (ETUI).

Vertesi, J. A., Goldstein, A., Enriquez, D., & Liu, L. (2020). Pre-Automation: Insourcing and Automating the Gig Economy. *Sociologica, 14*(3), 1–27. DOI: 10.6092/issn.1971-8853/11657

Vyas, N. (2021). 'Gender inequality-now available on digital platform': An interplay between gender equality and the gig economy in the European Union. *European Labour Law Journal, 12*(1), 37–51. DOI: 10.1177/2031952520953856

Waldkirch, M., Bucher, E., Schou, P. K., & Grünwald, E. (2021). Controlled by the algorithm, coached by the crowd—How HRM activities take shape on digital work platforms in the gig economy. *International Journal of Human Resource Management, 32*(12), 2643–2682. DOI: 10.1080/09585192.2021.1914129

Waldman, D. A., & Sparr, J. L. (2023). Rethinking diversity strategies: An application of paradox and positive organization behavior theories. *The Academy of Management Perspectives*, *37*(2), 174–192. DOI: 10.5465/amp.2021.0183

Wallenstein, J., de Chalendar, A., Reeves, M., & Bailey, A. (2019). *The new freelancers: Tapping talent in the gig economy.*

Walters, D. D. D. (2023). *DEI, Here I Come! Five Lessons From Organizational Dynamics For DEI* (Doctoral dissertation, University of Pennsylvania).

Wan, Z., Zhang, L., Wang, L., & Zhang, F. (2024). Navigating autonomy: Unraveling the dual influence of job autonomy on workplace well-being in the gig economy. *Frontiers in Psychology*, *15*, 1369495. DOI: 10.3389/fpsyg.2024.1369495 PMID: 39118837

Warren, T. (2021). Work–life balance and gig work: 'Where are we now' and 'where to next' with the work–life balance agenda? *The Journal of Industrial Relations*, *63*(4), 522–545. Advance online publication. DOI: 10.1177/00221856211007161

Wascher, E., Kaletka, C., & Schultze, J. (2019). SI-Labs: A Seedbed for Social Innovation. In J. Howaldt, C. Kaletka, A. Schröder, & M. Zirngiebl (Eds.), Atlas of Social Innovation – 2nd Volume: A World of New Practices (pp. 22-25). oekom verlag GmbH. https://www.socialinnovationatlas.net/articles/

Watkins, E. A. (2023). *Face Work: A Human-Centred Investigation into Facial Verification Technology in Gig Work.* Proceedings of the ACM on Human-Computer Interaction, 7(CSCW1), 52(1):1-24. DOI: 10.1145/3579485

Watson, G. (2019). Improving the Federal Tax System for Gig Economy Participants. *Tax Foundation*, *672*, 1–17.

Watson, G. P., Kistler, L. D., Graham, B. A., & Sinclair, R. R. (2021). Looking at the Gig Picture: Defining Gig Work and Explaining Profile Differences in Gig Workers' Job Demands and Resources. *Group & Organization Management*, *46*(2), 327–361. DOI: 10.1177/1059601121996548

Webb, A. (2022). A trade between flexibility and security: Examining the evolution of non-standard work arrangements and ways to rebalance the position of platform workers in the labor exchange. In *Platform Labour and Global Logistics* (pp. 89–107). Routledge. DOI: 10.4324/9781003351764-9

Webster, J. (2016). Microworkers of the Gig Economy. *New Labor Forum*, *25*(3), 56–64. DOI: 10.1177/1095796016661511

WiEat. (2024). *Wieat Terms and Conditions.*https://wieat.com/terms-condition/

Wiener, M., Cram, W., & Benlian, A. (2021). Algorithmic control and gig workers: A legitimacy perspective of Uber drivers. *European Journal of Information Systems*. Advance online publication. DOI: 10.1080/0960085X.2021.1977729

Wigfield, A., Turner, R., Alden, S., Green, M., & Karania, V. K. (2022). Developing a New Conceptual Framework of Meaningful Interaction for Understanding Social Isolation and Loneliness. *Social Policy and Society*, *21*(2), 172–193. DOI: 10.1017/S147474642000055X

Williams, P., McDonald, P., & Mayes, R. (2023). Recruitment in the gig economy: Attraction and selection on digital platforms. In *Technologically Mediated Human Resource Management* (pp. 142–168). Routledge. DOI: 10.4324/9781003388203-6

Woldoff, R. A., Woldoff, R., & Litchfield, R. C. (2021). *Digital nomads: In search of freedom, community, and meaningful work in the new economy*. Oxford University Press.

Wood, A., & Lehdonvirta, V. (2021). Platform Precarity: Surviving Algorithmic Insecurity in the Gig Economy. SSRN *Electronic Journal*. https://doi.org/DOI: 10.2139/SSRN.3795375

Wood, A. J., Graham, M., Lehdonvirta, V., & Hjorth, I. (2018). Good Gig, Bad Gig: Autonomy and Algorithmic Control in the Global Gig Economy. *Work, Employment and Society*, *33*(1), 56–75. DOI: 10.1177/0950017018785616 PMID: 30886460

Woodcock, J. (2021). *The fight against platform capitalism: an inquiry into the global struggles of the gig economy*. University of Westminster Press. DOI: 10.2307/j.ctv1ktbdrm

Woodcock, J., & Graham, M. (2020). *The gig economy: A critical introduction*. Polity.

Woodside, J., Vinodrai, T., & Moos, M. (2021). Bottom-up strategies, platform worker power and local action: Learning from ride hailing drivers. Local Economy. *Local Economy*, *36*(4), 325–343. https://doi.org/https://doi.org/10.1177/02690942211040170. DOI: 10.1177/02690942211040170

World Bank (WB). (2023). *Demand for Online Gig Work Rapidly Rising in Developing Countries*. Washington DC, United States: WB.

World Bank (WB). (2024). *Ease of Doing Business Rankings*. Washington DC, United States: WB. https://archive.doingbusiness.org/en/rankings

World Bank (WB). (2024). Rethinking Social Insurance for Self-Employed and Gig Workers. *Knowledge Brief Series*, *23*, 1–12.

World Bank. (2022). *Spotlight on gender gaps in online hourly rates*. https://documents1.worldbank.org/curated/en/099022224194519519/pdf/P1773021be8b0701d1a8e7167a651768f63.pdf

Xuan, Z. (2022). The innovation and value pursuit of the compensation system in the gig economy. *Acad. J. Bus Manag*, *4*, 50.

Yablonsky, S. (2020). A multidimensional platform ecosystem framework. *Kybernetes*, *49*(7), 2003–2035. DOI: 10.1108/K-07-2019-0447

Yadav, P. (2022). The gig and labour law reform: Balancing flexibility and workers' rights in changing employment landscape.

Yang, L., & Panyagometh, A. (2024). Factors influencing gig workers' satisfaction and commitment in the knowledge service providing platforms based on the self-determination theory: The case study in China. *Kasetsart Journal of Social Sciences*, *45*(1). Advance online publication. DOI: 10.34044/j.kjss.2024.45.1.29

Yaroshenko, O. M., Tkachenko, V. S., Puntus, D. A., Yakovleva, G. O., & Konopelt-seva, O. O. (2024). Models of Social Protection for Workers in the Gig Economy: Legal Challenges and Prospects. *Science of Law*, *2024*(3), 1–7. DOI: 10.55284/sol.v2024i3.139

Yasih, D. W. P. (2024). Precarious Workers in the Gig Economy.

Youssef, S. K., & Sikdar, A. (2020). The Role of Gig Economy in Supporting SME Internationalisation. In Zakaria, N., Abdul-Talib, A. N., & Amelinckx, A. (Eds.), *Transcending Cultural Frontiers* (pp. 91–106). Springer., DOI: 10.1007/978-981-15-4454-5_6

Zampoukos, K., Butler, O., & Mitchell, D. (2024). Who's got time for social reproduction? Migrant service workers as embodied infrastructures of the algorithmic city. *Journal of Ethnic and Migration Studies*, *50*(15), 3805–3821. DOI: 10.1080/1369183X.2024.2379647

Zhang, A., Boltz, A., Wang, C. W., & Lee, M. K. (2022). Algorithmic management reimagined for workers and by workers: Centering worker well-being in gig work. In *Proceedings of the 2022 CHI Conference on Human Factors in Computing Systems,* 14: 1-20. DOI: 10.1145/3491102.3501866

Zhou, C., He, X., Wu, R., & Zhang, G. (2022). Using Food Delivery Data to Identify Urban-Rural Areas: A Case Study of Guangzhou, China. *Frontiers in Earth Science (Lausanne)*, *1*(860361), 1–11. DOI: 10.3389/feart.2022.860361

Zhuo, Y., He, J., Li, W., Deng, J., & Lin, Q. (2023). A review on takeaway packaging waste: Types, ecological impact, and disposal route. *Environmental Pollution, 122518*, 122518. Advance online publication. DOI: 10.1016/j.envpol.2023.122518 PMID: 37678737

Zipo. (2022). *Filters.*https://zipotech.com/service-provider

Zipo. (2022a). *Filters.*https://zipotech.com/service-provider

Zipo. (2022b). *Terms and Conditions.*https://zipotech.com/assets/Frontend/images/terms-and-conditions.pdf

Zipper, B., McNicholas, C., Poydock, M., Schneider, D., & Harknett, K. (2022). *A national survey of gig workers paints a picture of poor working conditions and low pay*. Economic Policy Institute.

Zwick, A. (2022). Entrepreneurial Finance Capital and the gig economy. In Ness, I. (Ed.), *The Routledge Handbook of the Gig Economy*. Routledge., DOI: 10.4324/9781003161875-5

About the Contributors

Roshnie Doon is the Secretary of the Caribbean Academy of Sciences (CAS) Regional Executive at The University of the West Indies (UWI), St. Augustine, Trinidad and Tobago. In this role, she oversees all chapters across the Caribbean, including those in Trinidad and Tobago, Guyana, Jamaica, Guadeloupe, Antigua and Barbuda, and Barbados. Additionally, she is a research affiliate with the Global Labor Organization (GLO) in Essen, Germany, where her primary area of expertise lies in Labor Economics. Dr. Doon earned her PhD in Economic Development Policy, MSc in Economics, and BSc in Economics from UWI, St. Augustine, Trinidad & Tobago. She also completed a PhD Masterclass in International Business at the Henley Business School at the University of Reading, United Kingdom (UK). Dr. Doon currently leads six research clusters focused on Labor Economics, Social Policy, Migration, COVID-19, Climate Change, and Industry 4.0.

***

Zyed Achour is a committed scholar and researcher, holding a PhD in Management Science and currently serving as assistant professor at the National Institute of Labor and Social Studies, University of Carthage. He is also a research associate at the GEF2A Laboratory, Higher Institute of Management, University of Tunis. With over 20 years of experience in higher education and academic research, Dr. Achour's work spans a wide array of themes, including corporate social responsibility, sustainability, labor sciences, trade unionism, gender diversity, finance, human resource management, and strategic management. He is the author of numerous peer-reviewed articles and has contributed to several collective academic works. His innovative approach to exploring the complex interrelationships between organizational, social, and managerial dynamics distinguishes his research.

Rachit Agarwal is working as an Assistant Professor at University School of Business, Chandigarh University, Mohali. He is having more than 7 years of work experience in teaching and research. He is UGC-NET qualified and also completed executive financial data analytics from IIM Kashipur. His areas of interest are financial analysis, investment behavior analysis and behavioral study. He has published various papers in national and international journals including Scopus and ABDC listed journals. He has also organized many workshops and Faculty Development Programme on Research Methodology and on different statistical tools.

Arpan Anand serves as an Assistant Professor and Program Chair at Jaipuria Institute of Management, Noida, India. An alumnus of NIT Kurukshetra and UBS Chandigarh, Panjab University, Dr. Anand transitioned from a distinguished corporate career in banking to academia, where he has received multiple Best Faculty awards in recognition of his contributions to teaching, research, and institutional development. Dr. Anand specializes in Family Business and Marketing, with numerous publications in ABDC-listed, Scopus, and WoS-indexed journals. He has edited five books on contemporary management topics and served as guest faculty at institutions such as IIT Kanpur and AIMA. His expertise extends to training and development, with workshops conducted for organizations like Axis Bank, BHEL, IOCL and Airtel. Dr. Anand is a recognized academician, corporate trainer, and researcher committed to advancing management education and practice.

Reccia N. Charles is a Professor Emerita of International Business at St. George's University, dedicated to advancing academic excellence and fostering global understanding, holding a Doctorate in International Business from Nova Southeastern University and an MBA in Finance from Barry University. A trusted advisor to senior leadership in the Corporate and Non-Governmental Organizations, with the ability to see through complexities and develop a clear path forward. Expert in developing comprehensive curricula, conducting groundbreaking research, and providing exceptional mentorship to PhD students. Skilled in strategic analysis of global trade, cross-cultural management, and international relations. Leverages a profound understanding of global economic policies and international business to create engaging and relevant academic programs. Successfully leads cross-functional academic teams and collaborates with international organizations to enhance educational experiences and research opportunities. Effectively integrates practical experience opportunities to prepare students for impactful careers in the global arena.

Iris-Panagiota Efthymiou is a Lecturer at Greenwich University, formerly affiliated with the University of East London. She is an executive leader, author, and keynote speaker with over 20 years of experience in entrepreneurship, international affairs, and executive leadership. Her expertise spans research, strategic development, consultancy, and institutional management. Iris has held roles as a college director and founder of a Public Affairs consultancy, working alongside politicians, diplomats, entrepreneurs, academics, and journalists. She has spoken at prestigious venues, including the UN Headquarters in Geneva, and serves as a Board Member of HAPSc and a member of the Academic Board at the University of Piraeus's LabHEM. With 17 published books and over 40 peer-reviewed articles and chapters, Iris is also the Chief Editor of the Journal of Politics and Ethics in New Technologies and AI. Her academic background includes a Ph.D. in Behavioral Economics, a Master's in Health Economics and Management, and a Bachelor's in Economics.

Gunjan Tuteja is an Assistant Professor at Gargi College, University of Delhi. She is currently pursuing research at Dr. B.R. Ambedkar University, Agra. With a keen interest in research, her area of expertise lies in rural non-farm economies. Passionate about empowering students, Gunjan is dedicated to imparting academic and research skills. Her academic endeavors reflect her commitment to fostering intellectual growth and contributing meaningfully to her field.

Ashish Gupta is currently working as an Assistant Professor in the Department of Business Management, Maharishi University of Information Technology, Noida, U.P. He has completed his Ph.D. in Commerce from Department of Commerce, University of Lucknow, Lucknow, U.P (NAAC A++). He has qualified UGC-JRF in Commerce and UGC-NET in Management. His academic credentials include M.COM as well as MBA (Financial Management). He has authored and published a total of 24 research articles in various areas of Commerce and Management. These works have been included in both national and international journals, particularly in Scopus, UGC care and ABDC indexed journals. He has co-authored 4 books in the commerce and management domain. He has served as a subject matter expert in numerous workshops focused on commerce and management. He has been engaged in teaching and conducting research for over 7 years. He has also received the Best Paper award in International Conference.

Wako Jio is a PhD Scholar in the College of Business and Economics, Department of Management, Bule Hora University, Ethiopia.

Pooja Kalbalia is a Ph.D. Scholar at Christ University, Department of Media Studies in Bangalore, with an interest in communication, health, well-being, and gig work. With a fervent enthusiasm for health and media, her career is devoted to unravelling the influence of mass media on health-seeking behaviours and their subsequent outcomes. Currently, her passion lies in exploring the well-being of gig workers within the modern workplace, encompassing dimensions such as job satisfaction, social security, and interaction. Through her research endeavours, she seeks to shed light on the unique healthcare challenges faced by gig workers and devise innovative strategies for enhancing their overall well-being.

Shashi Kant is an Assistant Professor, College of Business and Economics, Department of Management, Bule Hora University, Ethiopia.

Nitish Khurana is a dedicated educator currently teaching at DAV College, Sector 10, Chandigarh. He holds a Ph.D. in Agricultural Economics from Panjab University, Chandigarh, showcasing his expertise in the field. With a keen interest in research, Dr. Khurana is actively engaged in academic endeavors that foster intellectual growth. His passion for teaching and research enables him to inspire students and contribute meaningfully to the academic community.

Tanya Kumar is working at Chandigarh Group of Colleges, Landran, Mohali. She has experience in teaching and research. She completed her Ph.D. in commerce from MAU, Baddi. Her areas of interest are financial analysis, investment behavior analysis, and behavioural study. She has published various papers in national and international journals, including Scopus and ABDC-listed journals.

Razia Nagina is currently working as Associate Professor at Mittal School of Business, Lovely Professional University, Phagwara, Punjab (India). In academic career spanning over 11 years, she has served at Lovely Professional University, Phagwara, Punjab (India). As a Faculty member, she has developed 6 online Courses in the area of Accounting and Business Laws. She has published more than 30 papers in indexed journals (Scopus, ABDC and UGC care). Her keen research areas are Financial Markets Anomalies, Institutional Investment Behavior, Cointegration of markets, Financial Reporting, Financial Statement Analysis and Behavioral studies.

Nazly Nardi is a Professor at Purdue Global University, specializing in graduate and undergraduate courses in Marketing Research and International Marketing. Her research is deeply rooted in cross-cultural management, negotiations, entrepreneurship, and international business, focusing on emerging markets and the Caribbean. Holding a Doctorate in International Business from Nova Southeastern University and a Master of Science in International Business from the University of the West Indies, Dr. Nardi combines academic rigor with a profound passion for international business, management, marketing, and qualitative research methods. This enthusiasm is not confined to the academic realm, where she extends it to her students, engaging in diverse academic presentations and publications; she applies her extensive knowledge to practical scenarios in the international business sphere, effectively bridging the gap between theory and real-world application.

Tanya Rabban is a dedicated PhD scholar at Chandigarh University, specializing in Business Management. With over four years of experience as a management consultant, she brings practical insights to her research on HR practices and their impact on gig workers in India's digital platform ecosystem. An entrepreneur at heart, Tanya is the founder of Bare, a self-care brand inspired by Indian Ayurveda, aimed at promoting holistic well-being. Her journey embodies a passion for innovation, academic excellence, and creating meaningful contributions to both the business and academic worlds.

Muhammad Usman Tariq has more than 16+ year's experience in industry and academia. He has authored more than 200+ research articles, 110+ case studies, 115+ book chapters and several books other than 4 patents. He is founder and CEO of The Case HQ, a unique repository for courses, narrative and video case studies. He has been working as a consultant and trainer for industries representing six sigma, quality, health and safety, environmental systems, project management, and information security standards. His work has encompassed sectors in aviation, manufacturing, food, hospitality, education, finance, research, software and transportation. He has diverse and significant experience working with accreditation agencies of ABET, ACBSP, AACSB, WASC, CAA, EFQM and NCEAC. Additionally, Dr. Tariq has operational experience in incubators, research labs, government research projects, private sector startups, program creation and management at various industrial and academic levels. He is Certified Higher Education Teacher from Harvard University, USA, Certified Online Educator from HMBSU, Certified Six Sigma Master Black Belt and has been awarded PFHEA, SFSEDA, SMIEEE, and CMBE.

Index

A

C

D

E

F

G

H

I

L

M

O

P

Q

R

S

T

V

W

www.ingramcontent.com/pod-product-compliance
Lightning Source LLC
LaVergne TN
LVHW080344011026
849161LV00009B/2184